CORPSE TALK

Groundbreaking SCIENTISTS

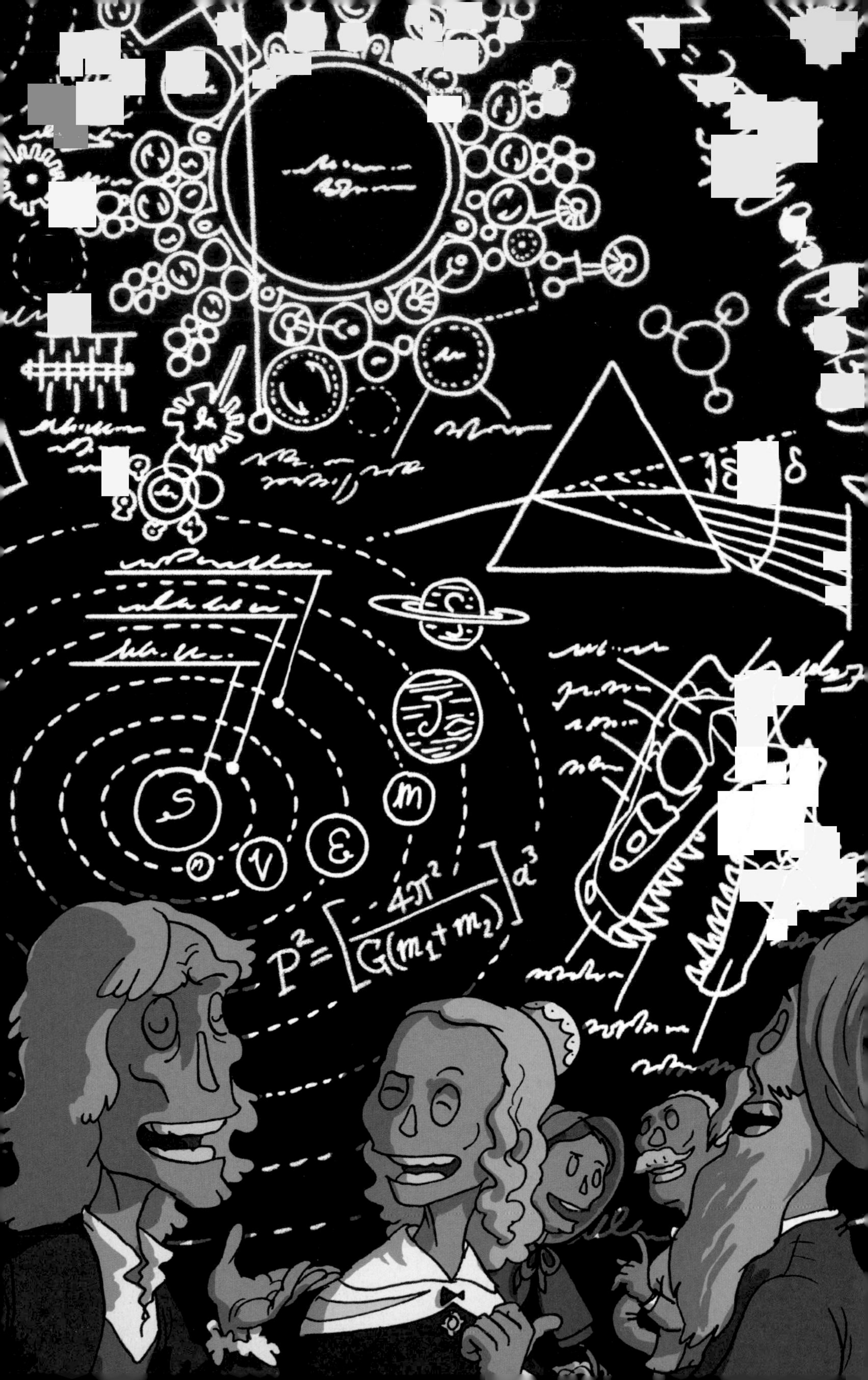
$P^2 = \left[\frac{4\pi^2}{G(m_1 + m_2)}\right] a^3$

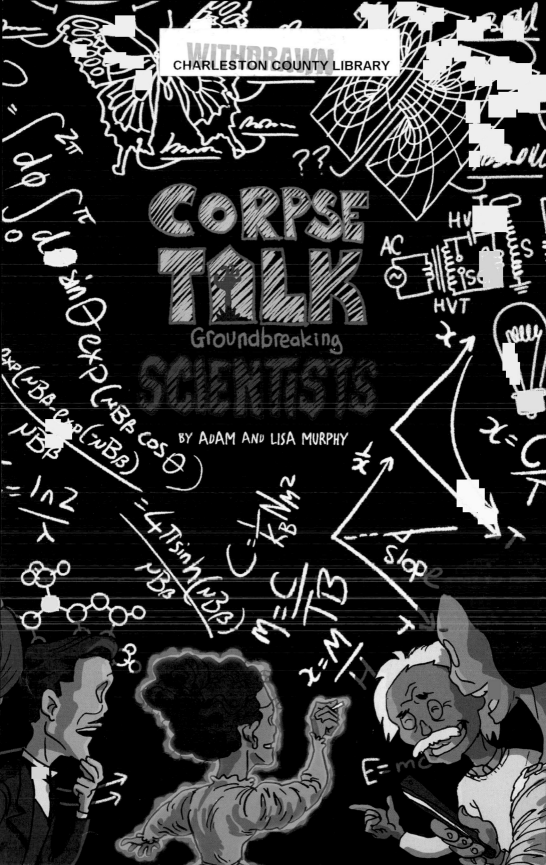

CORPSE TALK

Groundbreaking

SCIENTISTS

BY ADAM AND LISA MURPHY

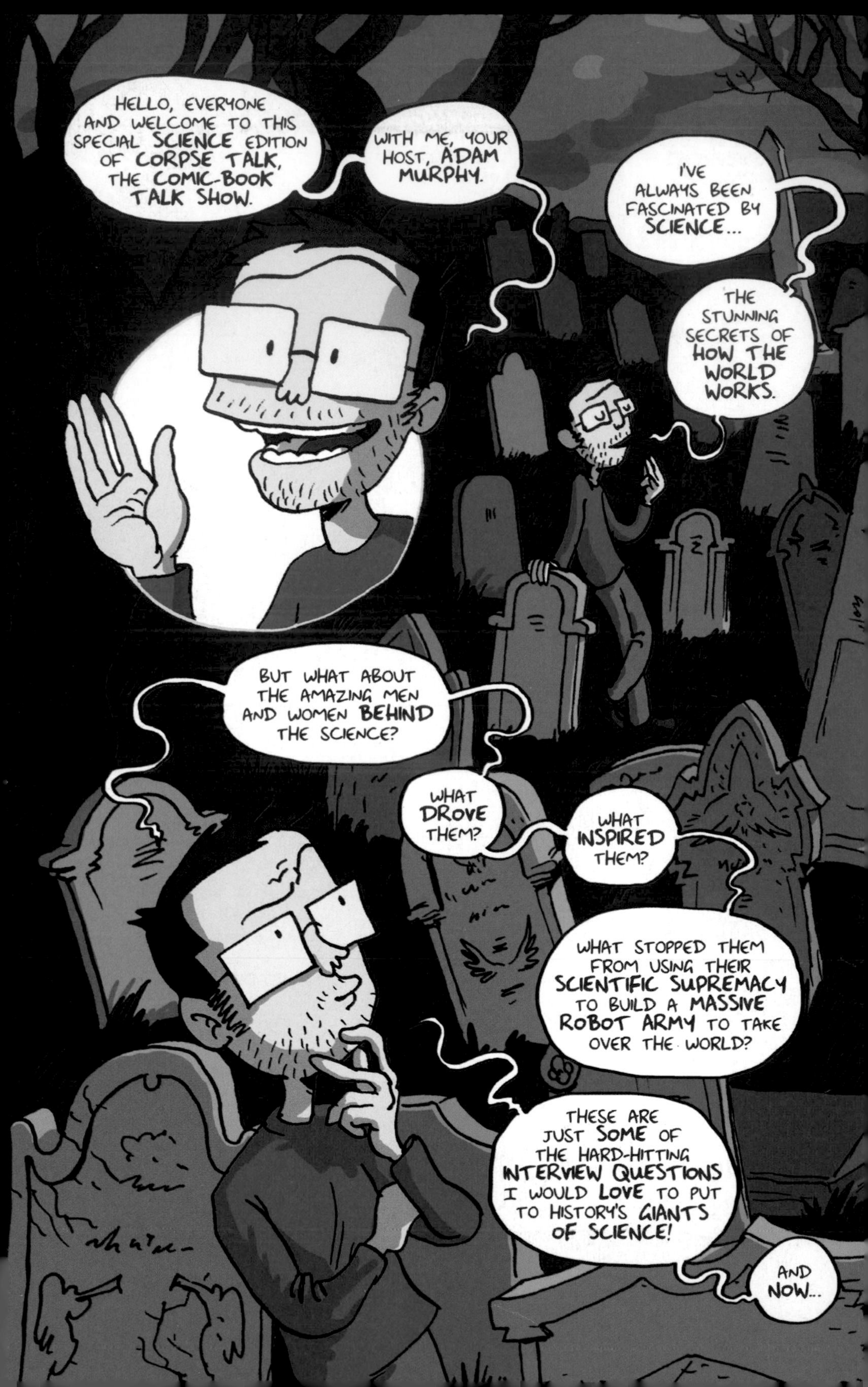
HELLO, EVERYONE AND WELCOME TO THIS SPECIAL SCIENCE EDITION OF CORPSE TALK, THE COMIC-BOOK TALK SHOW.
WITH ME, YOUR HOST, ADAM MURPHY.
I'VE ALWAYS BEEN FASCINATED BY SCIENCE...
THE STUNNING SECRETS OF HOW THE WORLD WORKS.
BUT WHAT ABOUT THE AMAZING MEN AND WOMEN BEHIND THE SCIENCE?
WHAT DROVE THEM?
WHAT INSPIRED THEM?
WHAT STOPPED THEM FROM USING THEIR SCIENTIFIC SUPREMACY TO BUILD A MASSIVE ROBOT ARMY TO TAKE OVER THE WORLD?
THESE ARE JUST SOME OF THE HARD-HITTING INTERVIEW QUESTIONS I WOULD LOVE TO PUT TO HISTORY'S GIANTS OF SCIENCE!
AND NOW...

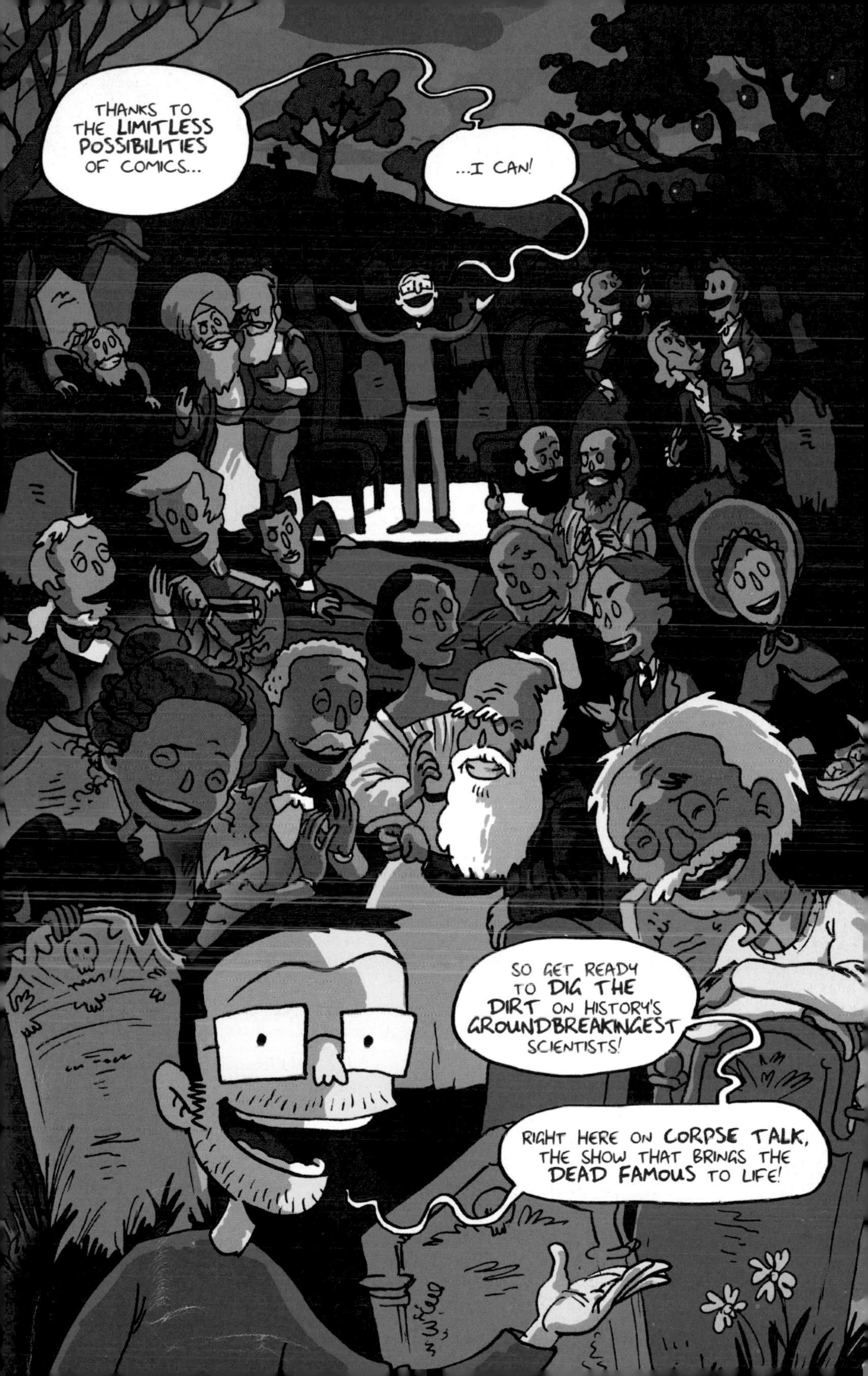
THANKS TO THE LIMITLESS POSSIBILITIES OF COMICS...
...I CAN!
SO GET READY TO DIG THE DIRT ON HISTORY'S GROUNDBREAKINGEST SCIENTISTS!
RIGHT HERE ON CORPSE TALK, THE SHOW THAT BRINGS THE DEAD FAMOUS TO LIFE!

CONTENTS

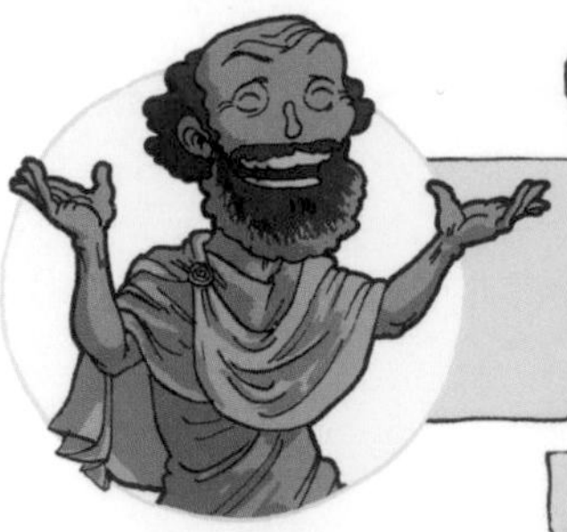

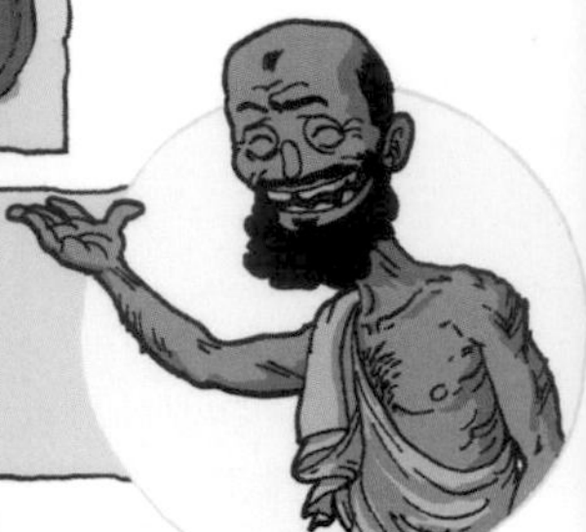

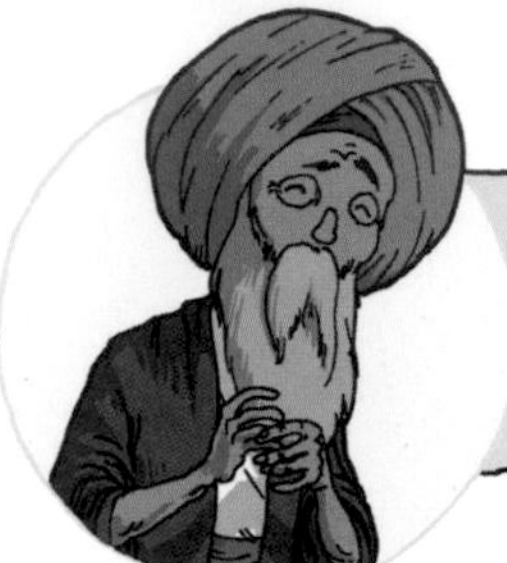

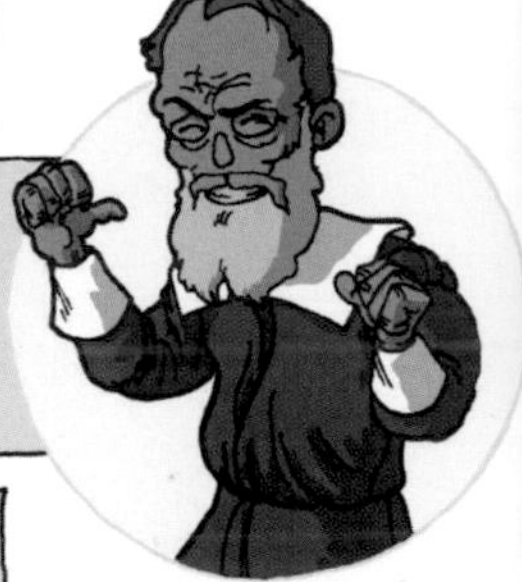

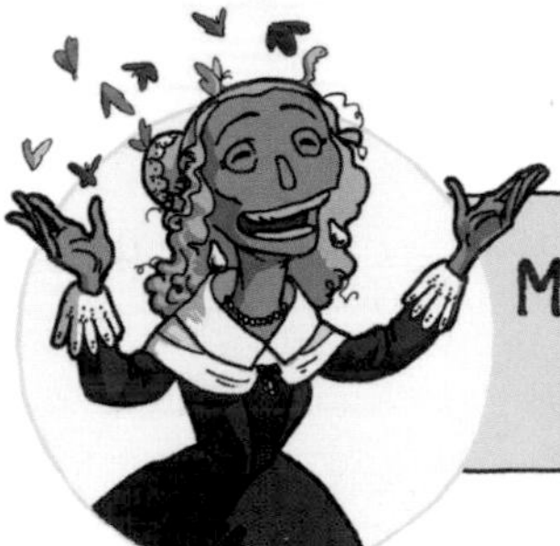

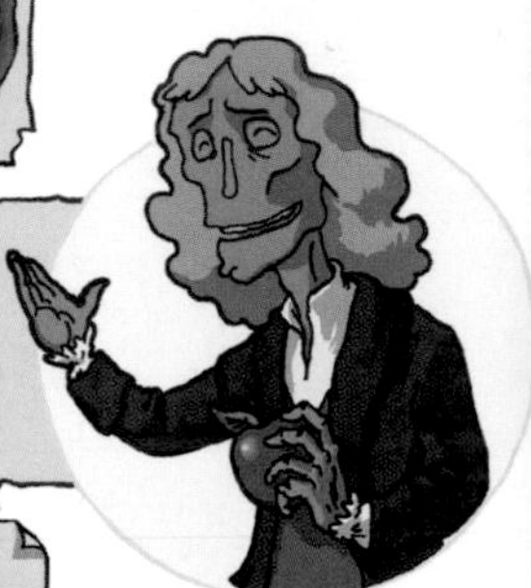

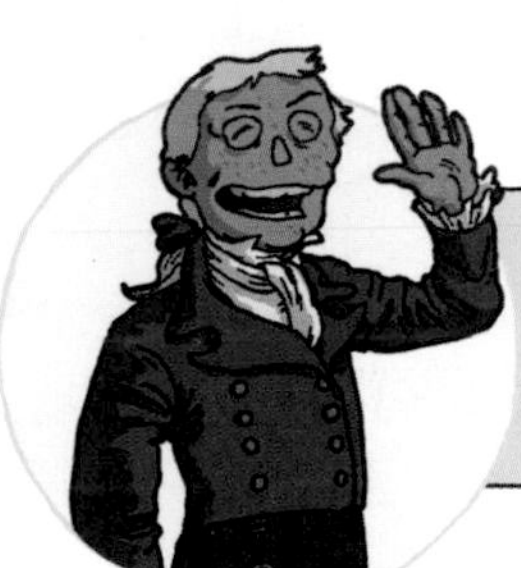

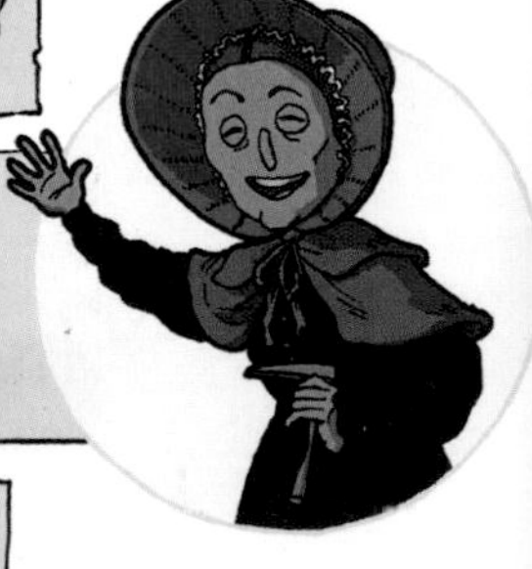

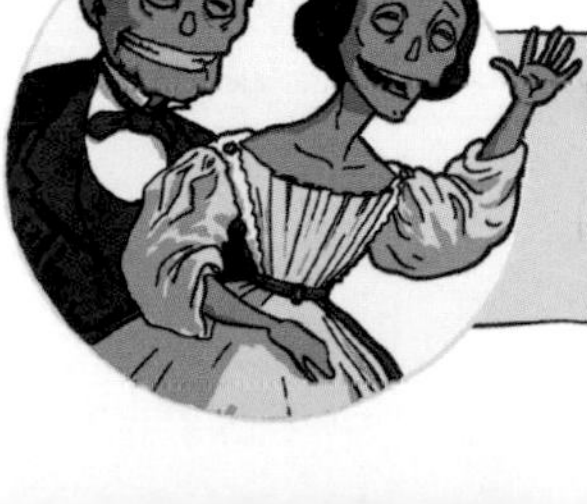

VON HUMBOLDT
EXPLORER, NATURALIST, GEOGRAPHER, ETC... 1769–1859
68

JAMES BARRY
DOCTOR 1790S–1865
72

CHARLES DARWIN
NATURALIST 1809–1882
78

DMITRI MENDELEEV
CHEMIST 1834–1907
88

MARIE CURIE
CHEMIST & PHYSICIST 1867–1934
94

GEORGE WASHINGTON CARVER
BOTANIST & INVENTOR 1860S–1943
98

NIKOLA TESLA
INVENTOR 1856–1943
104

ALAN TURING
COMPUTER SCIENTIST 1912–1954
110

ALBERT EINSTEIN
PHYSICIST 1879–1955
116

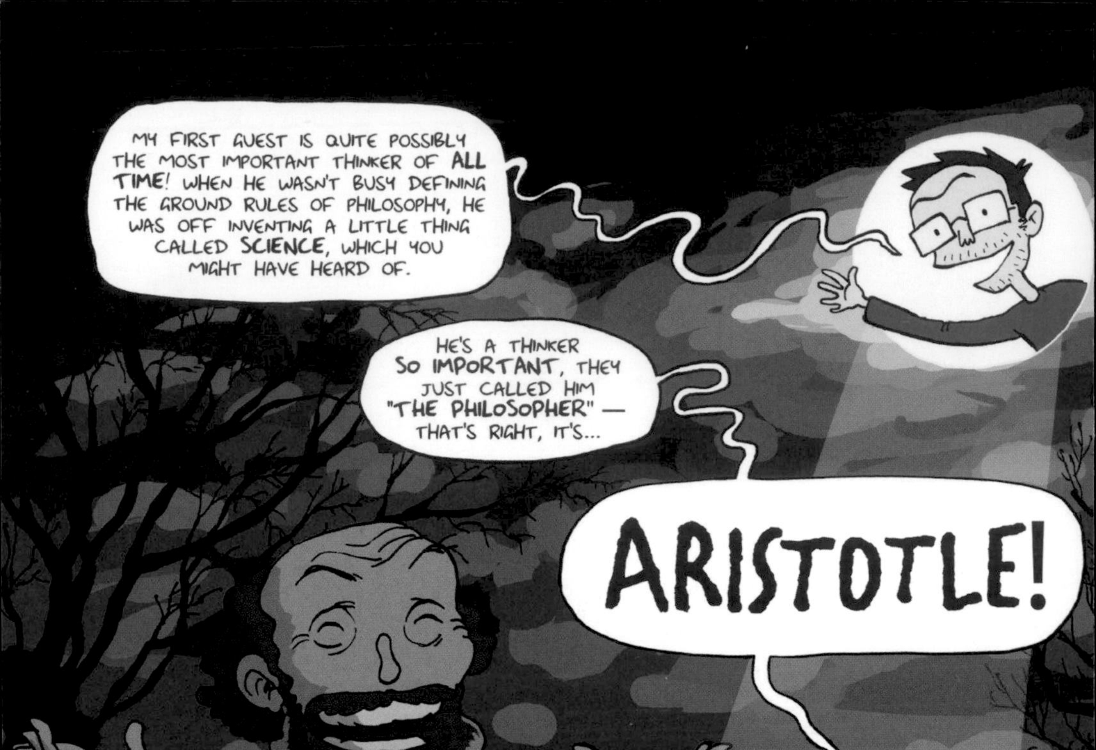
MY FIRST GUEST IS QUITE POSSIBLY THE MOST IMPORTANT THINKER OF **ALL TIME**! WHEN HE WASN'T BUSY DEFINING THE GROUND RULES OF PHILOSOPHY, HE WAS OFF INVENTING A LITTLE THING CALLED **SCIENCE**, WHICH YOU MIGHT HAVE HEARD OF.
HE'S A THINKER SO **IMPORTANT**, THEY JUST CALLED HIM **"THE PHILOSOPHER"** — THAT'S RIGHT, IT'S...
ARISTOTLE!
ARISTOTLE
PHILOSOPHER
384–322BCE

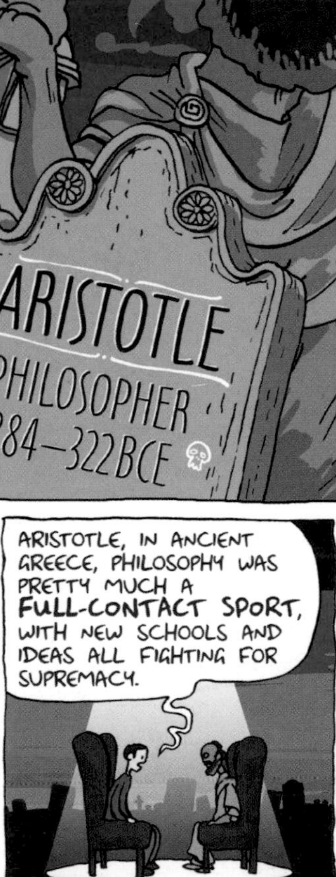
ARISTOTLE, IN ANCIENT GREECE, PHILOSOPHY WAS PRETTY MUCH A **FULL-CONTACT SPORT**, WITH NEW SCHOOLS AND IDEAS ALL FIGHTING FOR SUPREMACY.

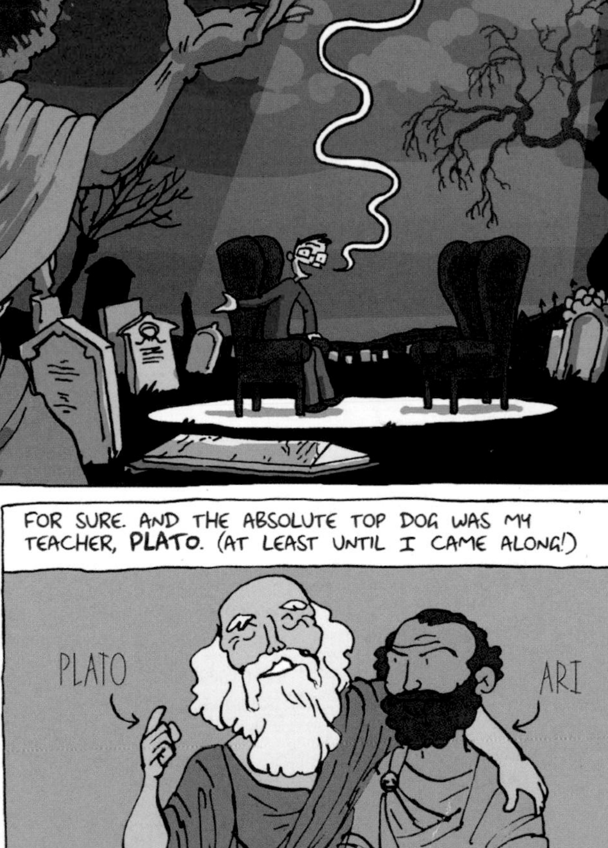
FOR SURE. AND THE ABSOLUTE TOP DOG WAS MY TEACHER, **PLATO**. (AT LEAST UNTIL I CAME ALONG!)
PLATO
ARI

PLATO'S WHOLE PHILOSOPHICAL SYSTEM WAS BUILT ON THE IDEA THAT THERE ARE THESE PURE, UNCHANGING, PERFECT IDEALS—OR FORMS—WHICH ONLY EXIST IN HEAVEN, OR THE MIND OF THE PHILOSOPHER.

SO, FOR EXAMPLE, THERE ARE LOTS OF **TRIANGLES** IN THE WORLD AND NONE OF THEM IS PERFECT. THEY'LL ALWAYS BE OFF-KILTER OR SKEWY IN SOME WAY...

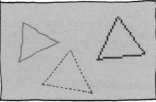

BUT EACH OF THEM IS AN **IMPERFECT COPY** OF THE PERFECT **IDEA** OF "TRIANGLE," WHICH WE CAN ONLY EVER SEE IN OUR MINDS...

AND IT'S THE SAME FOR OTHER ABSTRACT IDEALS, LIKE TRUTH OR JUSTICE OR BEAUTY; THEY MIGHT NEVER BE PERFECT IN **THIS** WORLD, BUT THEY **DO** EXIST IN A PLACE **BEYOND HEAVEN**...

WHICH, I'LL BE HONEST, ALWAYS STRUCK ME AS A LOT OF **NONSENSE**.

THE WORLD'S NOT PERFECT; IT'S WEIRD AND WACKY AND DIRTY AND UGLY AND MESSY. BUT THINGS HAPPEN FOR **REASONS**.

INSTEAD OF THESE SILLY BRAIN GAMES, WHY CAN'T THERE BE **REAL** REASONS WHY THINGS ARE THE WAY THEY ARE?

UH. YOU LOST ME...

OK. HERE'S A BASIC QUESTION: WHY DO SOME ANIMALS HAVE NECKS, AND SOME NOT?

UH... DON'T THEY ALL?

NO! FISH DON'T! NOR DO OCTOPUSES!

I STARTED THINKING MAYBE THERE'S SOMETHING THAT **CAUSES** SOME ANIMALS TO HAVE NECKS. NOT BECAUSE THEY'RE BEAUTIFUL, OR WHATEVER, BUT A REAL, PHYSICAL CAUSE IN THE REAL WORLD.

IF WE WANT TO UNDERSTAND THINGS, WE CAN'T JUST **THINK** ABOUT THEM. WE HAVE TO **STUDY** THEM.

9

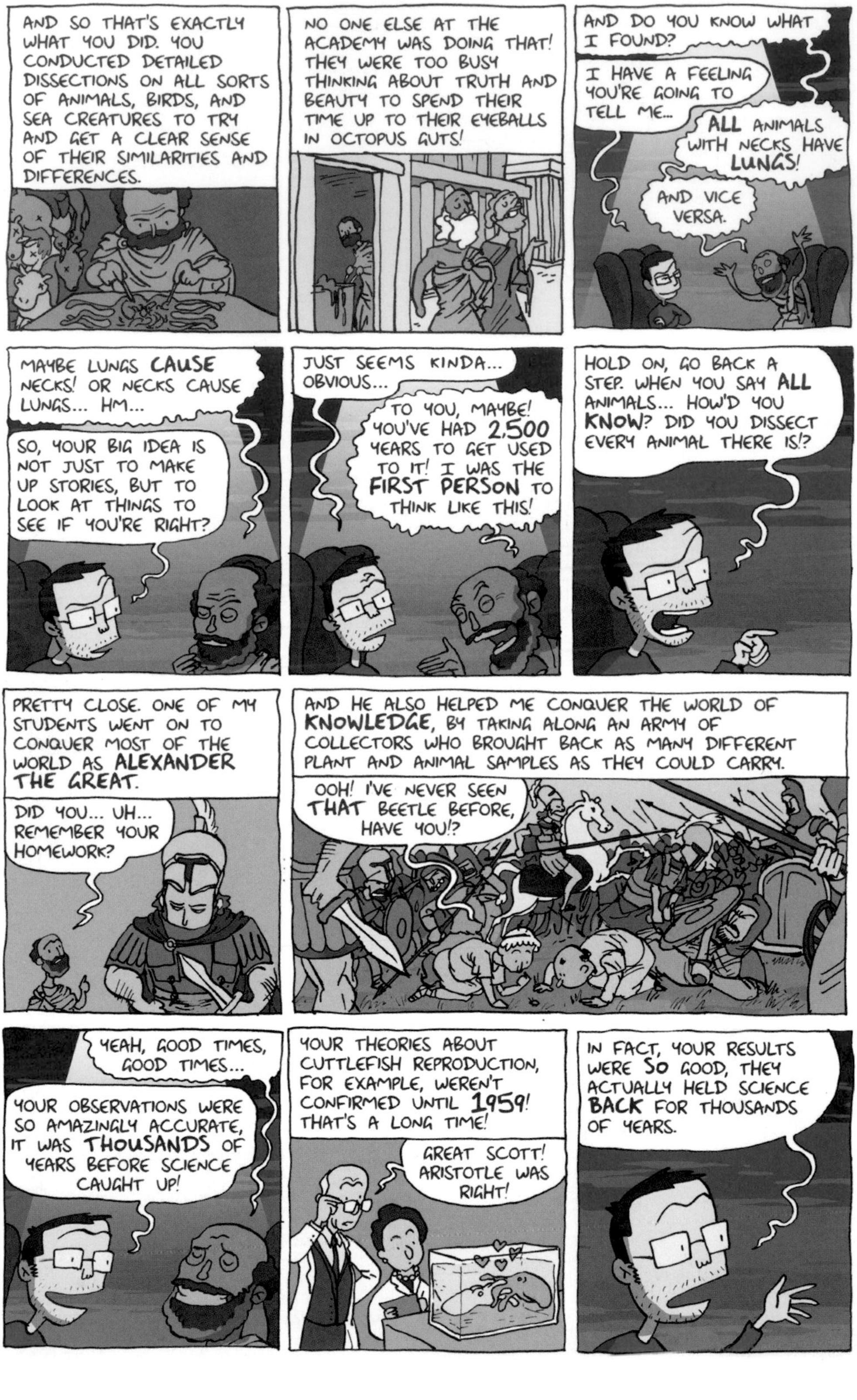
AND SO THAT'S EXACTLY WHAT YOU DID. YOU CONDUCTED DETAILED DISSECTIONS ON ALL SORTS OF ANIMALS, BIRDS, AND SEA CREATURES TO TRY AND GET A CLEAR SENSE OF THEIR SIMILARITIES AND DIFFERENCES.
NO ONE ELSE AT THE ACADEMY WAS DOING THAT! THEY WERE TOO BUSY THINKING ABOUT TRUTH AND BEAUTY TO SPEND THEIR TIME UP TO THEIR EYEBALLS IN OCTOPUS GUTS!
AND DO YOU KNOW WHAT I FOUND?
I HAVE A FEELING YOU'RE GOING TO TELL ME...
ALL ANIMALS WITH NECKS HAVE LUNGS!
AND VICE VERSA.
MAYBE LUNGS CAUSE NECKS! OR NECKS CAUSE LUNGS... HM...
SO, YOUR BIG IDEA IS NOT JUST TO MAKE UP STORIES, BUT TO LOOK AT THINGS TO SEE IF YOU'RE RIGHT?
JUST SEEMS KINDA... OBVIOUS...
TO YOU, MAYBE! YOU'VE HAD 2,500 YEARS TO GET USED TO IT! I WAS THE FIRST PERSON TO THINK LIKE THIS!
HOLD ON, GO BACK A STEP. WHEN YOU SAY ALL ANIMALS... HOW'D YOU KNOW? DID YOU DISSECT EVERY ANIMAL THERE IS!?
PRETTY CLOSE. ONE OF MY STUDENTS WENT ON TO CONQUER MOST OF THE WORLD AS ALEXANDER THE GREAT.
DID YOU... UH... REMEMBER YOUR HOMEWORK?
AND HE ALSO HELPED ME CONQUER THE WORLD OF KNOWLEDGE, BY TAKING ALONG AN ARMY OF COLLECTORS WHO BROUGHT BACK AS MANY DIFFERENT PLANT AND ANIMAL SAMPLES AS THEY COULD CARRY.
OOH! I'VE NEVER SEEN THAT BEETLE BEFORE, HAVE YOU!?
YEAH, GOOD TIMES, GOOD TIMES...
YOUR OBSERVATIONS WERE SO AMAZINGLY ACCURATE, IT WAS THOUSANDS OF YEARS BEFORE SCIENCE CAUGHT UP!
YOUR THEORIES ABOUT CUTTLEFISH REPRODUCTION, FOR EXAMPLE, WEREN'T CONFIRMED UNTIL 1959! THAT'S A LONG TIME!
GREAT SCOTT! ARISTOTLE WAS RIGHT!
IN FACT, YOUR RESULTS WERE SO GOOD, THEY ACTUALLY HELD SCIENCE BACK FOR THOUSANDS OF YEARS.

INSTEAD OF STUDYING THE WORLD AROUND THEM, PEOPLE JUST TOOK YOUR WORD FOR IT!

WHAT?! BUT THAT'S **EXACTLY** WHAT I TOLD THEM **NOT** TO DO!

AND I NEVER CLAIMED I'D GOT **EVERYTHING** RIGHT...

LIKE THE WHOLE INSECTS-APPEARING-OUT-OF-NOWHERE THING?

AH, NUTS. NOT THE INSECTS THING...

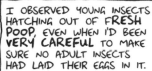

I OBSERVED YOUNG INSECTS HATCHING OUT OF **FRESH POOP**, EVEN WHEN I'D BEEN **VERY CAREFUL** TO MAKE SURE NO ADULT INSECTS HAD LAID THEIR EGGS IN IT.

AH, BUT THERE COULD HAVE BEEN EGGS ALREADY IN THE POOPING ANIMAL'S **DIGESTIVE TRACT!**

BAH. DIDN'T THINK OF THAT...

THE TRUE STORY WASN'T DISCOVERED UNTIL MARIA SIBYLLA MERIAN IN THE **17**TH CENTURY!*

BUT, HEY, DON'T WORRY. WE CAUGHT UP EVENTUALLY!

*SEE PAGE **32**

AND TODAY YOU'RE REVERED, NOT JUST AS THE FATHER OF SCIENCE, BUT ALSO LOGIC, ETHICS, POLITICAL THEORY, PHILOSOPHY AND EVEN WRITING!

WHOA. NICE PECS!

HOLLYWOOD SCRIPTWRITERS STUDY YOUR BOOK ON **DRAMA** LIKE IT WAS **THE BIBLE** FOR TIPS ON HOW TO STRUCTURE THE STORIES OF THEIR MOVIES!

HM... WHAT DID ARISTOTLE SAY?

JUST THE DRAMA? WHAT ABOUT MY BOOK ON **COMEDY?**

NOT ALL OF YOUR WRITINGS SURVIVED—IT **WAS** A LONG TIME AGO, AFTER ALL...

BUT SINCE YOU'RE HERE, YOU DON'T HAVE A FUNNY ENDING, BY ANY CHANCE...?

HEY, IT'S **YOUR** COMIC...

SCHOOL OF LIFE

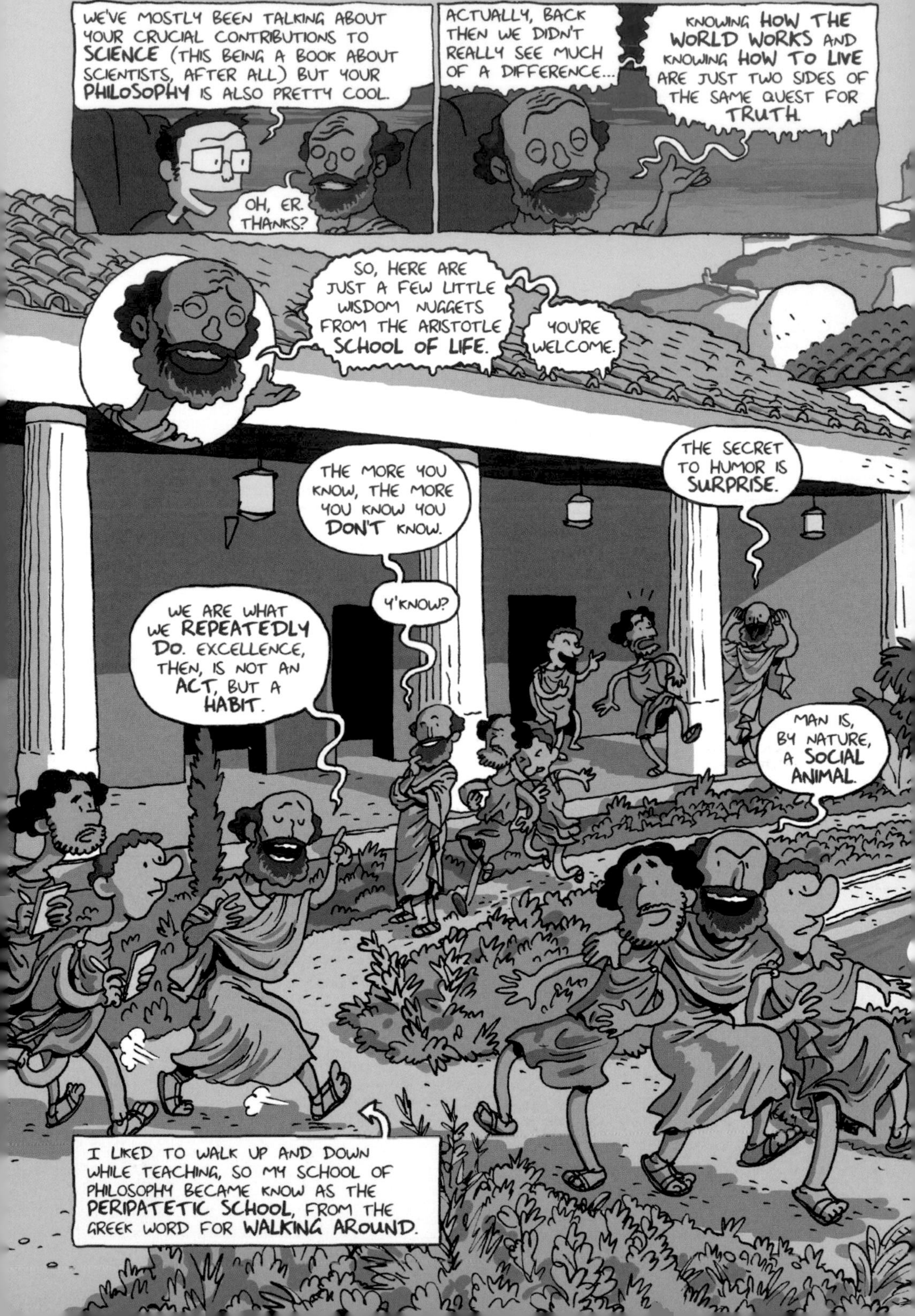
WE'VE MOSTLY BEEN TALKING ABOUT YOUR CRUCIAL CONTRIBUTIONS TO SCIENCE (THIS BEING A BOOK ABOUT SCIENTISTS, AFTER ALL) BUT YOUR PHILOSOPHY IS ALSO PRETTY COOL.
OH, ER. THANKS?
ACTUALLY, BACK THEN WE DIDN'T REALLY SEE MUCH OF A DIFFERENCE...
KNOWING HOW THE WORLD WORKS AND KNOWING HOW TO LIVE ARE JUST TWO SIDES OF THE SAME QUEST FOR TRUTH.
SO, HERE ARE JUST A FEW LITTLE WISDOM NUGGETS FROM THE ARISTOTLE SCHOOL OF LIFE.
YOU'RE WELCOME.
THE MORE YOU KNOW, THE MORE YOU KNOW YOU DON'T KNOW.
Y'KNOW?
THE SECRET TO HUMOR IS SURPRISE.
WE ARE WHAT WE REPEATEDLY DO. EXCELLENCE, THEN, IS NOT AN ACT, BUT A HABIT.
MAN IS, BY NATURE, A SOCIAL ANIMAL.
I LIKED TO WALK UP AND DOWN WHILE TEACHING, SO MY SCHOOL OF PHILOSOPHY BECAME KNOW AS THE PERIPATETIC SCHOOL, FROM THE GREEK WORD FOR WALKING AROUND.

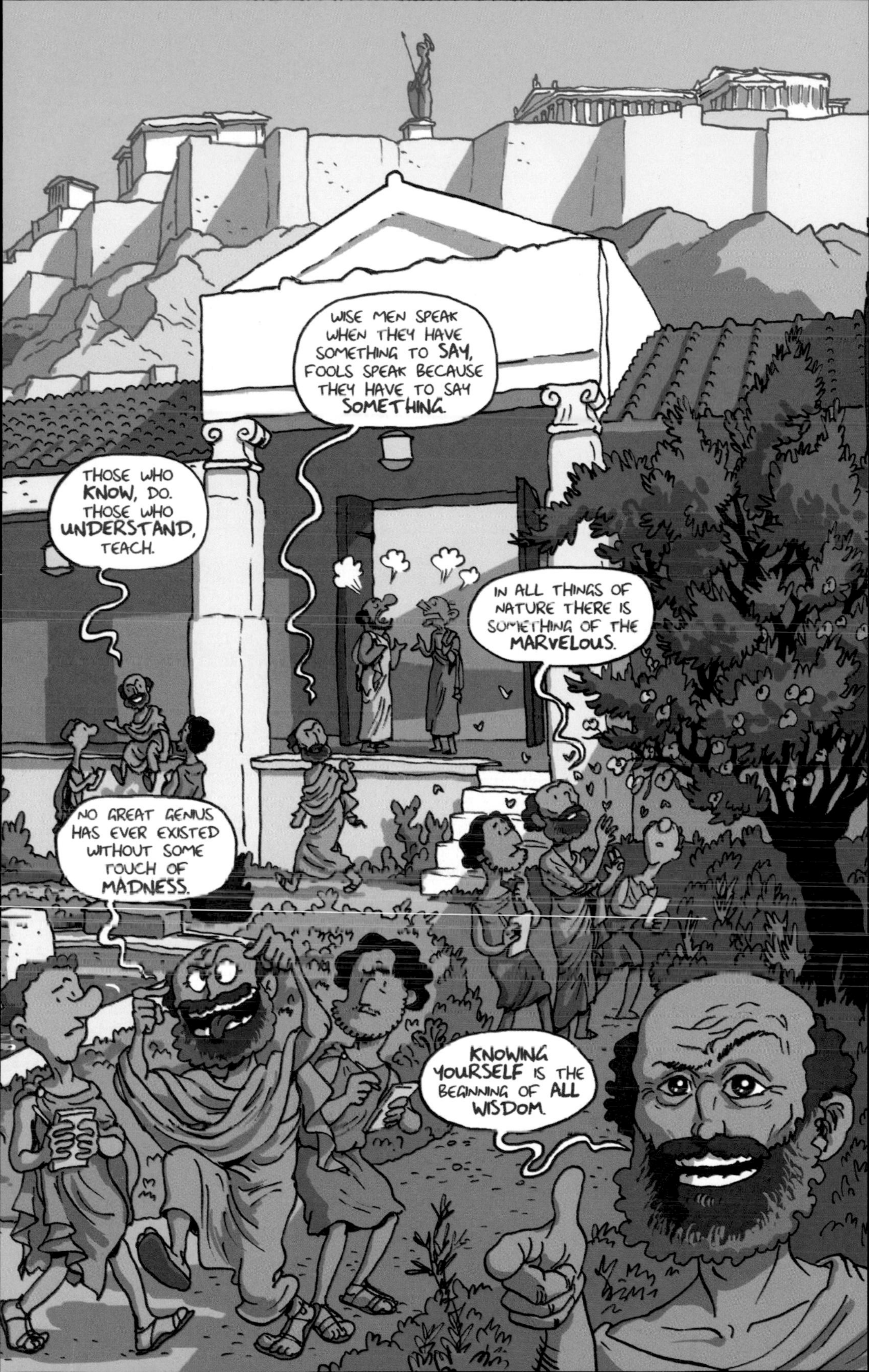
WISE MEN SPEAK WHEN THEY HAVE SOMETHING TO SAY, FOOLS SPEAK BECAUSE THEY HAVE TO SAY SOMETHING.
THOSE WHO KNOW, DO. THOSE WHO UNDERSTAND, TEACH.
IN ALL THINGS OF NATURE THERE IS SOMETHING OF THE MARVELOUS.
NO GREAT GENIUS HAS EVER EXISTED WITHOUT SOME TOUCH OF MADNESS.
KNOWING YOURSELF IS THE BEGINNING OF ALL WISDOM.

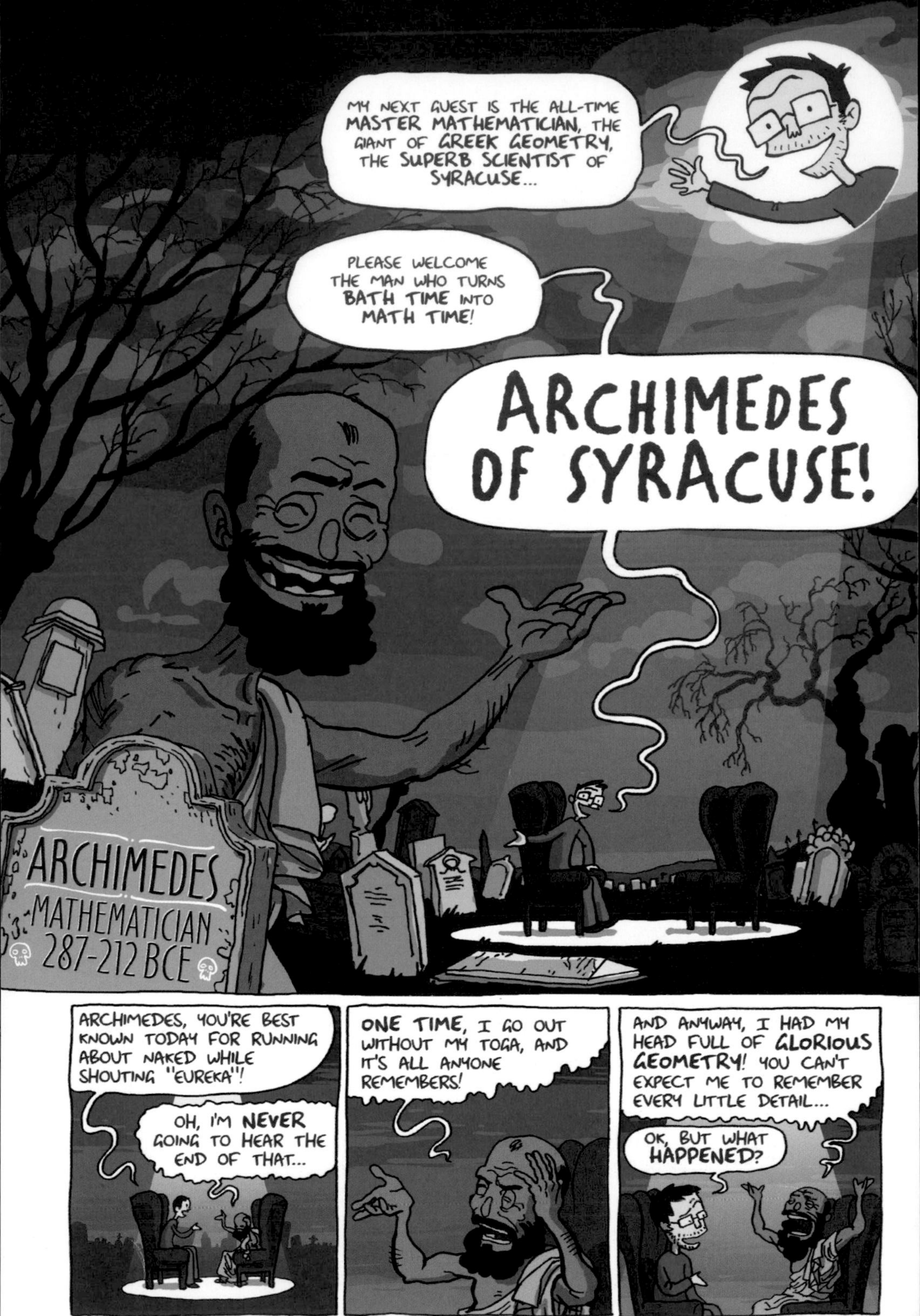
MY NEXT GUEST IS THE ALL-TIME MASTER MATHEMATICIAN, THE GIANT OF GREEK GEOMETRY, THE SUPERB SCIENTIST OF SYRACUSE...
PLEASE WELCOME THE MAN WHO TURNS BATH TIME INTO MATH TIME!
ARCHIMEDES OF SYRACUSE!
ARCHIMEDES
MATHEMATICIAN
287-212 BCE
ARCHIMEDES, YOU'RE BEST KNOWN TODAY FOR RUNNING ABOUT NAKED WHILE SHOUTING "EUREKA"!
OH, I'M NEVER GOING TO HEAR THE END OF THAT...
ONE TIME, I GO OUT WITHOUT MY TOGA, AND IT'S ALL ANYONE REMEMBERS!
AND ANYWAY, I HAD MY HEAD FULL OF GLORIOUS GEOMETRY! YOU CAN'T EXPECT ME TO REMEMBER EVERY LITTLE DETAIL...
OK, BUT WHAT HAPPENED?

KING HIERON OF SYRACUSE HAD A GOLD CROWN MADE, BUT HE WAS AFRAID THE GOLDSMITH HAD CHEATED HIM BY MIXING IN SOME CHEAPER SILVER.

HEH HEH HEH

1KG (2.2LB) OF SILVER TAKES UP **MORE SPACE** THAN 1KG (2.2LB) OF GOLD, SO THE EASY SOLUTION WOULD HAVE BEEN TO MELT IT DOWN AND MAKE A COMPARISON

BUT THIS CROWN WAS A **SACRED OFFERING** TO THE GODS. IT COULDN'T BE DAMAGED!

MMM. QUITE A PICKLE...

YOU'RE MY MATHEMATICIAN! **UNPICKLE** IT!

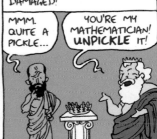

MAN! I SPENT **AGES** TRYING TO FIGURE THAT ONE OUT!

WAIT! YOU COULD...

NO.

MAYBE...

NO, NO, THAT'LL NEVER WORK!

HMMM

HOW ABOUT..?

BUT THEN, THE ANSWER CAME TO ME WHERE I LEAST EXPECTED IT... IN THE BATH!

THE TUB WAS FULL, SO WHEN I GOT IN, WATER GOT **OUT**.

I COULD DO THE SAME WITH THE CROWN! IF IT CONTAINED SILVER, IT WOULD **DISPLACE** MORE WATER THAN THE SAME WEIGHT OF PURE GOLD...

AND IN MY ENTHUSIASM, IT'S POSSIBLE I MAY HAVE OMITTED TO PUT MY CLOTHES ON...

EUREKA!

YOU ALSO INVENTED LOTS OF OTHER THINGS; LIKE THE **LEVER**!

I DIDN'T ACTUALLY **INVENT** IT, PER SE, BUT EXPLAINED THE MATHEMATICS OF HOW IT WORKS, WHICH IS KIND OF **MORE** AWESOME, IF YOU THINK ABOUT IT...

IF YOU HAVE TWO THINGS OF **EQUAL WEIGHT**, YOU CAN BALANCE THEM ON A CENTRAL POINT...

BUT IF ONE SIDE IS **HEAVIER**, IT WILL PUSH THE OTHER SIDE UP.

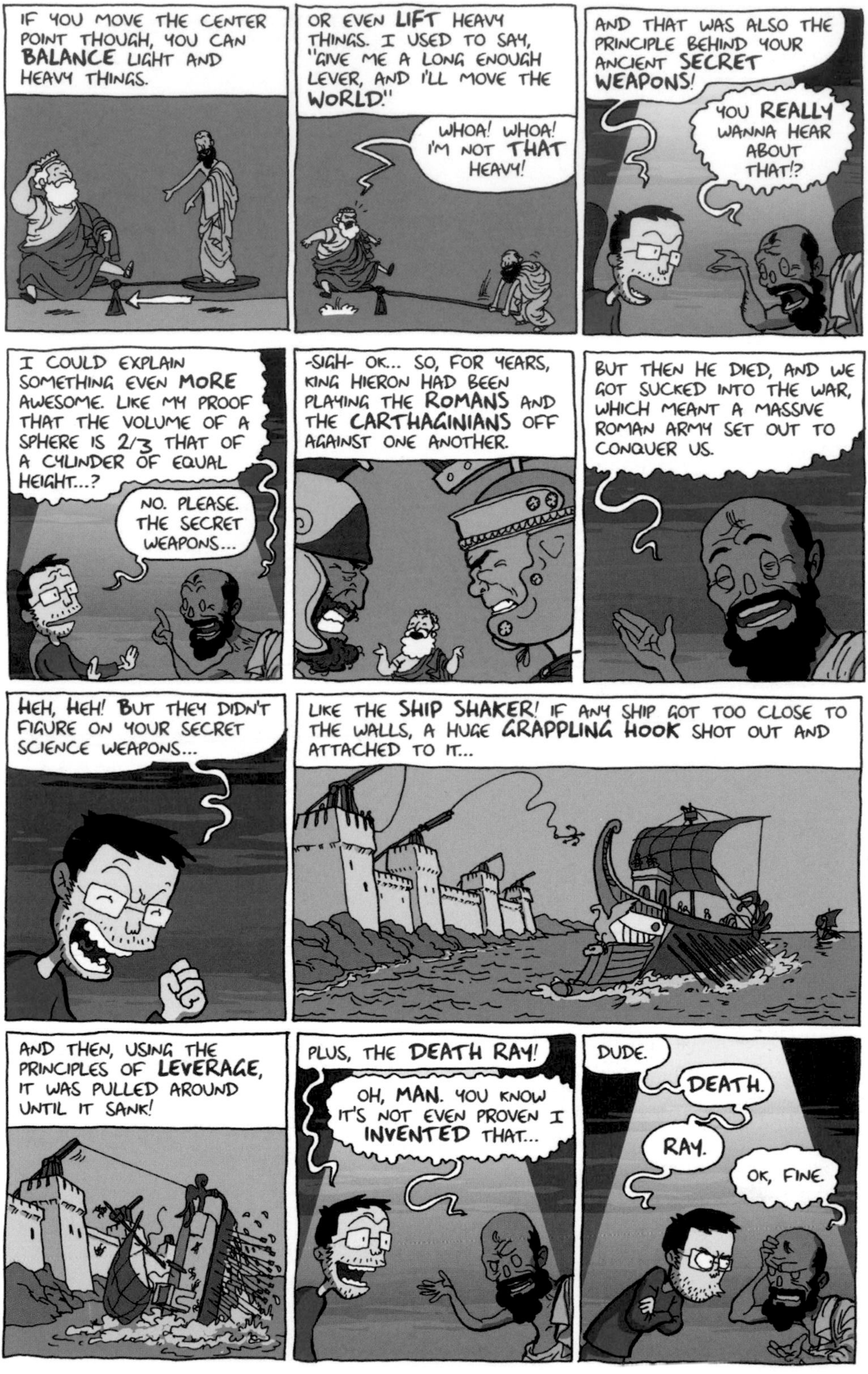
IF YOU MOVE THE CENTER POINT THOUGH, YOU CAN BALANCE LIGHT AND HEAVY THINGS.
OR EVEN LIFT HEAVY THINGS. I USED TO SAY, "GIVE ME A LONG ENOUGH LEVER, AND I'LL MOVE THE WORLD."
WHOA! WHOA! I'M NOT THAT HEAVY!
AND THAT WAS ALSO THE PRINCIPLE BEHIND YOUR ANCIENT SECRET WEAPONS!
YOU REALLY WANNA HEAR ABOUT THAT!?
I COULD EXPLAIN SOMETHING EVEN MORE AWESOME. LIKE MY PROOF THAT THE VOLUME OF A SPHERE IS 2/3 THAT OF A CYLINDER OF EQUAL HEIGHT...?
NO. PLEASE. THE SECRET WEAPONS...
-SIGH- OK... SO, FOR YEARS, KING HIERON HAD BEEN PLAYING THE ROMANS AND THE CARTHAGINIANS OFF AGAINST ONE ANOTHER.
BUT THEN HE DIED, AND WE GOT SUCKED INTO THE WAR, WHICH MEANT A MASSIVE ROMAN ARMY SET OUT TO CONQUER US.
HEH, HEH! BUT THEY DIDN'T FIGURE ON YOUR SECRET SCIENCE WEAPONS...
LIKE THE SHIP SHAKER! IF ANY SHIP GOT TOO CLOSE TO THE WALLS, A HUGE GRAPPLING HOOK SHOT OUT AND ATTACHED TO IT...
AND THEN, USING THE PRINCIPLES OF LEVERAGE, IT WAS PULLED AROUND UNTIL IT SANK!
PLUS, THE DEATH RAY!
OH, MAN. YOU KNOW IT'S NOT EVEN PROVEN I INVENTED THAT...
DUDE.
DEATH.
RAY.
OK, FINE.

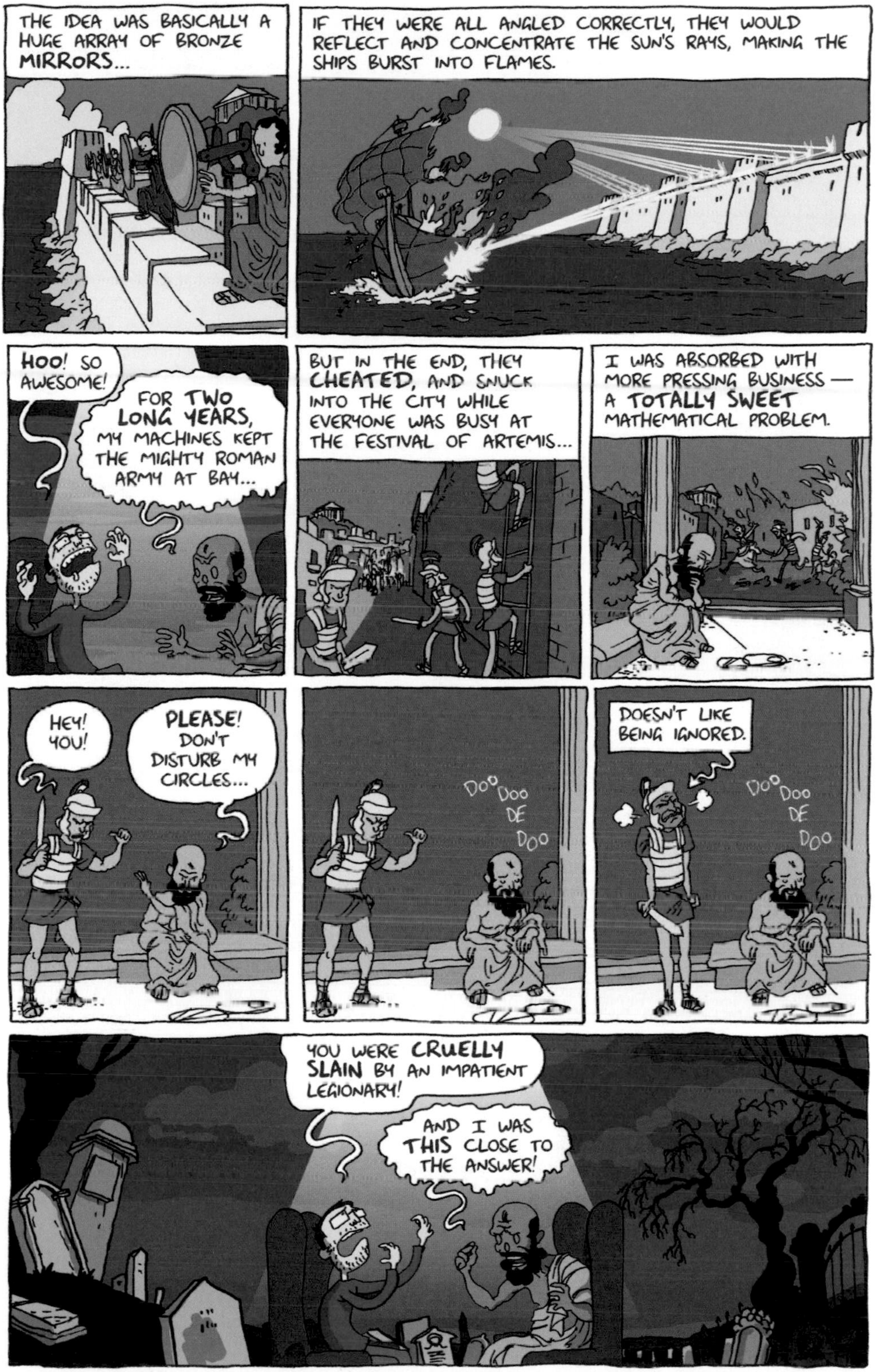
THE IDEA WAS BASICALLY A HUGE ARRAY OF BRONZE MIRRORS...
IF THEY WERE ALL ANGLED CORRECTLY, THEY WOULD REFLECT AND CONCENTRATE THE SUN'S RAYS, MAKING THE SHIPS BURST INTO FLAMES.
HOO! SO AWESOME!
FOR TWO LONG YEARS, MY MACHINES KEPT THE MIGHTY ROMAN ARMY AT BAY...
BUT IN THE END, THEY CHEATED, AND SNUCK INTO THE CITY WHILE EVERYONE WAS BUSY AT THE FESTIVAL OF ARTEMIS...
I WAS ABSORBED WITH MORE PRESSING BUSINESS — A TOTALLY SWEET MATHEMATICAL PROBLEM.
HEY! YOU!
PLEASE! DON'T DISTURB MY CIRCLES...
DOO DOO DE DOO
DOESN'T LIKE BEING IGNORED.
DOO DOO DE DOO
YOU WERE CRUELLY SLAIN BY AN IMPATIENT LEGIONARY!
AND I WAS THIS CLOSE TO THE ANSWER!

CALCULATED AGGRESSION

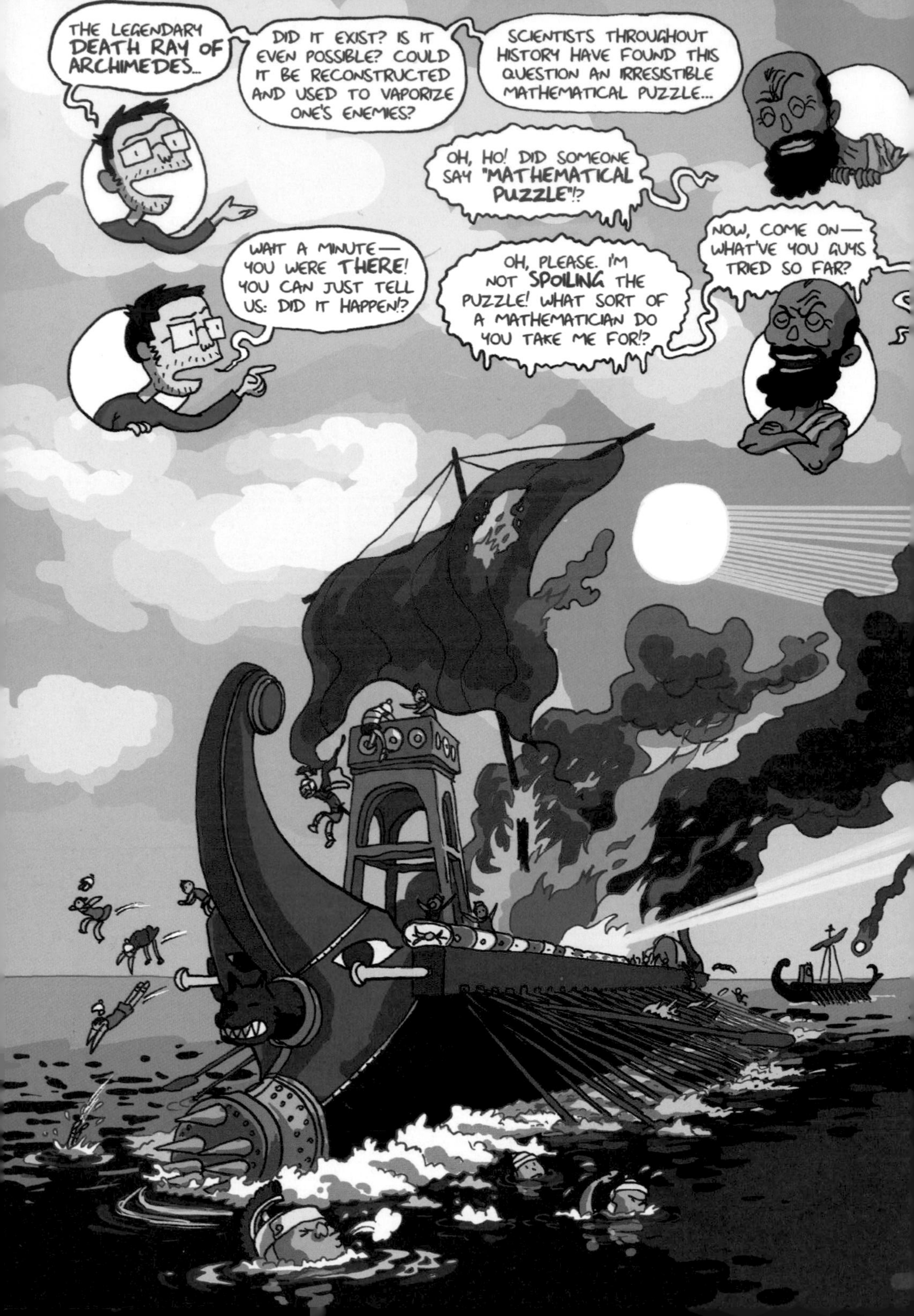
THE LEGENDARY DEATH RAY OF ARCHIMEDES...
DID IT EXIST? IS IT EVEN POSSIBLE? COULD IT BE RECONSTRUCTED AND USED TO VAPORIZE ONE'S ENEMIES?
SCIENTISTS THROUGHOUT HISTORY HAVE FOUND THIS QUESTION AN IRRESISTIBLE MATHEMATICAL PUZZLE...
OH, HO! DID SOMEONE SAY "MATHEMATICAL PUZZLE"!?
WAIT A MINUTE— YOU WERE THERE! YOU CAN JUST TELL US: DID IT HAPPEN!?
OH, PLEASE. I'M NOT SPOILING THE PUZZLE! WHAT SORT OF A MATHEMATICIAN DO YOU TAKE ME FOR!?
NOW, COME ON— WHAT'VE YOU GUYS TRIED SO FAR?

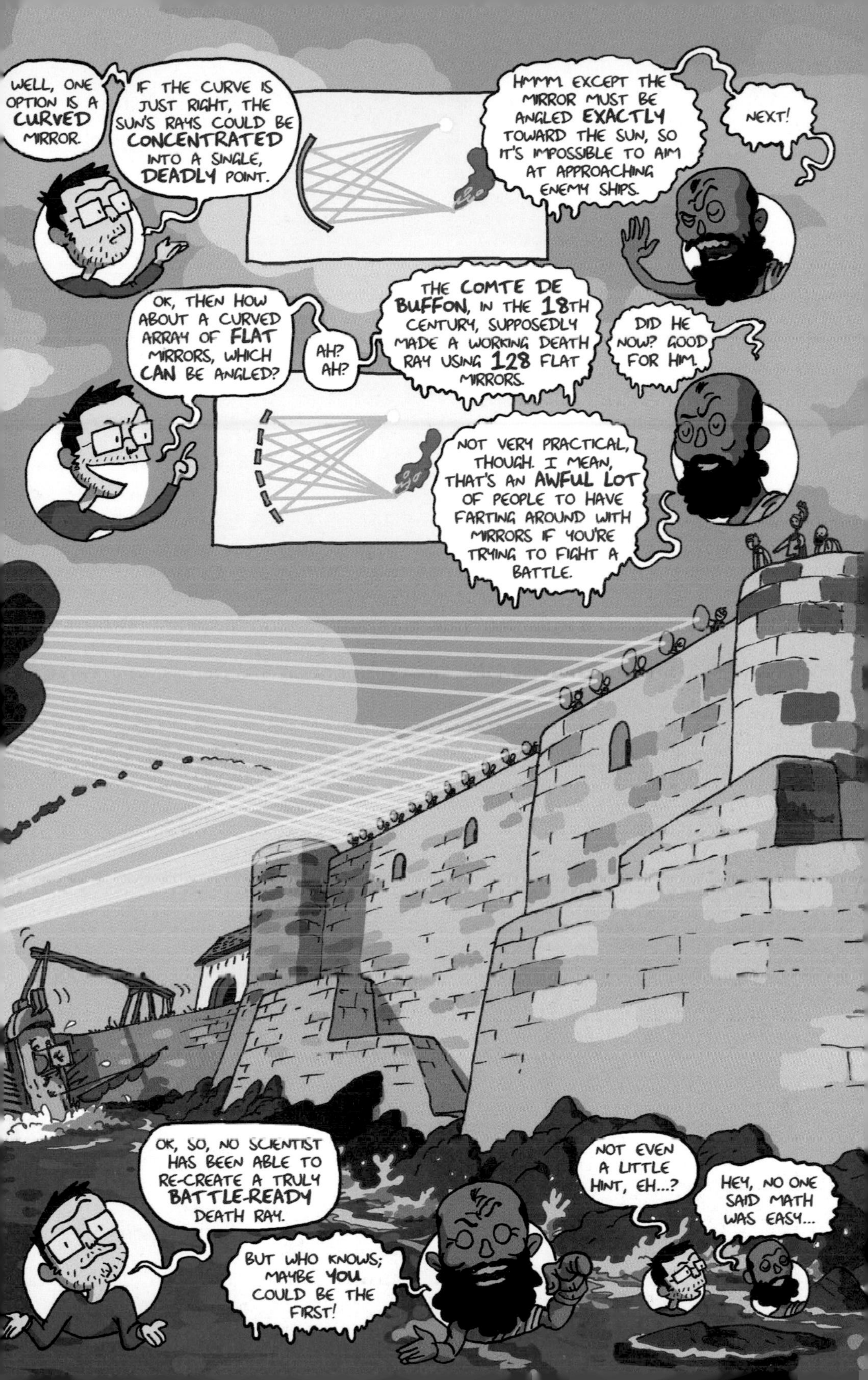
WELL, ONE OPTION IS A CURVED MIRROR.
IF THE CURVE IS JUST RIGHT, THE SUN'S RAYS COULD BE CONCENTRATED INTO A SINGLE, DEADLY POINT.
HMMM. EXCEPT THE MIRROR MUST BE ANGLED EXACTLY TOWARD THE SUN, SO IT'S IMPOSSIBLE TO AIM AT APPROACHING ENEMY SHIPS.
NEXT!
OK, THEN HOW ABOUT A CURVED ARRAY OF FLAT MIRRORS, WHICH CAN BE ANGLED?
AH? AH?
THE COMTE DE BUFFON, IN THE 18TH CENTURY, SUPPOSEDLY MADE A WORKING DEATH RAY USING 128 FLAT MIRRORS.
DID HE NOW? GOOD FOR HIM.
NOT VERY PRACTICAL, THOUGH. I MEAN, THAT'S AN AWFUL LOT OF PEOPLE TO HAVE FARTING AROUND WITH MIRRORS IF YOU'RE TRYING TO FIGHT A BATTLE.
OK, SO, NO SCIENTIST HAS BEEN ABLE TO RE-CREATE A TRULY BATTLE-READY DEATH RAY.
BUT WHO KNOWS; MAYBE YOU COULD BE THE FIRST!
NOT EVEN A LITTLE HINT, EH...?
HEY, NO ONE SAID MATH WAS EASY...

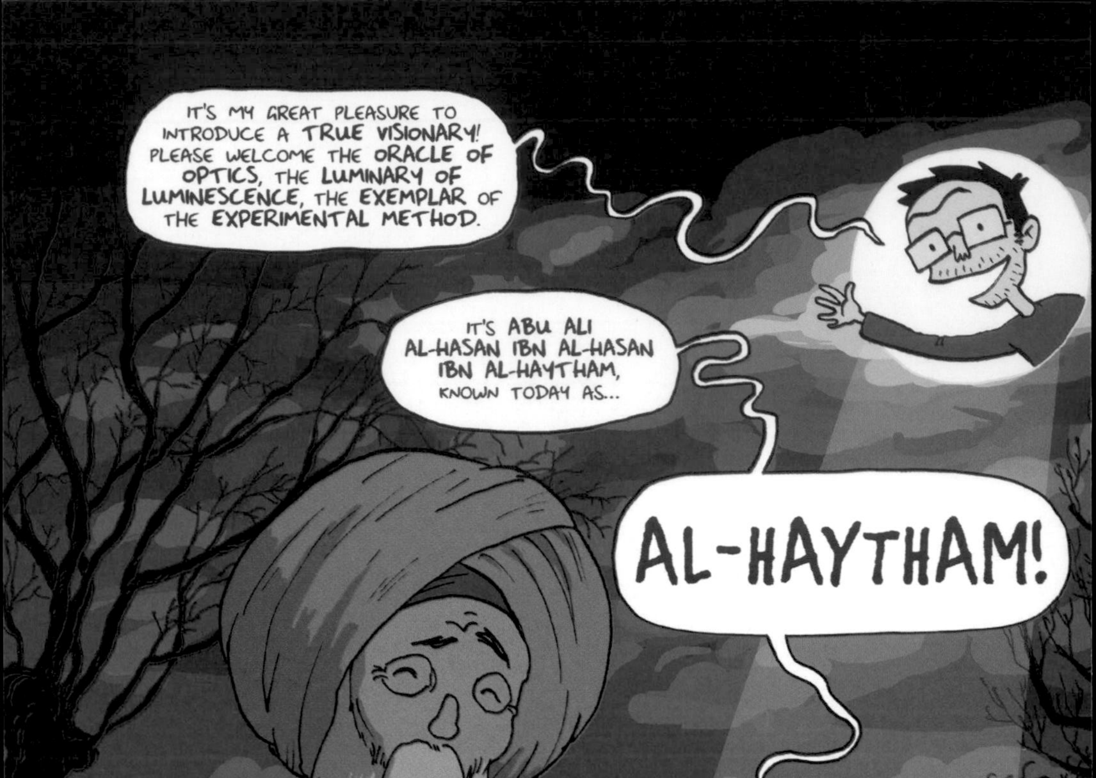
IT'S MY GREAT PLEASURE TO INTRODUCE A TRUE VISIONARY! PLEASE WELCOME THE ORACLE OF OPTICS, THE LUMINARY OF LUMINESCENCE, THE EXEMPLAR OF THE EXPERIMENTAL METHOD.
IT'S ABU ALI AL-HASAN IBN AL-HASAN IBN AL-HAYTHAM, KNOWN TODAY AS...
AL-HAYTHAM!
IBN AL-HAYTHAM
NATURAL PHILOSOPHER
965–1040

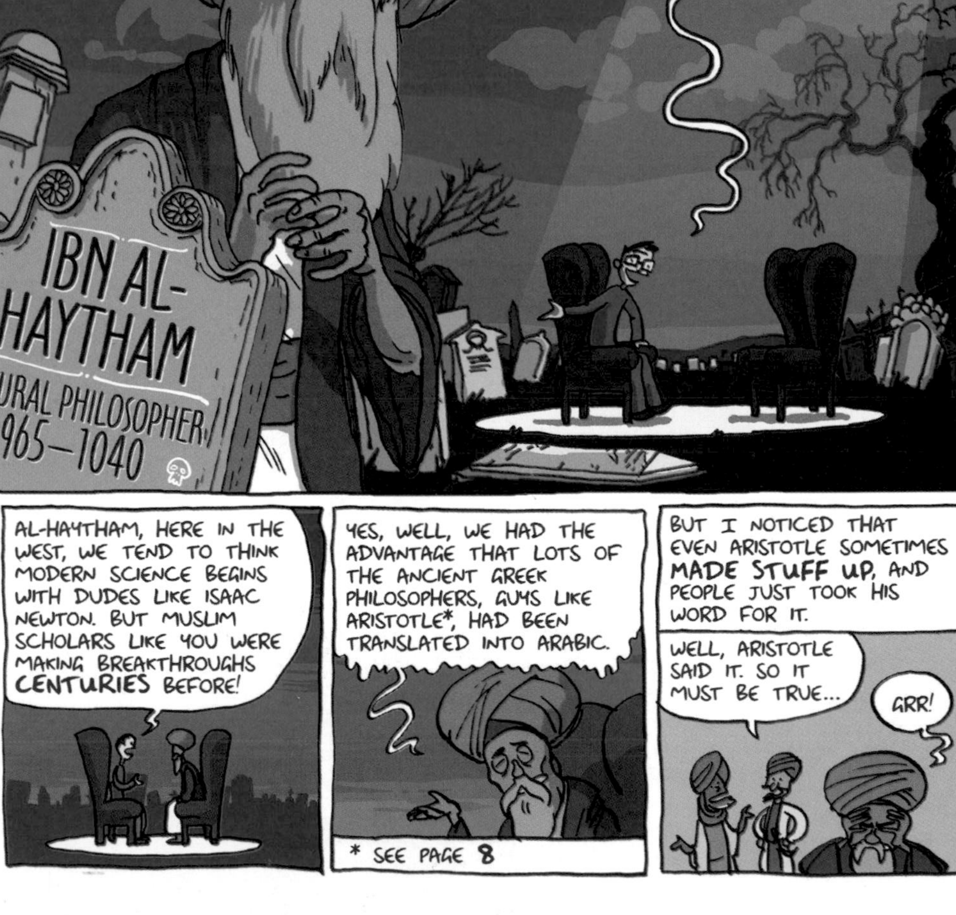
AL-HAYTHAM, HERE IN THE WEST, WE TEND TO THINK MODERN SCIENCE BEGINS WITH DUDES LIKE ISAAC NEWTON. BUT MUSLIM SCHOLARS LIKE YOU WERE MAKING BREAKTHROUGHS CENTURIES BEFORE!
YES, WELL, WE HAD THE ADVANTAGE THAT LOTS OF THE ANCIENT GREEK PHILOSOPHERS, GUYS LIKE ARISTOTLE*, HAD BEEN TRANSLATED INTO ARABIC.
* SEE PAGE 8
BUT I NOTICED THAT EVEN ARISTOTLE SOMETIMES MADE STUFF UP, AND PEOPLE JUST TOOK HIS WORD FOR IT.
WELL, ARISTOTLE SAID IT. SO IT MUST BE TRUE...
GRR!

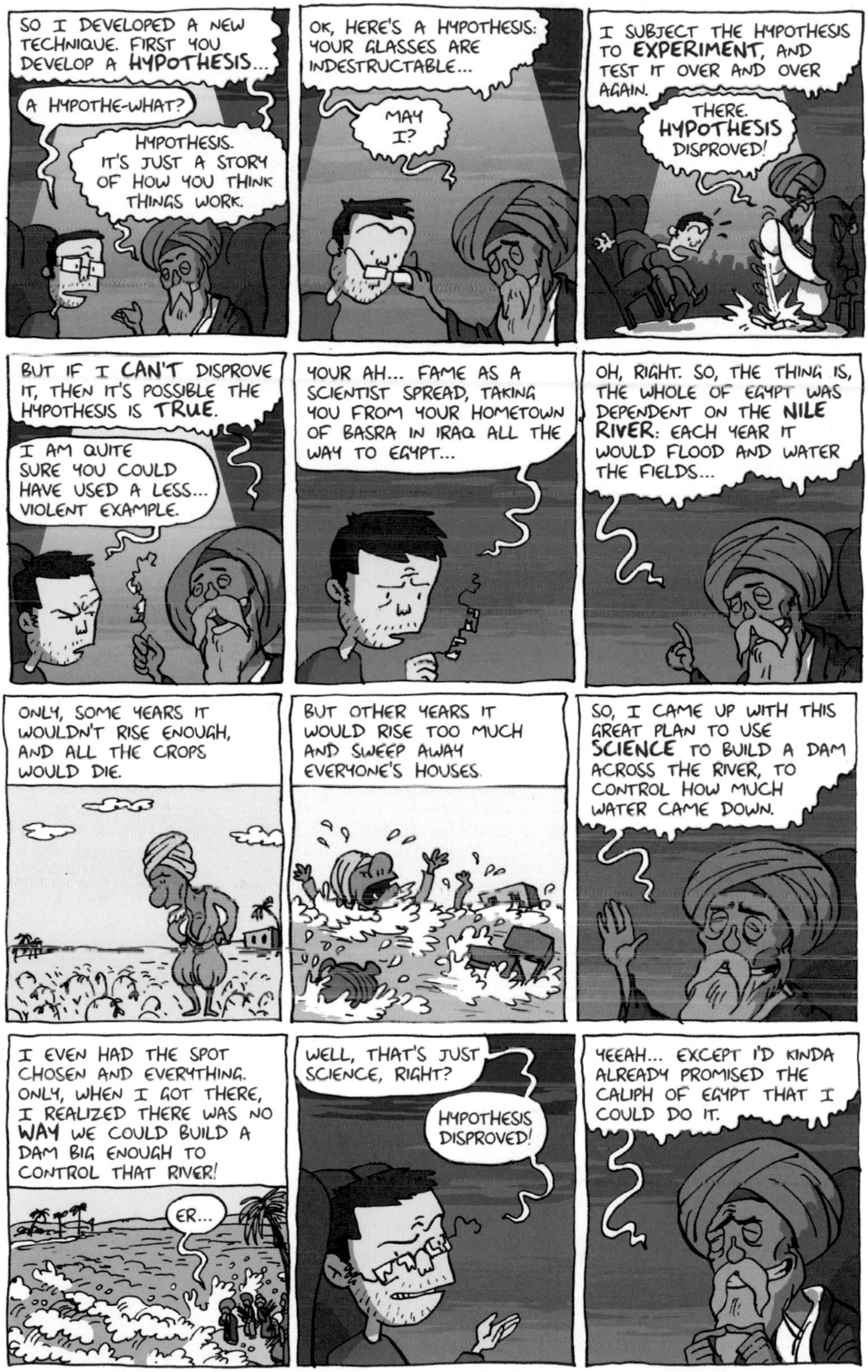
SO I DEVELOPED A NEW TECHNIQUE. FIRST YOU DEVELOP A HYPOTHESIS...
A HYPOTHE-WHAT?
HYPOTHESIS. IT'S JUST A STORY OF HOW YOU THINK THINGS WORK.
OK, HERE'S A HYPOTHESIS: YOUR GLASSES ARE INDESTRUCTABLE...
MAY I?
I SUBJECT THE HYPOTHESIS TO EXPERIMENT, AND TEST IT OVER AND OVER AGAIN.
THERE. HYPOTHESIS DISPROVED!
BUT IF I CAN'T DISPROVE IT, THEN IT'S POSSIBLE THE HYPOTHESIS IS TRUE.
I AM QUITE SURE YOU COULD HAVE USED A LESS... VIOLENT EXAMPLE.
YOUR AH... FAME AS A SCIENTIST SPREAD, TAKING YOU FROM YOUR HOMETOWN OF BASRA IN IRAQ ALL THE WAY TO EGYPT...
OH, RIGHT. SO, THE THING IS, THE WHOLE OF EGYPT WAS DEPENDENT ON THE NILE RIVER: EACH YEAR IT WOULD FLOOD AND WATER THE FIELDS...
ONLY, SOME YEARS IT WOULDN'T RISE ENOUGH, AND ALL THE CROPS WOULD DIE.
BUT OTHER YEARS IT WOULD RISE TOO MUCH AND SWEEP AWAY EVERYONE'S HOUSES.
SO, I CAME UP WITH THIS GREAT PLAN TO USE SCIENCE TO BUILD A DAM ACROSS THE RIVER, TO CONTROL HOW MUCH WATER CAME DOWN.
I EVEN HAD THE SPOT CHOSEN AND EVERYTHING. ONLY, WHEN I GOT THERE, I REALIZED THERE WAS NO WAY WE COULD BUILD A DAM BIG ENOUGH TO CONTROL THAT RIVER!
ER...
WELL, THAT'S JUST SCIENCE, RIGHT?
HYPOTHESIS DISPROVED!
YEEAH... EXCEPT I'D KINDA ALREADY PROMISED THE CALIPH OF EGYPT THAT I COULD DO IT.

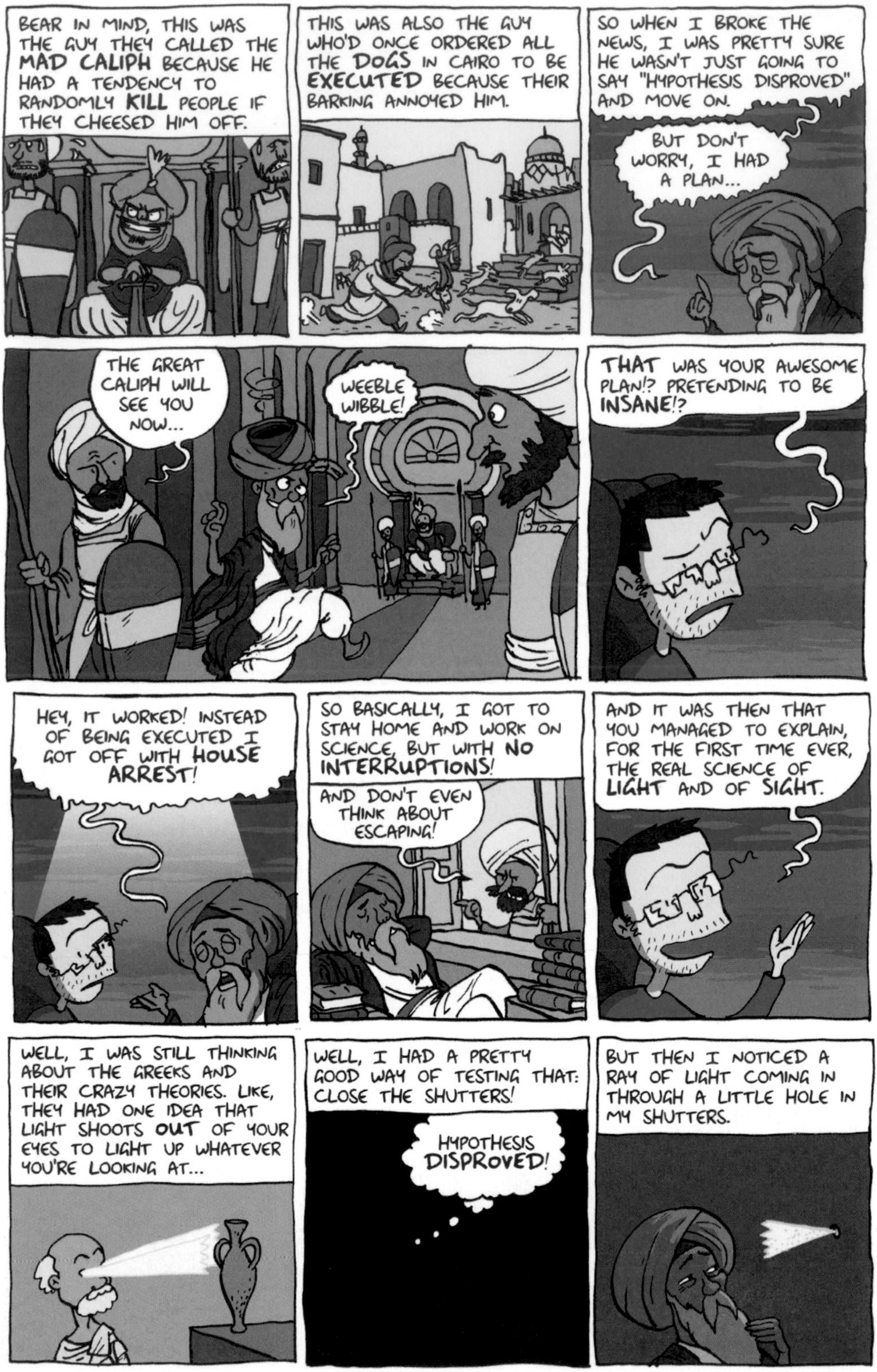
BEAR IN MIND, THIS WAS THE GUY THEY CALLED THE MAD CALIPH BECAUSE HE HAD A TENDENCY TO RANDOMLY KILL PEOPLE IF THEY CHEESED HIM OFF.
THIS WAS ALSO THE GUY WHO'D ONCE ORDERED ALL THE DOGS IN CAIRO TO BE EXECUTED BECAUSE THEIR BARKING ANNOYED HIM.
SO WHEN I BROKE THE NEWS, I WAS PRETTY SURE HE WASN'T JUST GOING TO SAY "HYPOTHESIS DISPROVED" AND MOVE ON.
BUT DON'T WORRY, I HAD A PLAN...
THE GREAT CALIPH WILL SEE YOU NOW...
WEEBLE WIBBLE!
THAT WAS YOUR AWESOME PLAN!? PRETENDING TO BE INSANE!?
HEY, IT WORKED! INSTEAD OF BEING EXECUTED I GOT OFF WITH HOUSE ARREST!
SO BASICALLY, I GOT TO STAY HOME AND WORK ON SCIENCE, BUT WITH NO INTERRUPTIONS!
AND DON'T EVEN THINK ABOUT ESCAPING!
AND IT WAS THEN THAT YOU MANAGED TO EXPLAIN, FOR THE FIRST TIME EVER, THE REAL SCIENCE OF LIGHT AND OF SIGHT.
WELL, I WAS STILL THINKING ABOUT THE GREEKS AND THEIR CRAZY THEORIES. LIKE, THEY HAD ONE IDEA THAT LIGHT SHOOTS OUT OF YOUR EYES TO LIGHT UP WHATEVER YOU'RE LOOKING AT...
WELL, I HAD A PRETTY GOOD WAY OF TESTING THAT: CLOSE THE SHUTTERS!
HYPOTHESIS DISPROVED!
BUT THEN I NOTICED A RAY OF LIGHT COMING IN THROUGH A LITTLE HOLE IN MY SHUTTERS.

AND **THEN** I SAW SOMETHING **REALLY** WEIRD—ON THE OPPOSITE WALL, I COULD SEE WHAT WAS OUTSIDE, ONLY IT WAS **UPSIDE DOWN!**

NOW, THERE'S ONLY **ONE** THEORY THAT COULD EXPLAIN **THAT!**

REALLY?

I MEAN, YES! OBVIOUSLY!

ER... WHAT IS IT...?

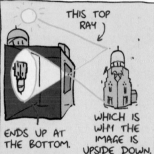

LIGHT MUST BE TRAVELING IN A **STRAIGHT LINE** FROM THE SUN, AND THEN BOUNCING OFF THE OBJECTS OUTSIDE.

ANYBODY LOOKING AT SOMETHING WILL HAVE **SOME** OF THOSE RAYS BOUNCING IN THEIR DIRECTION, ALLOWING THEM TO SEE IT.

BUT ONLY A FEW RAYS GET THROUGH THE LITTLE HOLE.

THIS TOP RAY

ENDS UP AT THE BOTTOM.

WHICH IS WHY THE IMAGE IS UPSIDE DOWN.

AND I ALSO REALIZED IT'S THE SAME THING THAT'S HAPPENING IN YOUR EYE!

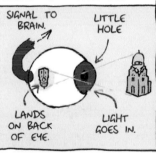

SIGNAL TO BRAIN.

LITTLE HOLE

LANDS ON BACK OF EYE.

LIGHT GOES IN.

AND IT'S THE SAME THING THAT HAPPENS IN A **CAMERA**, ONLY WITH SOME HIGH-TECH ADDED EXTRAS...

THE **WORD** "CAMERA" IS SHORT FOR **CAMERA OBSCURA**, LATIN FOR "DARK ROOM"!

SO, NOW, IF YOU COULD JUST USE YOUR OCULAR ABILITIES TO **FIX THESE GLASSES**...

SORRY, GLASSES WEREN'T INVENTED FOR ANOTHER TWO CENTURIES.

23

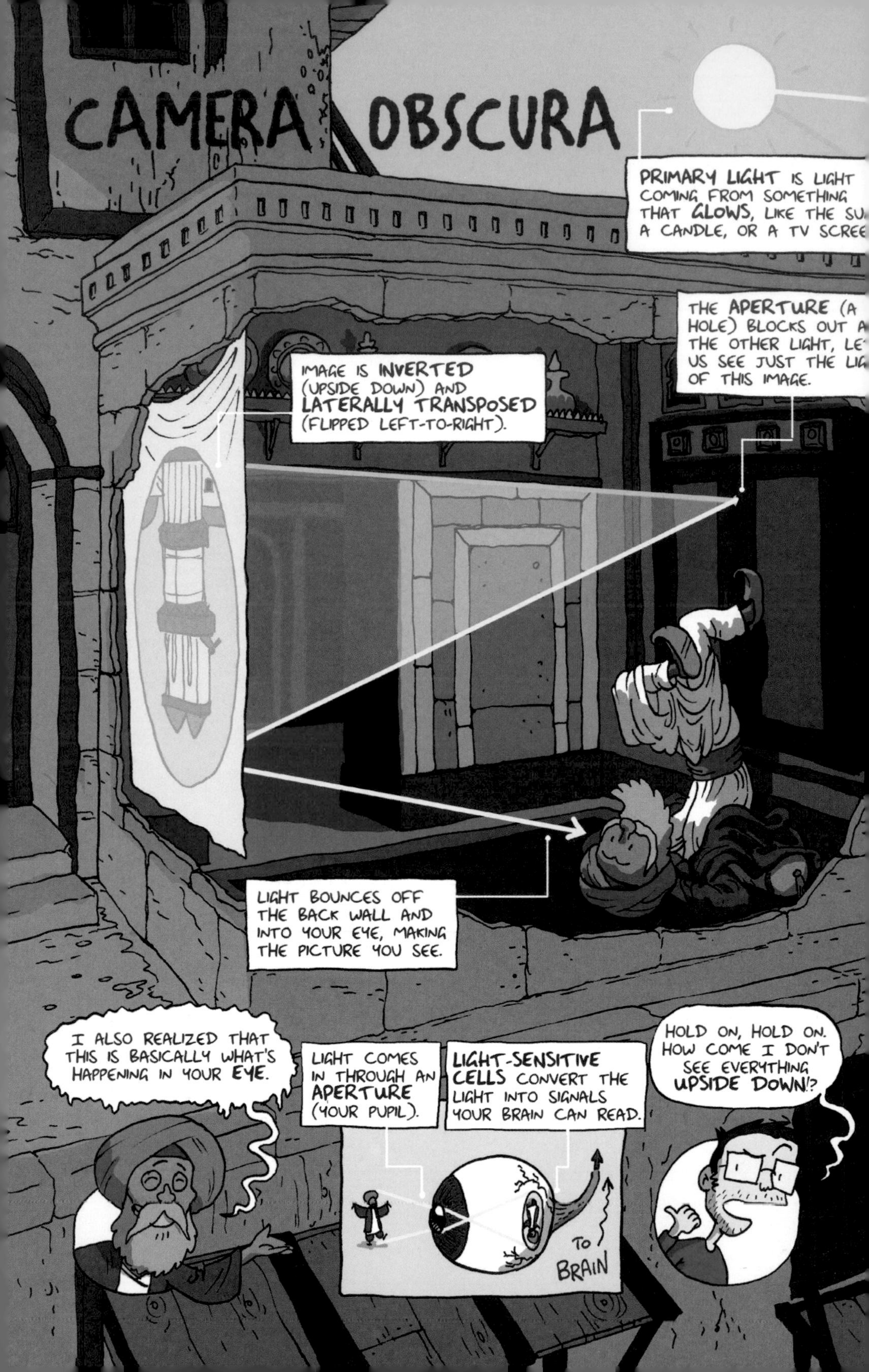
CAMERA OBSCURA
PRIMARY LIGHT IS LIGHT COMING FROM SOMETHING THAT GLOWS, LIKE THE SU A CANDLE, OR A TV SCREE
THE APERTURE (A HOLE) BLOCKS OUT A THE OTHER LIGHT, LE US SEE JUST THE LIG OF THIS IMAGE.
IMAGE IS INVERTED (UPSIDE DOWN) AND LATERALLY TRANSPOSED (FLIPPED LEFT-TO-RIGHT).
LIGHT BOUNCES OFF THE BACK WALL AND INTO YOUR EYE, MAKING THE PICTURE YOU SEE.
I ALSO REALIZED THAT THIS IS BASICALLY WHAT'S HAPPENING IN YOUR EYE.
LIGHT COMES IN THROUGH AN APERTURE (YOUR PUPIL).
LIGHT-SENSITIVE CELLS CONVERT THE LIGHT INTO SIGNALS YOUR BRAIN CAN READ.
TO BRAIN
HOLD ON, HOLD ON. HOW COME I DON'T SEE EVERYTHING UPSIDE DOWN!?

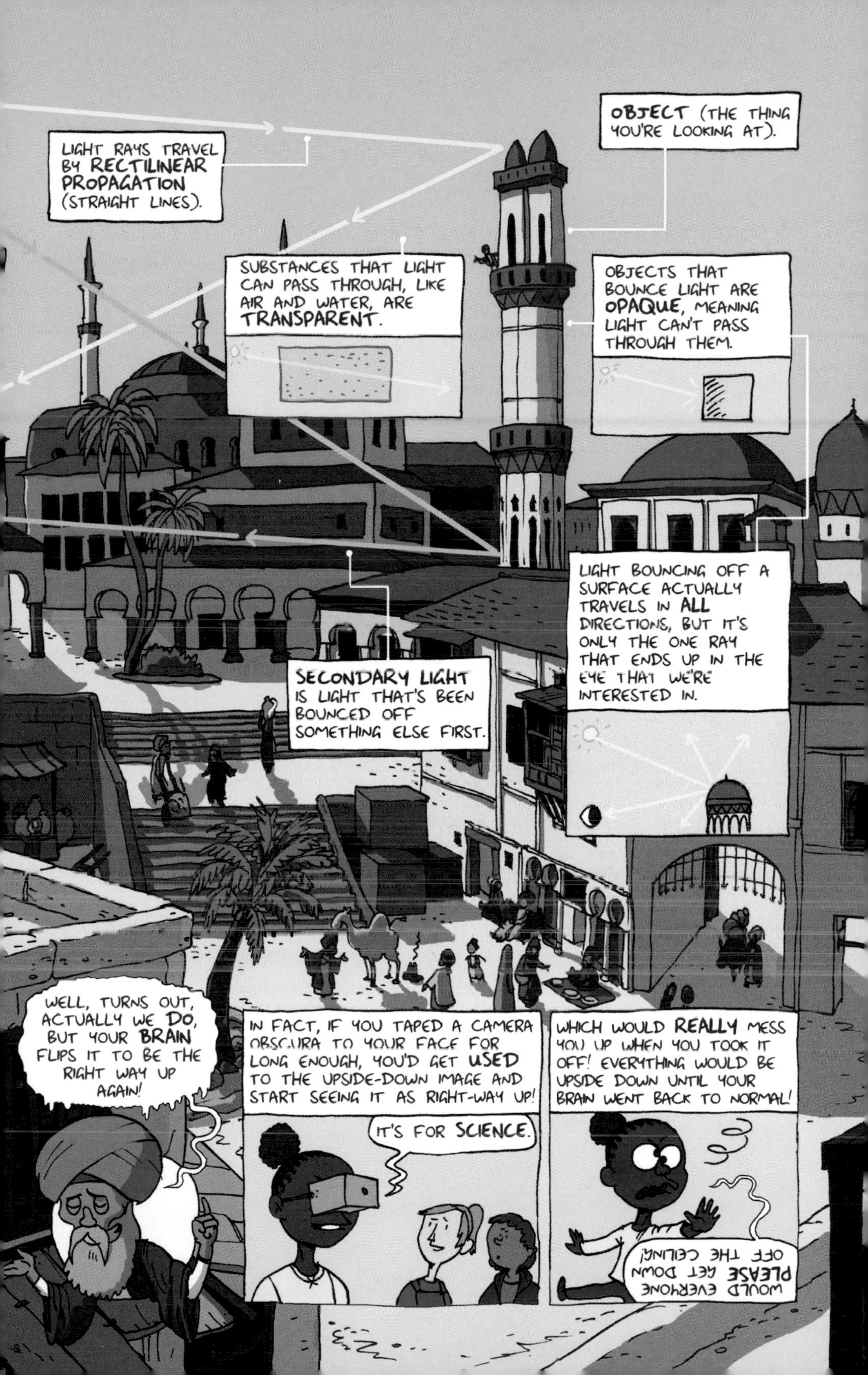
LIGHT RAYS TRAVEL BY RECTILINEAR PROPAGATION (STRAIGHT LINES).
OBJECT (THE THING YOU'RE LOOKING AT).
SUBSTANCES THAT LIGHT CAN PASS THROUGH, LIKE AIR AND WATER, ARE TRANSPARENT.
OBJECTS THAT BOUNCE LIGHT ARE OPAQUE, MEANING LIGHT CAN'T PASS THROUGH THEM.
LIGHT BOUNCING OFF A SURFACE ACTUALLY TRAVELS IN ALL DIRECTIONS, BUT IT'S ONLY THE ONE RAY THAT ENDS UP IN THE EYE THAT WE'RE INTERESTED IN.
SECONDARY LIGHT IS LIGHT THAT'S BEEN BOUNCED OFF SOMETHING ELSE FIRST.
WELL, TURNS OUT, ACTUALLY WE DO, BUT YOUR BRAIN FLIPS IT TO BE THE RIGHT WAY UP AGAIN!
IN FACT, IF YOU TAPED A CAMERA OBSCURA TO YOUR FACE FOR LONG ENOUGH, YOU'D GET USED TO THE UPSIDE-DOWN IMAGE AND START SEEING IT AS RIGHT-WAY UP!
IT'S FOR SCIENCE.
WHICH WOULD REALLY MESS YOU UP WHEN YOU TOOK IT OFF! EVERYTHING WOULD BE UPSIDE DOWN UNTIL YOUR BRAIN WENT BACK TO NORMAL!
WOULD EVERYONE PLEASE GET DOWN OFF THE CEILING!

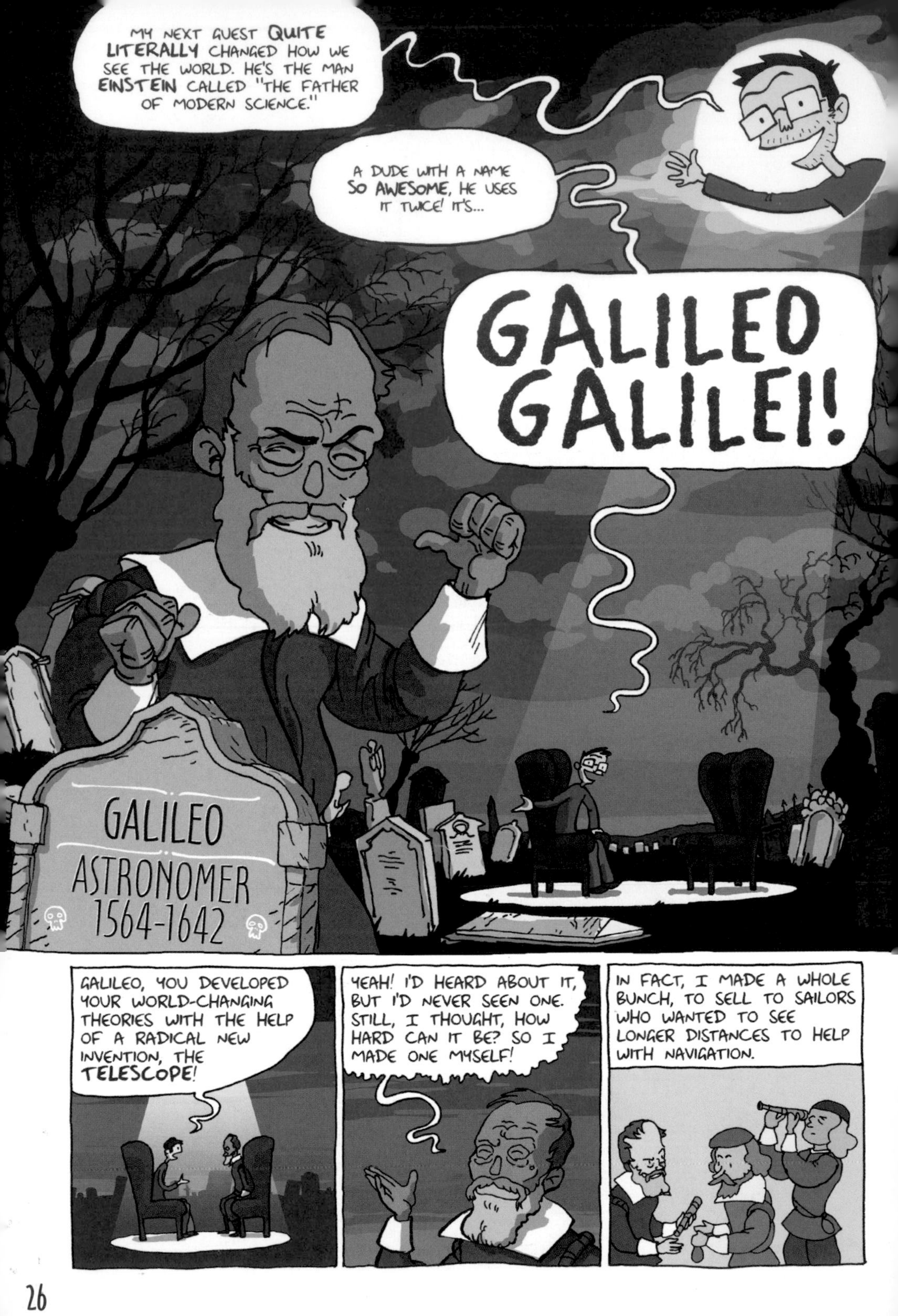
MY NEXT GUEST QUITE LITERALLY CHANGED HOW WE SEE THE WORLD. HE'S THE MAN EINSTEIN CALLED "THE FATHER OF MODERN SCIENCE."
A DUDE WITH A NAME SO AWESOME, HE USES IT TWICE! IT'S...
GALILEO GALILEI!
GALILEO
ASTRONOMER
1564-1642
GALILEO, YOU DEVELOPED YOUR WORLD-CHANGING THEORIES WITH THE HELP OF A RADICAL NEW INVENTION, THE TELESCOPE!
YEAH! I'D HEARD ABOUT IT, BUT I'D NEVER SEEN ONE. STILL, I THOUGHT, HOW HARD CAN IT BE? SO I MADE ONE MYSELF!
IN FACT, I MADE A WHOLE BUNCH, TO SELL TO SAILORS WHO WANTED TO SEE LONGER DISTANCES TO HELP WITH NAVIGATION.

BUT **I** HAD ANOTHER IDEA. I WOULD USE THIS NEW INVENTION TO PROBE THE SECRETS OF THE **UNIVERSE!**

O M G!

SEEN UP CLOSE, I REALIZED THAT THOSE GRAY SPLOTCHES ON THE MOON ARE REALLY **SHADOWS** CAST BY MASSIVE MOUNTAIN RANGES!

I FOUND A COLLECTION OF TINY LIGHTS THAT I REALIZED WERE **OTHER MOONS**, CIRCLING THE VAST PLANET **JUPITER.**

AND, MOST STRIKINGLY, I SAW THE PLANET **VENUS** UP CLOSE. TURNS OUT, IT HAS **PHASES**, JUST LIKE OUR MOON!

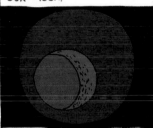

BUT THAT WAS KIND OF A PROBLEM. EVERYONE BELIEVED THE **EARTH** WAS THE CENTER OF THE UNIVERSE, AND EVERYTHING ELSE CIRCLED AROUND IT.

VENUS — SUN — EARTH — DOME OF FIXED STARS

WHAT? NO! THE **EARTH** GOES AROUND THE **SUN!**

DOESN'T IT...?

WELL, THAT'S WHAT MY FINDINGS SUGGESTED.

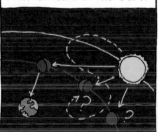

IT'S NOT **POSSIBLE** FOR THE SUN TO CAST THOSE SHADOWS ON VENUS IF THEY BOTH GO AROUND THE EARTH.

BUT THIS WAS THE **TOTAL OPPOSITE** OF WHAT EVERYONE HAD BELIEVED FOR **THOUSANDS** OF YEARS!

THE CHURCH GOT WIND OF IT, AND THEY STARTED **FREAKING OUT.**

WHAT HAS THE **CHURCH** GOT TO DO WITH IT?

ARE YOU KIDDING? BACK THEN, THE CHURCH HAD **EVERYTHING** TO DO WITH **EVERYTHING!**

AND THEY WERE PARTICULARLY CONCERNED THAT THIS NEW THEORY **CONTRADICTED** SOME PASSAGES IN THE BIBLE.

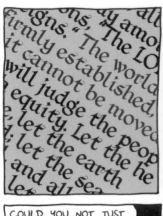

...igns." The LO... ...irmly established, it cannot be moved. ...will judge the peop... ...e equity. Let the... ...let the earth... ...and the sea... ...Let all...

...and generation... go, but the earth remains forever. The sun also arises, and sets, and hurries back to where it rises. The wind blows to the south and turns to the...

HOLY SCRIPTURE CAN'T POSSIBLY BE WRONG! IT MUST BE THESE NEW THEORIES!

COULD YOU NOT JUST SAY THOSE BITS WERE "POETICAL" OR SOMETHING?

I TRIED THAT.

POETICAL? TRY HERETICAL.

A HERETIC WAS SOMEONE WHO BELIEVED ILLEGAL IDEAS THAT WERE BANNED BY THE CHURCH.

AND THEY HAD A SPECIAL PUNISHMENT RESERVED FOR THAT...

SO I KEPT QUIET ABOUT MY FINDINGS, BUT THEN AN OLD BUDDY OF MINE GOT ELECTED POPE.

IT'S COOL, GG. WHY DON'T YOU WRITE A BOOK THAT EXPLAINS BOTH SIDES, LET PEOPLE DECIDE FOR THEMSELVES...

BUT THAT'S... NOT REALLY WHAT YOU DID...

SURE IT IS! MY BOOK HAD TWO CHARACTERS. EACH PUTTING FORWARD ONE SIDE OF THE ARGUMENT.

YEAH, BUT YOU MADE THE SUN-GOES-AROUND-THE-EARTH GUY SOUND REALLY STUPID.

ANYONE WHO BELIEVES THAT IS REALLY STUPID!

AND YOU CALLED HIM "SIMPLICIO," MEANING SIMPLETON!

IT'S THE NAME OF AN ANCIENT GREEK PHILOSOPHER!

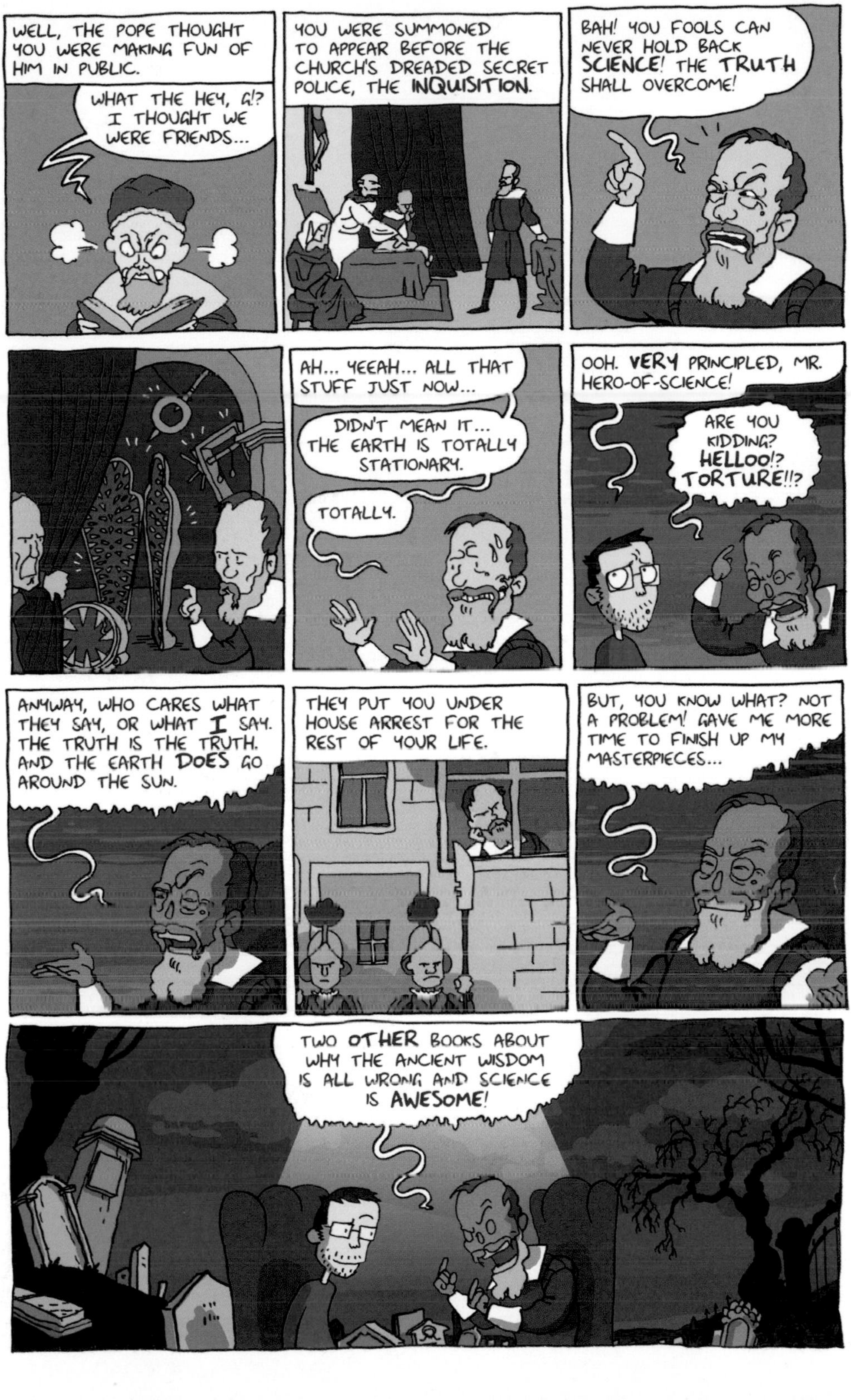
WELL, THE POPE THOUGHT YOU WERE MAKING FUN OF HIM IN PUBLIC.
WHAT THE HEY, G!? I THOUGHT WE WERE FRIENDS...
YOU WERE SUMMONED TO APPEAR BEFORE THE CHURCH'S DREADED SECRET POLICE, THE INQUISITION.
BAH! YOU FOOLS CAN NEVER HOLD BACK SCIENCE! THE TRUTH SHALL OVERCOME!
AH... YEEAH... ALL THAT STUFF JUST NOW...
DIDN'T MEAN IT... THE EARTH IS TOTALLY STATIONARY.
TOTALLY.
OOH. VERY PRINCIPLED, MR. HERO-OF-SCIENCE!
ARE YOU KIDDING? HELLOO!? TORTURE!!?
ANYWAY, WHO CARES WHAT THEY SAY, OR WHAT I SAY. THE TRUTH IS THE TRUTH. AND THE EARTH DOES GO AROUND THE SUN.
THEY PUT YOU UNDER HOUSE ARREST FOR THE REST OF YOUR LIFE.
BUT, YOU KNOW WHAT? NOT A PROBLEM! GAVE ME MORE TIME TO FINISH UP MY MASTERPIECES...
TWO OTHER BOOKS ABOUT WHY THE ANCIENT WISDOM IS ALL WRONG AND SCIENCE IS AWESOME!

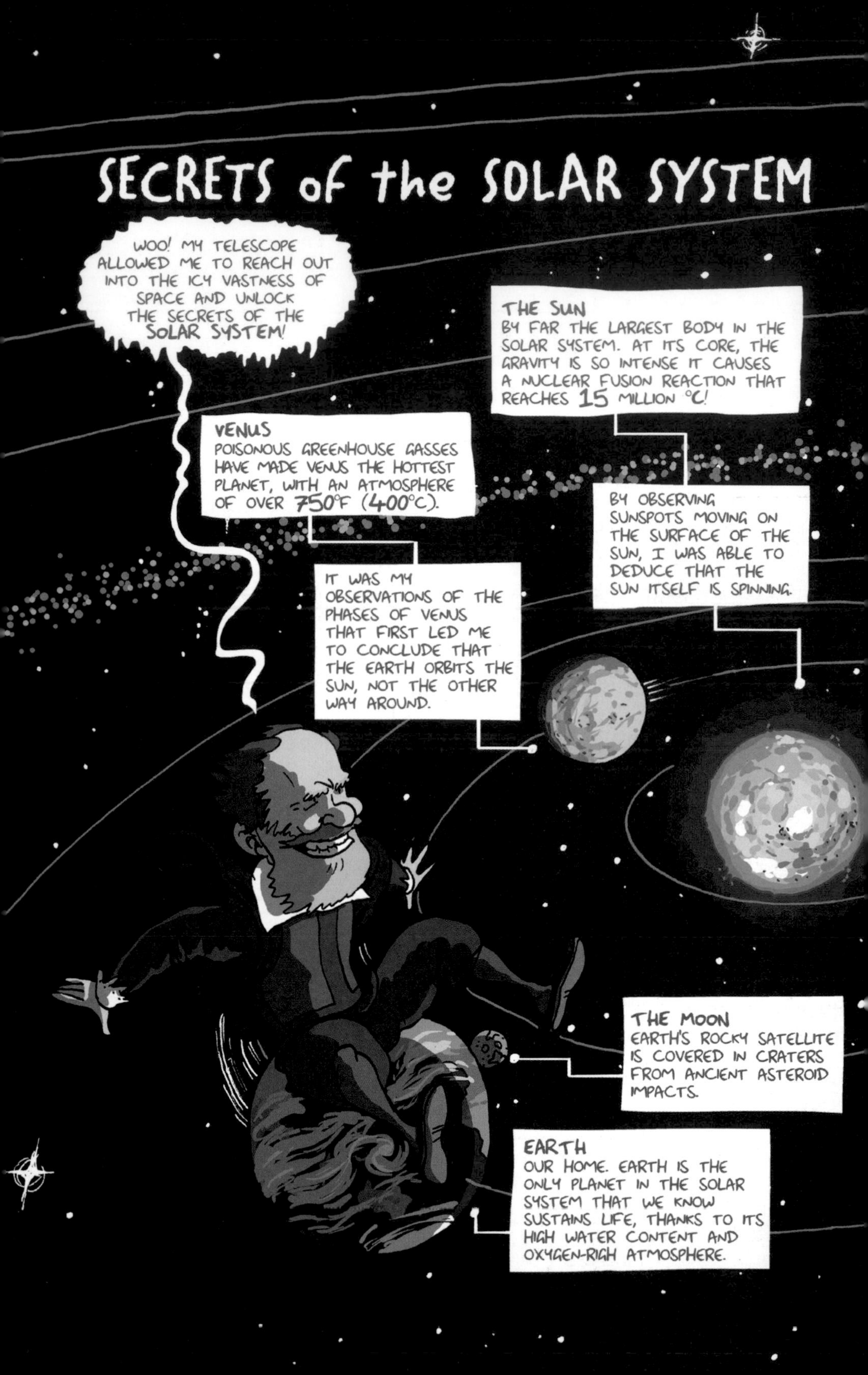
SECRETS of the SOLAR SYSTEM
WOO! MY TELESCOPE ALLOWED ME TO REACH OUT INTO THE ICY VASTNESS OF SPACE AND UNLOCK THE SECRETS OF THE SOLAR SYSTEM!
THE SUN
BY FAR THE LARGEST BODY IN THE SOLAR SYSTEM. AT ITS CORE, THE GRAVITY IS SO INTENSE IT CAUSES A NUCLEAR FUSION REACTION THAT REACHES 15 MILLION °C!
VENUS
POISONOUS GREENHOUSE GASSES HAVE MADE VENUS THE HOTTEST PLANET, WITH AN ATMOSPHERE OF OVER 750°F (400°C).
BY OBSERVING SUNSPOTS MOVING ON THE SURFACE OF THE SUN, I WAS ABLE TO DEDUCE THAT THE SUN ITSELF IS SPINNING.
IT WAS MY OBSERVATIONS OF THE PHASES OF VENUS THAT FIRST LED ME TO CONCLUDE THAT THE EARTH ORBITS THE SUN, NOT THE OTHER WAY AROUND.
THE MOON
EARTH'S ROCKY SATELLITE IS COVERED IN CRATERS FROM ANCIENT ASTEROID IMPACTS.
EARTH
OUR HOME. EARTH IS THE ONLY PLANET IN THE SOLAR SYSTEM THAT WE KNOW SUSTAINS LIFE, THANKS TO ITS HIGH WATER CONTENT AND OXYGEN-RIGH ATMOSPHERE.

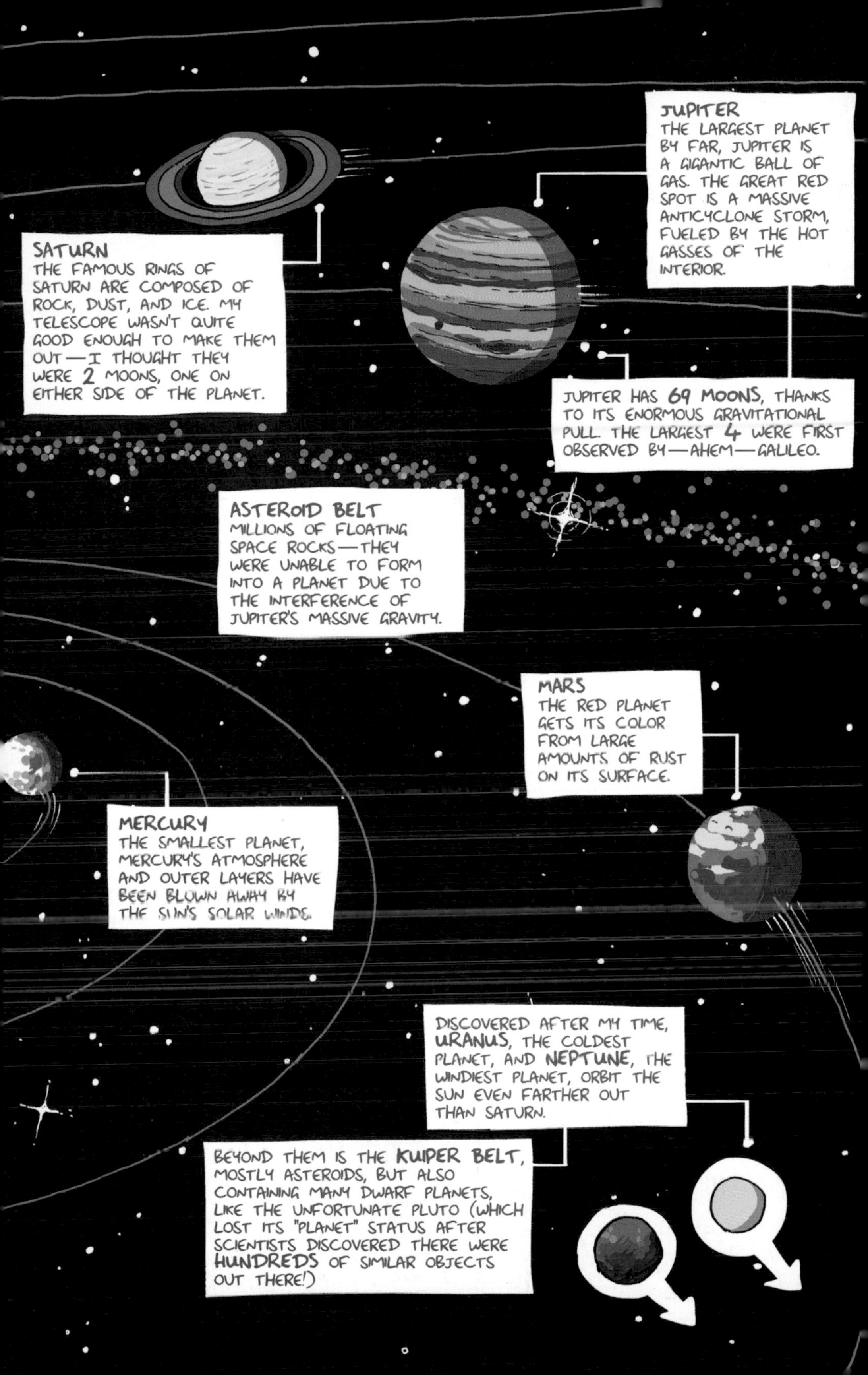
JUPITER
THE LARGEST PLANET BY FAR, JUPITER IS A GIGANTIC BALL OF GAS. THE GREAT RED SPOT IS A MASSIVE ANTICYCLONE STORM, FUELED BY THE HOT GASSES OF THE INTERIOR.
SATURN
THE FAMOUS RINGS OF SATURN ARE COMPOSED OF ROCK, DUST, AND ICE. MY TELESCOPE WASN'T QUITE GOOD ENOUGH TO MAKE THEM OUT—I THOUGHT THEY WERE 2 MOONS, ONE ON EITHER SIDE OF THE PLANET.
JUPITER HAS 69 MOONS, THANKS TO ITS ENORMOUS GRAVITATIONAL PULL. THE LARGEST 4 WERE FIRST OBSERVED BY—AHEM—GALILEO.
ASTEROID BELT
MILLIONS OF FLOATING SPACE ROCKS—THEY WERE UNABLE TO FORM INTO A PLANET DUE TO THE INTERFERENCE OF JUPITER'S MASSIVE GRAVITY.
MARS
THE RED PLANET GETS ITS COLOR FROM LARGE AMOUNTS OF RUST ON ITS SURFACE.
MERCURY
THE SMALLEST PLANET, MERCURY'S ATMOSPHERE AND OUTER LAYERS HAVE BEEN BLOWN AWAY BY THE SUN'S SOLAR WINDS.
DISCOVERED AFTER MY TIME, URANUS, THE COLDEST PLANET, AND NEPTUNE, THE WINDIEST PLANET, ORBIT THE SUN EVEN FARTHER OUT THAN SATURN.
BEYOND THEM IS THE KUIPER BELT, MOSTLY ASTEROIDS, BUT ALSO CONTAINING MANY DWARF PLANETS, LIKE THE UNFORTUNATE PLUTO (WHICH LOST ITS "PLANET" STATUS AFTER SCIENTISTS DISCOVERED THERE WERE HUNDREDS OF SIMILAR OBJECTS OUT THERE!)

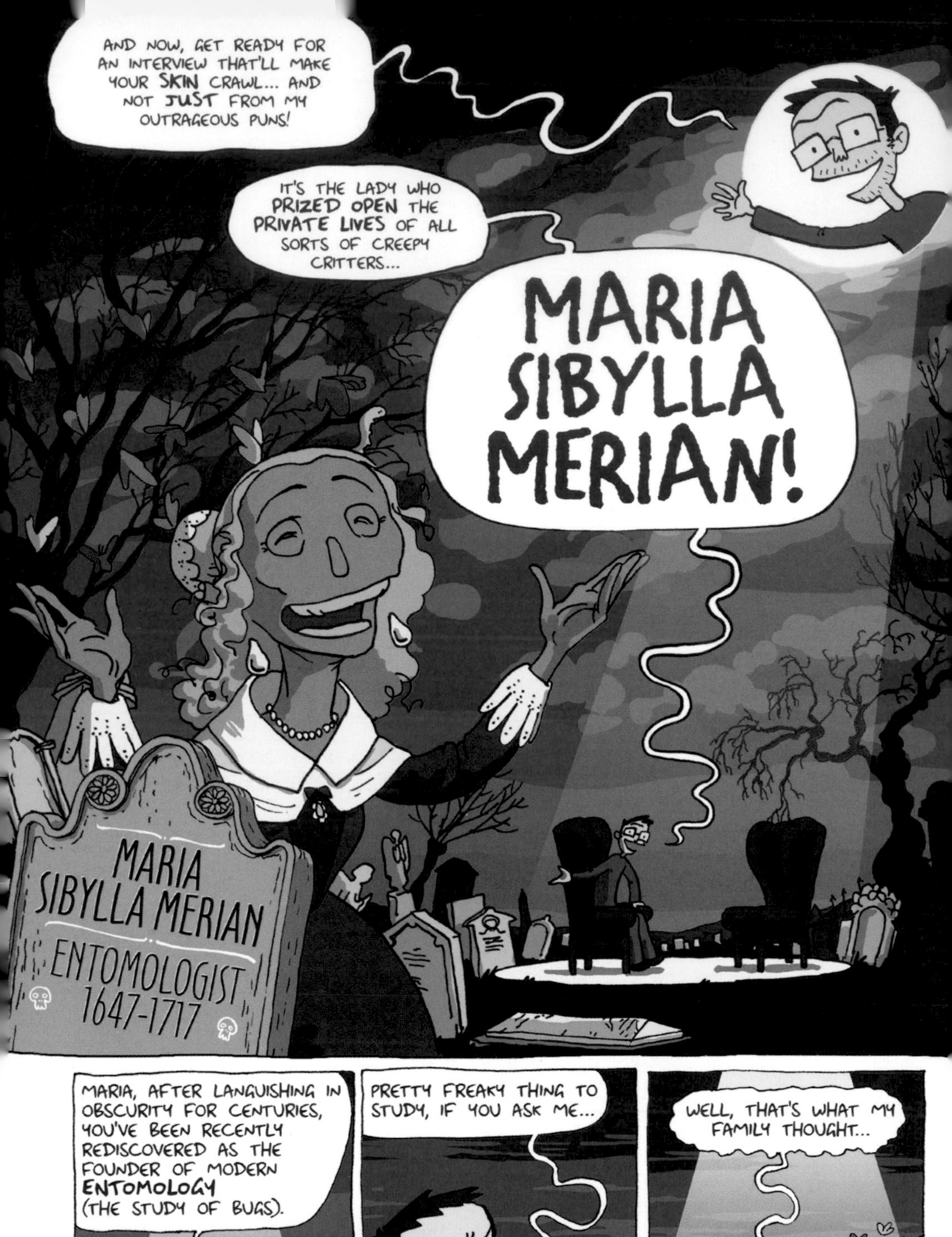
AND NOW, GET READY FOR AN INTERVIEW THAT'LL MAKE YOUR SKIN CRAWL... AND NOT JUST FROM MY OUTRAGEOUS PUNS!
IT'S THE LADY WHO PRIZED OPEN THE PRIVATE LIVES OF ALL SORTS OF CREEPY CRITTERS...
MARIA SIBYLLA MERIAN!
MARIA SIBYLLA MERIAN
ENTOMOLOGIST 1647-1717

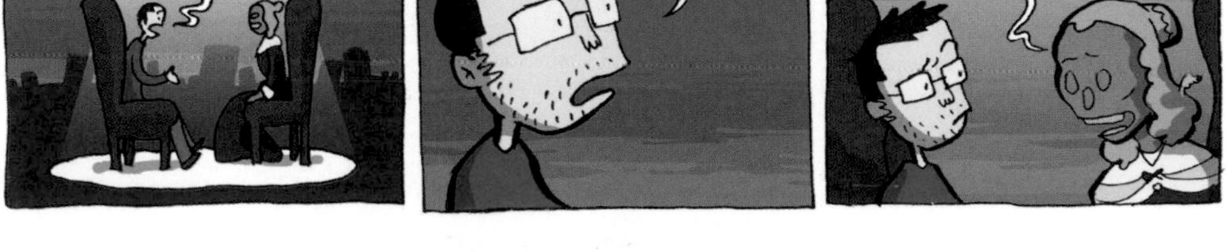
MARIA, AFTER LANGUISHING IN OBSCURITY FOR CENTURIES, YOU'VE BEEN RECENTLY REDISCOVERED AS THE FOUNDER OF MODERN ENTOMOLOGY (THE STUDY OF BUGS).
PRETTY FREAKY THING TO STUDY, IF YOU ASK ME...
WELL, THAT'S WHAT MY FAMILY THOUGHT...

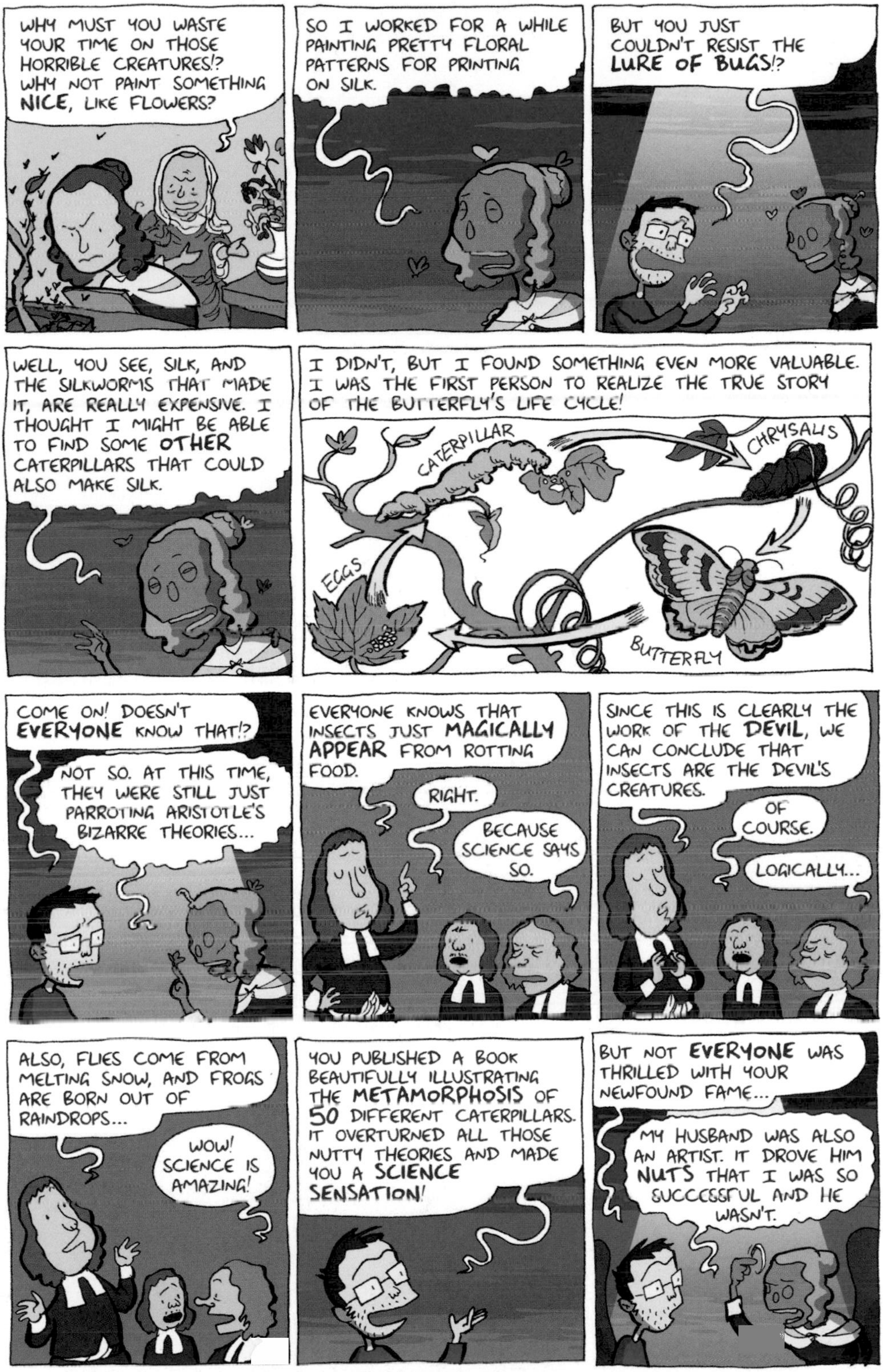

WHY MUST YOU WASTE YOUR TIME ON THOSE HORRIBLE CREATURES!? WHY NOT PAINT SOMETHING NICE, LIKE FLOWERS?
SO I WORKED FOR A WHILE PAINTING PRETTY FLORAL PATTERNS FOR PRINTING ON SILK.
BUT YOU JUST COULDN'T RESIST THE LURE OF BUGS!?
WELL, YOU SEE, SILK, AND THE SILKWORMS THAT MADE IT, ARE REALLY EXPENSIVE. I THOUGHT I MIGHT BE ABLE TO FIND SOME OTHER CATERPILLARS THAT COULD ALSO MAKE SILK.
I DIDN'T, BUT I FOUND SOMETHING EVEN MORE VALUABLE. I WAS THE FIRST PERSON TO REALIZE THE TRUE STORY OF THE BUTTERFLY'S LIFE CYCLE!
CATERPILLAR
CHRYSALIS
EGGS
BUTTERFLY
COME ON! DOESN'T EVERYONE KNOW THAT!?
NOT SO. AT THIS TIME, THEY WERE STILL JUST PARROTING ARISTOTLE'S BIZARRE THEORIES...
EVERYONE KNOWS THAT INSECTS JUST MAGICALLY APPEAR FROM ROTTING FOOD.
RIGHT.
BECAUSE SCIENCE SAYS SO.
SINCE THIS IS CLEARLY THE WORK OF THE DEVIL, WE CAN CONCLUDE THAT INSECTS ARE THE DEVIL'S CREATURES.
OF COURSE.
LOGICALLY...
ALSO, FLIES COME FROM MELTING SNOW, AND FROGS ARE BORN OUT OF RAINDROPS...
WOW! SCIENCE IS AMAZING!
YOU PUBLISHED A BOOK BEAUTIFULLY ILLUSTRATING THE METAMORPHOSIS OF 50 DIFFERENT CATERPILLARS. IT OVERTURNED ALL THOSE NUTTY THEORIES AND MADE YOU A SCIENCE SENSATION!
BUT NOT EVERYONE WAS THRILLED WITH YOUR NEWFOUND FAME...
MY HUSBAND WAS ALSO AN ARTIST. IT DROVE HIM NUTS THAT I WAS SO SUCCESSFUL AND HE WASN'T.

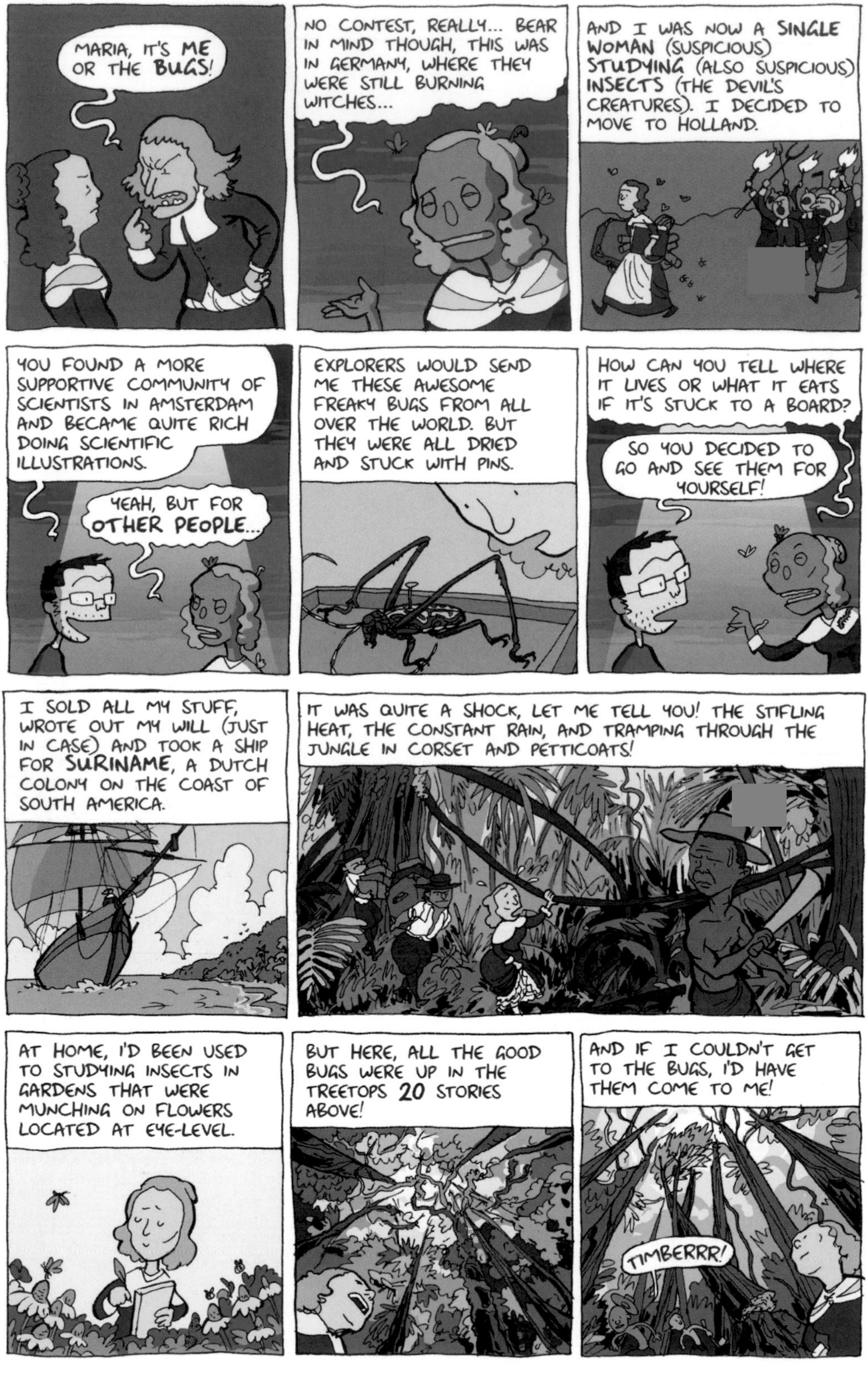
MARIA, IT'S ME OR THE BUGS!
NO CONTEST, REALLY... BEAR IN MIND THOUGH, THIS WAS IN GERMANY, WHERE THEY WERE STILL BURNING WITCHES...
AND I WAS NOW A SINGLE WOMAN (SUSPICIOUS) STUDYING (ALSO SUSPICIOUS) INSECTS (THE DEVIL'S CREATURES). I DECIDED TO MOVE TO HOLLAND.
YOU FOUND A MORE SUPPORTIVE COMMUNITY OF SCIENTISTS IN AMSTERDAM AND BECAME QUITE RICH DOING SCIENTIFIC ILLUSTRATIONS.
YEAH, BUT FOR OTHER PEOPLE...
EXPLORERS WOULD SEND ME THESE AWESOME FREAKY BUGS FROM ALL OVER THE WORLD. BUT THEY WERE ALL DRIED AND STUCK WITH PINS.
HOW CAN YOU TELL WHERE IT LIVES OR WHAT IT EATS IF IT'S STUCK TO A BOARD?
SO YOU DECIDED TO GO AND SEE THEM FOR YOURSELF!
I SOLD ALL MY STUFF, WROTE OUT MY WILL (JUST IN CASE) AND TOOK A SHIP FOR SURINAME, A DUTCH COLONY ON THE COAST OF SOUTH AMERICA.
IT WAS QUITE A SHOCK, LET ME TELL YOU! THE STIFLING HEAT, THE CONSTANT RAIN, AND TRAMPING THROUGH THE JUNGLE IN CORSET AND PETTICOATS!
AT HOME, I'D BEEN USED TO STUDYING INSECTS IN GARDENS THAT WERE MUNCHING ON FLOWERS LOCATED AT EYE-LEVEL.
BUT HERE, ALL THE GOOD BUGS WERE UP IN THE TREETOPS 20 STORIES ABOVE!
AND IF I COULDN'T GET TO THE BUGS, I'D HAVE THEM COME TO ME!
TIMBERRR!

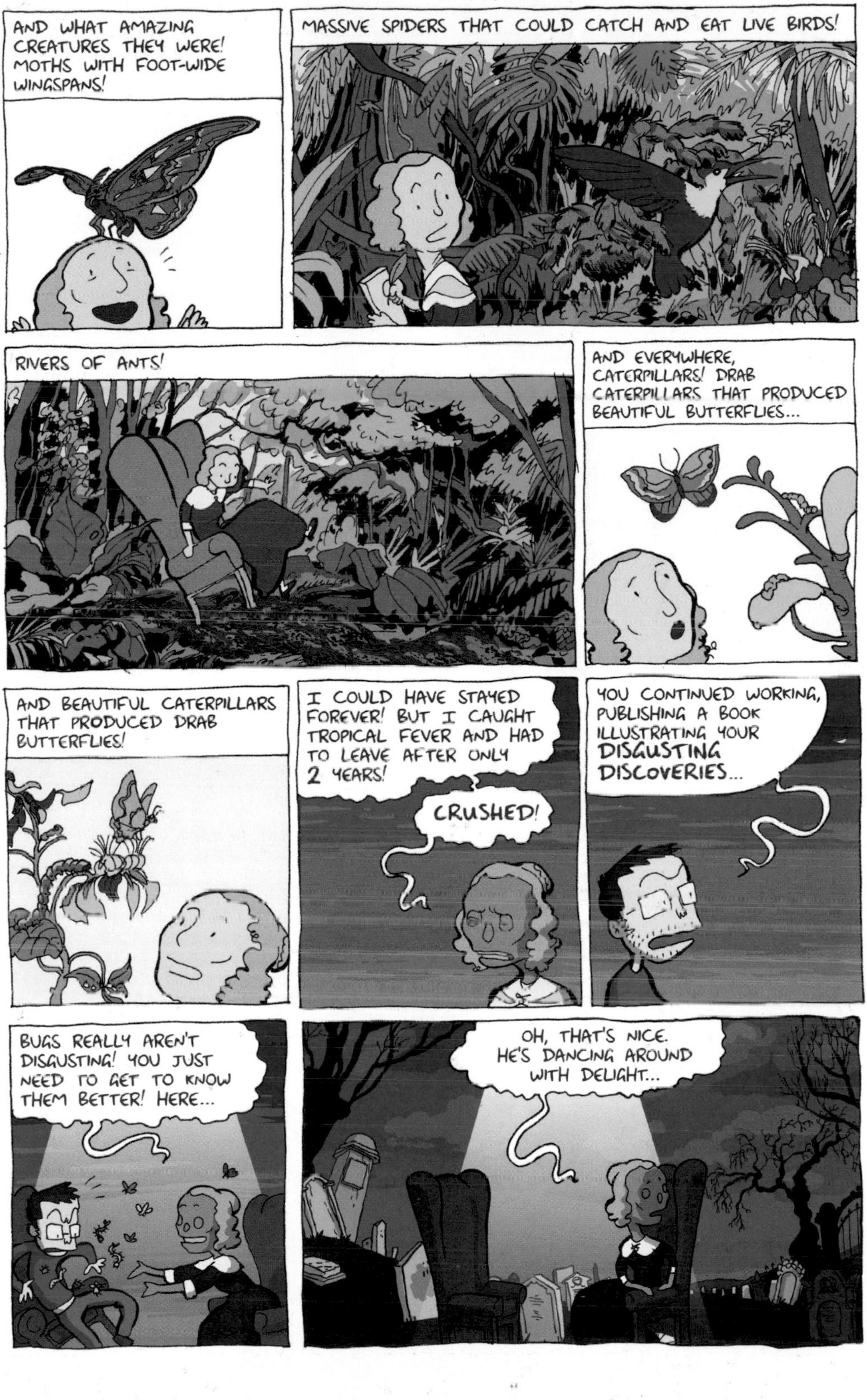
AND WHAT AMAZING CREATURES THEY WERE! MOTHS WITH FOOT-WIDE WINGSPANS!
MASSIVE SPIDERS THAT COULD CATCH AND EAT LIVE BIRDS!
RIVERS OF ANTS!
AND EVERYWHERE, CATERPILLARS! DRAB CATERPILLARS THAT PRODUCED BEAUTIFUL BUTTERFLIES...
AND BEAUTIFUL CATERPILLARS THAT PRODUCED DRAB BUTTERFLIES!
I COULD HAVE STAYED FOREVER! BUT I CAUGHT TROPICAL FEVER AND HAD TO LEAVE AFTER ONLY 2 YEARS!
CRUSHED!
YOU CONTINUED WORKING, PUBLISHING A BOOK ILLUSTRATING YOUR DISGUSTING DISCOVERIES...
BUGS REALLY AREN'T DISGUSTING! YOU JUST NEED TO GET TO KNOW THEM BETTER! HERE...
OH, THAT'S NICE. HE'S DANCING AROUND WITH DELIGHT...

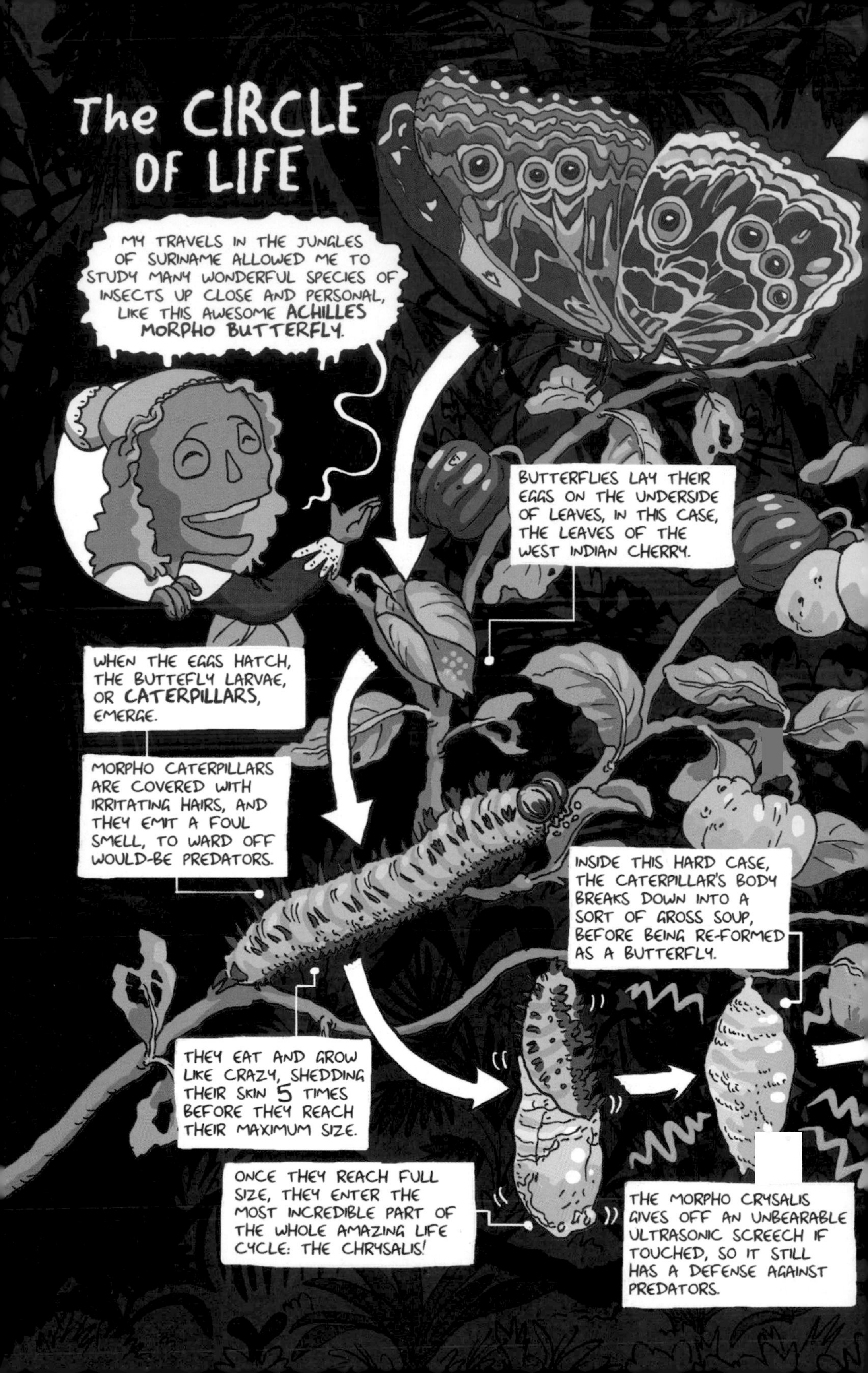
The CIRCLE OF LIFE
MY TRAVELS IN THE JUNGLES OF SURINAME ALLOWED ME TO STUDY MANY WONDERFUL SPECIES OF INSECTS UP CLOSE AND PERSONAL, LIKE THIS AWESOME ACHILLES MORPHO BUTTERFLY.
BUTTERFLIES LAY THEIR EGGS ON THE UNDERSIDE OF LEAVES, IN THIS CASE, THE LEAVES OF THE WEST INDIAN CHERRY.
WHEN THE EGGS HATCH, THE BUTTEFLY LARVAE, OR CATERPILLARS, EMERGE.
MORPHO CATERPILLARS ARE COVERED WITH IRRITATING HAIRS, AND THEY EMIT A FOUL SMELL, TO WARD OFF WOULD-BE PREDATORS.
THEY EAT AND GROW LIKE CRAZY, SHEDDING THEIR SKIN 5 TIMES BEFORE THEY REACH THEIR MAXIMUM SIZE.
ONCE THEY REACH FULL SIZE, THEY ENTER THE MOST INCREDIBLE PART OF THE WHOLE AMAZING LIFE CYCLE: THE CHRYSALIS!
INSIDE THIS HARD CASE, THE CATERPILLAR'S BODY BREAKS DOWN INTO A SORT OF GROSS SOUP, BEFORE BEING RE-FORMED AS A BUTTERFLY.
THE MORPHO CRYSALIS GIVES OFF AN UNBEARABLE ULTRASONIC SCREECH IF TOUCHED, SO IT STILL HAS A DEFENSE AGAINST PREDATORS.

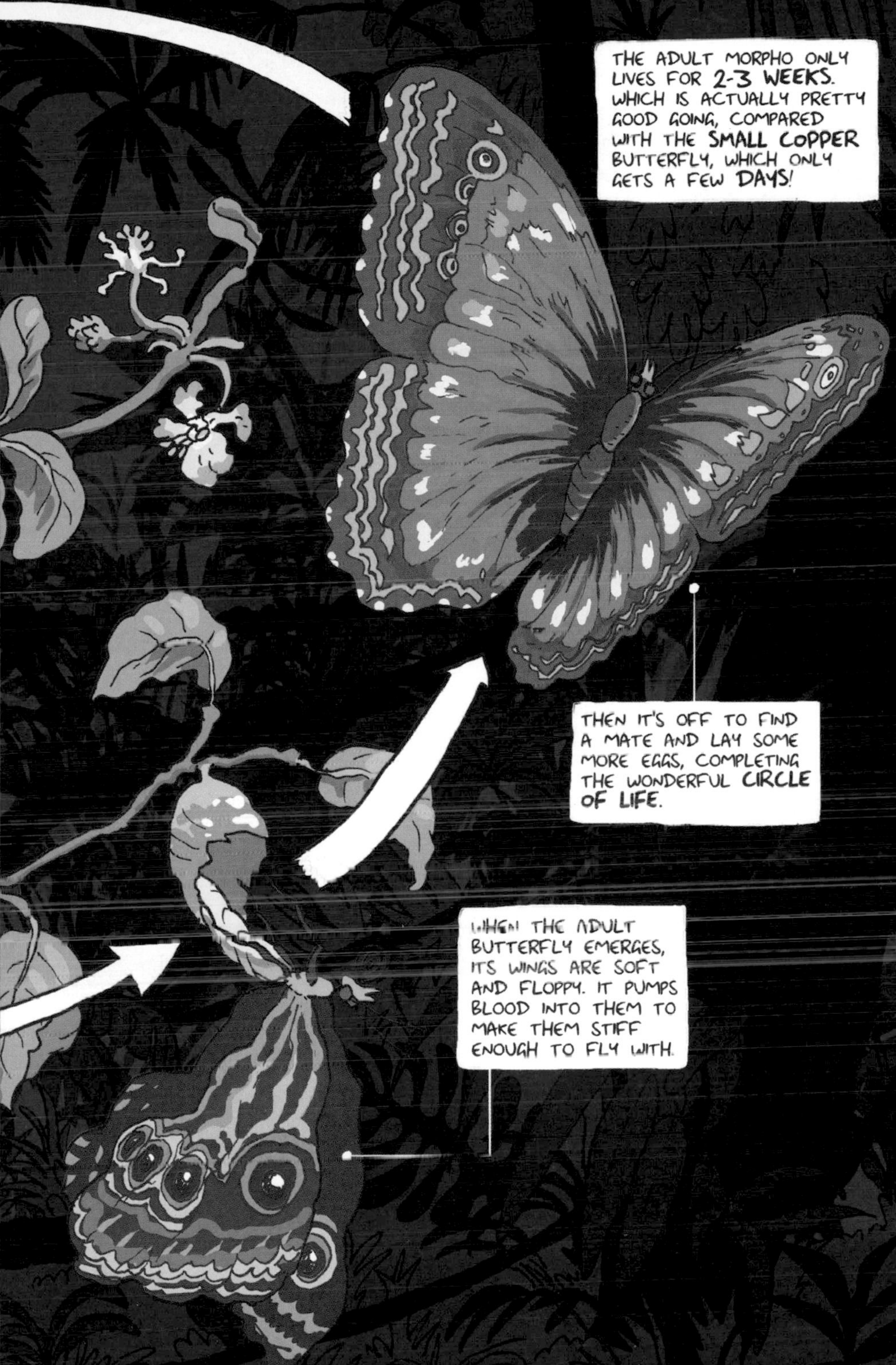
THE ADULT MORPHO ONLY LIVES FOR 2-3 WEEKS. WHICH IS ACTUALLY PRETTY GOOD GOING, COMPARED WITH THE SMALL COPPER BUTTERFLY, WHICH ONLY GETS A FEW DAYS!
THEN IT'S OFF TO FIND A MATE AND LAY SOME MORE EGGS, COMPLETING THE WONDERFUL CIRCLE OF LIFE.
WHEN THE ADULT BUTTERFLY EMERGES, ITS WINGS ARE SOFT AND FLOPPY. IT PUMPS BLOOD INTO THEM TO MAKE THEM STIFF ENOUGH TO FLY WITH.

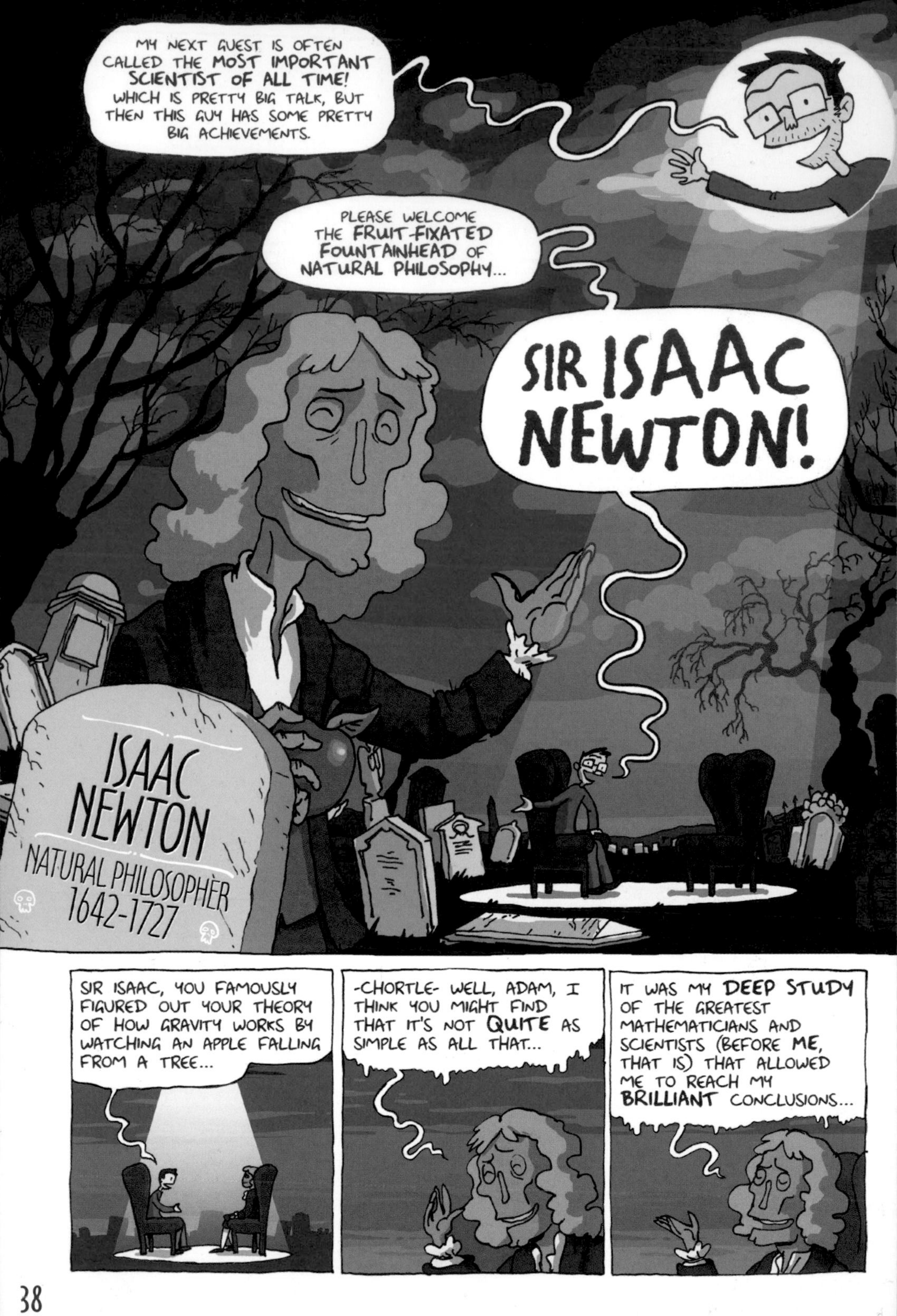
MY NEXT GUEST IS OFTEN CALLED THE MOST IMPORTANT SCIENTIST OF ALL TIME! WHICH IS PRETTY BIG TALK, BUT THEN THIS GUY HAS SOME PRETTY BIG ACHIEVEMENTS.
PLEASE WELCOME THE FRUIT-FIXATED FOUNTAINHEAD OF NATURAL PHILOSOPHY...
SIR ISAAC NEWTON!
ISAAC NEWTON
NATURAL PHILOSOPHER
1642-1727
SIR ISAAC, YOU FAMOUSLY FIGURED OUT YOUR THEORY OF HOW GRAVITY WORKS BY WATCHING AN APPLE FALLING FROM A TREE...
-CHORTLE- WELL, ADAM, I THINK YOU MIGHT FIND THAT IT'S NOT QUITE AS SIMPLE AS ALL THAT...
IT WAS MY DEEP STUDY OF THE GREATEST MATHEMATICIANS AND SCIENTISTS (BEFORE ME, THAT IS) THAT ALLOWED ME TO REACH MY BRILLIANT CONCLUSIONS...

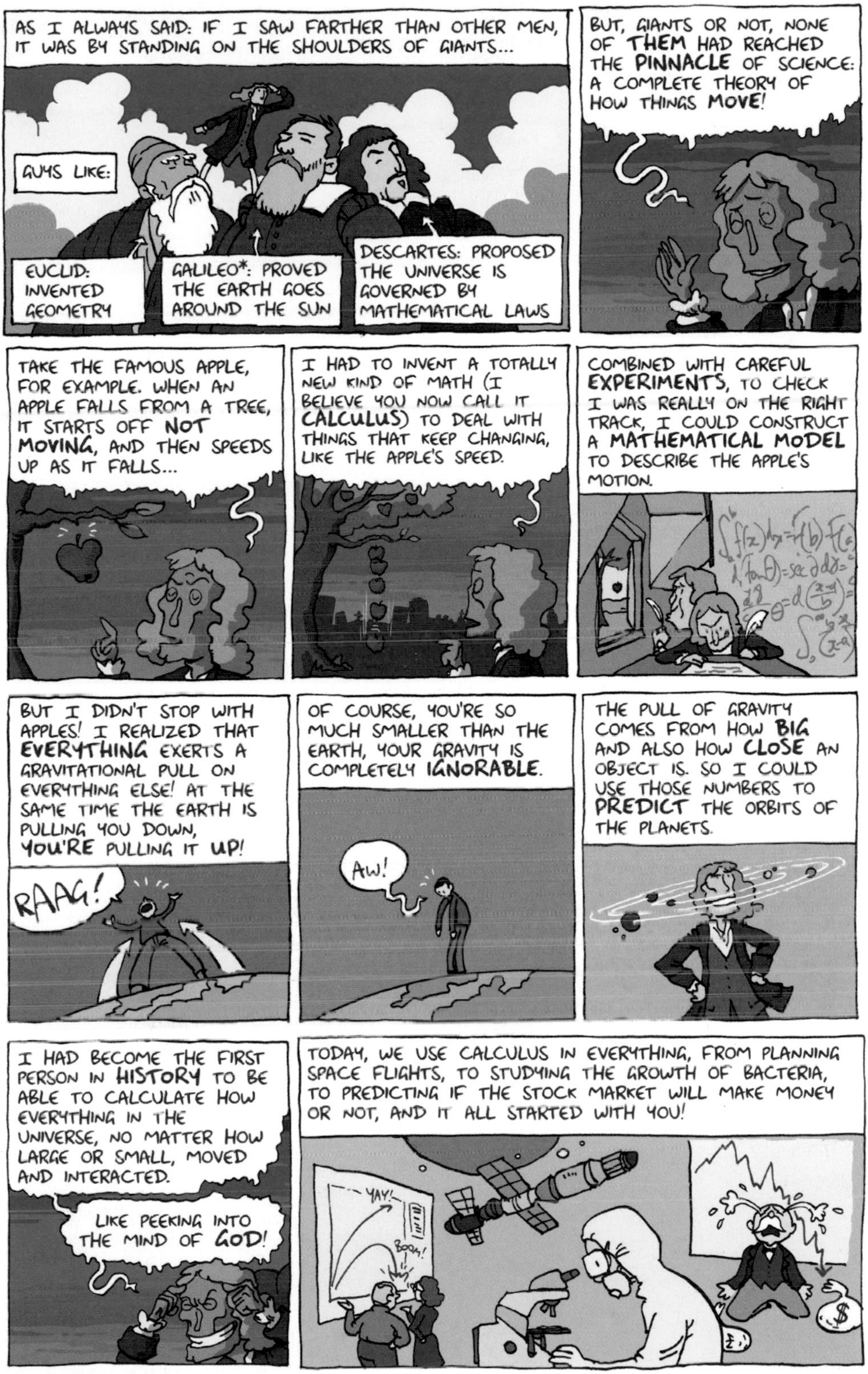
AS I ALWAYS SAID: IF I SAW FARTHER THAN OTHER MEN, IT WAS BY STANDING ON THE SHOULDERS OF GIANTS...
GUYS LIKE:
EUCLID: INVENTED GEOMETRY
GALILEO*: PROVED THE EARTH GOES AROUND THE SUN
DESCARTES: PROPOSED THE UNIVERSE IS GOVERNED BY MATHEMATICAL LAWS
BUT, GIANTS OR NOT, NONE OF THEM HAD REACHED THE PINNACLE OF SCIENCE: A COMPLETE THEORY OF HOW THINGS MOVE!
TAKE THE FAMOUS APPLE, FOR EXAMPLE. WHEN AN APPLE FALLS FROM A TREE, IT STARTS OFF NOT MOVING, AND THEN SPEEDS UP AS IT FALLS...
I HAD TO INVENT A TOTALLY NEW KIND OF MATH (I BELIEVE YOU NOW CALL IT CALCULUS) TO DEAL WITH THINGS THAT KEEP CHANGING, LIKE THE APPLE'S SPEED.
COMBINED WITH CAREFUL EXPERIMENTS, TO CHECK I WAS REALLY ON THE RIGHT TRACK, I COULD CONSTRUCT A MATHEMATICAL MODEL TO DESCRIBE THE APPLE'S MOTION.
BUT I DIDN'T STOP WITH APPLES! I REALIZED THAT EVERYTHING EXERTS A GRAVITATIONAL PULL ON EVERYTHING ELSE! AT THE SAME TIME THE EARTH IS PULLING YOU DOWN, YOU'RE PULLING IT UP!
RAAG!
OF COURSE, YOU'RE SO MUCH SMALLER THAN THE EARTH, YOUR GRAVITY IS COMPLETELY IGNORABLE.
AW!
THE PULL OF GRAVITY COMES FROM HOW BIG AND ALSO HOW CLOSE AN OBJECT IS. SO I COULD USE THOSE NUMBERS TO PREDICT THE ORBITS OF THE PLANETS.
I HAD BECOME THE FIRST PERSON IN HISTORY TO BE ABLE TO CALCULATE HOW EVERYTHING IN THE UNIVERSE, NO MATTER HOW LARGE OR SMALL, MOVED AND INTERACTED.
LIKE PEEKING INTO THE MIND OF GOD!
TODAY, WE USE CALCULUS IN EVERYTHING, FROM PLANNING SPACE FLIGHTS, TO STUDYING THE GROWTH OF BACTERIA, TO PREDICTING IF THE STOCK MARKET WILL MAKE MONEY OR NOT, AND IT ALL STARTED WITH YOU!
YAY!
BOOM!
$

*SEE PAGE 26

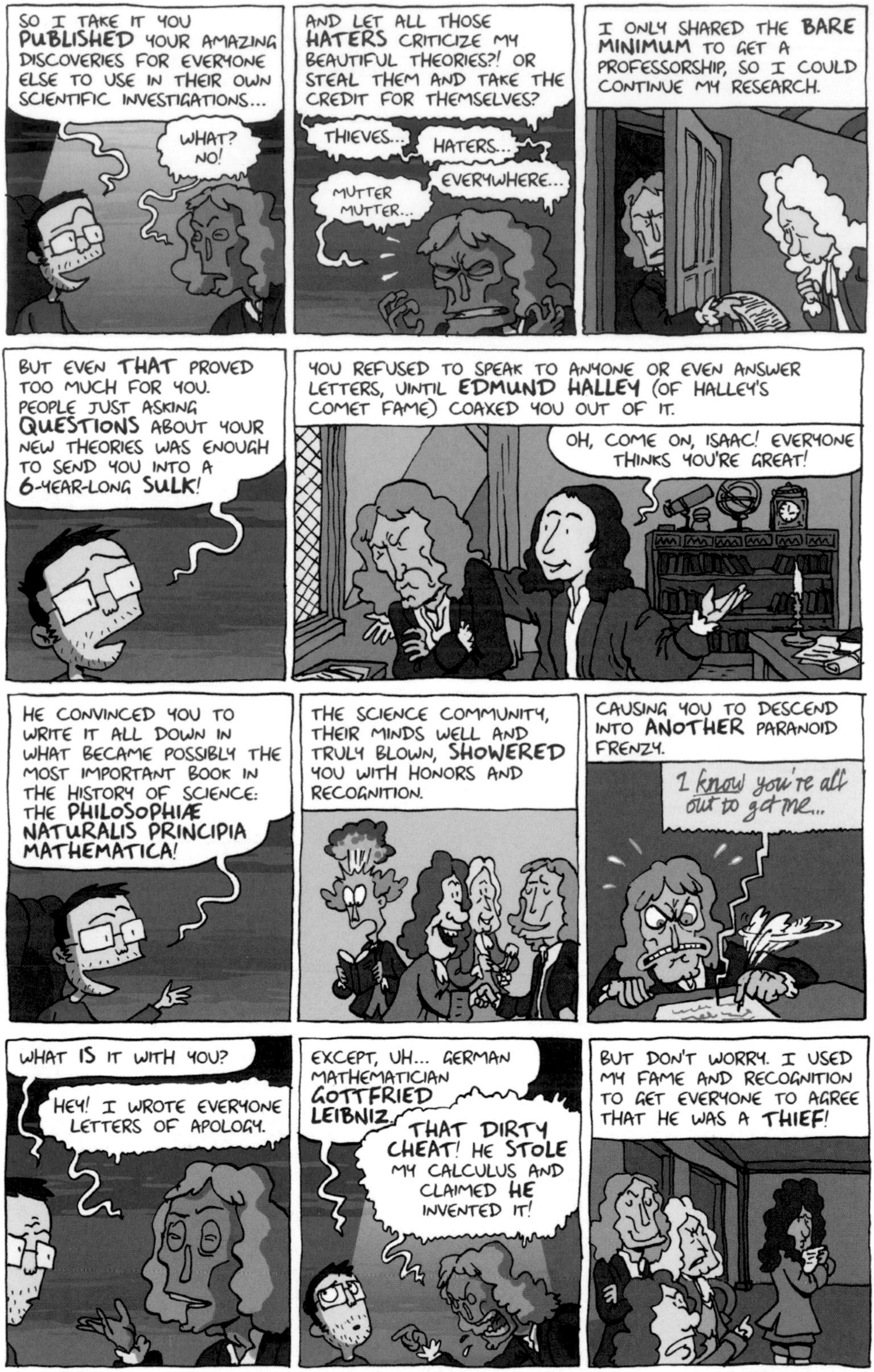
SO I TAKE IT YOU PUBLISHED YOUR AMAZING DISCOVERIES FOR EVERYONE ELSE TO USE IN THEIR OWN SCIENTIFIC INVESTIGATIONS...
WHAT? NO!
AND LET ALL THOSE HATERS CRITICIZE MY BEAUTIFUL THEORIES?! OR STEAL THEM AND TAKE THE CREDIT FOR THEMSELVES?
THIEVES...
HATERS...
EVERYWHERE...
MUTTER MUTTER...
I ONLY SHARED THE BARE MINIMUM TO GET A PROFESSORSHIP, SO I COULD CONTINUE MY RESEARCH.
BUT EVEN THAT PROVED TOO MUCH FOR YOU. PEOPLE JUST ASKING QUESTIONS ABOUT YOUR NEW THEORIES WAS ENOUGH TO SEND YOU INTO A 6-YEAR-LONG SULK!
YOU REFUSED TO SPEAK TO ANYONE OR EVEN ANSWER LETTERS, UNTIL EDMUND HALLEY (OF HALLEY'S COMET FAME) COAXED YOU OUT OF IT.
OH, COME ON, ISAAC! EVERYONE THINKS YOU'RE GREAT!
HE CONVINCED YOU TO WRITE IT ALL DOWN IN WHAT BECAME POSSIBLY THE MOST IMPORTANT BOOK IN THE HISTORY OF SCIENCE: THE PHILOSOPHIÆ NATURALIS PRINCIPIA MATHEMATICA!
THE SCIENCE COMMUNITY, THEIR MINDS WELL AND TRULY BLOWN, SHOWERED YOU WITH HONORS AND RECOGNITION.
CAUSING YOU TO DESCEND INTO ANOTHER PARANOID FRENZY.
I know you're all out to get me...
WHAT IS IT WITH YOU?
HEY! I WROTE EVERYONE LETTERS OF APOLOGY.
EXCEPT, UH... GERMAN MATHEMATICIAN GOTTFRIED LEIBNIZ.
THAT DIRTY CHEAT! HE STOLE MY CALCULUS AND CLAIMED HE INVENTED IT!
BUT DON'T WORRY. I USED MY FAME AND RECOGNITION TO GET EVERYONE TO AGREE THAT HE WAS A THIEF!

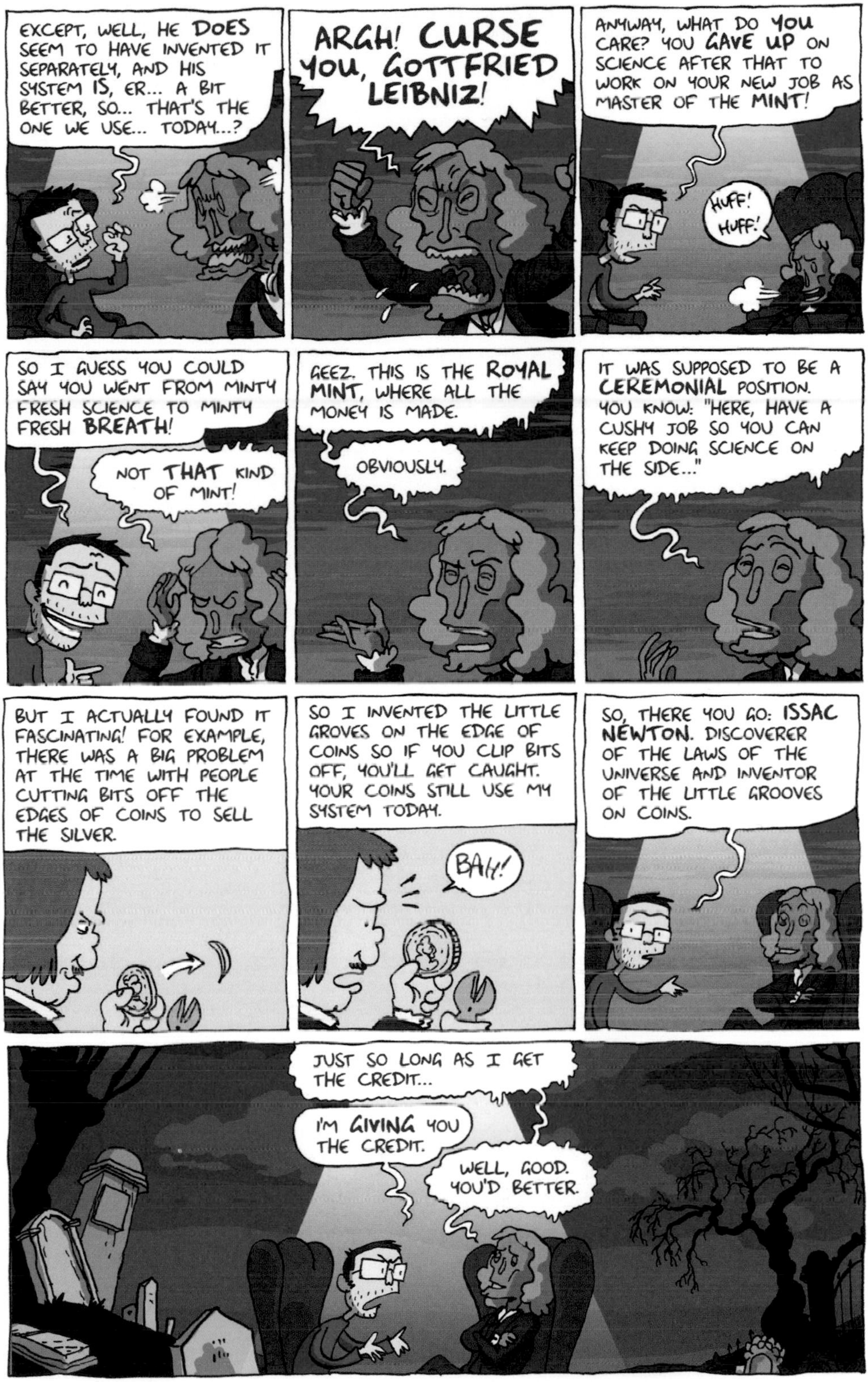

EXCEPT, WELL, HE DOES SEEM TO HAVE INVENTED IT SEPARATELY, AND HIS SYSTEM IS, ER... A BIT BETTER, SO... THAT'S THE ONE WE USE... TODAY...?
ARGH! CURSE YOU, GOTTFRIED LEIBNIZ!
ANYWAY, WHAT DO YOU CARE? YOU GAVE UP ON SCIENCE AFTER THAT TO WORK ON YOUR NEW JOB AS MASTER OF THE MINT!
HUFF! HUFF!
SO I GUESS YOU COULD SAY YOU WENT FROM MINTY FRESH SCIENCE TO MINTY FRESH BREATH!
NOT THAT KIND OF MINT!
GEEZ. THIS IS THE ROYAL MINT, WHERE ALL THE MONEY IS MADE.
OBVIOUSLY.
IT WAS SUPPOSED TO BE A CEREMONIAL POSITION. YOU KNOW: "HERE, HAVE A CUSHY JOB SO YOU CAN KEEP DOING SCIENCE ON THE SIDE..."
BUT I ACTUALLY FOUND IT FASCINATING! FOR EXAMPLE, THERE WAS A BIG PROBLEM AT THE TIME WITH PEOPLE CUTTING BITS OFF THE EDGES OF COINS TO SELL THE SILVER.
SO I INVENTED THE LITTLE GROVES ON THE EDGE OF COINS SO IF YOU CLIP BITS OFF, YOU'LL GET CAUGHT. YOUR COINS STILL USE MY SYSTEM TODAY.
BAH!
SO, THERE YOU GO: ISSAC NEWTON. DISCOVERER OF THE LAWS OF THE UNIVERSE AND INVENTOR OF THE LITTLE GROOVES ON COINS.
JUST SO LONG AS I GET THE CREDIT...
I'M GIVING YOU THE CREDIT.
WELL, GOOD. YOU'D BETTER.

LAYING DOWN THE LAWS

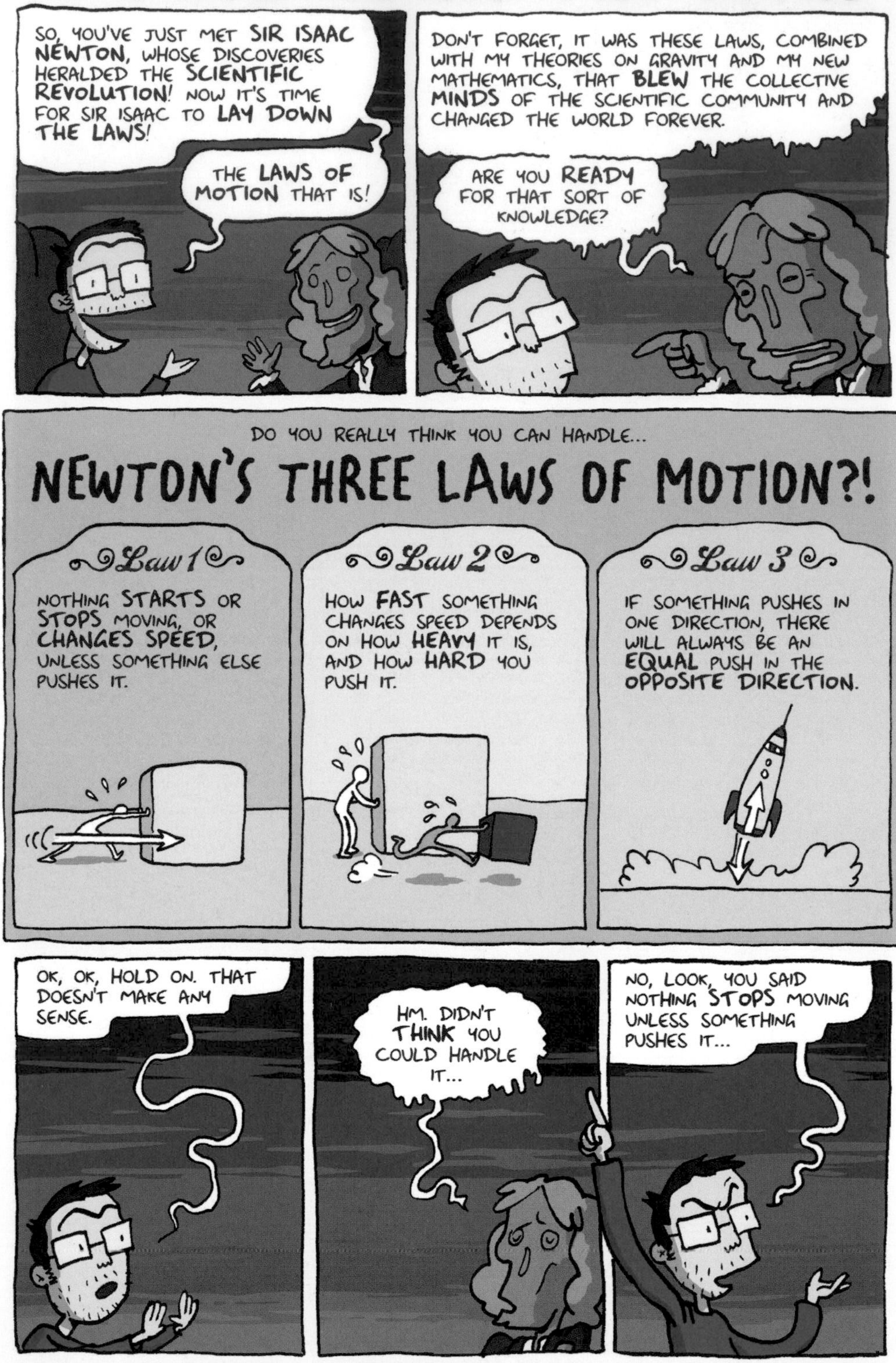
SO, YOU'VE JUST MET SIR ISAAC NEWTON, WHOSE DISCOVERIES HERALDED THE SCIENTIFIC REVOLUTION! NOW IT'S TIME FOR SIR ISAAC TO LAY DOWN THE LAWS!
THE LAWS OF MOTION THAT IS!
DON'T FORGET, IT WAS THESE LAWS, COMBINED WITH MY THEORIES ON GRAVITY AND MY NEW MATHEMATICS, THAT BLEW THE COLLECTIVE MINDS OF THE SCIENTIFIC COMMUNITY AND CHANGED THE WORLD FOREVER.
ARE YOU READY FOR THAT SORT OF KNOWLEDGE?
DO YOU REALLY THINK YOU CAN HANDLE...
NEWTON'S THREE LAWS OF MOTION?!
Law 1
NOTHING STARTS OR STOPS MOVING, OR CHANGES SPEED, UNLESS SOMETHING ELSE PUSHES IT.
Law 2
HOW FAST SOMETHING CHANGES SPEED DEPENDS ON HOW HEAVY IT IS, AND HOW HARD YOU PUSH IT.
Law 3
IF SOMETHING PUSHES IN ONE DIRECTION, THERE WILL ALWAYS BE AN EQUAL PUSH IN THE OPPOSITE DIRECTION.
OK, OK, HOLD ON. THAT DOESN'T MAKE ANY SENSE.
HM. DIDN'T THINK YOU COULD HANDLE IT...
NO, LOOK, YOU SAID NOTHING STOPS MOVING UNLESS SOMETHING PUSHES IT...

BUT EVERYTHING STOPS MOVING **EVENTUALLY.** EVEN IF IT DOESN'T HIT AN OBSTACLE, IT'LL JUST SLOW DOWN AND STOP ON ITS OWN.

AHA! YES, BUT ONLY HERE ON EARTH!

IN SPACE THERE'S NOTHING TO BUMP AGAINST, NOT EVEN **AIR,** SO IF YOU PUSH SOMETHING, IT JUST KEEPS GOING. FOREVER.

THANK GOODNESS I HAVE THIS SAFETY LINE...

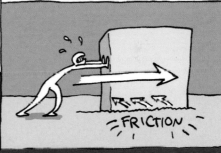

BUT ON EARTH, THINGS SLOW DOWN DUE TO **FRICTION,** WHICH IS OTHER STUFF (LIKE THE GROUND OR THE AIR) **RUBBING** THE MOVING OBJECT, AND THAT'S WHAT PUSHES AGAINST IT.

FRICTION

WHICH IS WHY, IF YOU WANT TO ENJOY MY THREE LAWS IN THEIR **PUREST** FORM, YOU NEED TO BUILD SOMETHING LIKE...

A Homemade Hovercraft!

WHAT YOU WILL NEED:

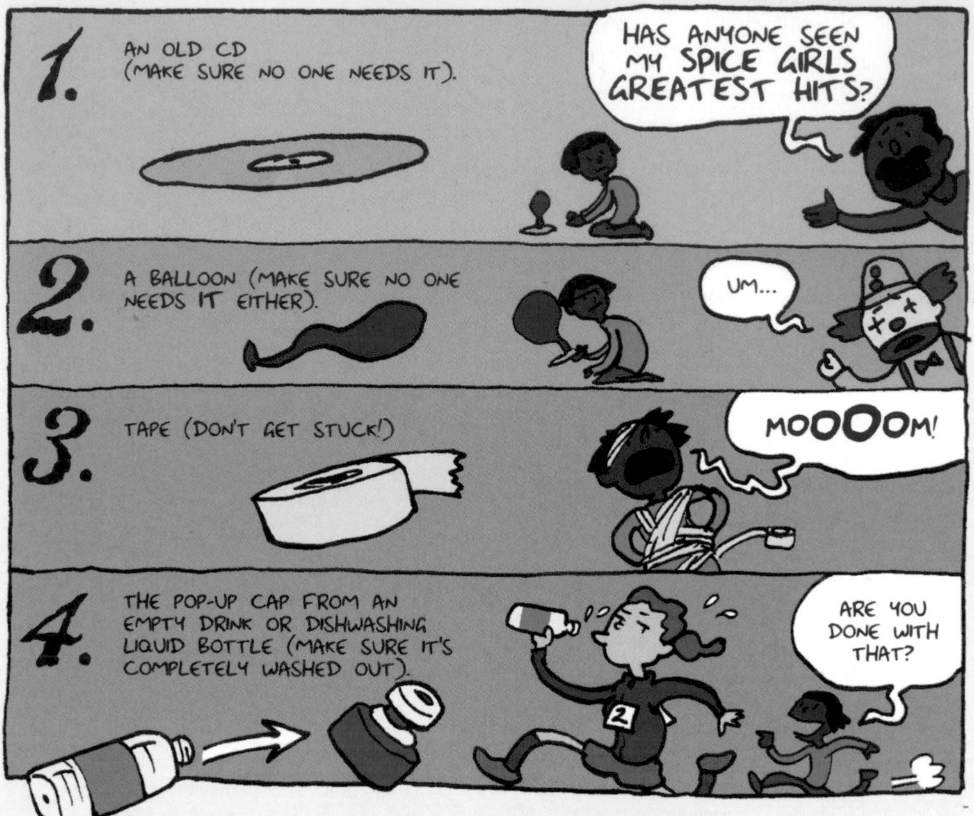
1. AN OLD CD (MAKE SURE NO ONE NEEDS IT).
HAS ANYONE SEEN MY SPICE GIRLS GREATEST HITS?
2. A BALLOON (MAKE SURE NO ONE NEEDS IT EITHER).
UM...
3. TAPE (DON'T GET STUCK!)
MOOOOOM!
4. THE POP-UP CAP FROM AN EMPTY DRINK OR DISHWASHING LIQUID BOTTLE (MAKE SURE IT'S COMPLETELY WASHED OUT).
ARE YOU DONE WITH THAT?
2

HOW TO MAKE IT:

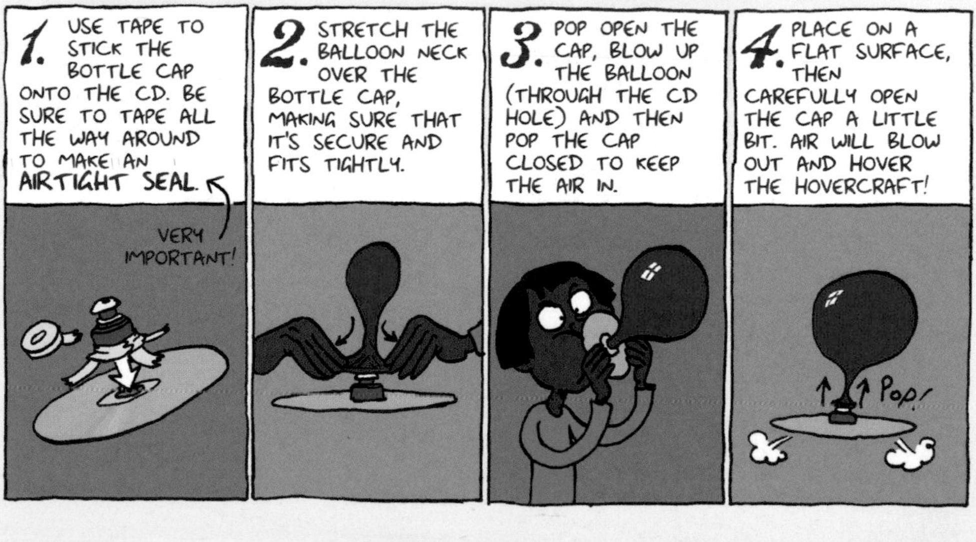
1. USE TAPE TO STICK THE BOTTLE CAP ONTO THE CD. BE SURE TO TAPE ALL THE WAY AROUND TO MAKE AN AIRTIGHT SEAL.
VERY IMPORTANT!
2. STRETCH THE BALLOON NECK OVER THE BOTTLE CAP, MAKING SURE THAT IT'S SECURE AND FITS TIGHTLY.
3. POP OPEN THE CAP, BLOW UP THE BALLOON (THROUGH THE CD HOLE) AND THEN POP THE CAP CLOSED TO KEEP THE AIR IN.
4. PLACE ON A FLAT SURFACE, THEN CAREFULLY OPEN THE CAP A LITTLE BIT. AIR WILL BLOW OUT AND HOVER THE HOVERCRAFT!
POP!

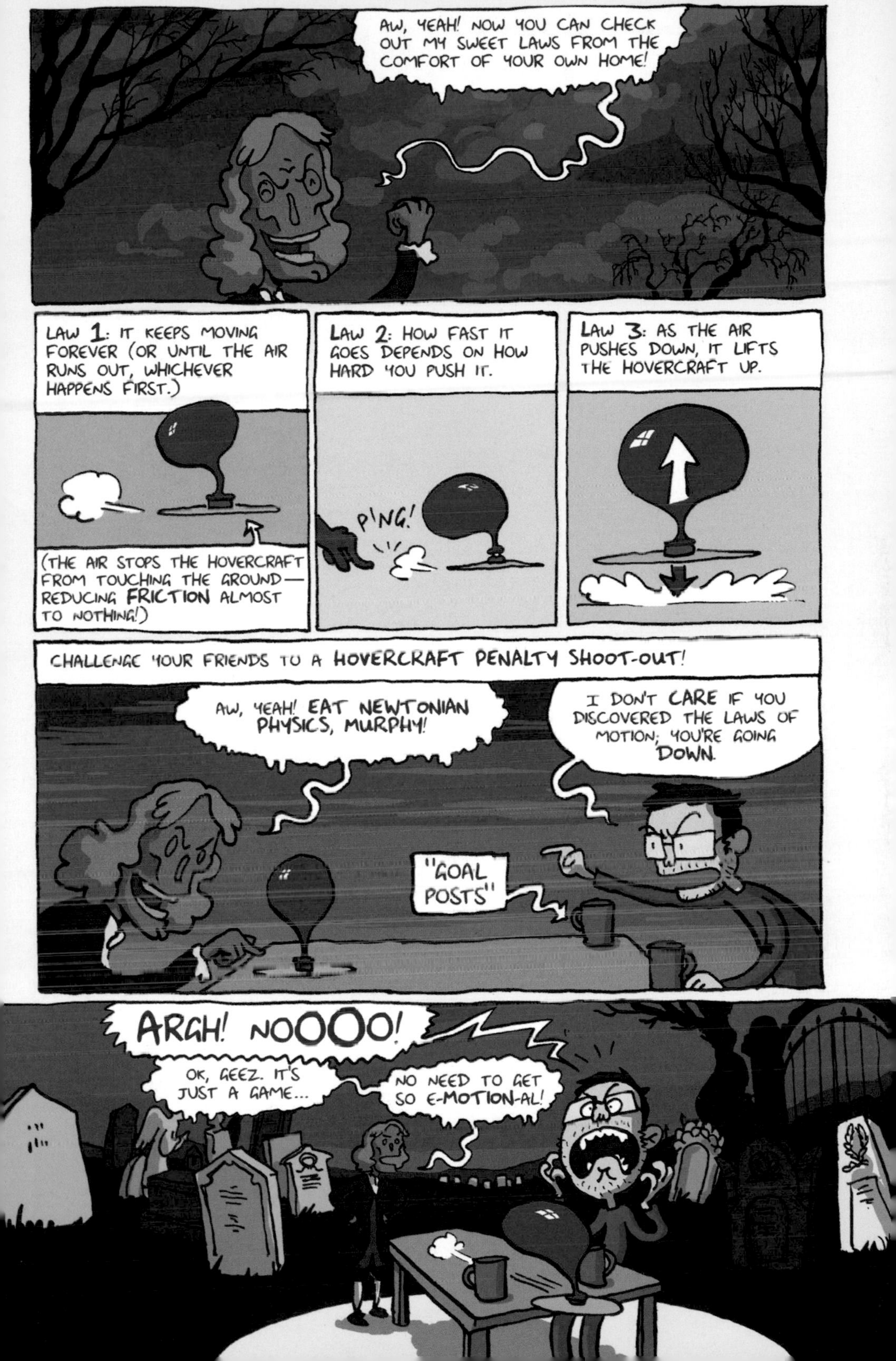
AW, YEAH! NOW YOU CAN CHECK OUT MY SWEET LAWS FROM THE COMFORT OF YOUR OWN HOME!
LAW 1: IT KEEPS MOVING FOREVER (OR UNTIL THE AIR RUNS OUT, WHICHEVER HAPPENS FIRST.)
(THE AIR STOPS THE HOVERCRAFT FROM TOUCHING THE GROUND— REDUCING FRICTION ALMOST TO NOTHING!)
LAW 2: HOW FAST IT GOES DEPENDS ON HOW HARD YOU PUSH IT.
PING!
LAW 3: AS THE AIR PUSHES DOWN, IT LIFTS THE HOVERCRAFT UP.
CHALLENGE YOUR FRIENDS TO A HOVERCRAFT PENALTY SHOOT-OUT!
AW, YEAH! EAT NEWTONIAN PHYSICS, MURPHY!
I DON'T CARE IF YOU DISCOVERED THE LAWS OF MOTION; YOU'RE GOING DOWN.
"GOAL POSTS"
ARGH! NOOOO!
OK, GEEZ. IT'S JUST A GAME...
NO NEED TO GET SO E-MOTION-AL!

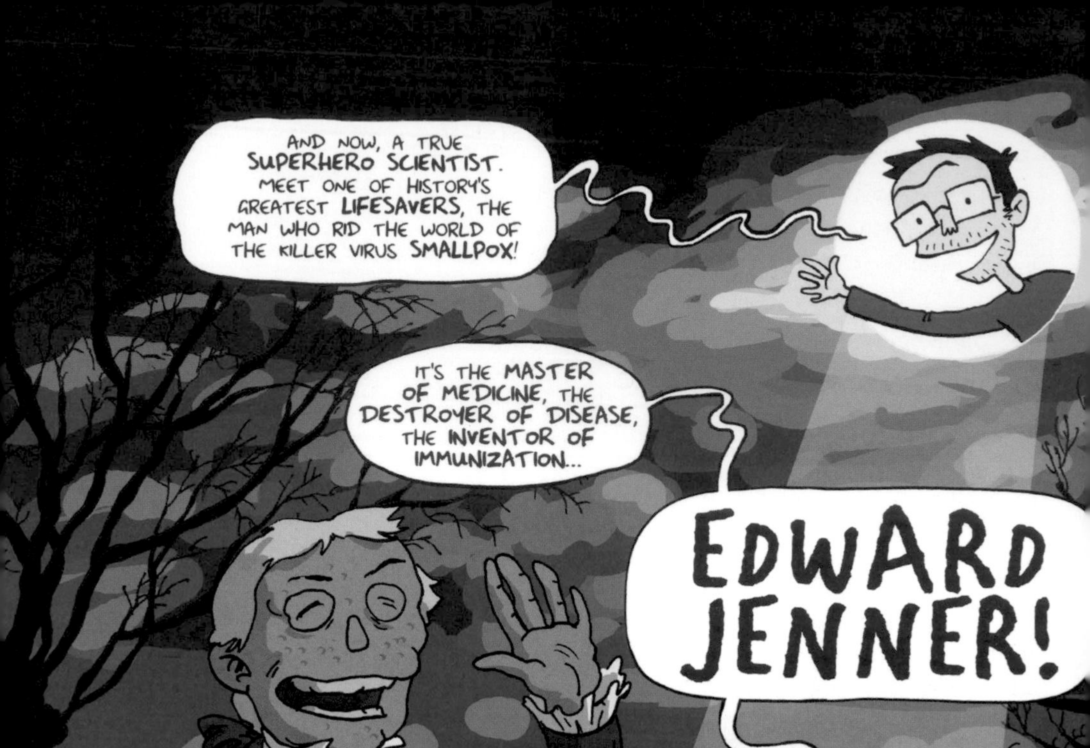
AND NOW, A TRUE SUPERHERO SCIENTIST. MEET ONE OF HISTORY'S GREATEST LIFESAVERS, THE MAN WHO RID THE WORLD OF THE KILLER VIRUS SMALLPOX!
IT'S THE MASTER OF MEDICINE, THE DESTROYER OF DISEASE, THE INVENTOR OF IMMUNIZATION...
EDWARD JENNER!
EDWARD JENNER PHYSICIAN 1749-1823

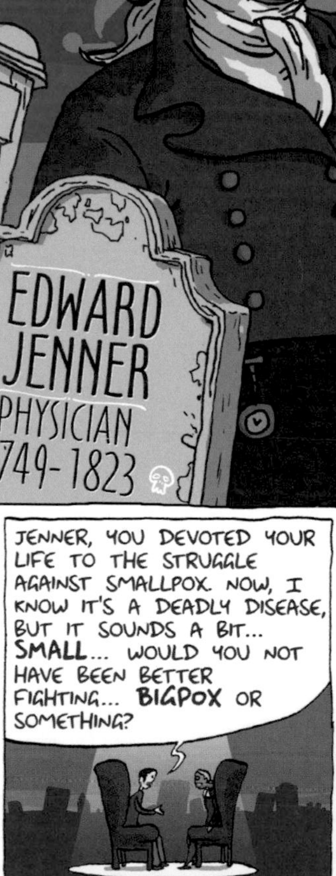
JENNER, YOU DEVOTED YOUR LIFE TO THE STRUGGLE AGAINST SMALLPOX. NOW, I KNOW IT'S A DEADLY DISEASE, BUT IT SOUNDS A BIT... SMALL... WOULD YOU NOT HAVE BEEN BETTER FIGHTING... BIGPOX OR SOMETHING?

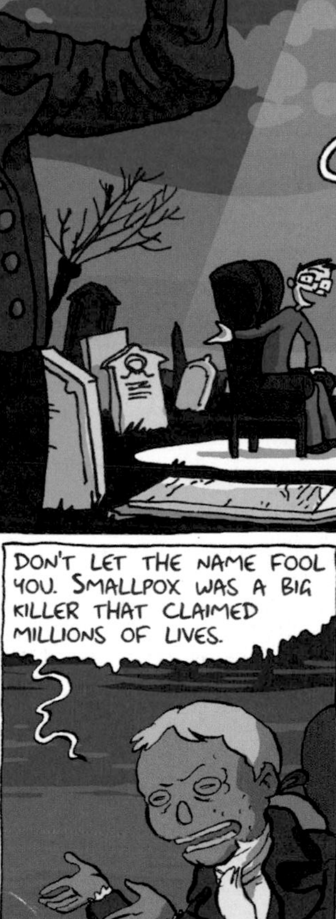
DON'T LET THE NAME FOOL YOU. SMALLPOX WAS A BIG KILLER THAT CLAIMED MILLIONS OF LIVES.

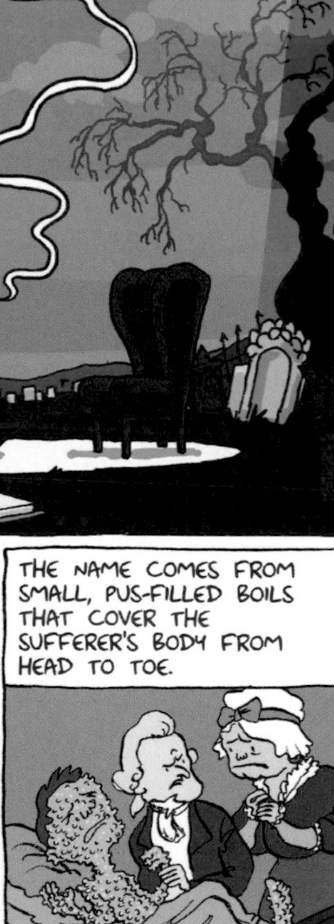
THE NAME COMES FROM SMALL, PUS-FILLED BOILS THAT COVER THE SUFFERER'S BODY FROM HEAD TO TOE.

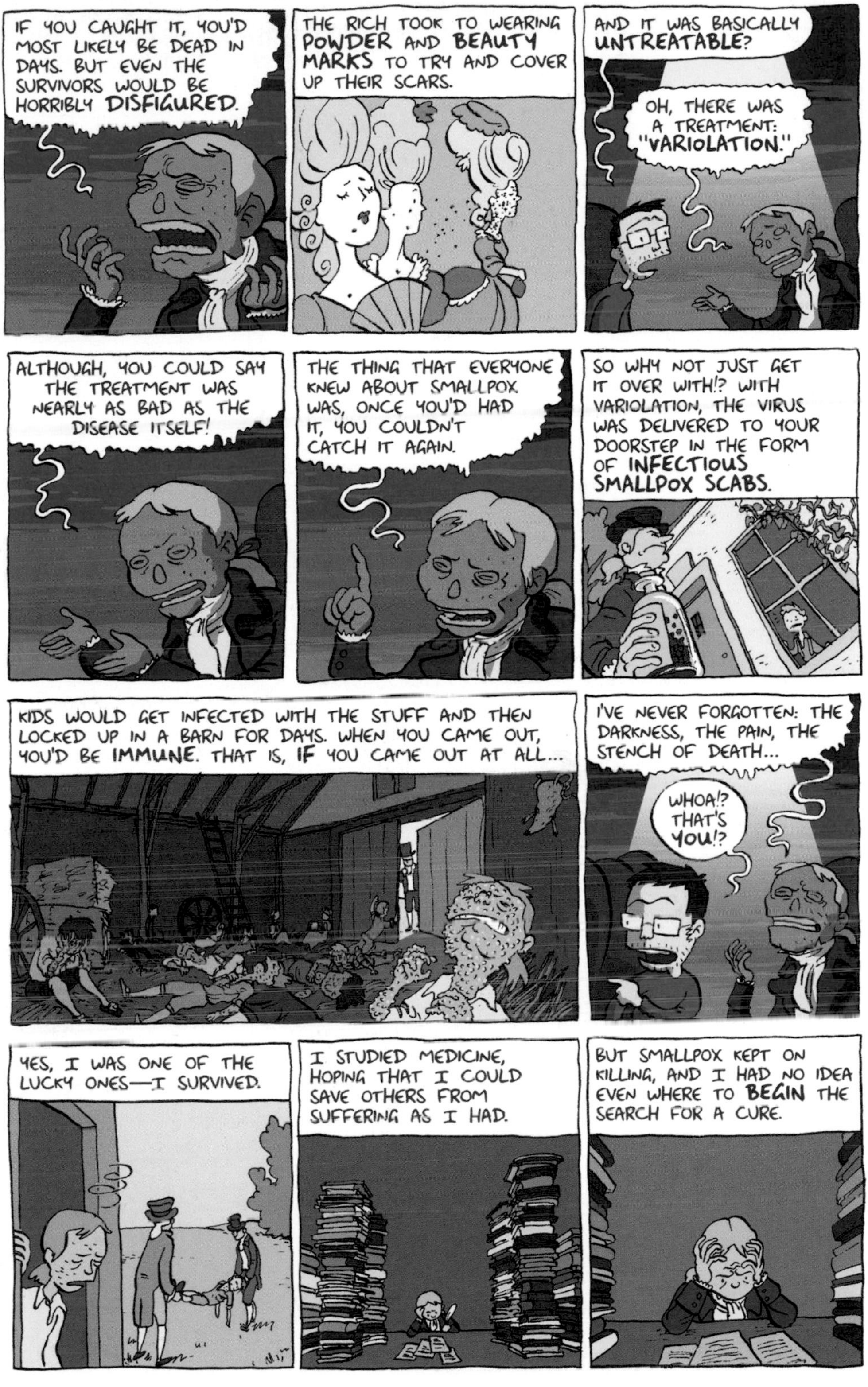
IF YOU CAUGHT IT, YOU'D MOST LIKELY BE DEAD IN DAYS. BUT EVEN THE SURVIVORS WOULD BE HORRIBLY DISFIGURED.
THE RICH TOOK TO WEARING POWDER AND BEAUTY MARKS TO TRY AND COVER UP THEIR SCARS.
AND IT WAS BASICALLY UNTREATABLE?
OH, THERE WAS A TREATMENT: "VARIOLATION."
ALTHOUGH, YOU COULD SAY THE TREATMENT WAS NEARLY AS BAD AS THE DISEASE ITSELF!
THE THING THAT EVERYONE KNEW ABOUT SMALLPOX WAS, ONCE YOU'D HAD IT, YOU COULDN'T CATCH IT AGAIN.
SO WHY NOT JUST GET IT OVER WITH!? WITH VARIOLATION, THE VIRUS WAS DELIVERED TO YOUR DOORSTEP IN THE FORM OF INFECTIOUS SMALLPOX SCABS.
KIDS WOULD GET INFECTED WITH THE STUFF AND THEN LOCKED UP IN A BARN FOR DAYS. WHEN YOU CAME OUT, YOU'D BE IMMUNE. THAT IS, IF YOU CAME OUT AT ALL...
I'VE NEVER FORGOTTEN: THE DARKNESS, THE PAIN, THE STENCH OF DEATH...
WHOA!? THAT'S YOU!?
YES, I WAS ONE OF THE LUCKY ONES—I SURVIVED.
I STUDIED MEDICINE, HOPING THAT I COULD SAVE OTHERS FROM SUFFERING AS I HAD.
BUT SMALLPOX KEPT ON KILLING, AND I HAD NO IDEA EVEN WHERE TO BEGIN THE SEARCH FOR A CURE.

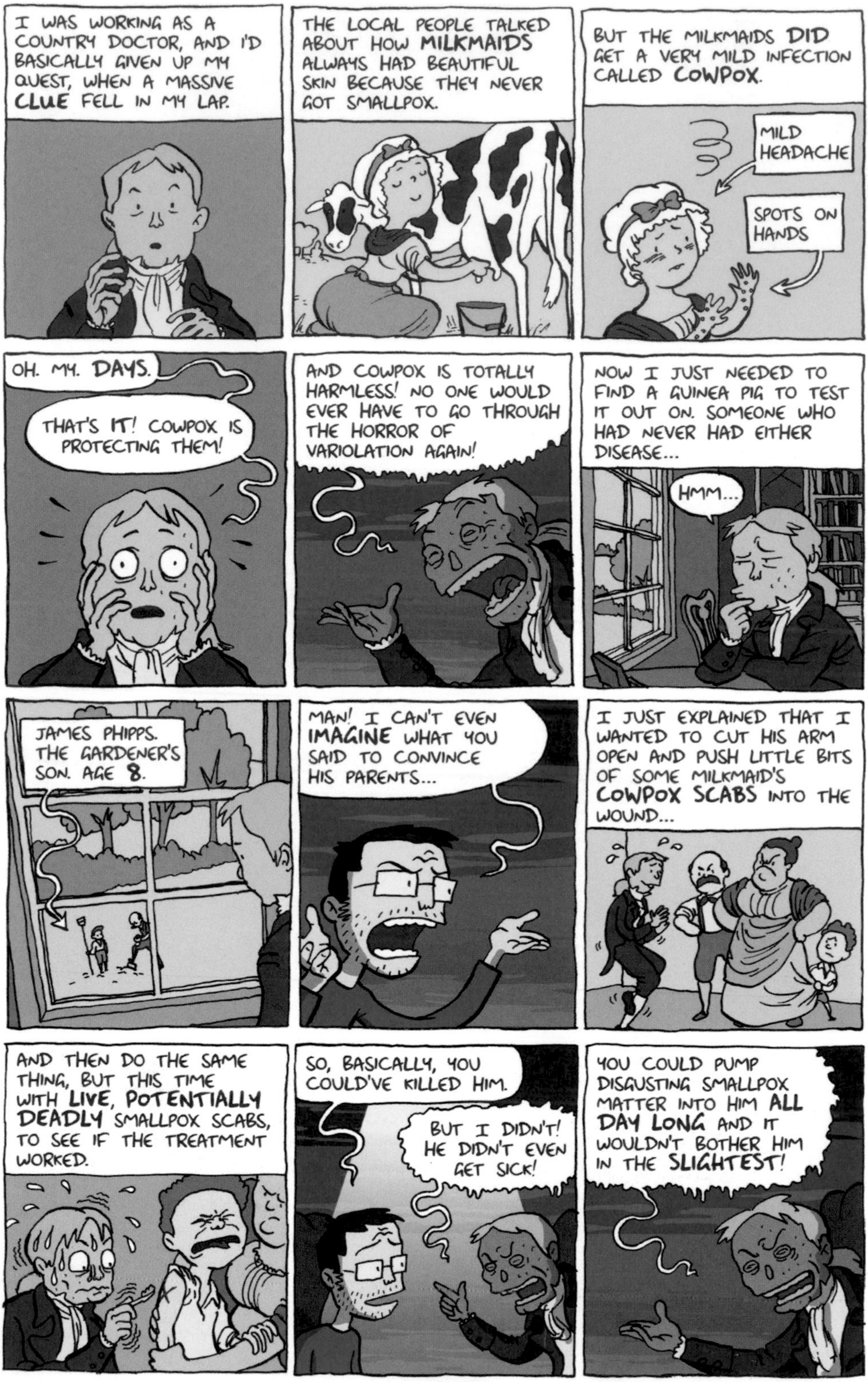
I WAS WORKING AS A COUNTRY DOCTOR, AND I'D BASICALLY GIVEN UP MY QUEST, WHEN A MASSIVE CLUE FELL IN MY LAP.
THE LOCAL PEOPLE TALKED ABOUT HOW MILKMAIDS ALWAYS HAD BEAUTIFUL SKIN BECAUSE THEY NEVER GOT SMALLPOX.
BUT THE MILKMAIDS DID GET A VERY MILD INFECTION CALLED COWPOX.
MILD HEADACHE
SPOTS ON HANDS
OH. MY. DAYS.
THAT'S IT! COWPOX IS PROTECTING THEM!
AND COWPOX IS TOTALLY HARMLESS! NO ONE WOULD EVER HAVE TO GO THROUGH THE HORROR OF VARIOLATION AGAIN!
NOW I JUST NEEDED TO FIND A GUINEA PIG TO TEST IT OUT ON. SOMEONE WHO HAD NEVER HAD EITHER DISEASE...
HMM...
JAMES PHIPPS. THE GARDENER'S SON. AGE 8.
MAN! I CAN'T EVEN IMAGINE WHAT YOU SAID TO CONVINCE HIS PARENTS...
I JUST EXPLAINED THAT I WANTED TO CUT HIS ARM OPEN AND PUSH LITTLE BITS OF SOME MILKMAID'S COWPOX SCABS INTO THE WOUND...
AND THEN DO THE SAME THING, BUT THIS TIME WITH LIVE, POTENTIALLY DEADLY SMALLPOX SCABS, TO SEE IF THE TREATMENT WORKED.
SO, BASICALLY, YOU COULD'VE KILLED HIM.
BUT I DIDN'T! HE DIDN'T EVEN GET SICK!
YOU COULD PUMP DISGUSTING SMALLPOX MATTER INTO HIM ALL DAY LONG AND IT WOULDN'T BOTHER HIM IN THE SLIGHTEST!

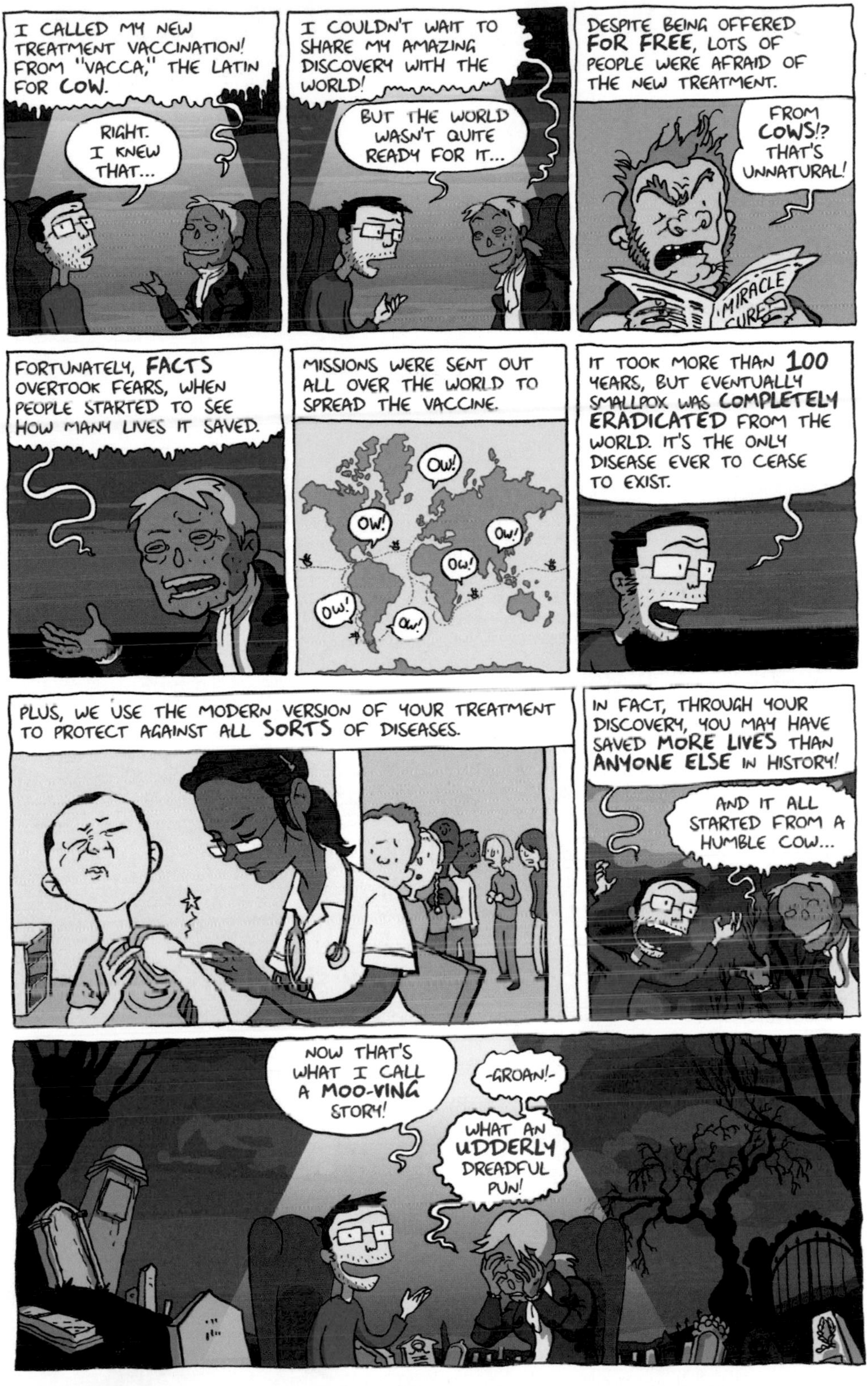
I CALLED MY NEW TREATMENT VACCINATION! FROM "VACCA," THE LATIN FOR COW.
RIGHT. I KNEW THAT...
I COULDN'T WAIT TO SHARE MY AMAZING DISCOVERY WITH THE WORLD!
BUT THE WORLD WASN'T QUITE READY FOR IT...
DESPITE BEING OFFERED FOR FREE, LOTS OF PEOPLE WERE AFRAID OF THE NEW TREATMENT.
FROM COWS!? THAT'S UNNATURAL!
MIRACLE CURES
FORTUNATELY, FACTS OVERTOOK FEARS, WHEN PEOPLE STARTED TO SEE HOW MANY LIVES IT SAVED.
MISSIONS WERE SENT OUT ALL OVER THE WORLD TO SPREAD THE VACCINE.
OW!
OW!
OW!
OW!
OW!
OW!
IT TOOK MORE THAN 100 YEARS, BUT EVENTUALLY SMALLPOX WAS COMPLETELY ERADICATED FROM THE WORLD. IT'S THE ONLY DISEASE EVER TO CEASE TO EXIST.
PLUS, WE USE THE MODERN VERSION OF YOUR TREATMENT TO PROTECT AGAINST ALL SORTS OF DISEASES.
IN FACT, THROUGH YOUR DISCOVERY, YOU MAY HAVE SAVED MORE LIVES THAN ANYONE ELSE IN HISTORY!
AND IT ALL STARTED FROM A HUMBLE COW...
NOW THAT'S WHAT I CALL A MOO-VING STORY!
-GROAN!-
WHAT AN UDDERLY DREADFUL PUN!

VACCINATION STATIONS

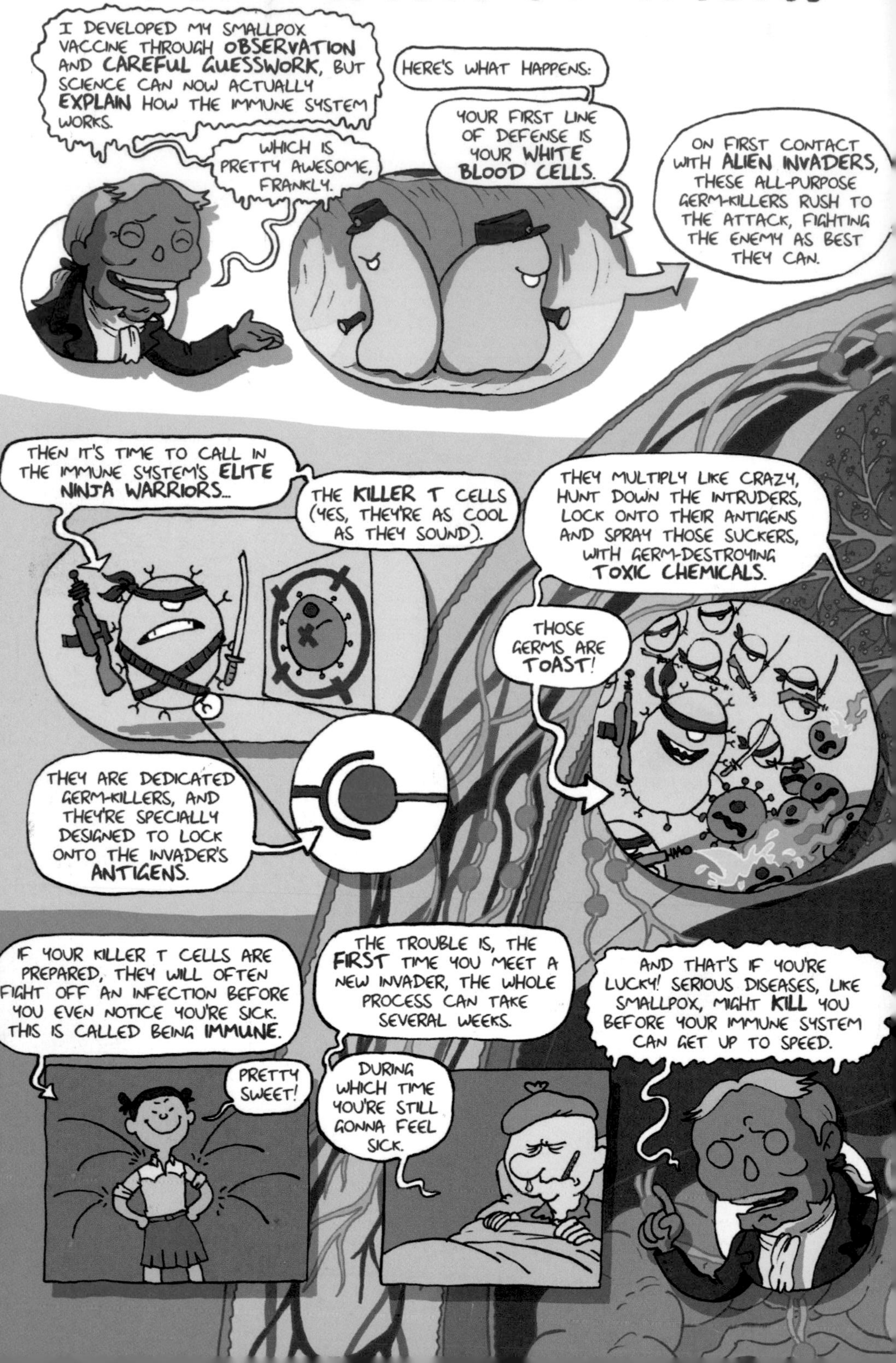

I DEVELOPED MY SMALLPOX VACCINE THROUGH **OBSERVATION** AND **CAREFUL GUESSWORK**, BUT SCIENCE CAN NOW ACTUALLY **EXPLAIN** HOW THE IMMUNE SYSTEM WORKS.
WHICH IS PRETTY AWESOME, FRANKLY.
HERE'S WHAT HAPPENS:
YOUR FIRST LINE OF DEFENSE IS YOUR **WHITE BLOOD CELLS**.
ON FIRST CONTACT WITH **ALIEN INVADERS**, THESE ALL-PURPOSE GERM-KILLERS RUSH TO THE ATTACK, FIGHTING THE ENEMY AS BEST THEY CAN.
THEN IT'S TIME TO CALL IN THE IMMUNE SYSTEM'S **ELITE NINJA WARRIORS**...
THE **KILLER T** CELLS (YES, THEY'RE AS COOL AS THEY SOUND).
THEY ARE DEDICATED GERM-KILLERS, AND THEY'RE SPECIALLY DESIGNED TO LOCK ONTO THE INVADER'S **ANTIGENS**.
THEY MULTIPLY LIKE CRAZY, HUNT DOWN THE INTRUDERS, LOCK ONTO THEIR ANTIGENS AND SPRAY THOSE SUCKERS, WITH GERM-DESTROYING **TOXIC CHEMICALS**.
THOSE GERMS ARE **TOAST**!
IF YOUR KILLER T CELLS ARE PREPARED, THEY WILL OFTEN FIGHT OFF AN INFECTION BEFORE YOU EVEN NOTICE YOU'RE SICK. THIS IS CALLED BEING **IMMUNE**.
PRETTY SWEET!
THE TROUBLE IS, THE **FIRST** TIME YOU MEET A NEW INVADER, THE WHOLE PROCESS CAN TAKE SEVERAL WEEKS.
DURING WHICH TIME YOU'RE STILL GONNA FEEL SICK.
AND THAT'S IF YOU'RE LUCKY! SERIOUS DISEASES, LIKE SMALLPOX, MIGHT **KILL** YOU BEFORE YOUR IMMUNE SYSTEM CAN GET UP TO SPEED.

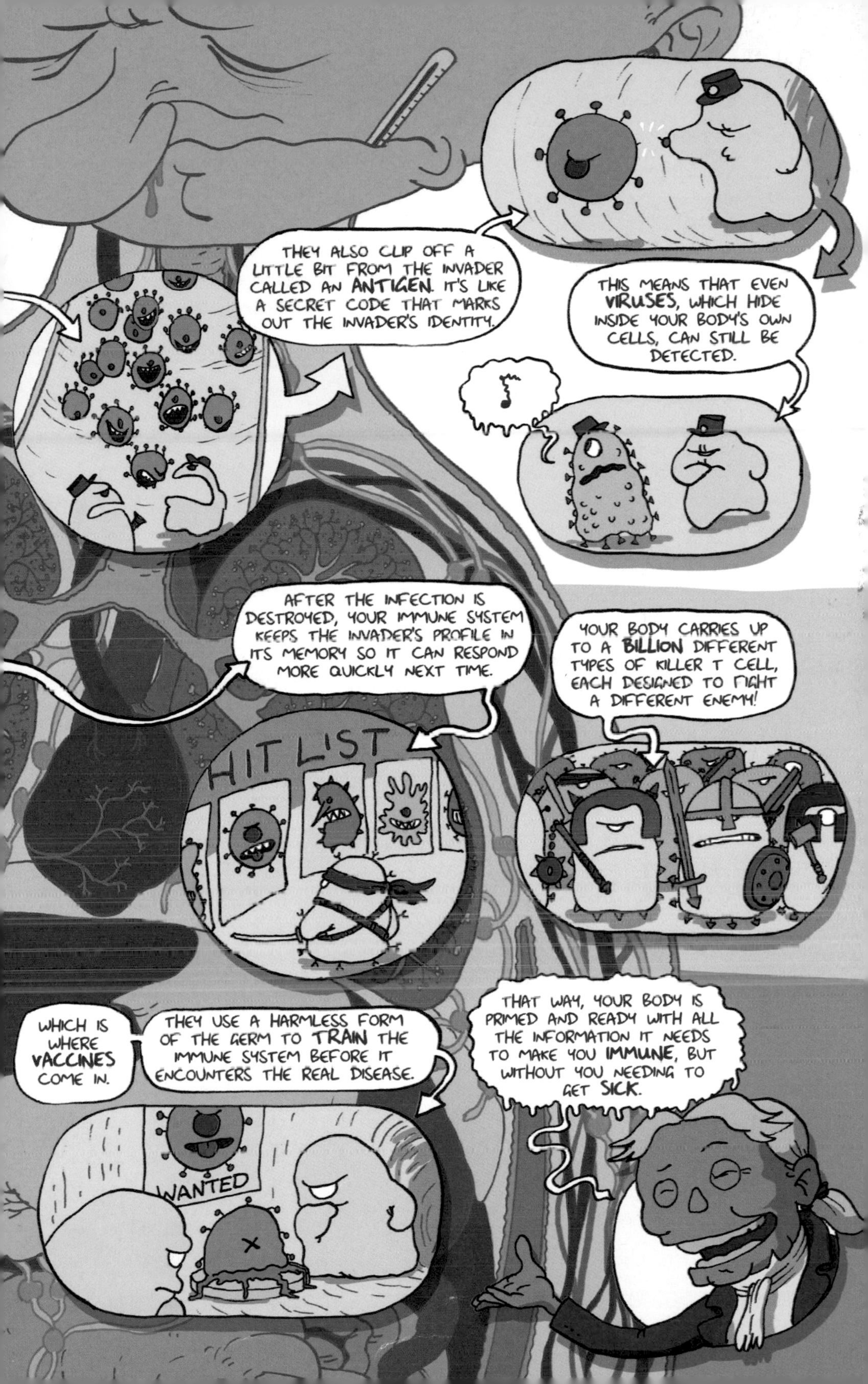
THEY ALSO CLIP OFF A LITTLE BIT FROM THE INVADER CALLED AN ANTIGEN. IT'S LIKE A SECRET CODE THAT MARKS OUT THE INVADER'S IDENTITY.
THIS MEANS THAT EVEN VIRUSES, WHICH HIDE INSIDE YOUR BODY'S OWN CELLS, CAN STILL BE DETECTED.
AFTER THE INFECTION IS DESTROYED, YOUR IMMUNE SYSTEM KEEPS THE INVADER'S PROFILE IN ITS MEMORY SO IT CAN RESPOND MORE QUICKLY NEXT TIME.
HIT LIST
YOUR BODY CARRIES UP TO A BILLION DIFFERENT TYPES OF KILLER T CELL, EACH DESIGNED TO FIGHT A DIFFERENT ENEMY!
WHICH IS WHERE VACCINES COME IN.
THEY USE A HARMLESS FORM OF THE GERM TO TRAIN THE IMMUNE SYSTEM BEFORE IT ENCOUNTERS THE REAL DISEASE.
THAT WAY, YOUR BODY IS PRIMED AND READY WITH ALL THE INFORMATION IT NEEDS TO MAKE YOU IMMUNE, BUT WITHOUT YOU NEEDING TO GET SICK.
WANTED

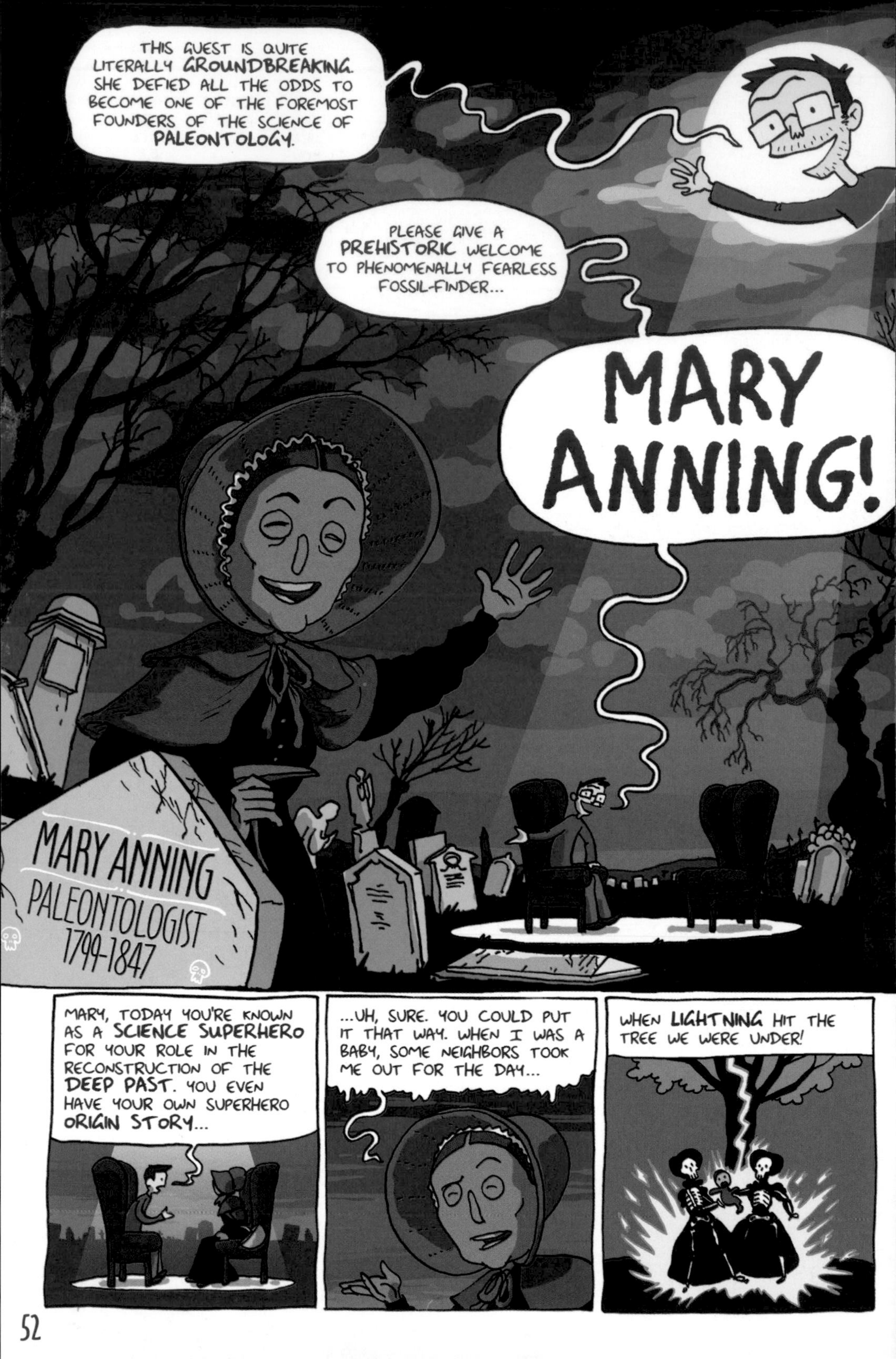
THIS GUEST IS QUITE LITERALLY GROUNDBREAKING. SHE DEFIED ALL THE ODDS TO BECOME ONE OF THE FOREMOST FOUNDERS OF THE SCIENCE OF PALEONTOLOGY.
PLEASE GIVE A PREHISTORIC WELCOME TO PHENOMENALLY FEARLESS FOSSIL-FINDER...
MARY ANNING!
MARY ANNING
PALEONTOLOGIST
1799-1847
MARY, TODAY YOU'RE KNOWN AS A SCIENCE SUPERHERO FOR YOUR ROLE IN THE RECONSTRUCTION OF THE DEEP PAST. YOU EVEN HAVE YOUR OWN SUPERHERO ORIGIN STORY...
...UH, SURE. YOU COULD PUT IT THAT WAY. WHEN I WAS A BABY, SOME NEIGHBORS TOOK ME OUT FOR THE DAY...
WHEN LIGHTNING HIT THE TREE WE WERE UNDER!

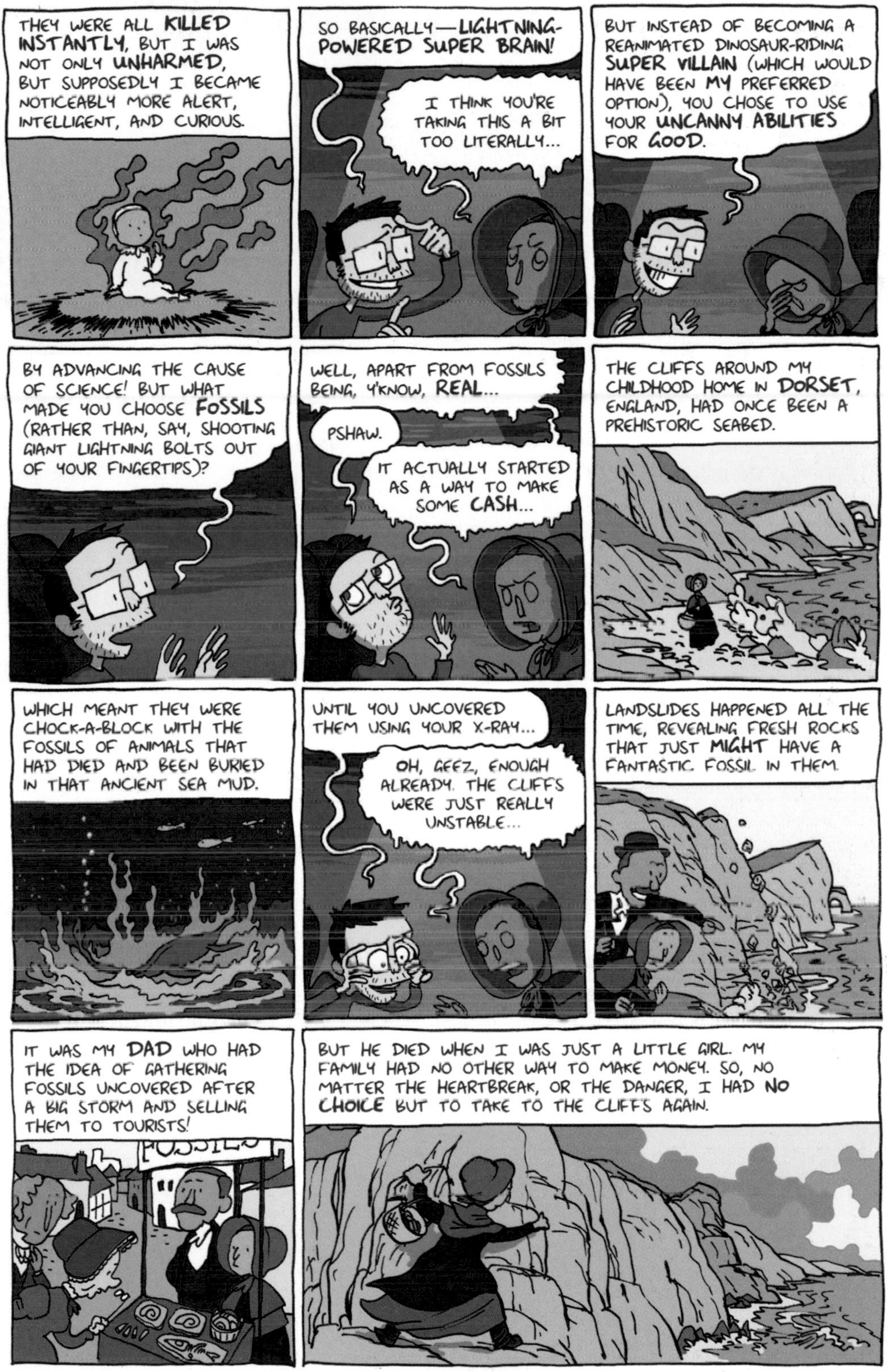
THEY WERE ALL KILLED INSTANTLY, BUT I WAS NOT ONLY UNHARMED, BUT SUPPOSEDLY I BECAME NOTICEABLY MORE ALERT, INTELLIGENT, AND CURIOUS.
SO BASICALLY—LIGHTNING-POWERED SUPER BRAIN!
I THINK YOU'RE TAKING THIS A BIT TOO LITERALLY...
BUT INSTEAD OF BECOMING A REANIMATED DINOSAUR-RIDING SUPER VILLAIN (WHICH WOULD HAVE BEEN MY PREFERRED OPTION), YOU CHOSE TO USE YOUR UNCANNY ABILITIES FOR GOOD.
BY ADVANCING THE CAUSE OF SCIENCE! BUT WHAT MADE YOU CHOOSE FOSSILS (RATHER THAN, SAY, SHOOTING GIANT LIGHTNING BOLTS OUT OF YOUR FINGERTIPS)?
WELL, APART FROM FOSSILS BEING, Y'KNOW, REAL...
PSHAW.
IT ACTUALLY STARTED AS A WAY TO MAKE SOME CASH...
THE CLIFFS AROUND MY CHILDHOOD HOME IN DORSET, ENGLAND, HAD ONCE BEEN A PREHISTORIC SEABED.
WHICH MEANT THEY WERE CHOCK-A-BLOCK WITH THE FOSSILS OF ANIMALS THAT HAD DIED AND BEEN BURIED IN THAT ANCIENT SEA MUD.
UNTIL YOU UNCOVERED THEM USING YOUR X-RAY...
OH, GEEZ, ENOUGH ALREADY. THE CLIFFS WERE JUST REALLY UNSTABLE...
LANDSLIDES HAPPENED ALL THE TIME, REVEALING FRESH ROCKS THAT JUST MIGHT HAVE A FANTASTIC FOSSIL IN THEM.
IT WAS MY DAD WHO HAD THE IDEA OF GATHERING FOSSILS UNCOVERED AFTER A BIG STORM AND SELLING THEM TO TOURISTS!
BUT HE DIED WHEN I WAS JUST A LITTLE GIRL. MY FAMILY HAD NO OTHER WAY TO MAKE MONEY. SO, NO MATTER THE HEARTBREAK, OR THE DANGER, I HAD NO CHOICE BUT TO TAKE TO THE CLIFFS AGAIN.

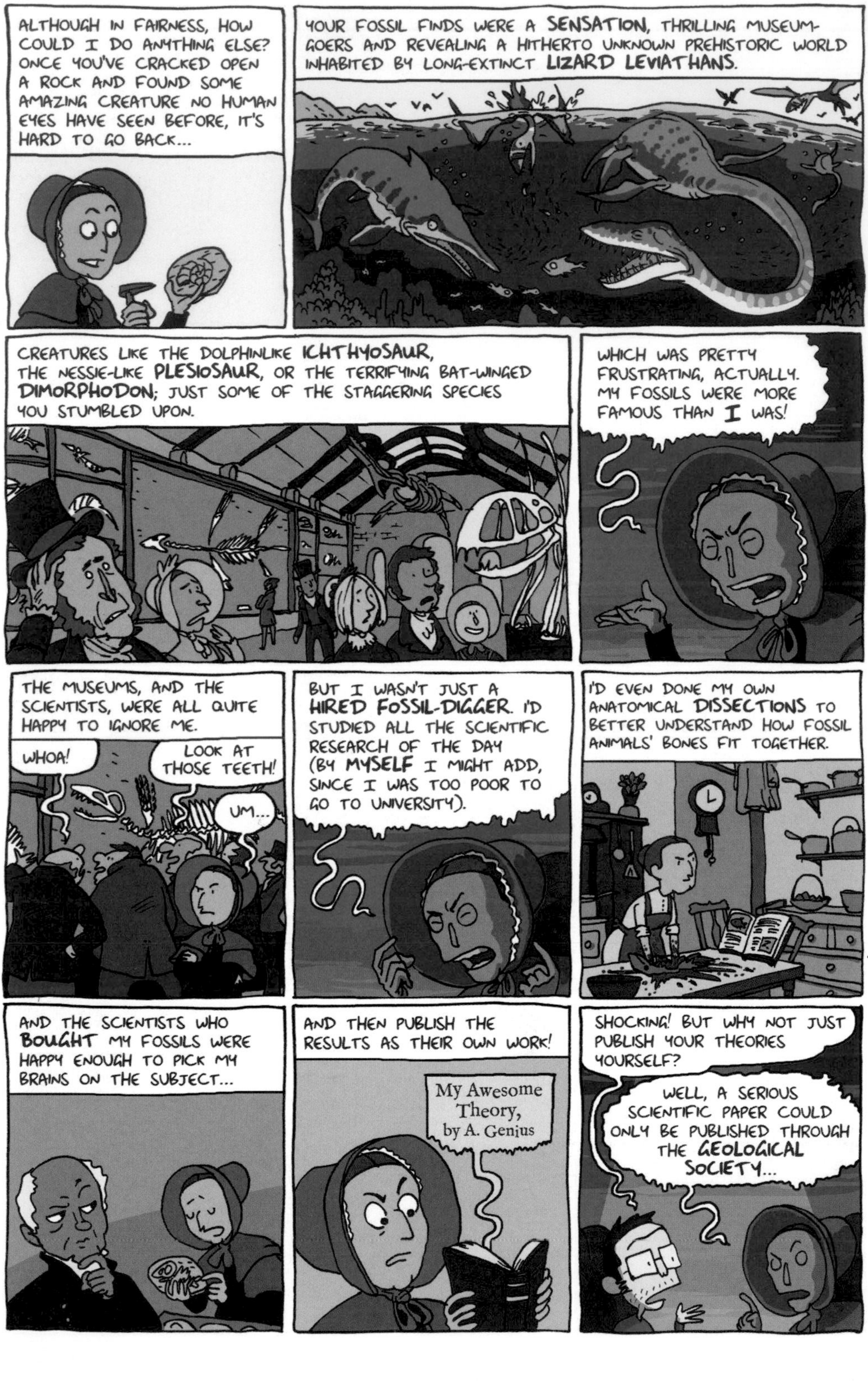
ALTHOUGH IN FAIRNESS, HOW COULD I DO ANYTHING ELSE? ONCE YOU'VE CRACKED OPEN A ROCK AND FOUND SOME AMAZING CREATURE NO HUMAN EYES HAVE SEEN BEFORE, IT'S HARD TO GO BACK...
YOUR FOSSIL FINDS WERE A SENSATION, THRILLING MUSEUM-GOERS AND REVEALING A HITHERTO UNKNOWN PREHISTORIC WORLD INHABITED BY LONG-EXTINCT LIZARD LEVIATHANS.
CREATURES LIKE THE DOLPHINLIKE ICHTHYOSAUR, THE NESSIE-LIKE PLESIOSAUR, OR THE TERRIFYING BAT-WINGED DIMORPHODON; JUST SOME OF THE STAGGERING SPECIES YOU STUMBLED UPON.
WHICH WAS PRETTY FRUSTRATING, ACTUALLY. MY FOSSILS WERE MORE FAMOUS THAN I WAS!
THE MUSEUMS, AND THE SCIENTISTS, WERE ALL QUITE HAPPY TO IGNORE ME.
WHOA!
LOOK AT THOSE TEETH!
UM...
BUT I WASN'T JUST A HIRED FOSSIL-DIGGER. I'D STUDIED ALL THE SCIENTIFIC RESEARCH OF THE DAY (BY MYSELF I MIGHT ADD, SINCE I WAS TOO POOR TO GO TO UNIVERSITY).
I'D EVEN DONE MY OWN ANATOMICAL DISSECTIONS TO BETTER UNDERSTAND HOW FOSSIL ANIMALS' BONES FIT TOGETHER.
AND THE SCIENTISTS WHO BOUGHT MY FOSSILS WERE HAPPY ENOUGH TO PICK MY BRAINS ON THE SUBJECT...
AND THEN PUBLISH THE RESULTS AS THEIR OWN WORK!
My Awesome Theory, by A. Genius
SHOCKING! BUT WHY NOT JUST PUBLISH YOUR THEORIES YOURSELF?
WELL, A SERIOUS SCIENTIFIC PAPER COULD ONLY BE PUBLISHED THROUGH THE GEOLOGICAL SOCIETY...

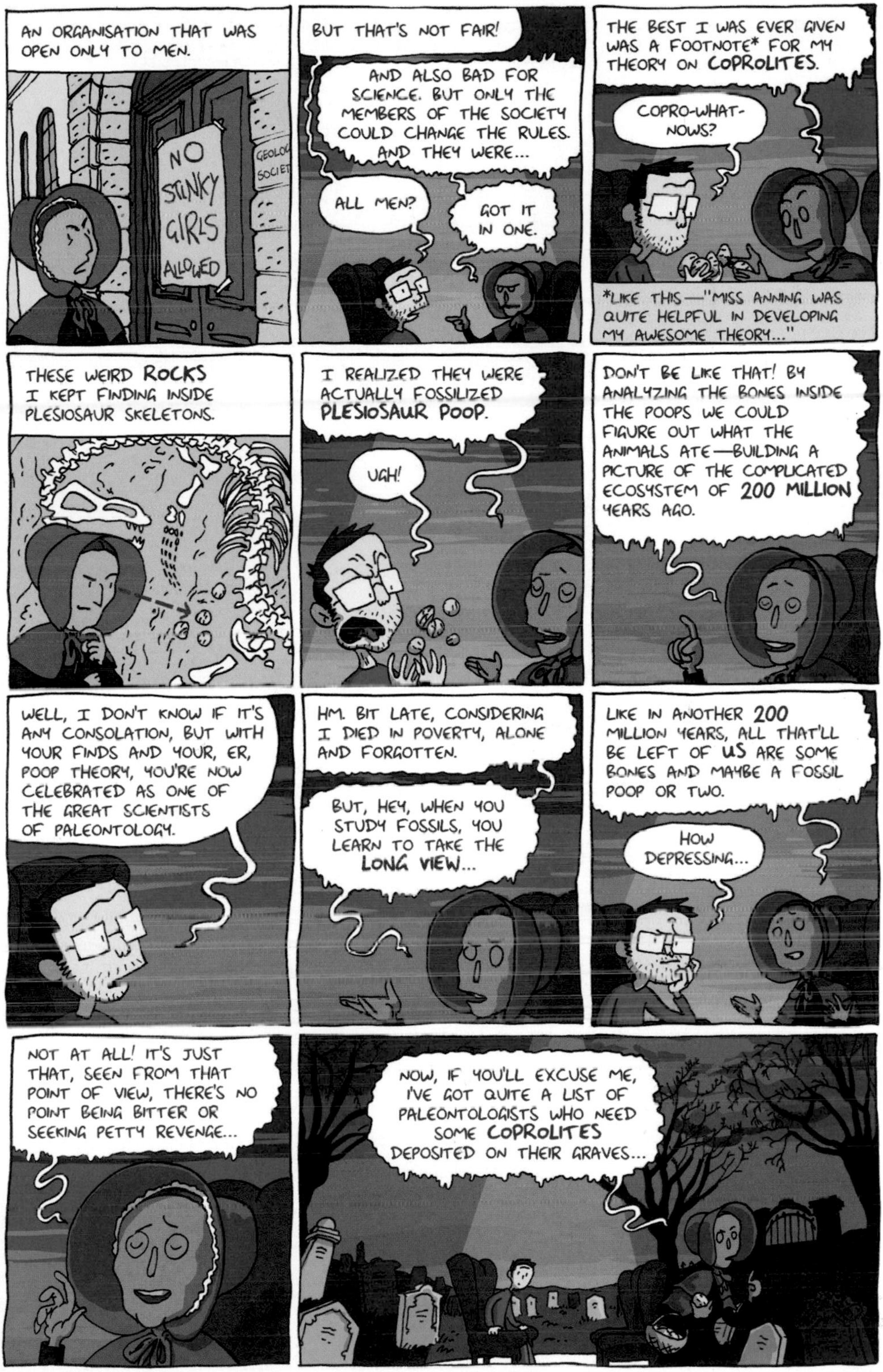
AN ORGANISATION THAT WAS OPEN ONLY TO MEN.
NO STINKY GIRLS ALLOWED
BUT THAT'S NOT FAIR!
AND ALSO BAD FOR SCIENCE. BUT ONLY THE MEMBERS OF THE SOCIETY COULD CHANGE THE RULES. AND THEY WERE...
ALL MEN?
GOT IT IN ONE.
THE BEST I WAS EVER GIVEN WAS A FOOTNOTE* FOR MY THEORY ON COPROLITES.
COPRO-WHAT-NOWS?
*LIKE THIS—"MISS ANNING WAS QUITE HELPFUL IN DEVELOPING MY AWESOME THEORY..."
THESE WEIRD ROCKS I KEPT FINDING INSIDE PLESIOSAUR SKELETONS.
I REALIZED THEY WERE ACTUALLY FOSSILIZED PLESIOSAUR POOP.
UGH!
DON'T BE LIKE THAT! BY ANALYZING THE BONES INSIDE THE POOPS WE COULD FIGURE OUT WHAT THE ANIMALS ATE—BUILDING A PICTURE OF THE COMPLICATED ECOSYSTEM OF 200 MILLION YEARS AGO.
WELL, I DON'T KNOW IF IT'S ANY CONSOLATION, BUT WITH YOUR FINDS AND YOUR, ER, POOP THEORY, YOU'RE NOW CELEBRATED AS ONE OF THE GREAT SCIENTISTS OF PALEONTOLOGY.
HM. BIT LATE, CONSIDERING I DIED IN POVERTY, ALONE AND FORGOTTEN.
BUT, HEY, WHEN YOU STUDY FOSSILS, YOU LEARN TO TAKE THE LONG VIEW...
LIKE IN ANOTHER 200 MILLION YEARS, ALL THAT'LL BE LEFT OF US ARE SOME BONES AND MAYBE A FOSSIL POOP OR TWO.
HOW DEPRESSING...
NOT AT ALL! IT'S JUST THAT, SEEN FROM THAT POINT OF VIEW, THERE'S NO POINT BEING BITTER OR SEEKING PETTY REVENGE...
NOW, IF YOU'LL EXCUSE ME, I'VE GOT QUITE A LIST OF PALEONTOLOGISTS WHO NEED SOME COPROLITES DEPOSITED ON THEIR GRAVES...

THE JURASSIC WORLD

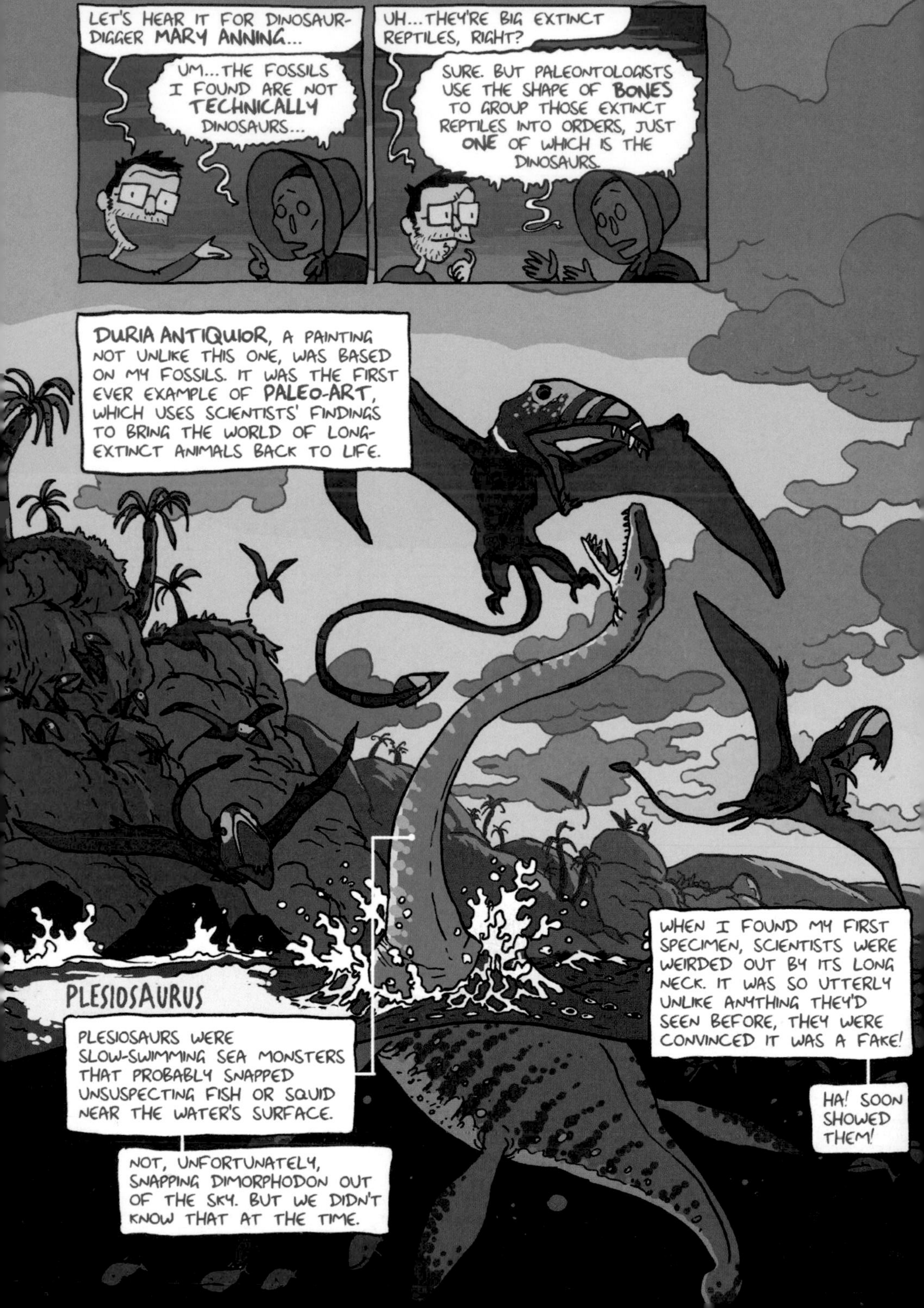

LET'S HEAR IT FOR DINOSAUR-DIGGER **MARY ANNING**...
UM... THE FOSSILS I FOUND ARE NOT **TECHNICALLY** DINOSAURS...
UH... THEY'RE BIG EXTINCT REPTILES, RIGHT?
SURE. BUT PALEONTOLOGISTS USE THE SHAPE OF **BONES** TO GROUP THOSE EXTINCT REPTILES INTO ORDERS, JUST **ONE** OF WHICH IS THE DINOSAURS.
DURIA ANTIQUIOR, A PAINTING NOT UNLIKE THIS ONE, WAS BASED ON MY FOSSILS. IT WAS THE FIRST EVER EXAMPLE OF **PALEO-ART**, WHICH USES SCIENTISTS' FINDINGS TO BRING THE WORLD OF LONG-EXTINCT ANIMALS BACK TO LIFE.
PLESIOSAURUS
PLESIOSAURS WERE SLOW-SWIMMING SEA MONSTERS THAT PROBABLY SNAPPED UNSUSPECTING FISH OR SQUID NEAR THE WATER'S SURFACE.
NOT, UNFORTUNATELY, SNAPPING DIMORPHODON OUT OF THE SKY. BUT WE DIDN'T KNOW THAT AT THE TIME.
WHEN I FOUND MY FIRST SPECIMEN, SCIENTISTS WERE WEIRDED OUT BY ITS LONG NECK. IT WAS SO UTTERLY UNLIKE ANYTHING THEY'D SEEN BEFORE, THEY WERE CONVINCED IT WAS A FAKE!
HA! SOON SHOWED THEM!

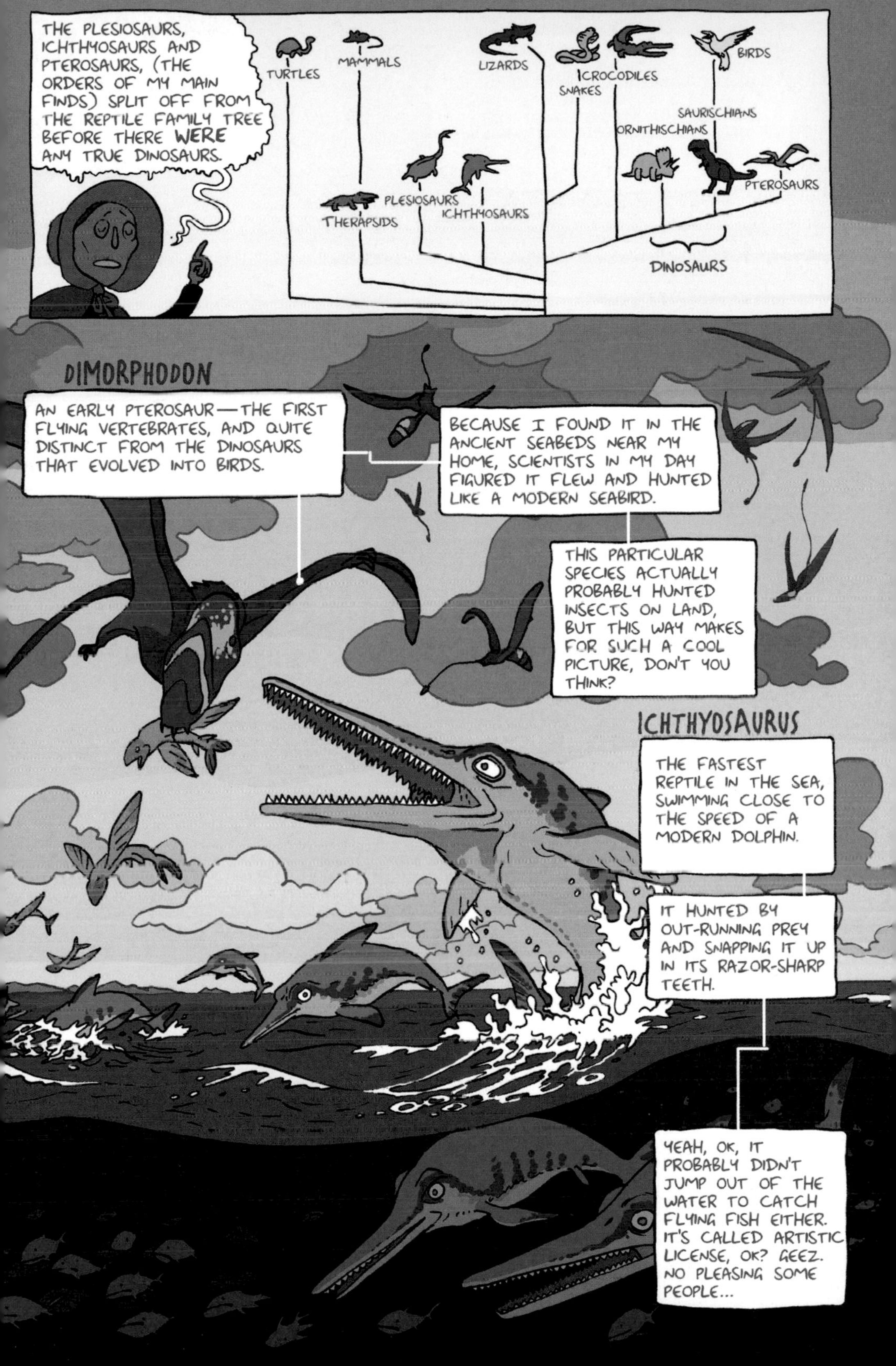
THE PLESIOSAURS, ICHTHYOSAURS AND PTEROSAURS, (THE ORDERS OF MY MAIN FINDS) SPLIT OFF FROM THE REPTILE FAMILY TREE BEFORE THERE WERE ANY TRUE DINOSAURS.
TURTLES
MAMMALS
LIZARDS
SNAKES
CROCODILES
BIRDS
SAURISCHIANS
ORNITHISCHIANS
PLESIOSAURS
THERAPSIDS
ICHTHYOSAURS
PTEROSAURS
DINOSAURS
DIMORPHODON
AN EARLY PTEROSAUR—THE FIRST FLYING VERTEBRATES, AND QUITE DISTINCT FROM THE DINOSAURS THAT EVOLVED INTO BIRDS.
BECAUSE I FOUND IT IN THE ANCIENT SEABEDS NEAR MY HOME, SCIENTISTS IN MY DAY FIGURED IT FLEW AND HUNTED LIKE A MODERN SEABIRD.
THIS PARTICULAR SPECIES ACTUALLY PROBABLY HUNTED INSECTS ON LAND, BUT THIS WAY MAKES FOR SUCH A COOL PICTURE, DON'T YOU THINK?
ICHTHYOSAURUS
THE FASTEST REPTILE IN THE SEA, SWIMMING CLOSE TO THE SPEED OF A MODERN DOLPHIN.
IT HUNTED BY OUT-RUNNING PREY AND SNAPPING IT UP IN ITS RAZOR-SHARP TEETH.
YEAH, OK, IT PROBABLY DIDN'T JUMP OUT OF THE WATER TO CATCH FLYING FISH EITHER. IT'S CALLED ARTISTIC LICENSE, OK? GEEZ. NO PLEASING SOME PEOPLE...

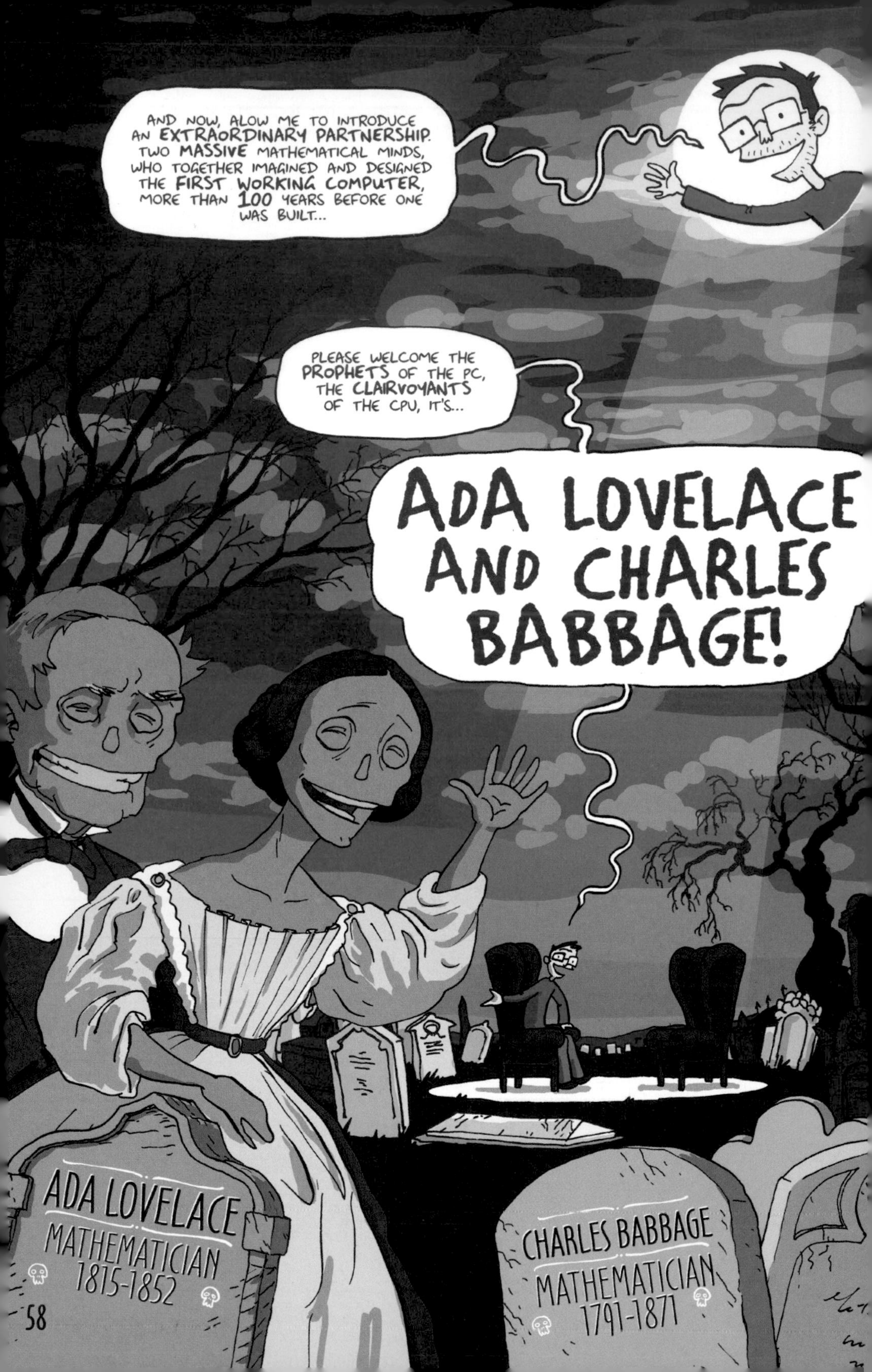
AND NOW, ALOW ME TO INTRODUCE AN EXTRAORDINARY PARTNERSHIP. TWO MASSIVE MATHEMATICAL MINDS, WHO TOGETHER IMAGINED AND DESIGNED THE FIRST WORKING COMPUTER, MORE THAN 100 YEARS BEFORE ONE WAS BUILT...
PLEASE WELCOME THE PROPHETS OF THE PC, THE CLAIRVOYANTS OF THE CPU, IT'S...
ADA LOVELACE AND CHARLES BABBAGE!
ADA LOVELACE
MATHEMATICIAN
1815-1852
CHARLES BABBAGE
MATHEMATICIAN
1791-1871

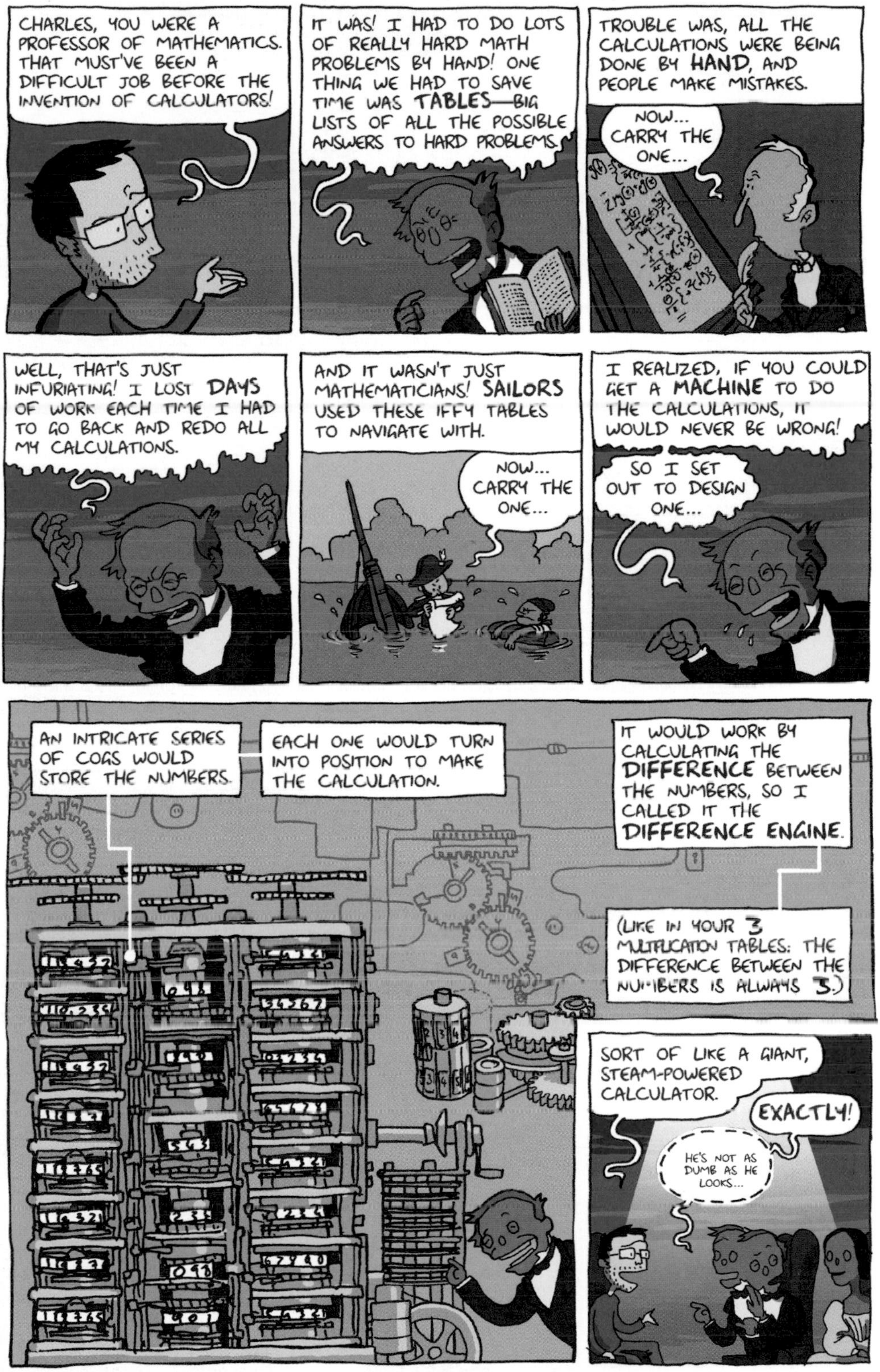
CHARLES, YOU WERE A PROFESSOR OF MATHEMATICS. THAT MUST'VE BEEN A DIFFICULT JOB BEFORE THE INVENTION OF CALCULATORS!
IT WAS! I HAD TO DO LOTS OF REALLY HARD MATH PROBLEMS BY HAND! ONE THING WE HAD TO SAVE TIME WAS TABLES—BIG LISTS OF ALL THE POSSIBLE ANSWERS TO HARD PROBLEMS.
TROUBLE WAS, ALL THE CALCULATIONS WERE BEING DONE BY HAND, AND PEOPLE MAKE MISTAKES.
NOW... CARRY THE ONE...
WELL, THAT'S JUST INFURIATING! I LOST DAYS OF WORK EACH TIME I HAD TO GO BACK AND REDO ALL MY CALCULATIONS.
AND IT WASN'T JUST MATHEMATICIANS! SAILORS USED THESE IFFY TABLES TO NAVIGATE WITH.
NOW... CARRY THE ONE...
I REALIZED, IF YOU COULD GET A MACHINE TO DO THE CALCULATIONS, IT WOULD NEVER BE WRONG!
SO I SET OUT TO DESIGN ONE...
AN INTRICATE SERIES OF COGS WOULD STORE THE NUMBERS.
EACH ONE WOULD TURN INTO POSITION TO MAKE THE CALCULATION.
IT WOULD WORK BY CALCULATING THE DIFFERENCE BETWEEN THE NUMBERS, SO I CALLED IT THE DIFFERENCE ENGINE.
(LIKE IN YOUR 3 MULTIPLICATION TABLES: THE DIFFERENCE BETWEEN THE NUMBERS IS ALWAYS 3.)
SORT OF LIKE A GIANT, STEAM-POWERED CALCULATOR.
EXACTLY!
HE'S NOT AS DUMB AS HE LOOKS...

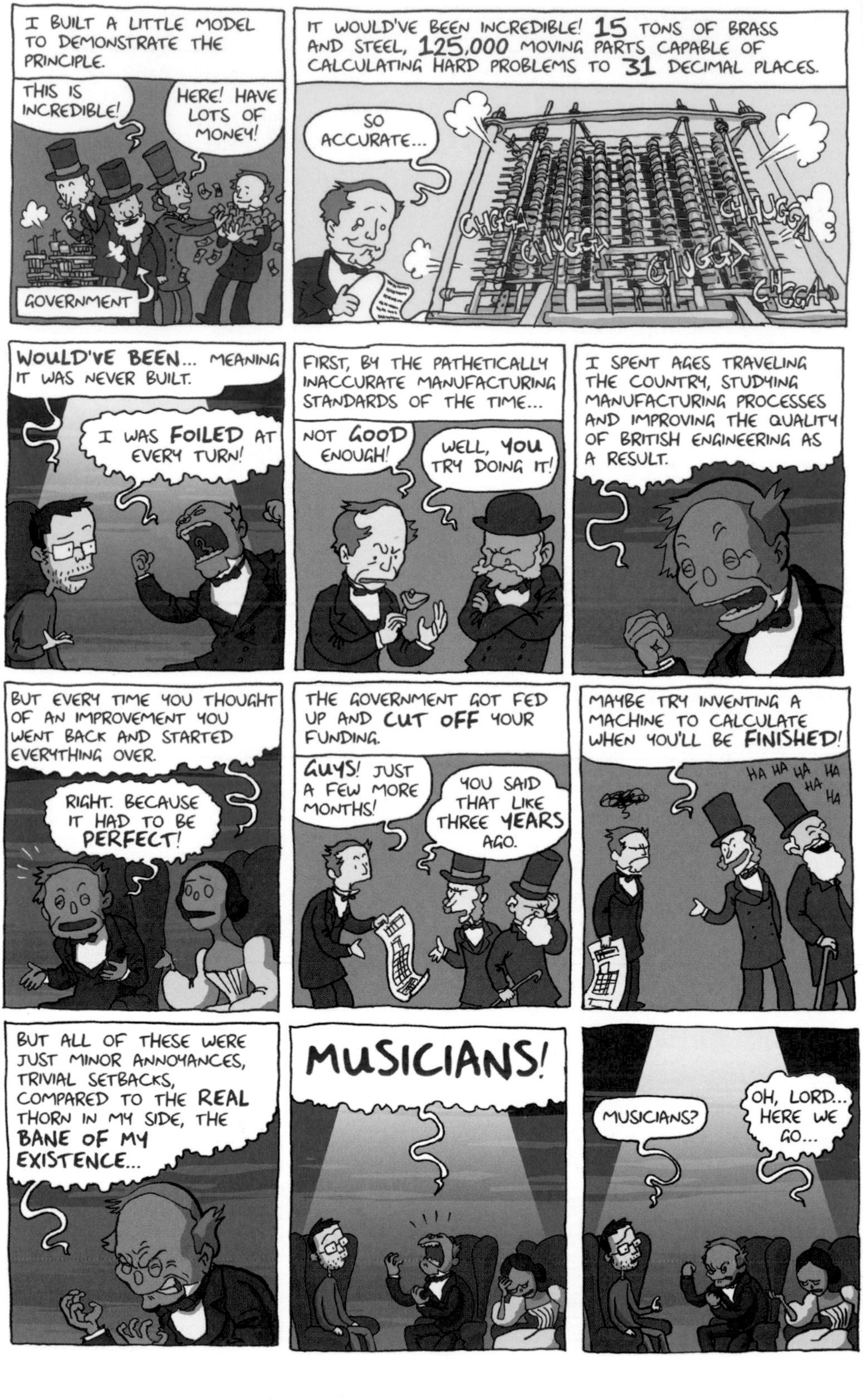
I BUILT A LITTLE MODEL TO DEMONSTRATE THE PRINCIPLE.
THIS IS INCREDIBLE!
HERE! HAVE LOTS OF MONEY!
GOVERNMENT
IT WOULD'VE BEEN INCREDIBLE! 15 TONS OF BRASS AND STEEL, 125,000 MOVING PARTS CAPABLE OF CALCULATING HARD PROBLEMS TO 31 DECIMAL PLACES.
SO ACCURATE...
CHUGGA CHUGGA CHUGGA CHUGGA CHUGGA
WOULD'VE BEEN... MEANING IT WAS NEVER BUILT.
I WAS FOILED AT EVERY TURN!
FIRST, BY THE PATHETICALLY INACCURATE MANUFACTURING STANDARDS OF THE TIME...
NOT GOOD ENOUGH!
WELL, YOU TRY DOING IT!
I SPENT AGES TRAVELING THE COUNTRY, STUDYING MANUFACTURING PROCESSES AND IMPROVING THE QUALITY OF BRITISH ENGINEERING AS A RESULT.
BUT EVERY TIME YOU THOUGHT OF AN IMPROVEMENT YOU WENT BACK AND STARTED EVERYTHING OVER.
RIGHT. BECAUSE IT HAD TO BE PERFECT!
THE GOVERNMENT GOT FED UP AND CUT OFF YOUR FUNDING.
GUYS! JUST A FEW MORE MONTHS!
YOU SAID THAT LIKE THREE YEARS AGO.
MAYBE TRY INVENTING A MACHINE TO CALCULATE WHEN YOU'LL BE FINISHED!
HA HA HA HA HA HA
BUT ALL OF THESE WERE JUST MINOR ANNOYANCES, TRIVIAL SETBACKS, COMPARED TO THE REAL THORN IN MY SIDE, THE BANE OF MY EXISTENCE...
MUSICIANS!
MUSICIANS?
OH, LORD... HERE WE GO...

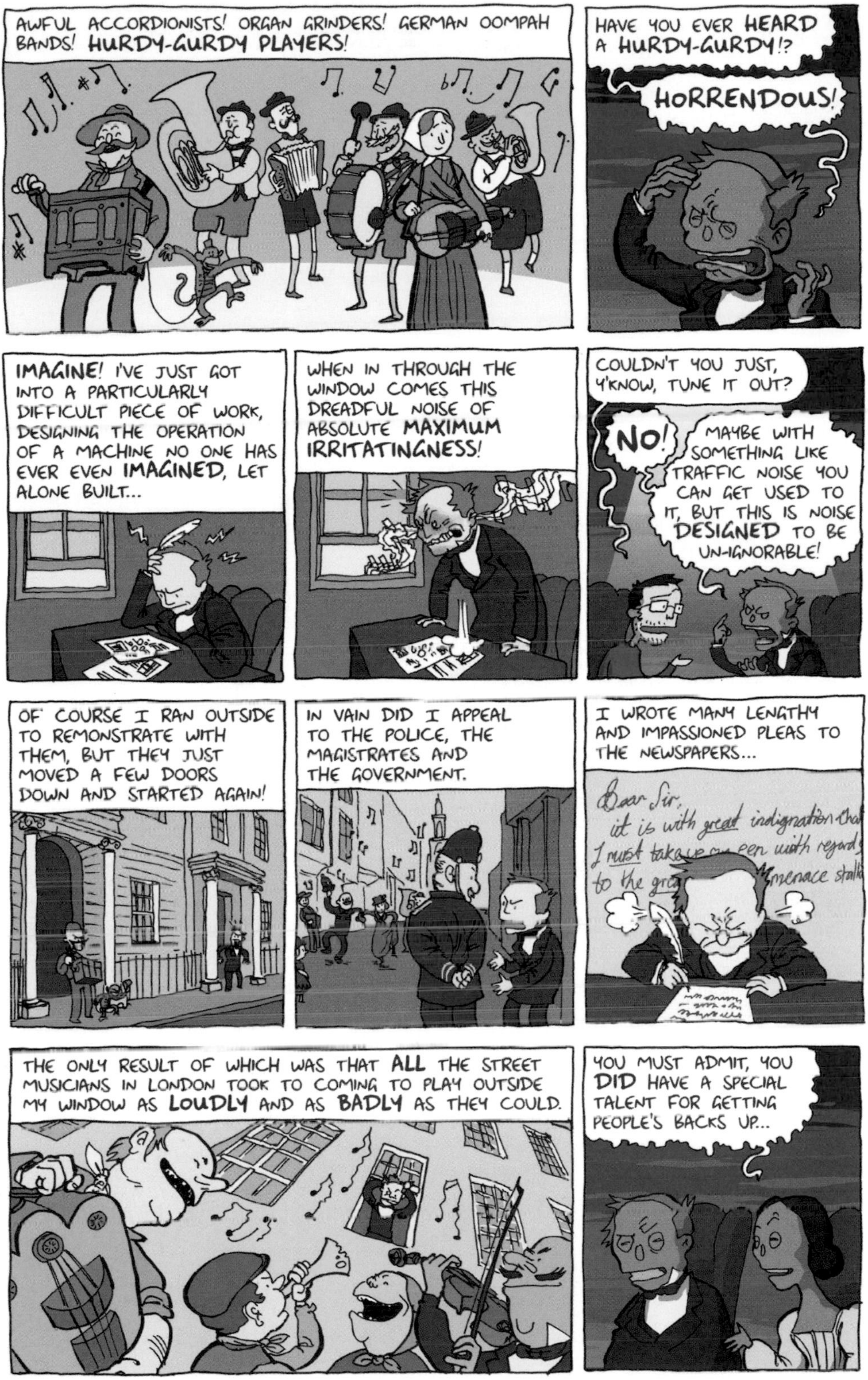
AWFUL ACCORDIONISTS! ORGAN GRINDERS! GERMAN OOMPAH BANDS! HURDY-GURDY PLAYERS!
HAVE YOU EVER HEARD A HURDY-GURDY!?
HORRENDOUS!
IMAGINE! I'VE JUST GOT INTO A PARTICULARLY DIFFICULT PIECE OF WORK, DESIGNING THE OPERATION OF A MACHINE NO ONE HAS EVER EVEN IMAGINED, LET ALONE BUILT...
WHEN IN THROUGH THE WINDOW COMES THIS DREADFUL NOISE OF ABSOLUTE MAXIMUM IRRITATINGNESS!
COULDN'T YOU JUST, Y'KNOW, TUNE IT OUT?
NO!
MAYBE WITH SOMETHING LIKE TRAFFIC NOISE YOU CAN GET USED TO IT, BUT THIS IS NOISE DESIGNED TO BE UN-IGNORABLE!
OF COURSE I RAN OUTSIDE TO REMONSTRATE WITH THEM, BUT THEY JUST MOVED A FEW DOORS DOWN AND STARTED AGAIN!
IN VAIN DID I APPEAL TO THE POLICE, THE MAGISTRATES AND THE GOVERNMENT.
I WROTE MANY LENGTHY AND IMPASSIONED PLEAS TO THE NEWSPAPERS...
Dear Sir,
it is with great indignation
THE ONLY RESULT OF WHICH WAS THAT ALL THE STREET MUSICIANS IN LONDON TOOK TO COMING TO PLAY OUTSIDE MY WINDOW AS LOUDLY AND AS BADLY AS THEY COULD.
YOU MUST ADMIT, YOU DID HAVE A SPECIAL TALENT FOR GETTING PEOPLE'S BACKS UP...

THEY WERE CLEARLY ALL STUNTED IMBECILES, JEALOUS OF MY VASTLY SUPERIOR INTELLIGENCE!

YOU SEE WHAT I'M TALKING ABOUT...

AND ALL THE WHILE YOUR DIFFERENCE ENGINE WAS LANGUISHING HALF-FINISHED...

BUT THEN I HAD A NEW IDEA!

I STARTED THINKING, IF I COULD BUILD A MACHINE TO DO ONE KIND OF CALCULATION...

BUT YOU DIDN'T...

NO, BUT I COULD HAVE. YOU DON'T GET TO BE THIS CLEVER WITHOUT BEING ABLE TO VISUALISE YOUR INVENTIONS BEFORE THEY'RE BUILT. I KNEW IT WORKED!

ANYWAY, THAT'S NOT THE POINT—I HAD THIS NEW IDEA—INSTEAD OF THE DIFFERENCE ENGINE, I WOULD BUILD THE ANALYTIC ENGINE!

WHAT'S THE DIFFERENCE?

WELL, THE DIFFERENCE ENGINE COULD ONLY DO ONE TYPE OF CALCULATION. THE ANALYTIC MACHINE COULD BE PROGRAMMED TO DO ANY TYPE OF CALCULATION AT ALL!

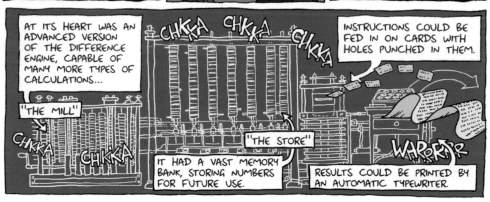

AT ITS HEART WAS AN ADVANCED VERSION OF THE DIFFERENCE ENGINE, CAPABLE OF MANY MORE TYPES OF CALCULATIONS...

"THE MILL"

CHKKA CHKKA

CHKKA CHKKA CHKKA

"THE STORE"

IT HAD A VAST MEMORY BANK, STORING NUMBERS FOR FUTURE USE.

INSTRUCTIONS COULD BE FED IN ON CARDS WITH HOLES PUNCHED IN THEM.

WARRRRR

RESULTS COULD BE PRINTED BY AN AUTOMATIC TYPEWRITER.

WAIT, WAIT. IT STILL SOUNDS LIKE A CALCULATOR. MAYBE ONE OF THOSE FANCY ONES WITH ALL THE EXTRA BUTTONS...

WELL, THAT'S WHERE ADA COMES IN...

ABOUT TIME! I BECAME THE HIGH PRIESTESS OF CHARLES'S AMAZING MACHINE, USING THE MAGIC OF MATH TO FIGHT THE EVILS OF POETRY.

HOLD ON. WHAT!?

MY FATHER WAS LORD BYRON, THE FAMOUS POET.

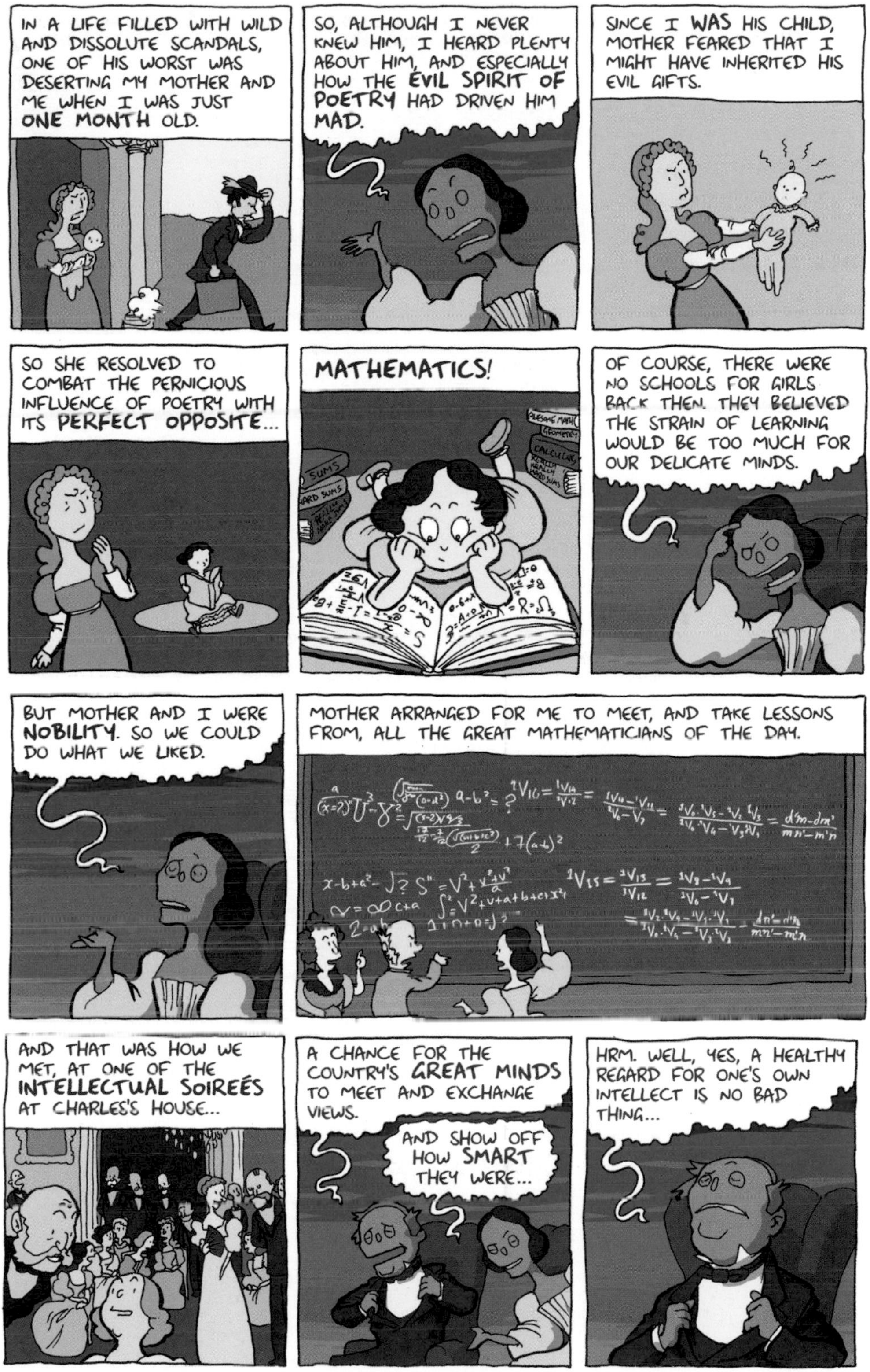
IN A LIFE FILLED WITH WILD AND DISSOLUTE SCANDALS, ONE OF HIS WORST WAS DESERTING MY MOTHER AND ME WHEN I WAS JUST ONE MONTH OLD.
SO, ALTHOUGH I NEVER KNEW HIM, I HEARD PLENTY ABOUT HIM, AND ESPECIALLY HOW THE EVIL SPIRIT OF POETRY HAD DRIVEN HIM MAD.
SINCE I WAS HIS CHILD, MOTHER FEARED THAT I MIGHT HAVE INHERITED HIS EVIL GIFTS.
SO SHE RESOLVED TO COMBAT THE PERNICIOUS INFLUENCE OF POETRY WITH ITS PERFECT OPPOSITE...
MATHEMATICS!
SUMS
HARD SUMS
GEOMETRY
CALCULUS
OF COURSE, THERE WERE NO SCHOOLS FOR GIRLS BACK THEN. THEY BELIEVED THE STRAIN OF LEARNING WOULD BE TOO MUCH FOR OUR DELICATE MINDS.
BUT MOTHER AND I WERE NOBILITY. SO WE COULD DO WHAT WE LIKED.
MOTHER ARRANGED FOR ME TO MEET, AND TAKE LESSONS FROM, ALL THE GREAT MATHEMATICIANS OF THE DAY.
AND THAT WAS HOW WE MET, AT ONE OF THE INTELLECTUAL SOIREÉS AT CHARLES'S HOUSE...
A CHANCE FOR THE COUNTRY'S GREAT MINDS TO MEET AND EXCHANGE VIEWS.
AND SHOW OFF HOW SMART THEY WERE...
HRM. WELL, YES, A HEALTHY REGARD FOR ONE'S OWN INTELLECT IS NO BAD THING...

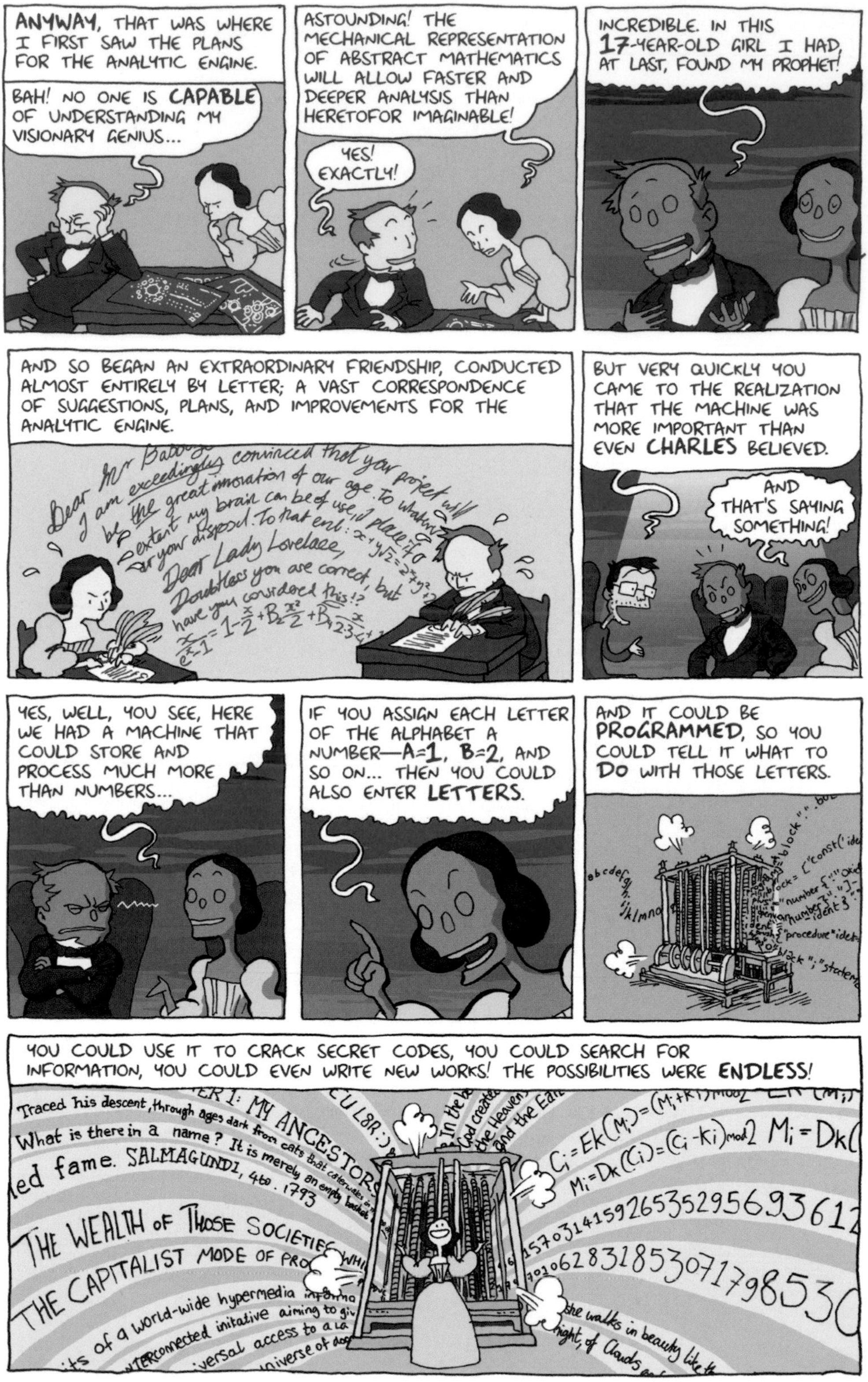
ANYWAY, THAT WAS WHERE I FIRST SAW THE PLANS FOR THE ANALYTIC ENGINE.
BAH! NO ONE IS CAPABLE OF UNDERSTANDING MY VISIONARY GENIUS...
ASTOUNDING! THE MECHANICAL REPRESENTATION OF ABSTRACT MATHEMATICS WILL ALLOW FASTER AND DEEPER ANALYSIS THAN HERETOFOR IMAGINABLE!
YES! EXACTLY!
INCREDIBLE. IN THIS 17-YEAR-OLD GIRL I HAD, AT LAST, FOUND MY PROPHET!
AND SO BEGAN AN EXTRAORDINARY FRIENDSHIP, CONDUCTED ALMOST ENTIRELY BY LETTER; A VAST CORRESPONDENCE OF SUGGESTIONS, PLANS, AND IMPROVEMENTS FOR THE ANALYTIC ENGINE.
Dear Lady Lovelace,
Doubtless you are correct, but have you considered this!?
BUT VERY QUICKLY YOU CAME TO THE REALIZATION THAT THE MACHINE WAS MORE IMPORTANT THAN EVEN CHARLES BELIEVED.
AND THAT'S SAYING SOMETHING!
YES, WELL, YOU SEE, HERE WE HAD A MACHINE THAT COULD STORE AND PROCESS MUCH MORE THAN NUMBERS...
IF YOU ASSIGN EACH LETTER OF THE ALPHABET A NUMBER—A=1, B=2, AND SO ON... THEN YOU COULD ALSO ENTER LETTERS.
AND IT COULD BE PROGRAMMED, SO YOU COULD TELL IT WHAT TO DO WITH THOSE LETTERS.
YOU COULD USE IT TO CRACK SECRET CODES, YOU COULD SEARCH FOR INFORMATION, YOU COULD EVEN WRITE NEW WORKS! THE POSSIBILITIES WERE ENDLESS!
Traced his descent, through ages dark
What is there in a name? It is merely an empty basket
ed fame. SALMAGUNDI, 4to. 1793
THE WEALTH OF THOSE SOCIETIES
THE CAPITALIST MODE OF PRO
THE CAPITALIST MODE OF PRO
its of a world-wide hypermedia
interconnected initiative aiming to giv
iversal access to a la
In the be
God created
the Heavens
and the Ear
$C_i = Ek(M_i) = (M_i + k_i) \bmod 2$
$M_i = Dk(C_i) = (C_i - k_i) \bmod 2$
she walks in beauty like th
night, of clouds

AND YOU COULD DO THE SAME WITH **ANY** INFORMATION THAT COULD BE CONVERTED TO NUMBERS.

FOR EXAMPLE, THE NOTES OF MUSICAL NOTATION...

NOOO!

NOT **MUSIC!** THAT **INFERNAL NOISE!**

CHARLES! DO CALM YOURSELF!

OH, YEAH? WELL, THEN WHAT IF IT WAS USED FOR... **POETRY!**

NOOO!

GUYS, GUYS! IT CAN BE USED FOR ALL THESE THINGS AND **MORE!**

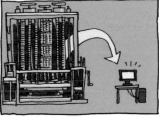

TODAY, WE USE **ELECTRICITY** INSTEAD OF STEAM, BUT THE BASIC PRINCIPLES OF YOUR ANALYTIC ENGINE ARE THE SAME AS THE MODERN **COMPUTER.**

AND WE CAN PROCESS NOT ONLY NUMBERS, TEXT, AND MUSIC, BUT PHOTOS, GAMES, VIDEO-CONFERENCE CALLS FROM AROUND THE WORLD...

EVEN **COMICS!** SOME OF OUR READERS MIGHT BE READING **THIS VERY BOOK** ON A TINY, PORTABLE VERSION OF THE ANALYTIC ENGINE!

PRETTY GOOD GOING FOR AN **IMAGINARY** MACHINE!

YESS! CALL ME A CRACKPOT WILL YOU? WELL, WHO'S LAUGHING NOW!? **ME!** HA HA HA HA HA!

VISIONARIES OF THE COMPUTER AGE!

AW, YEAH!

The DIFFERENCE ENGINE

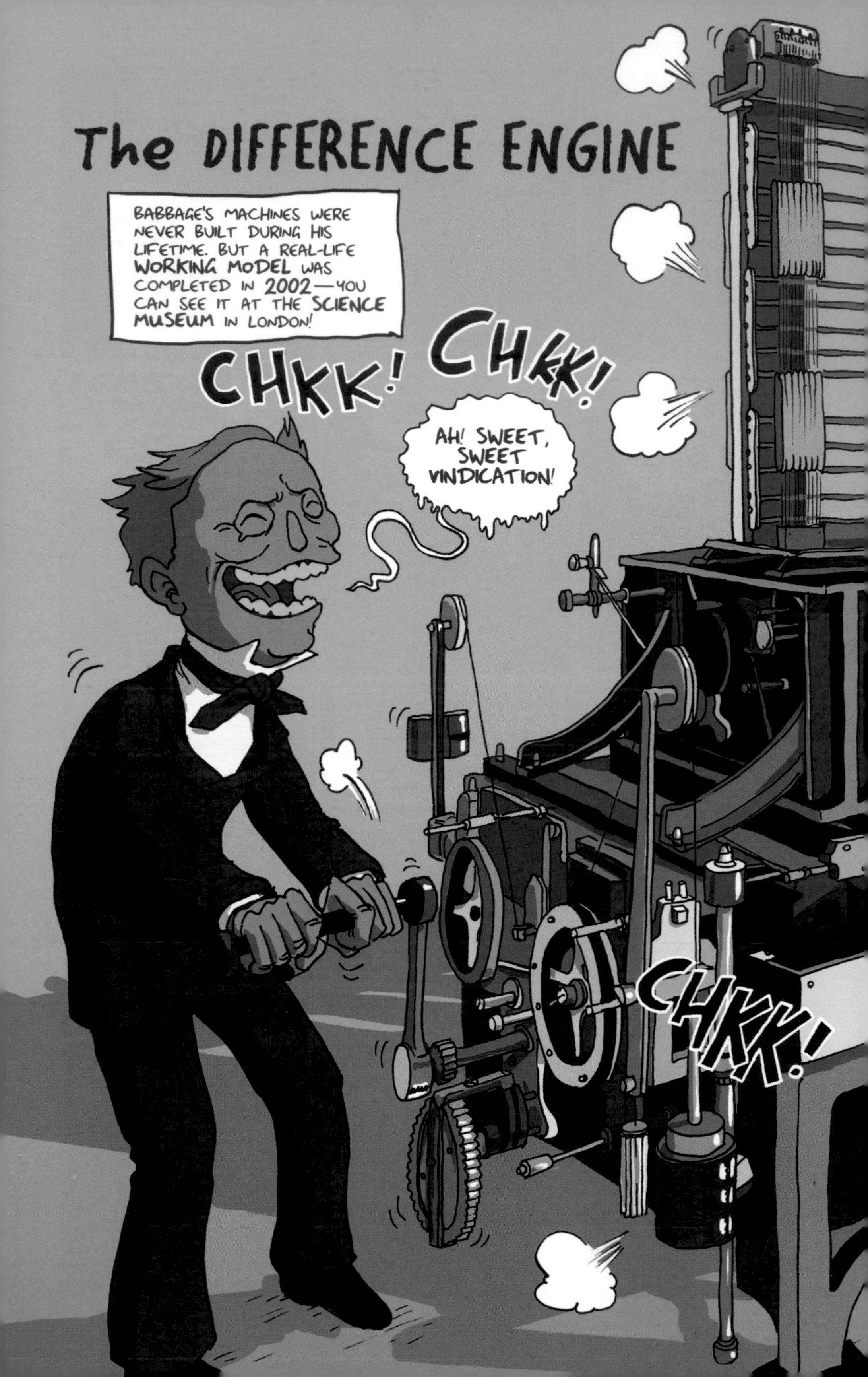
BABBAGE'S MACHINES WERE NEVER BUILT DURING HIS LIFETIME. BUT A REAL-LIFE WORKING MODEL WAS COMPLETED IN 2002—YOU CAN SEE IT AT THE SCIENCE MUSEUM IN LONDON!
CHKK! CHKK!
AH! SWEET, SWEET VINDICATION!
CHKK!

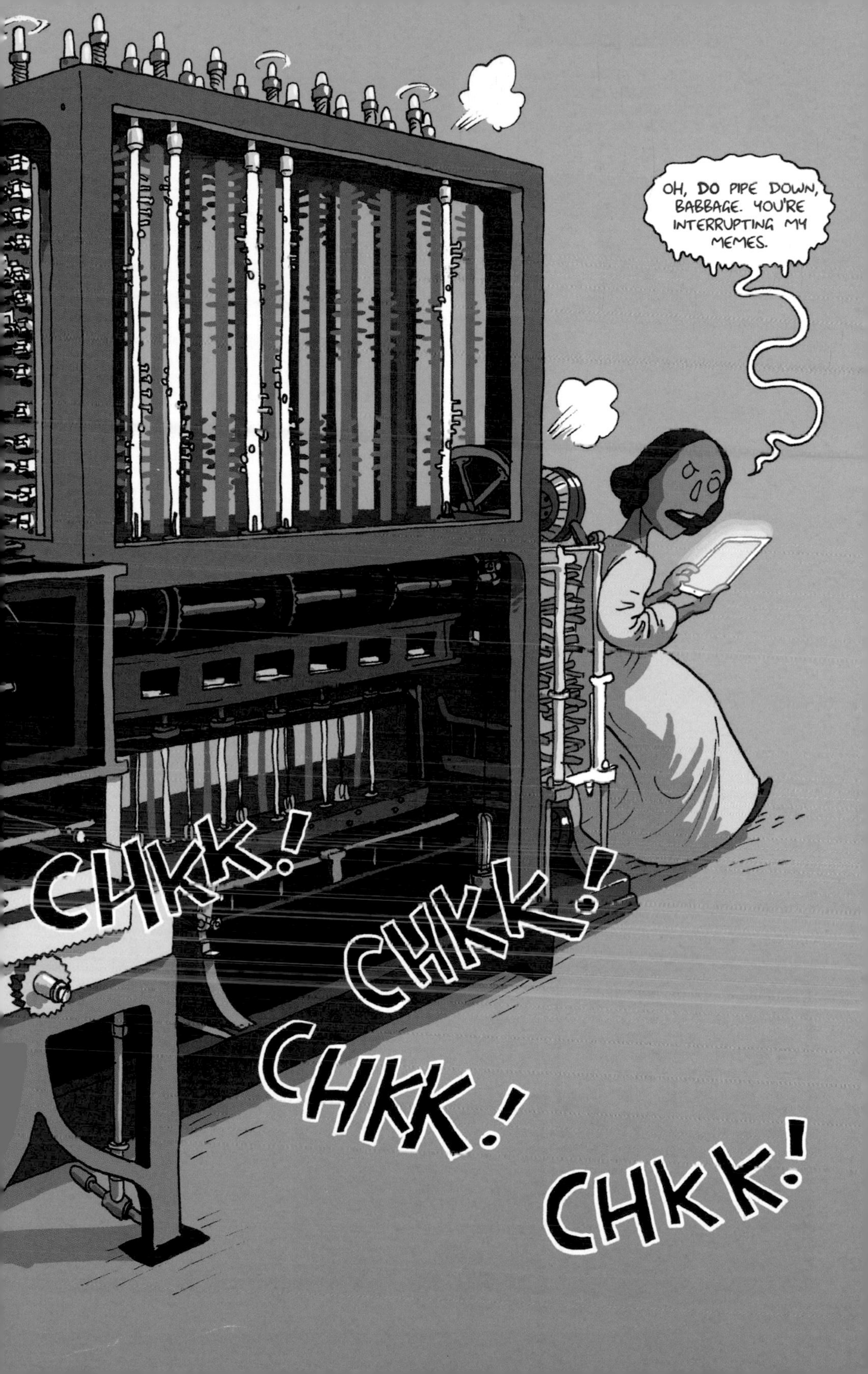
OH, DO PIPE DOWN, BABBAGE. YOU'RE INTERRUPTING MY MEMES.
CHKK!
CHKK!
CHKK!
CHKK!

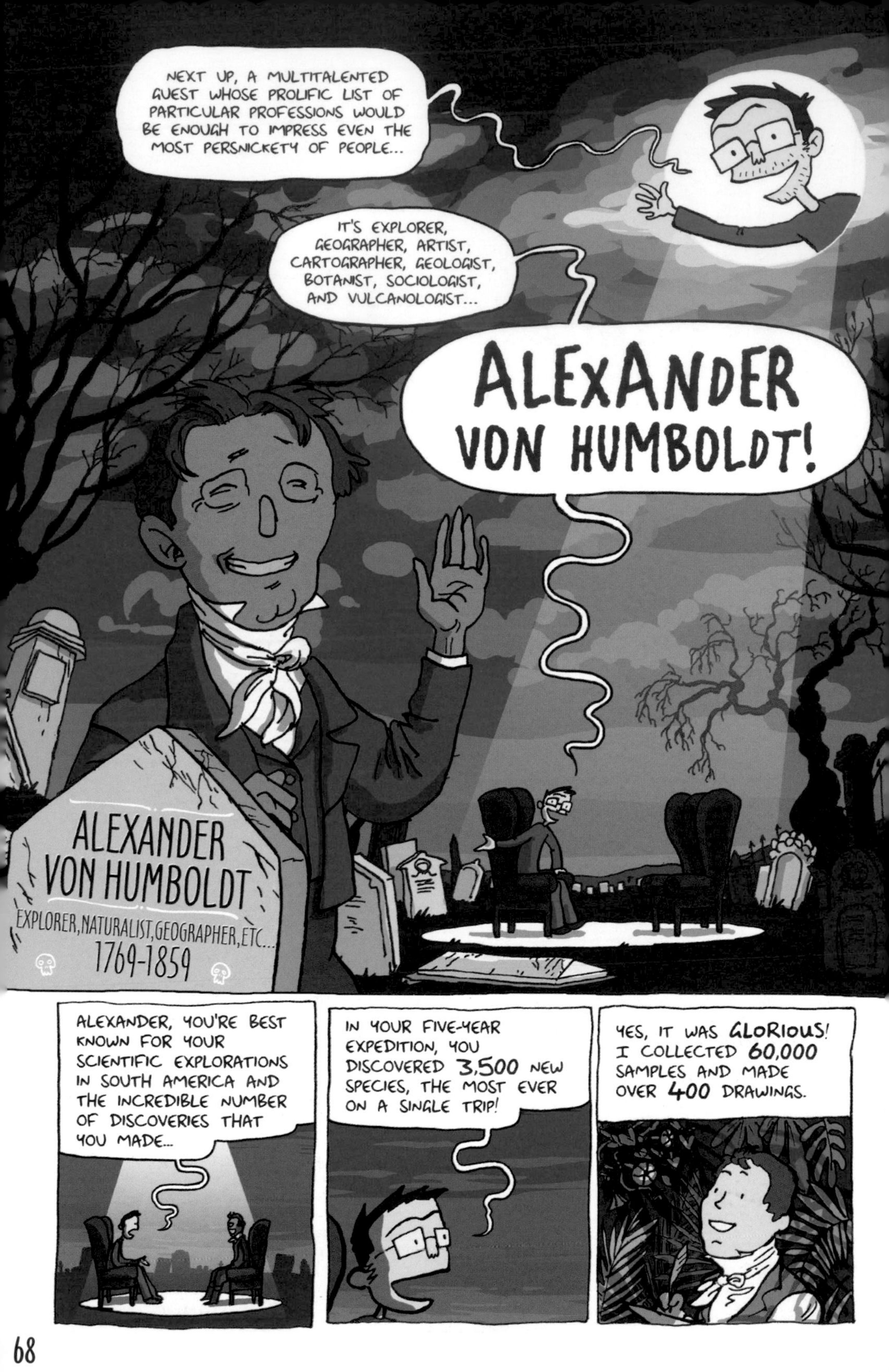
NEXT UP, A MULTITALENTED GUEST WHOSE PROLIFIC LIST OF PARTICULAR PROFESSIONS WOULD BE ENOUGH TO IMPRESS EVEN THE MOST PERSNICKETY OF PEOPLE...
IT'S EXPLORER, GEOGRAPHER, ARTIST, CARTOGRAPHER, GEOLOGIST, BOTANIST, SOCIOLOGIST, AND VULCANOLOGIST...
ALEXANDER VON HUMBOLDT!
ALEXANDER VON HUMBOLDT
EXPLORER, NATURALIST, GEOGRAPHER, ETC...
1769-1859
ALEXANDER, YOU'RE BEST KNOWN FOR YOUR SCIENTIFIC EXPLORATIONS IN SOUTH AMERICA AND THE INCREDIBLE NUMBER OF DISCOVERIES THAT YOU MADE...
IN YOUR FIVE-YEAR EXPEDITION, YOU DISCOVERED 3,500 NEW SPECIES, THE MOST EVER ON A SINGLE TRIP!
YES, IT WAS GLORIOUS! I COLLECTED 60,000 SAMPLES AND MADE OVER 400 DRAWINGS.

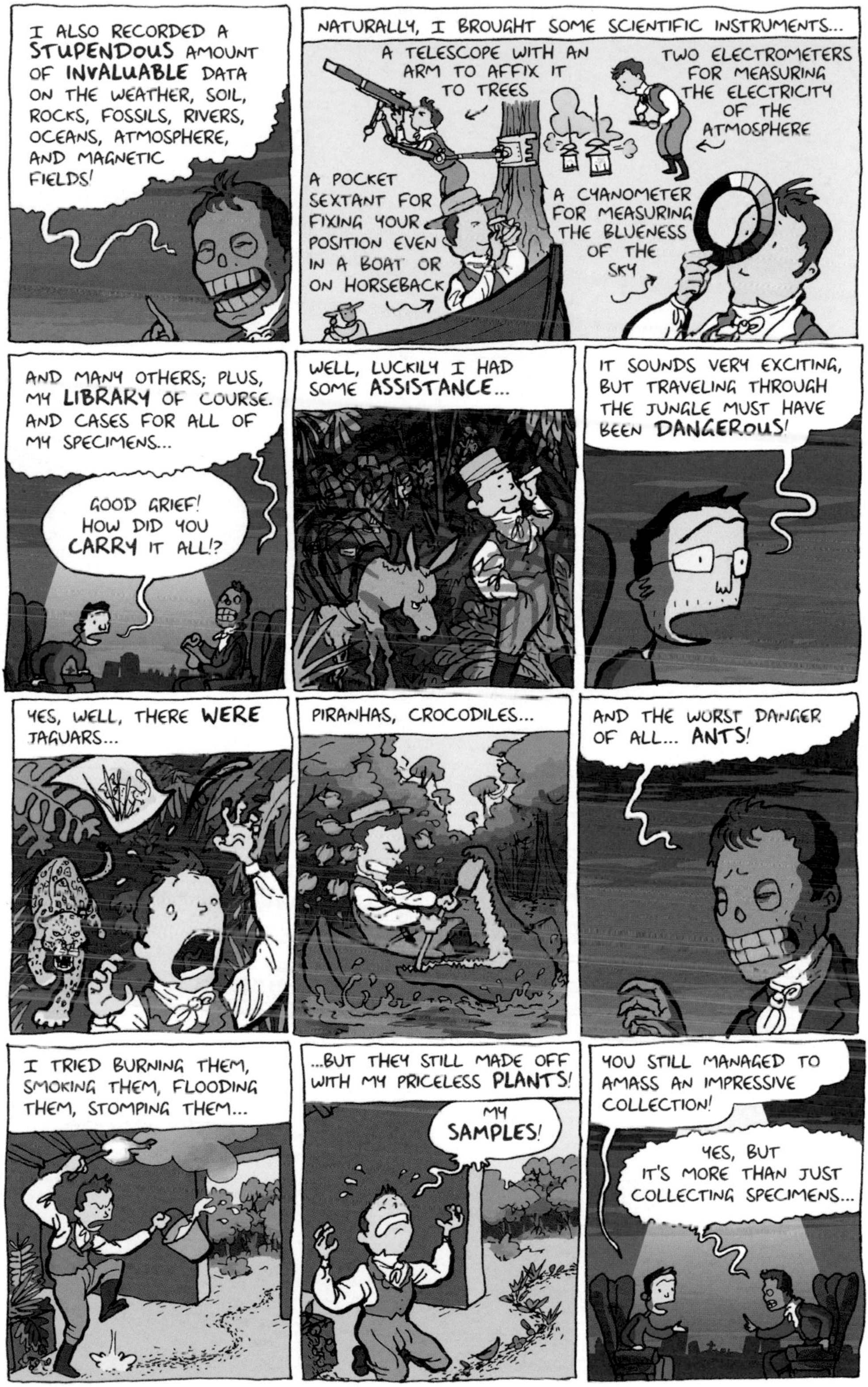

I ALSO RECORDED A STUPENDOUS AMOUNT OF INVALUABLE DATA ON THE WEATHER, SOIL, ROCKS, FOSSILS, RIVERS, OCEANS, ATMOSPHERE, AND MAGNETIC FIELDS!
NATURALLY, I BROUGHT SOME SCIENTIFIC INSTRUMENTS...
A TELESCOPE WITH AN ARM TO AFFIX IT TO TREES
TWO ELECTROMETERS FOR MEASURING THE ELECTRICITY OF THE ATMOSPHERE
A POCKET SEXTANT FOR FIXING YOUR POSITION EVEN IN A BOAT OR ON HORSEBACK
A CYANOMETER FOR MEASURING THE BLUENESS OF THE SKY
AND MANY OTHERS; PLUS, MY LIBRARY OF COURSE. AND CASES FOR ALL OF MY SPECIMENS...
GOOD GRIEF! HOW DID YOU CARRY IT ALL!?
WELL, LUCKILY I HAD SOME ASSISTANCE...
IT SOUNDS VERY EXCITING, BUT TRAVELING THROUGH THE JUNGLE MUST HAVE BEEN DANGEROUS!
YES, WELL, THERE WERE JAGUARS...
PIRANHAS, CROCODILES...
AND THE WORST DANGER OF ALL... ANTS!
I TRIED BURNING THEM, SMOKING THEM, FLOODING THEM, STOMPING THEM...
...BUT THEY STILL MADE OFF WITH MY PRICELESS PLANTS!
MY SAMPLES!
YOU STILL MANAGED TO AMASS AN IMPRESSIVE COLLECTION!
YES, BUT IT'S MORE THAN JUST COLLECTING SPECIMENS...

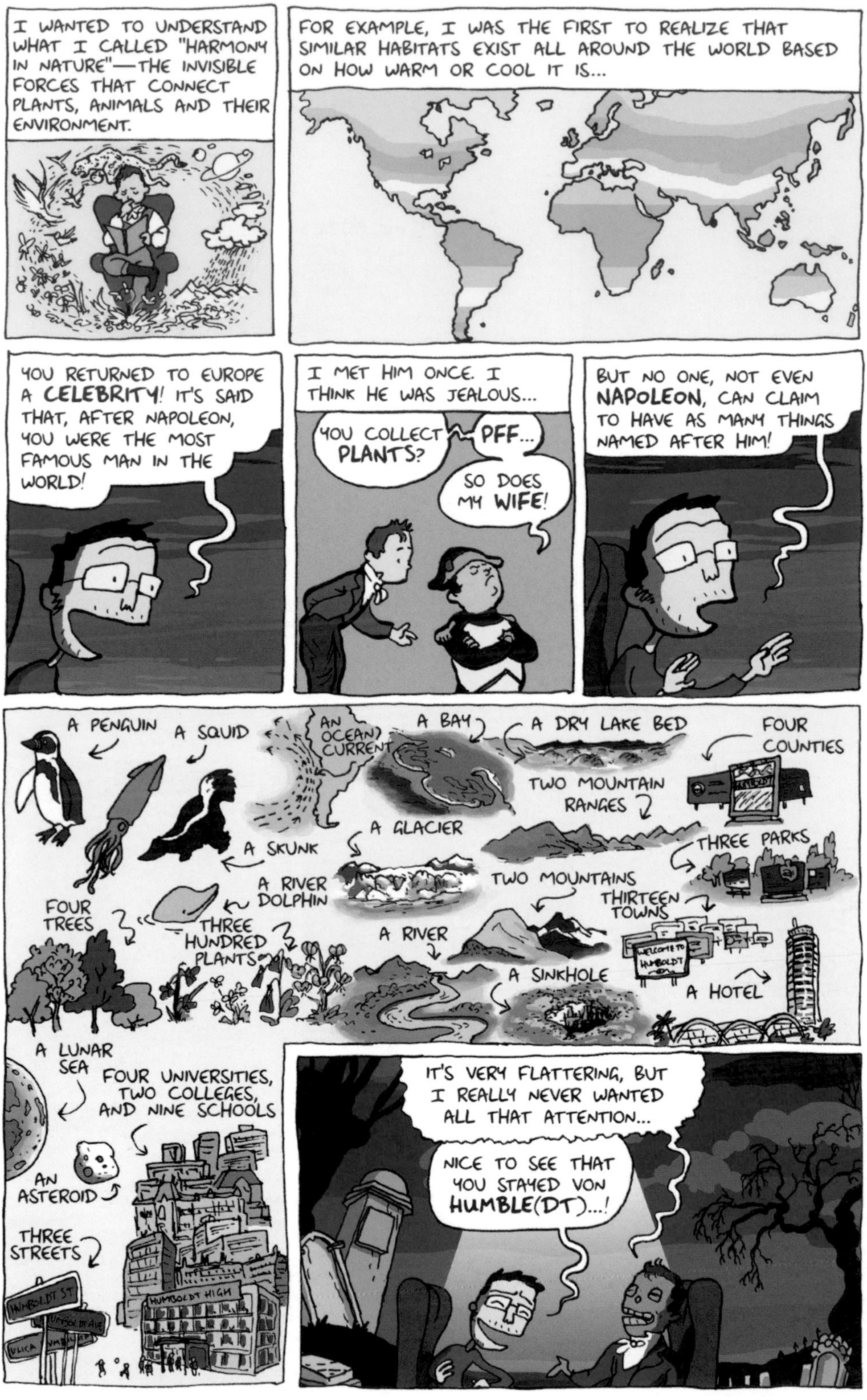

I WANTED TO UNDERSTAND WHAT I CALLED "HARMONY IN NATURE"—THE INVISIBLE FORCES THAT CONNECT PLANTS, ANIMALS AND THEIR ENVIRONMENT.
FOR EXAMPLE, I WAS THE FIRST TO REALIZE THAT SIMILAR HABITATS EXIST ALL AROUND THE WORLD BASED ON HOW WARM OR COOL IT IS...
YOU RETURNED TO EUROPE A **CELEBRITY**! IT'S SAID THAT, AFTER NAPOLEON, YOU WERE THE MOST FAMOUS MAN IN THE WORLD!
I MET HIM ONCE. I THINK HE WAS JEALOUS...
YOU COLLECT **PLANTS**?
PFF...
SO DOES MY **WIFE**!
BUT NO ONE, NOT EVEN **NAPOLEON**, CAN CLAIM TO HAVE AS MANY THINGS NAMED AFTER HIM!
A PENGUIN
A SQUID
AN OCEAN CURRENT
A BAY
A DRY LAKE BED
FOUR COUNTIES
TWO MOUNTAIN RANGES
A SKUNK
A GLACIER
THREE PARKS
A RIVER DOLPHIN
TWO MOUNTAINS
THIRTEEN TOWNS
FOUR TREES
THREE HUNDRED PLANTS
A RIVER
WELCOME TO HUMBOLDT
A SINKHOLE
A HOTEL
A LUNAR SEA
FOUR UNIVERSITIES, TWO COLLEGES, AND NINE SCHOOLS
AN ASTEROID
THREE STREETS
HUMBOLDT ST
HUMBOLDT HIGH
IT'S VERY FLATTERING, BUT I REALLY NEVER WANTED ALL THAT ATTENTION...
NICE TO SEE THAT YOU STAYED VON **HUMBLE(DT)**...!

WUTHERING HEIGHTS

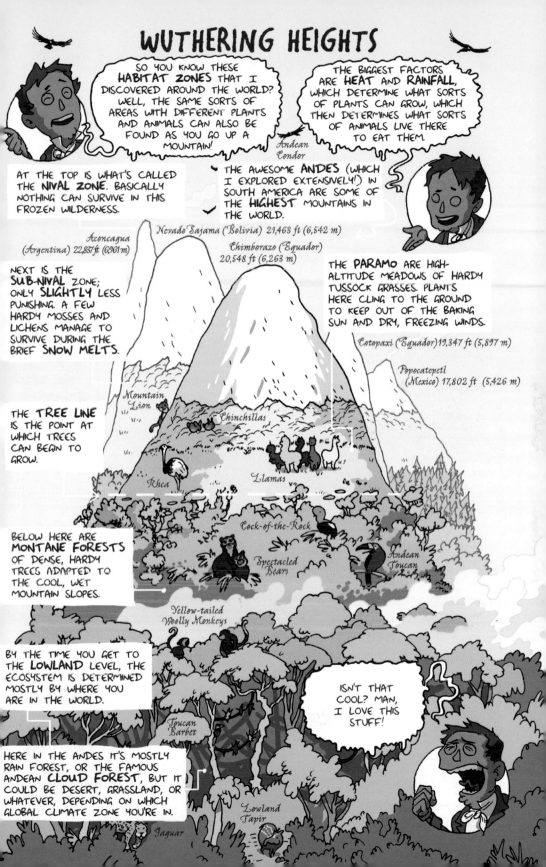

SO YOU KNOW THESE **HABITAT ZONES** THAT I DISCOVERED AROUND THE WORLD? WELL, THE SAME SORTS OF AREAS WITH DIFFERENT PLANTS AND ANIMALS CAN ALSO BE FOUND AS YOU GO UP A MOUNTAIN!

THE BIGGEST FACTORS ARE **HEAT** AND **RAINFALL**, WHICH DETERMINE WHAT SORTS OF PLANTS CAN GROW, WHICH THEN DETERMINES WHAT SORTS OF ANIMALS LIVE THERE TO EAT THEM.

Andean Condor

AT THE TOP IS WHAT'S CALLED THE **NIVAL ZONE**. BASICALLY NOTHING CAN SURVIVE IN THIS FROZEN WILDERNESS.

THE AWESOME **ANDES** (WHICH I EXPLORED EXTENSIVELY!) IN SOUTH AMERICA ARE SOME OF THE **HIGHEST** MOUNTAINS IN THE WORLD.

Aconcagua (Argentina) 22,837 ft (6961 m)

Nevado Sajama (Bolivia) 21,463 ft (6,542 m)

Chimborazo (Ecuador) 20,548 ft (6,263 m)

NEXT IS THE **SUB-NIVAL** ZONE; ONLY **SLIGHTLY** LESS PUNISHING. A FEW HARDY MOSSES AND LICHENS MANAGE TO SURVIVE DURING THE BRIEF **SNOW MELTS**.

THE **PARAMO** ARE HIGH-ALTITUDE MEADOWS OF HARDY TUSSOCK GRASSES. PLANTS HERE CLING TO THE GROUND TO KEEP OUT OF THE BAKING SUN AND DRY, FREEZING WINDS.

Cotopaxi (Ecuador) 19,347 ft (5,897 m)

Popocatepetl (Mexico) 17,802 ft (5,426 m)

THE **TREE LINE** IS THE POINT AT WHICH TREES CAN BEGIN TO GROW.

Mountain Lion

Chinchillas

Rhea

Llamas

Cock-of-the-Rock

BELOW HERE ARE **MONTANE FORESTS** OF DENSE, HARDY TREES ADAPTED TO THE COOL, WET MOUNTAIN SLOPES.

Spectacled Bears

Andean Toucan

Yellow-tailed Woolly Monkeys

BY THE TIME YOU GET TO THE **LOWLAND** LEVEL, THE ECOSYSTEM IS DETERMINED MOSTLY BY WHERE YOU ARE IN THE WORLD.

ISN'T THAT COOL? MAN, I LOVE THIS STUFF!

Toucan Barbet

HERE IN THE ANDES IT'S MOSTLY RAIN FOREST, OR THE FAMOUS ANDEAN **CLOUD FOREST**, BUT IT COULD BE DESERT, GRASSLAND, OR WHATEVER, DEPENDING ON WHICH GLOBAL CLIMATE ZONE YOU'RE IN.

Lowland Tapir

Jaguar

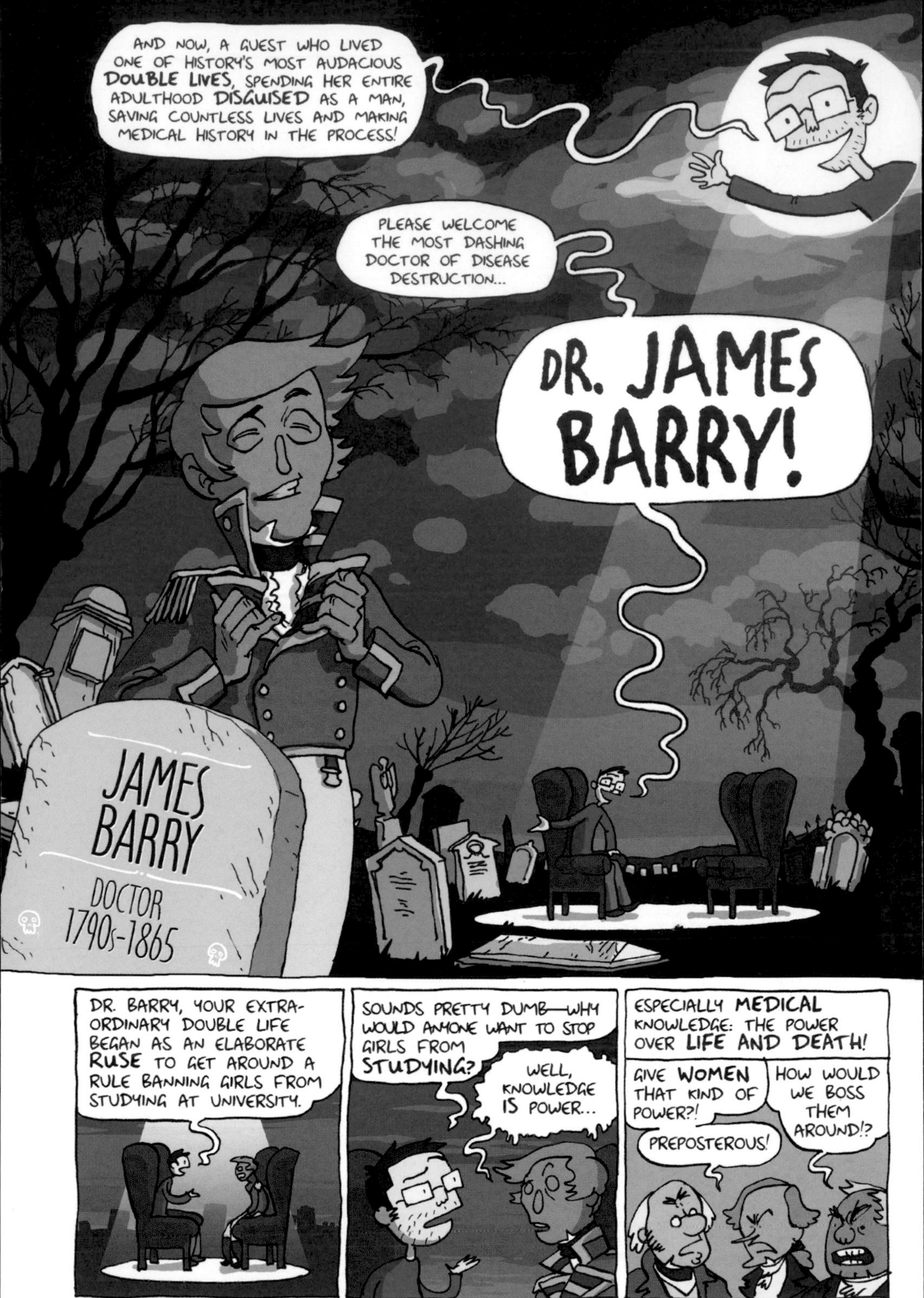
AND NOW, A GUEST WHO LIVED ONE OF HISTORY'S MOST AUDACIOUS DOUBLE LIVES, SPENDING HER ENTIRE ADULTHOOD DISGUISED AS A MAN, SAVING COUNTLESS LIVES AND MAKING MEDICAL HISTORY IN THE PROCESS!
PLEASE WELCOME THE MOST DASHING DOCTOR OF DISEASE DESTRUCTION...
DR. JAMES BARRY!
JAMES BARRY
DOCTOR
1790s-1865
DR. BARRY, YOUR EXTRAORDINARY DOUBLE LIFE BEGAN AS AN ELABORATE RUSE TO GET AROUND A RULE BANNING GIRLS FROM STUDYING AT UNIVERSITY.
SOUNDS PRETTY DUMB—WHY WOULD ANYONE WANT TO STOP GIRLS FROM STUDYING?
WELL, KNOWLEDGE IS POWER...
ESPECIALLY MEDICAL KNOWLEDGE: THE POWER OVER LIFE AND DEATH!
GIVE WOMEN THAT KIND OF POWER?!
HOW WOULD WE BOSS THEM AROUND!?
PREPOSTEROUS!

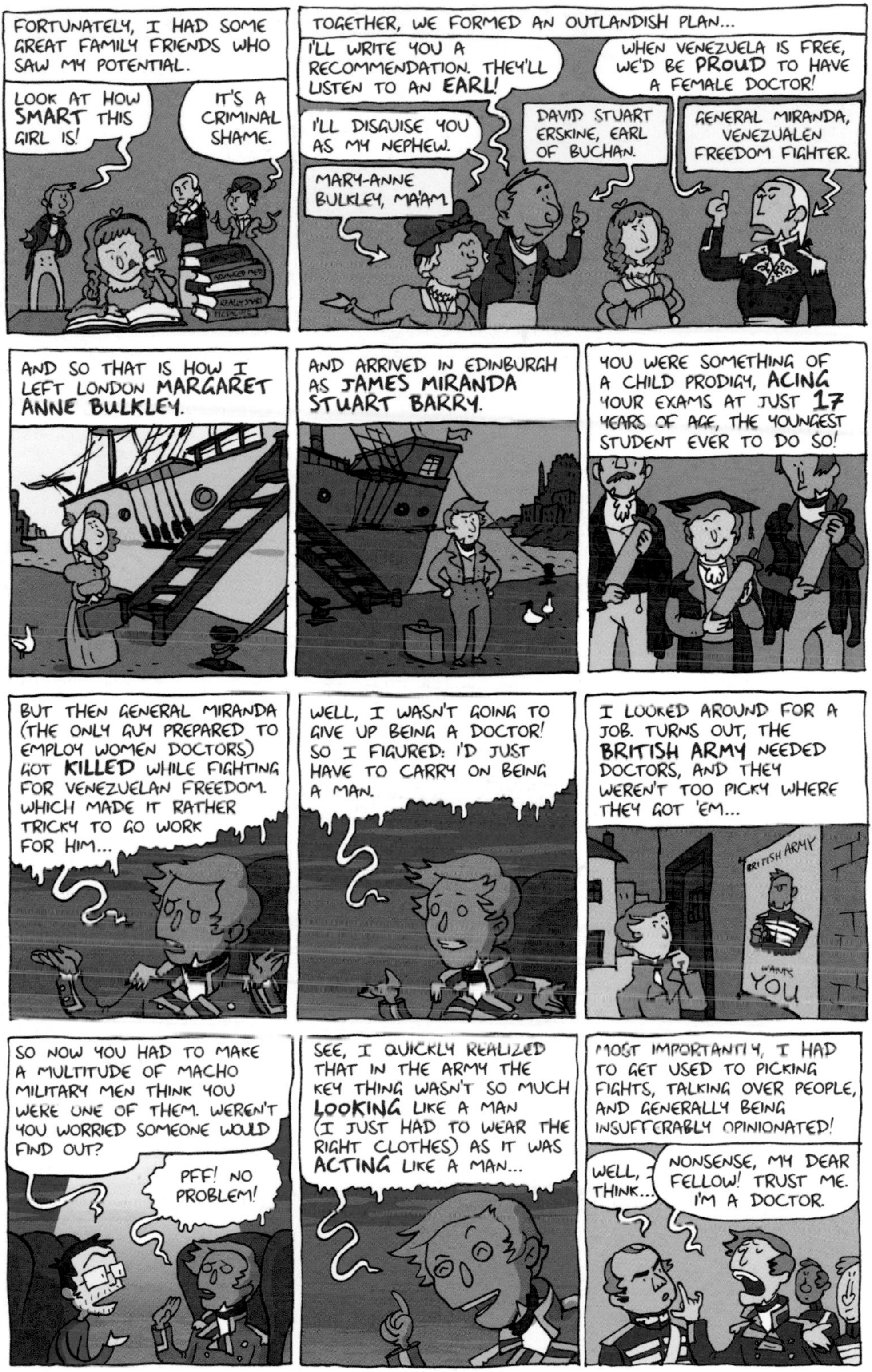

FORTUNATELY, I HAD SOME GREAT FAMILY FRIENDS WHO SAW MY POTENTIAL.
LOOK AT HOW SMART THIS GIRL IS!
IT'S A CRIMINAL SHAME.
ADVANCED MED
TOGETHER, WE FORMED AN OUTLANDISH PLAN...
I'LL WRITE YOU A RECOMMENDATION. THEY'LL LISTEN TO AN EARL!
WHEN VENEZUELA IS FREE, WE'D BE PROUD TO HAVE A FEMALE DOCTOR!
I'LL DISGUISE YOU AS MY NEPHEW.
DAVID STUART ERSKINE, EARL OF BUCHAN.
GENERAL MIRANDA, VENEZUALEN FREEDOM FIGHTER.
MARY-ANNE BULKLEY, MA'AM.
AND SO THAT IS HOW I LEFT LONDON MARGARET ANNE BULKLEY.
AND ARRIVED IN EDINBURGH AS JAMES MIRANDA STUART BARRY.
YOU WERE SOMETHING OF A CHILD PRODIGY, ACING YOUR EXAMS AT JUST 17 YEARS OF AGE, THE YOUNGEST STUDENT EVER TO DO SO!
BUT THEN GENERAL MIRANDA (THE ONLY GUY PREPARED TO EMPLOY WOMEN DOCTORS) GOT KILLED WHILE FIGHTING FOR VENEZUELAN FREEDOM. WHICH MADE IT RATHER TRICKY TO GO WORK FOR HIM...
WELL, I WASN'T GOING TO GIVE UP BEING A DOCTOR! SO I FIGURED: I'D JUST HAVE TO CARRY ON BEING A MAN.
I LOOKED AROUND FOR A JOB. TURNS OUT, THE BRITISH ARMY NEEDED DOCTORS, AND THEY WEREN'T TOO PICKY WHERE THEY GOT 'EM...
BRITISH ARMY
WANTS YOU
SO NOW YOU HAD TO MAKE A MULTITUDE OF MACHO MILITARY MEN THINK YOU WERE ONE OF THEM. WEREN'T YOU WORRIED SOMEONE WOULD FIND OUT?
PFF! NO PROBLEM!
SEE, I QUICKLY REALIZED THAT IN THE ARMY THE KEY THING WASN'T SO MUCH LOOKING LIKE A MAN (I JUST HAD TO WEAR THE RIGHT CLOTHES) AS IT WAS ACTING LIKE A MAN...
MOST IMPORTANTLY, I HAD TO GET USED TO PICKING FIGHTS, TALKING OVER PEOPLE, AND GENERALLY BEING INSUFFERABLY OPINIONATED!
WELL, I THINK...
NONSENSE, MY DEAR FELLOW! TRUST ME. I'M A DOCTOR.

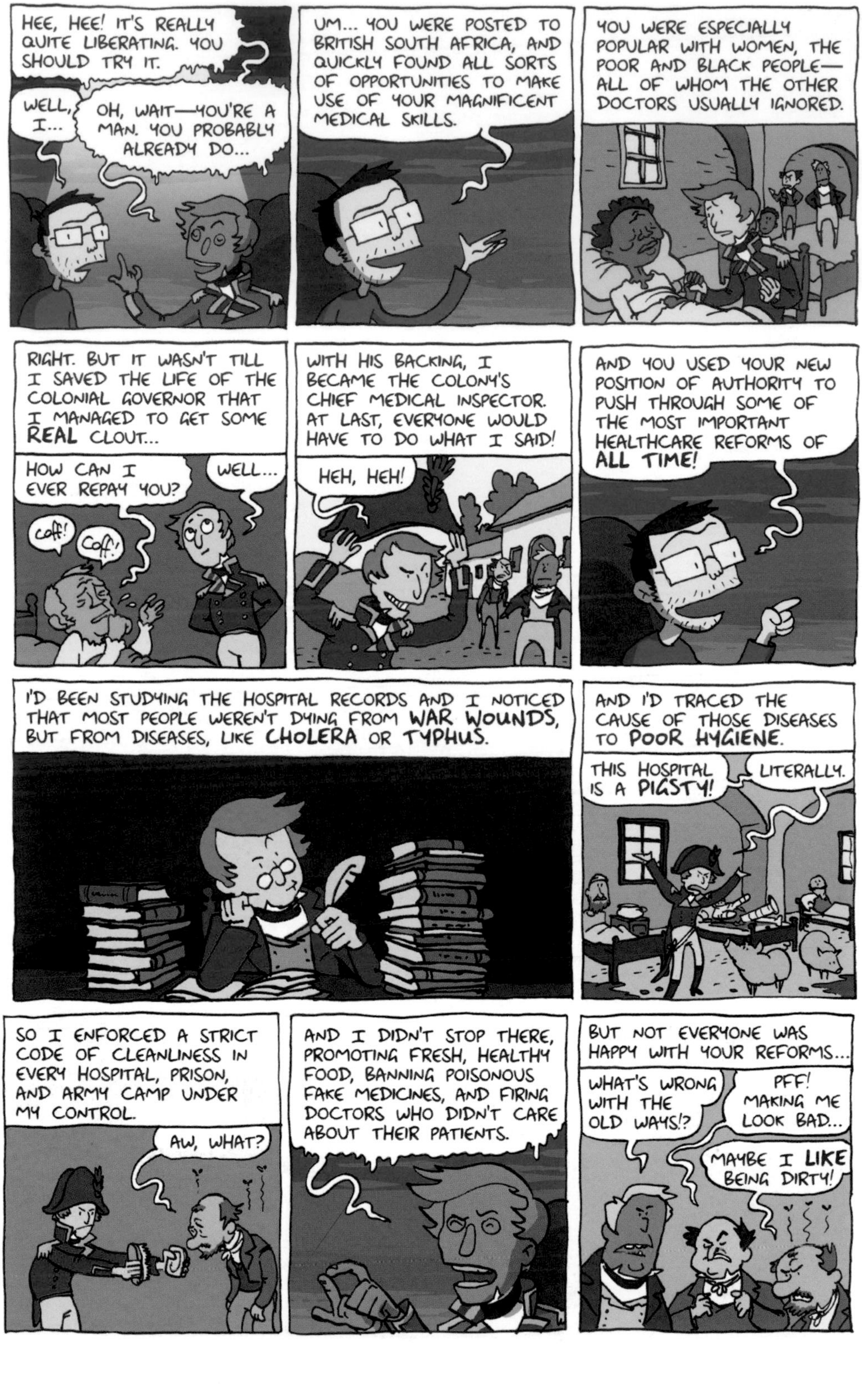
HEE, HEE! IT'S REALLY QUITE LIBERATING. YOU SHOULD TRY IT.
WELL, I...
OH, WAIT—YOU'RE A MAN. YOU PROBABLY ALREADY DO...
UM... YOU WERE POSTED TO BRITISH SOUTH AFRICA, AND QUICKLY FOUND ALL SORTS OF OPPORTUNITIES TO MAKE USE OF YOUR MAGNIFICENT MEDICAL SKILLS.
YOU WERE ESPECIALLY POPULAR WITH WOMEN, THE POOR AND BLACK PEOPLE—ALL OF WHOM THE OTHER DOCTORS USUALLY IGNORED.
RIGHT. BUT IT WASN'T TILL I SAVED THE LIFE OF THE COLONIAL GOVERNOR THAT I MANAGED TO GET SOME **REAL** CLOUT...
HOW CAN I EVER REPAY YOU?
WELL...
COFF!
COFF!
WITH HIS BACKING, I BECAME THE COLONY'S CHIEF MEDICAL INSPECTOR. AT LAST, EVERYONE WOULD HAVE TO DO WHAT I SAID!
HEH, HEH!
AND YOU USED YOUR NEW POSITION OF AUTHORITY TO PUSH THROUGH SOME OF THE MOST IMPORTANT HEALTHCARE REFORMS OF **ALL TIME!**
I'D BEEN STUDYING THE HOSPITAL RECORDS AND I NOTICED THAT MOST PEOPLE WEREN'T DYING FROM **WAR WOUNDS**, BUT FROM DISEASES, LIKE **CHOLERA** OR **TYPHUS**.
AND I'D TRACED THE CAUSE OF THOSE DISEASES TO **POOR HYGIENE**.
THIS HOSPITAL IS A **PIGSTY!**
LITERALLY.
SO I ENFORCED A STRICT CODE OF CLEANLINESS IN EVERY HOSPITAL, PRISON, AND ARMY CAMP UNDER MY CONTROL.
AW, WHAT?
AND I DIDN'T STOP THERE, PROMOTING FRESH, HEALTHY FOOD, BANNING POISONOUS FAKE MEDICINES, AND FIRING DOCTORS WHO DIDN'T CARE ABOUT THEIR PATIENTS.
BUT NOT EVERYONE WAS HAPPY WITH YOUR REFORMS...
WHAT'S WRONG WITH THE OLD WAYS!?
PFF! MAKING ME LOOK BAD...
MAYBE I **LIKE** BEING DIRTY!

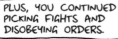

PLUS, YOU CONTINUED PICKING FIGHTS AND DISOBEYING ORDERS.

STOP CALLING YOUR BROTHER OFFICERS IDIOTS!

BUT THEY **ARE** IDIOTS!

A ROLLING CAVALCADE OF PROMOTIONS, DEMOTIONS, ACCOLADES, AND SCANDALS SAW YOU PING-PONGING AROUND THE BRITISH EMPIRE, SPREADING YOUR RADICAL REFORMS WHEREVER YOU WENT.

WHICH IS HOW YOU RAN ACROSS PIONEERING NURSE **FLORENCE NIGHTINGALE**.

BAH! THAT WOMAN!

HER "HOSPITAL" WAS ONE OF THE WORST I EVER SAW—**UTTERLY FILTHY!** I GAVE HER A GOOD PIECE OF MY MIND, I'LL TELL YOU THAT!

WELL, AFTER YOUR RANT, SHE **CLEANED UP** HER ACT AND WENT ON TO FOUND THE MODERN SCIENCE OF NURSING.

MODERN SCIENCE OF **STEALING MY THUNDER**, MORE LIKE IT...

YOU'RE **BOTH** GREAT, FOR DIFFERENT REASONS. SHE WORKED **WITHIN** THE RULES, **PUSHING THE ENVELOPE** OF WHAT WOMEN WERE ALLOWED TO DO...

WHEREAS YOU **TORE UP** THE ENVELOPE AND THREW IT IN THE TRASH, AND, IN DOING SO, **PROVED** HOW STUPID IT IS TO DIVIDE THE WORLD INTO BOYS' THINGS AND GIRLS' THINGS!

EXACTLY! WHY NOT JUST LET PEOPLE DO WHAT THEY LOVE!?

ESPECIALLY IF WHAT THEY LOVE IS SAVING LIVES, PICKING FIGHTS, AND LOOKING **FREAKING AWESOME** IN AN OFFICER'S JACKET...

A HISTORY OF INFECTION

YEAH, SO, I MANAGED TO SAVE A LOT OF LIVES BY ENFORCING **BASIC HYGIENE.** BUT EVEN **I** HAD NO **REAL** IDEA ABOUT WHAT ACTUALLY **CAUSED** THE DISEASES I WAS FIGHTING...

I'D NEVER EVEN **HEARD** OF BACTERIA! LIKE ALL THE DOCTORS IN MY DAY, I FOLLOWED THE **MIASMA** THEORY.

MAKES SENSE, RIGHT!? AND PEOPLE **DID** GET SICK IF THEY WENT NEAR STINKY GARBAGE, RUBBISH OR ROTTING CORPSES, SO IT LOOKED PRETTY CONVINCING.

CONVINCING, BUT **WRONG!** SOMETIMES INFECTIONS SEEMED TO PASS FROM **PERSON TO PERSON,** AT OTHER TIMES THEY COULD **TRAVEL** LONG DISTANCES. ANOTHER THEORY WAS NEEDED!

NOW, WAY BACK IN **1676**, A DUTCH SCIENTIST WITH THE IMPRESSIVE NAME OF **ANTONIE VAN LEEUWENHOEK** HAD SEEN BACTERIA IN HIS OWN **SPIT** USING A HOMEMADE MICROSCOPE.

OH, MAN! THAT'S TOTALLY GROSS!

BUT NO ONE REALIZED THESE MICROSCOPIC ORGANISMS WERE CONNECTED TO **DISEASE.**

-SIGH- I MET A LOT OF GUYS LIKE THAT...

THE **REAL** ANSWER WASN'T DISCOVERED UNTIL FRENCH SCIENTIST **LOUIS PASTEUR** DID HIS FAMOUS BACTERIA-KILLING EXPERIMENTS.

IF MILK WAS **SEALED** AND **HEATED**, NO **BACTERIA** WOULD BE LEFT TO TURN IT BAD.

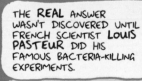

IT WAS PROPOSED BY **GALEN**, A FAMOUS DOCTOR DURING THE **ROMAN EMPIRE**, AND IT BASICALLY HADN'T BEEN UPDATED SINCE!

THE IDEA WAS THAT MIASMAS WERE **BAD SMELLS** FLOATING IN THE AIR AND THAT WAS WHAT GOT PEOPLE SICK.

THAT'S WHY THE MEDIEVAL PLAGUE DOCTORS WORE THOSE LONG-BEAKED MASKS FULL OF **FLOWERS**, SO THEY COULDN'T **SMELL** THE MIASMAS.

HEH, HEH. **TOTALLY** SAFE...

THEN, IN **1847**, A HUNGARIAN DOCTOR WITH THE EQUALLY IMPRESSIVE NAME OF **IGNAZ SEMMELWEIS** NOTICED THAT WOMEN GIVING BIRTH IN THE HOSPITAL WERE **WAY** MORE LIKELY TO DIE THAN WOMEN GIVING BIRTH AT HOME.

HE THOUGHT IT MIGHT HAVE TO DO WITH THE FACT THAT SURGEONS **DIDN'T WASH THEIR HANDS** IN BETWEEN CUTTING UP DEAD BODIES AND ASSISTING IN BIRTHS.

WHICH **SCANDALIZED** THE MEDICAL PROFESSION, WHICH ROUNDLY CONDEMNED HIM FOR SUGGESTING SOMETHING SO **INSULTING**.

"A DOCTOR IS A GENTLEMAN. AND A GENTLEMAN'S HANDS ARE **ALWAYS** CLEAN..."

AMERICAN DOCTOR **CHARLES MEIGS**.

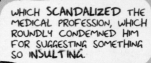

HIS DISCOVERY CONVINCED THE WORLD THESE BACTERIA THINGIES MIGHT BE IMPORTANT AFTER ALL.

ALL THE MILK WE DRINK TODAY IS **PASTEURIZED** TO KILL GERMS THIS WAY.

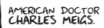

BEFORE LONG, THE BACTERIA BEHIND **ALL SORTS** OF HORRIBLE DISEASES HAD BEEN FOUND. THE MODERN **GERM THEORY** OF DISEASE WAS HERE TO STAY!

I CAN'T HELP BUT NOTICE ALL OF THESE GUYS ARE... WELL... GUYS.

YEAH, I NOTICED THAT, TOO. MAYBE IF THEY HADN'T **BANNED WOMEN FROM SCIENCE**, THEY'D HAVE FIGURED IT OUT SOONER...

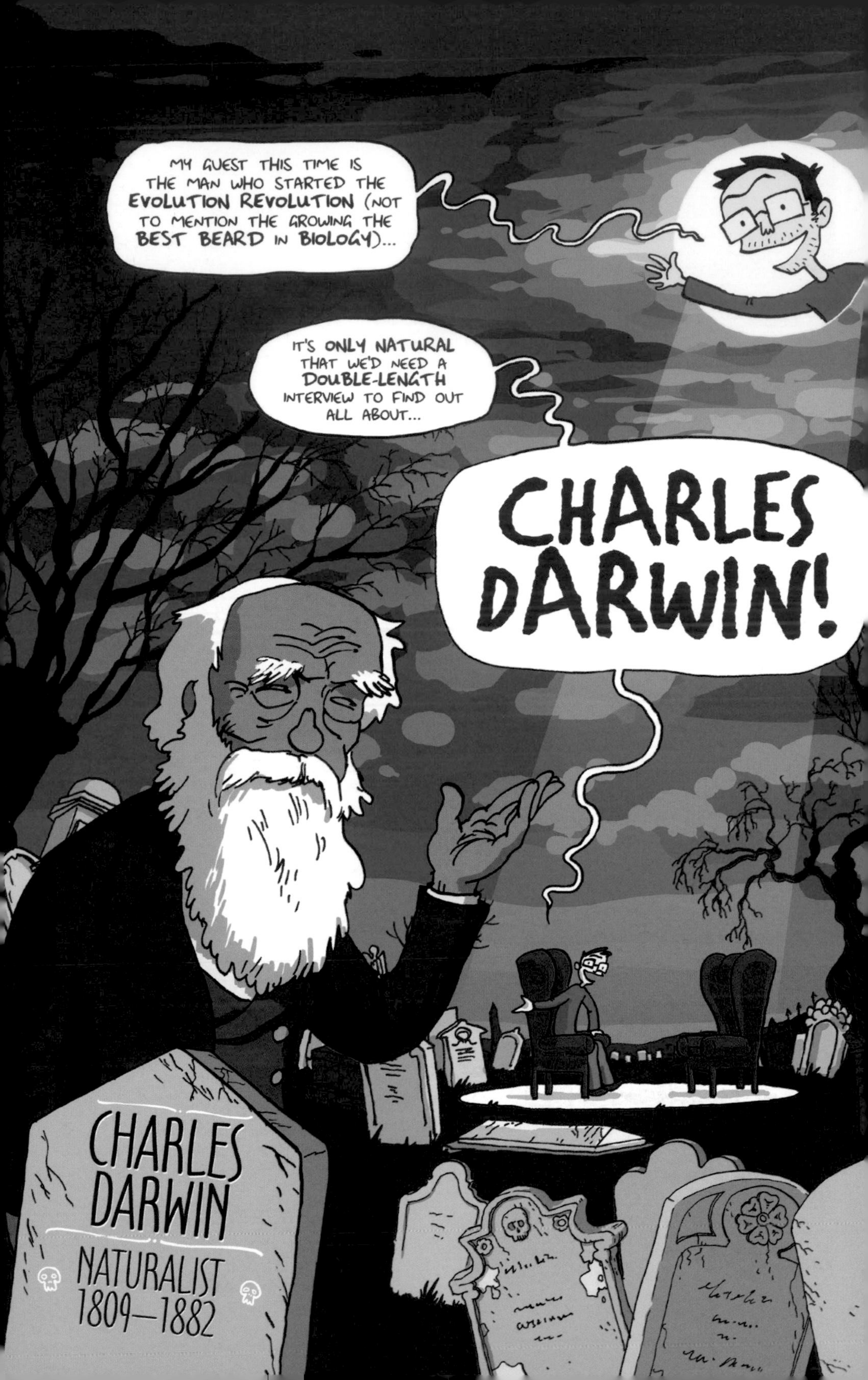

MY GUEST THIS TIME IS THE MAN WHO STARTED THE EVOLUTION REVOLUTION (NOT TO MENTION THE GROWING THE BEST BEARD IN BIOLOGY)...
IT'S ONLY NATURAL THAT WE'D NEED A DOUBLE-LENGTH INTERVIEW TO FIND OUT ALL ABOUT...
CHARLES DARWIN!
CHARLES DARWIN
NATURALIST
1809–1882

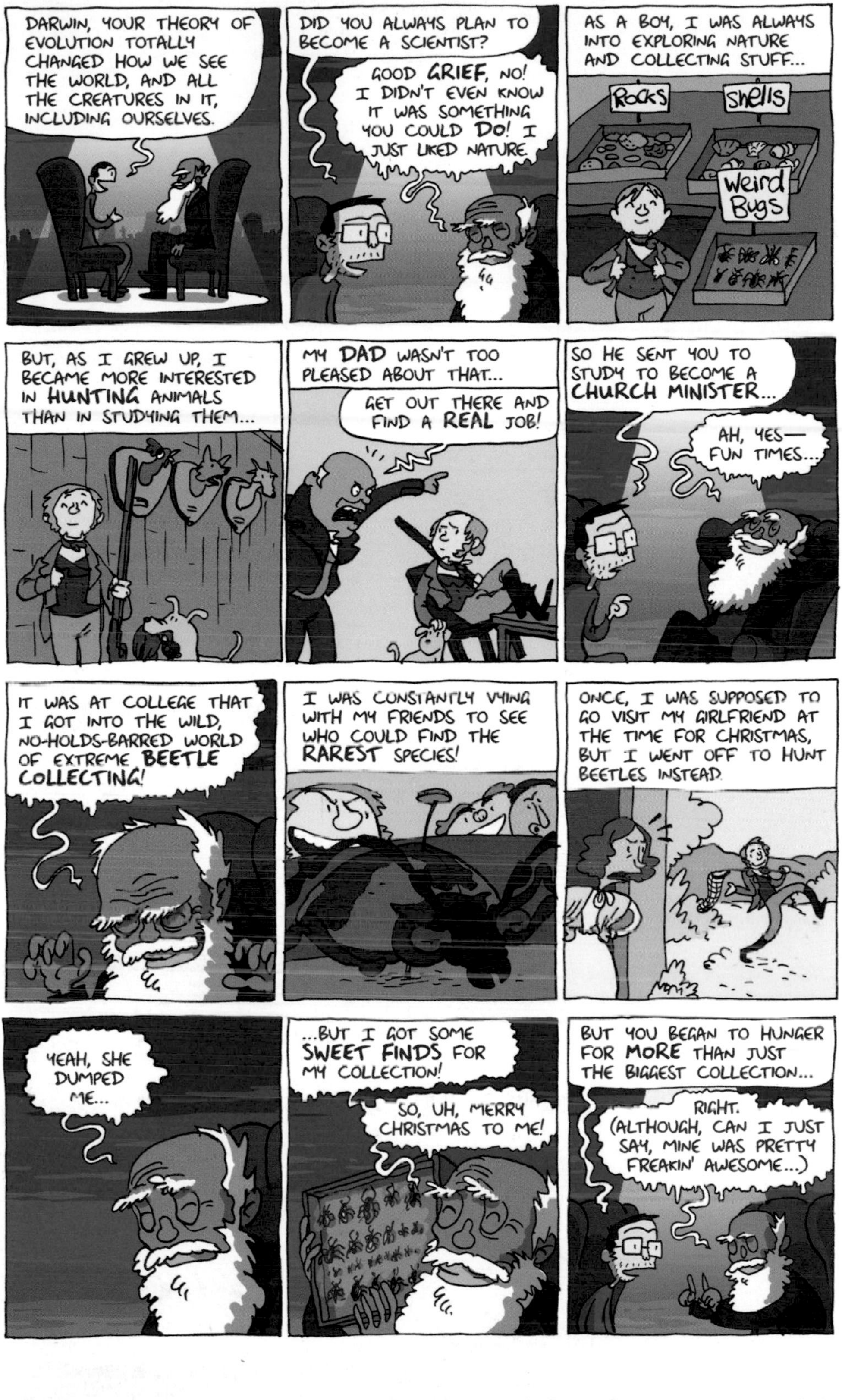

DARWIN, YOUR THEORY OF EVOLUTION TOTALLY CHANGED HOW WE SEE THE WORLD, AND ALL THE CREATURES IN IT, INCLUDING OURSELVES.
DID YOU ALWAYS PLAN TO BECOME A SCIENTIST?
GOOD GRIEF, NO! I DIDN'T EVEN KNOW IT WAS SOMETHING YOU COULD DO! I JUST LIKED NATURE.
AS A BOY, I WAS ALWAYS INTO EXPLORING NATURE AND COLLECTING STUFF...
Rocks
Shells
Weird Bugs
BUT, AS I GREW UP, I BECAME MORE INTERESTED IN HUNTING ANIMALS THAN IN STUDYING THEM...
MY DAD WASN'T TOO PLEASED ABOUT THAT...
GET OUT THERE AND FIND A REAL JOB!
SO HE SENT YOU TO STUDY TO BECOME A CHURCH MINISTER...
AH, YES— FUN TIMES...
IT WAS AT COLLEGE THAT I GOT INTO THE WILD, NO-HOLDS-BARRED WORLD OF EXTREME BEETLE COLLECTING!
I WAS CONSTANTLY VYING WITH MY FRIENDS TO SEE WHO COULD FIND THE RAREST SPECIES!
ONCE, I WAS SUPPOSED TO GO VISIT MY GIRLFRIEND AT THE TIME FOR CHRISTMAS, BUT I WENT OFF TO HUNT BEETLES INSTEAD.
YEAH, SHE DUMPED ME...
...BUT I GOT SOME SWEET FINDS FOR MY COLLECTION!
SO, UH, MERRY CHRISTMAS TO ME!
BUT YOU BEGAN TO HUNGER FOR MORE THAN JUST THE BIGGEST COLLECTION...
RIGHT. (ALTHOUGH, CAN I JUST SAY, MINE WAS PRETTY FREAKIN' AWESOME...)

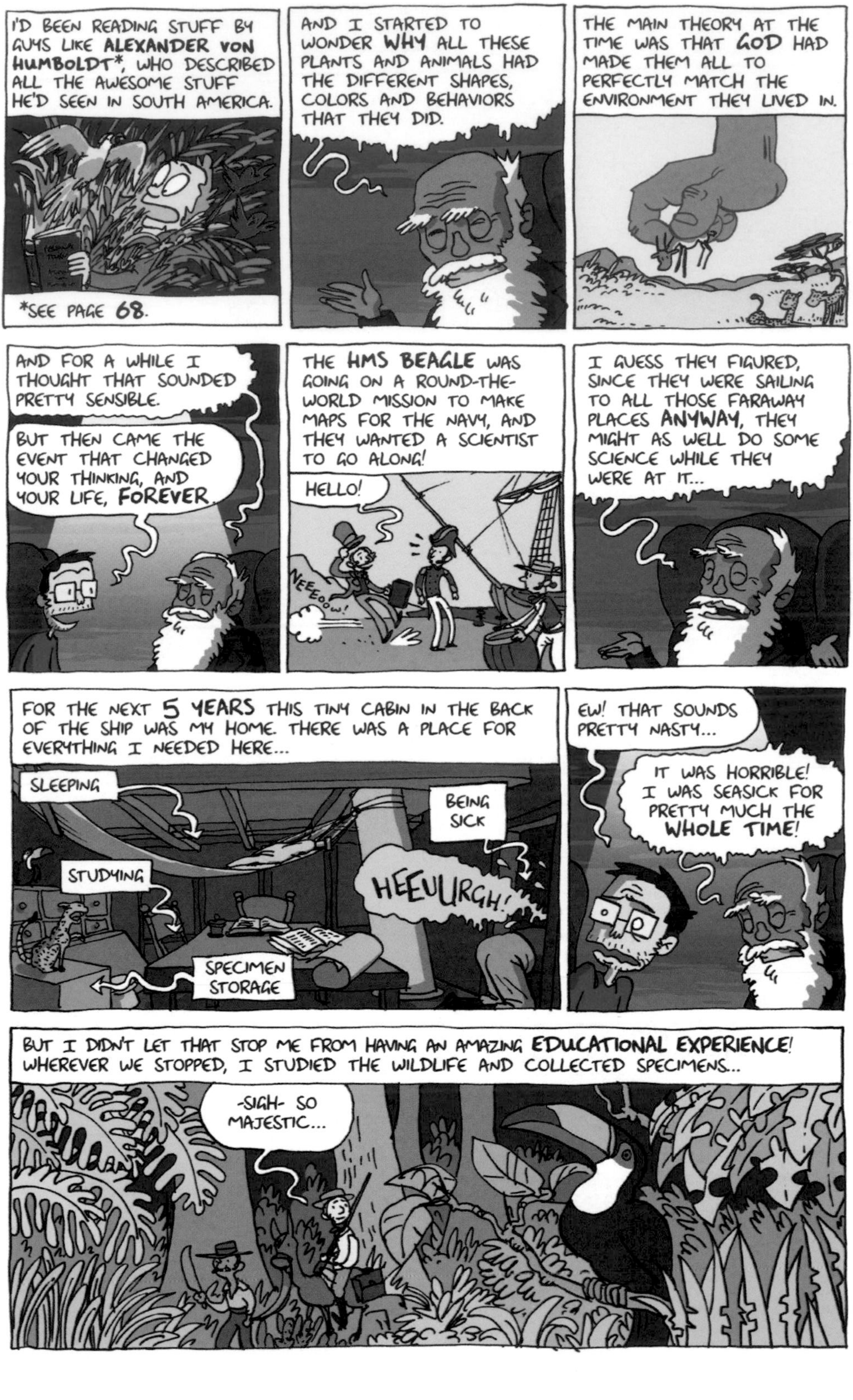
I'D BEEN READING STUFF BY GUYS LIKE ALEXANDER VON HUMBOLDT*, WHO DESCRIBED ALL THE AWESOME STUFF HE'D SEEN IN SOUTH AMERICA.
*SEE PAGE 68.
AND I STARTED TO WONDER WHY ALL THESE PLANTS AND ANIMALS HAD THE DIFFERENT SHAPES, COLORS AND BEHAVIORS THAT THEY DID.
THE MAIN THEORY AT THE TIME WAS THAT GOD HAD MADE THEM ALL TO PERFECTLY MATCH THE ENVIRONMENT THEY LIVED IN.
AND FOR A WHILE I THOUGHT THAT SOUNDED PRETTY SENSIBLE.
BUT THEN CAME THE EVENT THAT CHANGED YOUR THINKING, AND YOUR LIFE, FOREVER.
THE HMS BEAGLE WAS GOING ON A ROUND-THE-WORLD MISSION TO MAKE MAPS FOR THE NAVY, AND THEY WANTED A SCIENTIST TO GO ALONG!
HELLO!
NEEEOOW!
I GUESS THEY FIGURED, SINCE THEY WERE SAILING TO ALL THOSE FARAWAY PLACES ANYWAY, THEY MIGHT AS WELL DO SOME SCIENCE WHILE THEY WERE AT IT...
FOR THE NEXT 5 YEARS THIS TINY CABIN IN THE BACK OF THE SHIP WAS MY HOME. THERE WAS A PLACE FOR EVERYTHING I NEEDED HERE...
SLEEPING
BEING SICK
STUDYING
HEEULURGH!
SPECIMEN STORAGE
EW! THAT SOUNDS PRETTY NASTY...
IT WAS HORRIBLE! I WAS SEASICK FOR PRETTY MUCH THE WHOLE TIME!
BUT I DIDN'T LET THAT STOP ME FROM HAVING AN AMAZING EDUCATIONAL EXPERIENCE! WHEREVER WE STOPPED, I STUDIED THE WILDLIFE AND COLLECTED SPECIMENS...
-SIGH- SO MAJESTIC...

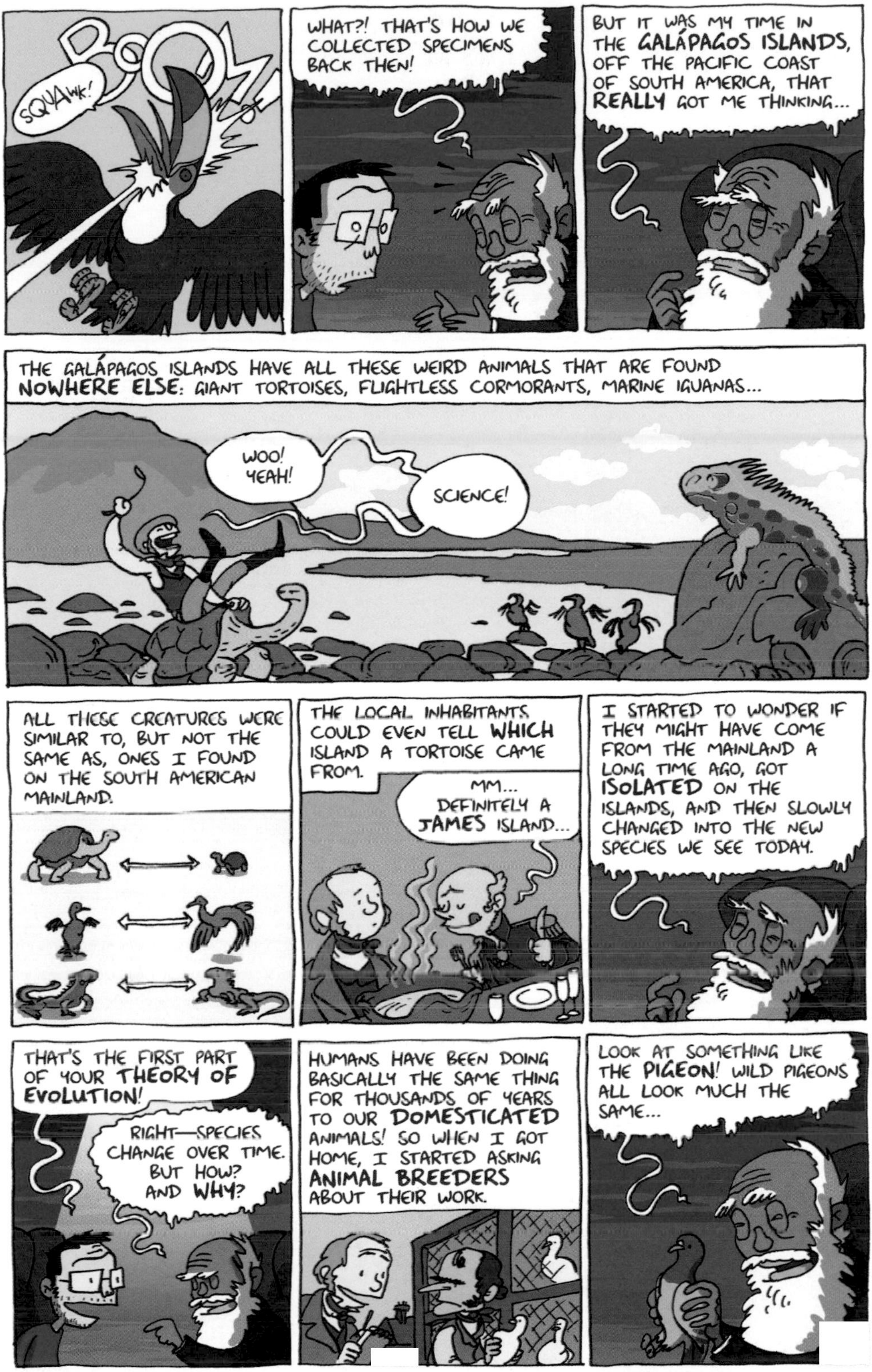
BOOM!
SQUAWK!
WHAT?! THAT'S HOW WE COLLECTED SPECIMENS BACK THEN!
BUT IT WAS MY TIME IN THE GALÁPAGOS ISLANDS, OFF THE PACIFIC COAST OF SOUTH AMERICA, THAT REALLY GOT ME THINKING...
THE GALÁPAGOS ISLANDS HAVE ALL THESE WEIRD ANIMALS THAT ARE FOUND NOWHERE ELSE: GIANT TORTOISES, FLIGHTLESS CORMORANTS, MARINE IGUANAS...
WOO! YEAH!
SCIENCE!
ALL THESE CREATURES WERE SIMILAR TO, BUT NOT THE SAME AS, ONES I FOUND ON THE SOUTH AMERICAN MAINLAND.
THE LOCAL INHABITANTS COULD EVEN TELL WHICH ISLAND A TORTOISE CAME FROM.
MM... DEFINITELY A JAMES ISLAND...
I STARTED TO WONDER IF THEY MIGHT HAVE COME FROM THE MAINLAND A LONG TIME AGO, GOT ISOLATED ON THE ISLANDS, AND THEN SLOWLY CHANGED INTO THE NEW SPECIES WE SEE TODAY.
THAT'S THE FIRST PART OF YOUR THEORY OF EVOLUTION!
RIGHT—SPECIES CHANGE OVER TIME. BUT HOW? AND WHY?
HUMANS HAVE BEEN DOING BASICALLY THE SAME THING FOR THOUSANDS OF YEARS TO OUR DOMESTICATED ANIMALS! SO WHEN I GOT HOME, I STARTED ASKING ANIMAL BREEDERS ABOUT THEIR WORK.
LOOK AT SOMETHING LIKE THE PIGEON! WILD PIGEONS ALL LOOK MUCH THE SAME...

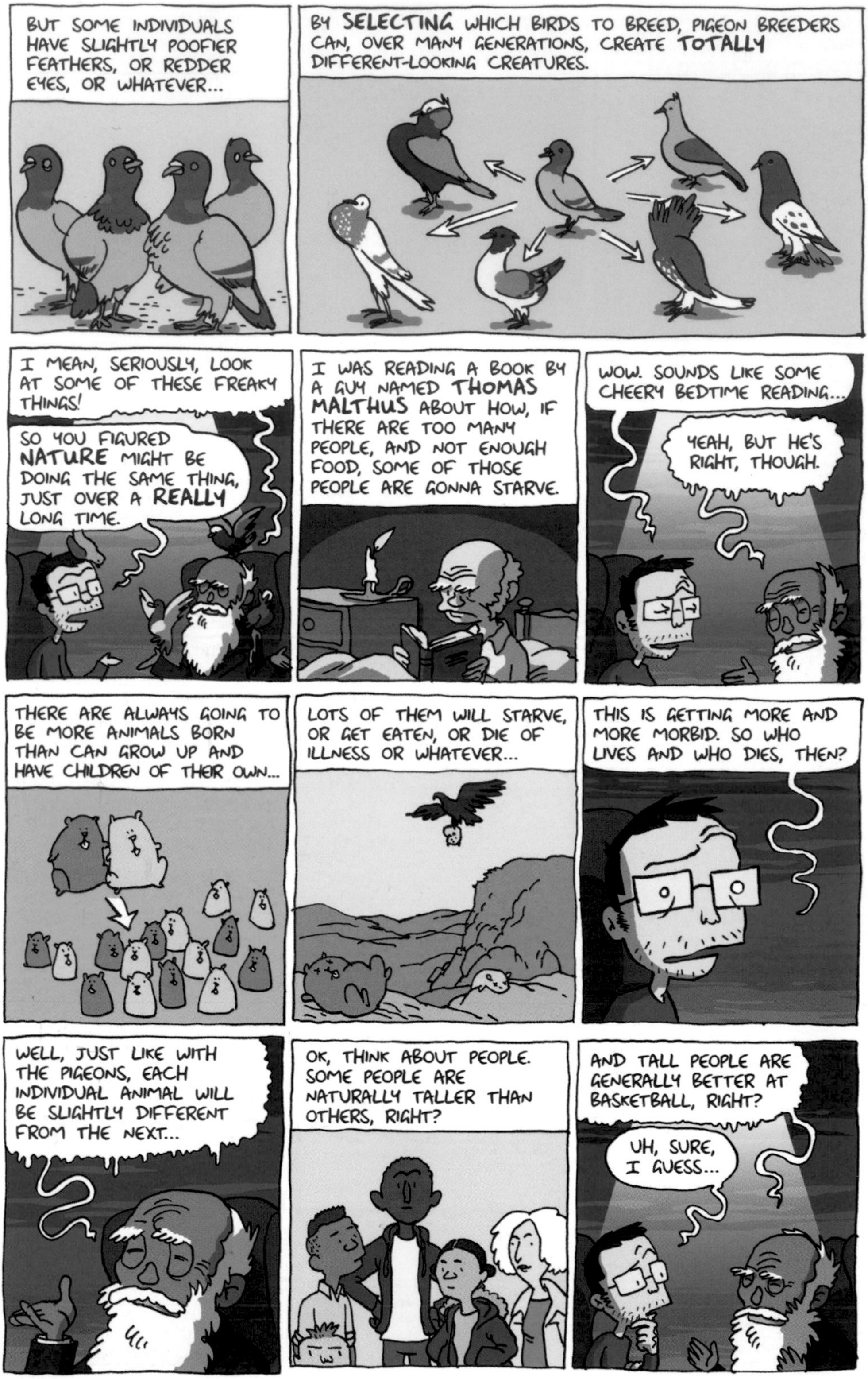
BUT SOME INDIVIDUALS HAVE SLIGHTLY POOFIER FEATHERS, OR REDDER EYES, OR WHATEVER...
BY SELECTING WHICH BIRDS TO BREED, PIGEON BREEDERS CAN, OVER MANY GENERATIONS, CREATE TOTALLY DIFFERENT-LOOKING CREATURES.
I MEAN, SERIOUSLY, LOOK AT SOME OF THESE FREAKY THINGS!
SO YOU FIGURED NATURE MIGHT BE DOING THE SAME THING, JUST OVER A REALLY LONG TIME.
I WAS READING A BOOK BY A GUY NAMED THOMAS MALTHUS ABOUT HOW, IF THERE ARE TOO MANY PEOPLE, AND NOT ENOUGH FOOD, SOME OF THOSE PEOPLE ARE GONNA STARVE.
WOW. SOUNDS LIKE SOME CHEERY BEDTIME READING...
YEAH, BUT HE'S RIGHT, THOUGH.
THERE ARE ALWAYS GOING TO BE MORE ANIMALS BORN THAN CAN GROW UP AND HAVE CHILDREN OF THEIR OWN...
LOTS OF THEM WILL STARVE, OR GET EATEN, OR DIE OF ILLNESS OR WHATEVER...
THIS IS GETTING MORE AND MORE MORBID. SO WHO LIVES AND WHO DIES, THEN?
WELL, JUST LIKE WITH THE PIGEONS, EACH INDIVIDUAL ANIMAL WILL BE SLIGHTLY DIFFERENT FROM THE NEXT...
OK, THINK ABOUT PEOPLE. SOME PEOPLE ARE NATURALLY TALLER THAN OTHERS, RIGHT?
AND TALL PEOPLE ARE GENERALLY BETTER AT BASKETBALL, RIGHT?
UH, SURE, I GUESS...

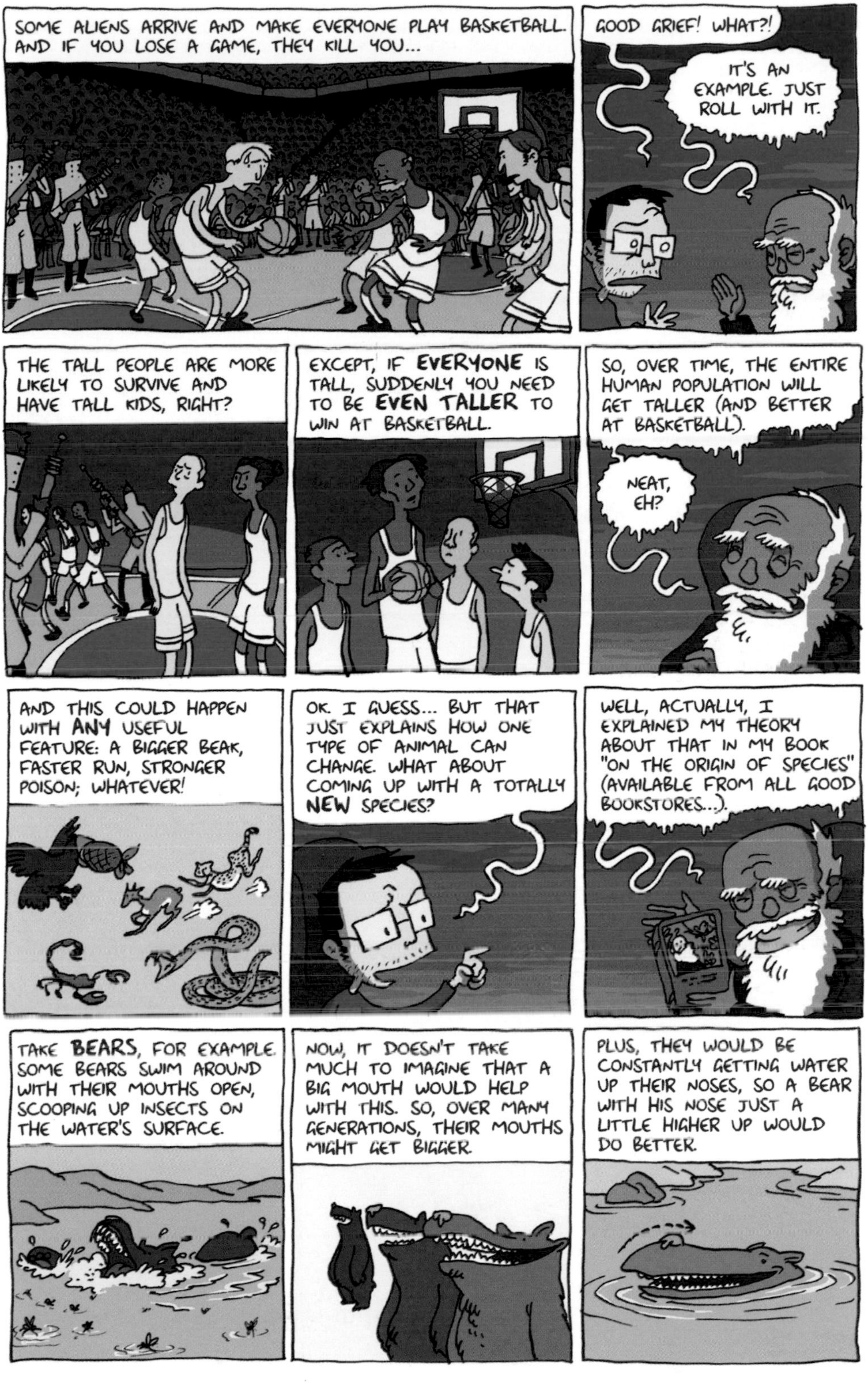
SOME ALIENS ARRIVE AND MAKE EVERYONE PLAY BASKETBALL. AND IF YOU LOSE A GAME, THEY KILL YOU...
GOOD GRIEF! WHAT?!
IT'S AN EXAMPLE. JUST ROLL WITH IT.
THE TALL PEOPLE ARE MORE LIKELY TO SURVIVE AND HAVE TALL KIDS, RIGHT?
EXCEPT, IF EVERYONE IS TALL, SUDDENLY YOU NEED TO BE EVEN TALLER TO WIN AT BASKETBALL.
SO, OVER TIME, THE ENTIRE HUMAN POPULATION WILL GET TALLER (AND BETTER AT BASKETBALL).
NEAT, EH?
AND THIS COULD HAPPEN WITH ANY USEFUL FEATURE: A BIGGER BEAK, FASTER RUN, STRONGER POISON; WHATEVER!
OK. I GUESS... BUT THAT JUST EXPLAINS HOW ONE TYPE OF ANIMAL CAN CHANGE. WHAT ABOUT COMING UP WITH A TOTALLY NEW SPECIES?
WELL, ACTUALLY, I EXPLAINED MY THEORY ABOUT THAT IN MY BOOK "ON THE ORIGIN OF SPECIES" (AVAILABLE FROM ALL GOOD BOOKSTORES...).
TAKE BEARS, FOR EXAMPLE. SOME BEARS SWIM AROUND WITH THEIR MOUTHS OPEN, SCOOPING UP INSECTS ON THE WATER'S SURFACE.
NOW, IT DOESN'T TAKE MUCH TO IMAGINE THAT A BIG MOUTH WOULD HELP WITH THIS. SO, OVER MANY GENERATIONS, THEIR MOUTHS MIGHT GET BIGGER.
PLUS, THEY WOULD BE CONSTANTLY GETTING WATER UP THEIR NOSES, SO A BEAR WITH HIS NOSE JUST A LITTLE HIGHER UP WOULD DO BETTER.

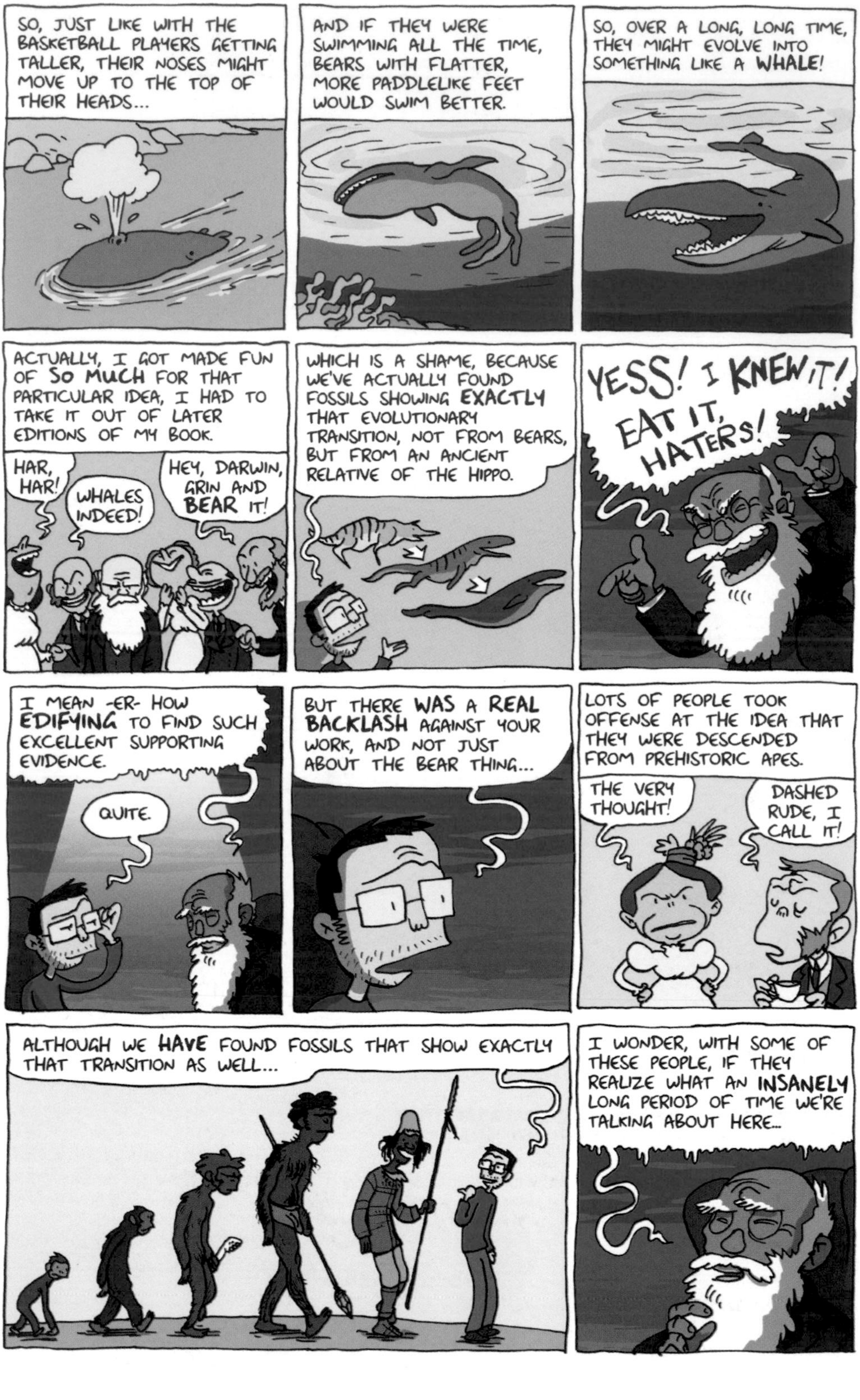
SO, JUST LIKE WITH THE BASKETBALL PLAYERS GETTING TALLER, THEIR NOSES MIGHT MOVE UP TO THE TOP OF THEIR HEADS...
AND IF THEY WERE SWIMMING ALL THE TIME, BEARS WITH FLATTER, MORE PADDLELIKE FEET WOULD SWIM BETTER.
SO, OVER A LONG, LONG TIME, THEY MIGHT EVOLVE INTO SOMETHING LIKE A WHALE!
ACTUALLY, I GOT MADE FUN OF SO MUCH FOR THAT PARTICULAR IDEA, I HAD TO TAKE IT OUT OF LATER EDITIONS OF MY BOOK.
HAR, HAR!
WHALES INDEED!
HEY, DARWIN, GRIN AND BEAR IT!
WHICH IS A SHAME, BECAUSE WE'VE ACTUALLY FOUND FOSSILS SHOWING EXACTLY THAT EVOLUTIONARY TRANSITION, NOT FROM BEARS, BUT FROM AN ANCIENT RELATIVE OF THE HIPPO.
YESS! I KNEW IT! EAT IT, HATERS!
I MEAN -ER- HOW EDIFYING TO FIND SUCH EXCELLENT SUPPORTING EVIDENCE.
QUITE.
BUT THERE WAS A REAL BACKLASH AGAINST YOUR WORK, AND NOT JUST ABOUT THE BEAR THING...
LOTS OF PEOPLE TOOK OFFENSE AT THE IDEA THAT THEY WERE DESCENDED FROM PREHISTORIC APES.
THE VERY THOUGHT!
DASHED RUDE, I CALL IT!
ALTHOUGH WE HAVE FOUND FOSSILS THAT SHOW EXACTLY THAT TRANSITION AS WELL...
I WONDER, WITH SOME OF THESE PEOPLE, IF THEY REALIZE WHAT AN INSANELY LONG PERIOD OF TIME WE'RE TALKING ABOUT HERE...

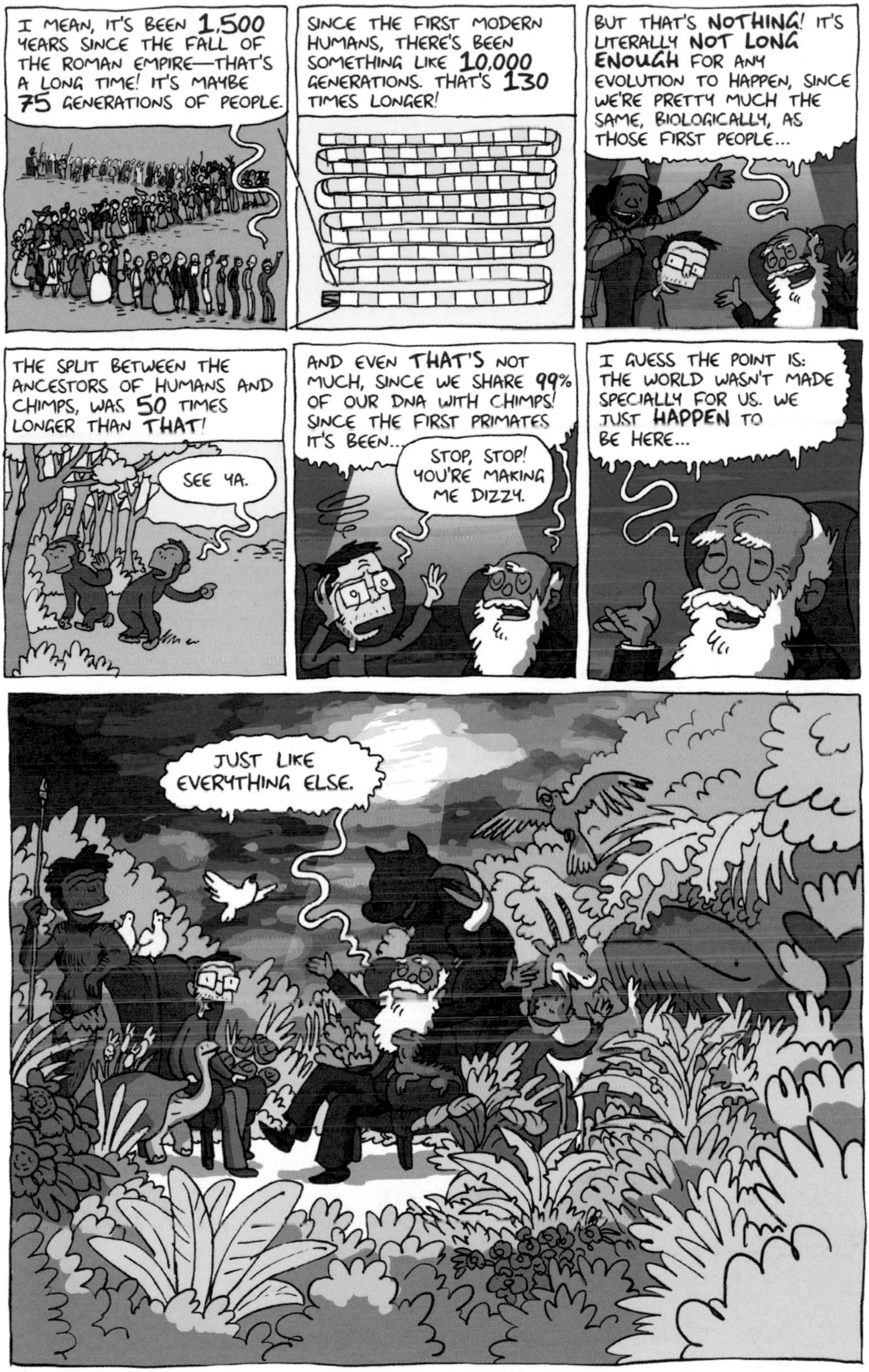
I MEAN, IT'S BEEN 1,500 YEARS SINCE THE FALL OF THE ROMAN EMPIRE—THAT'S A LONG TIME! IT'S MAYBE 75 GENERATIONS OF PEOPLE.
SINCE THE FIRST MODERN HUMANS, THERE'S BEEN SOMETHING LIKE 10,000 GENERATIONS. THAT'S 130 TIMES LONGER!
BUT THAT'S NOTHING! IT'S LITERALLY NOT LONG ENOUGH FOR ANY EVOLUTION TO HAPPEN, SINCE WE'RE PRETTY MUCH THE SAME, BIOLOGICALLY, AS THOSE FIRST PEOPLE...
THE SPLIT BETWEEN THE ANCESTORS OF HUMANS AND CHIMPS, WAS 50 TIMES LONGER THAN THAT!
SEE YA.
AND EVEN THAT'S NOT MUCH, SINCE WE SHARE 99% OF OUR DNA WITH CHIMPS! SINCE THE FIRST PRIMATES IT'S BEEN...
STOP, STOP! YOU'RE MAKING ME DIZZY.
I GUESS THE POINT IS: THE WORLD WASN'T MADE SPECIALLY FOR US. WE JUST HAPPEN TO BE HERE...
JUST LIKE EVERYTHING ELSE.

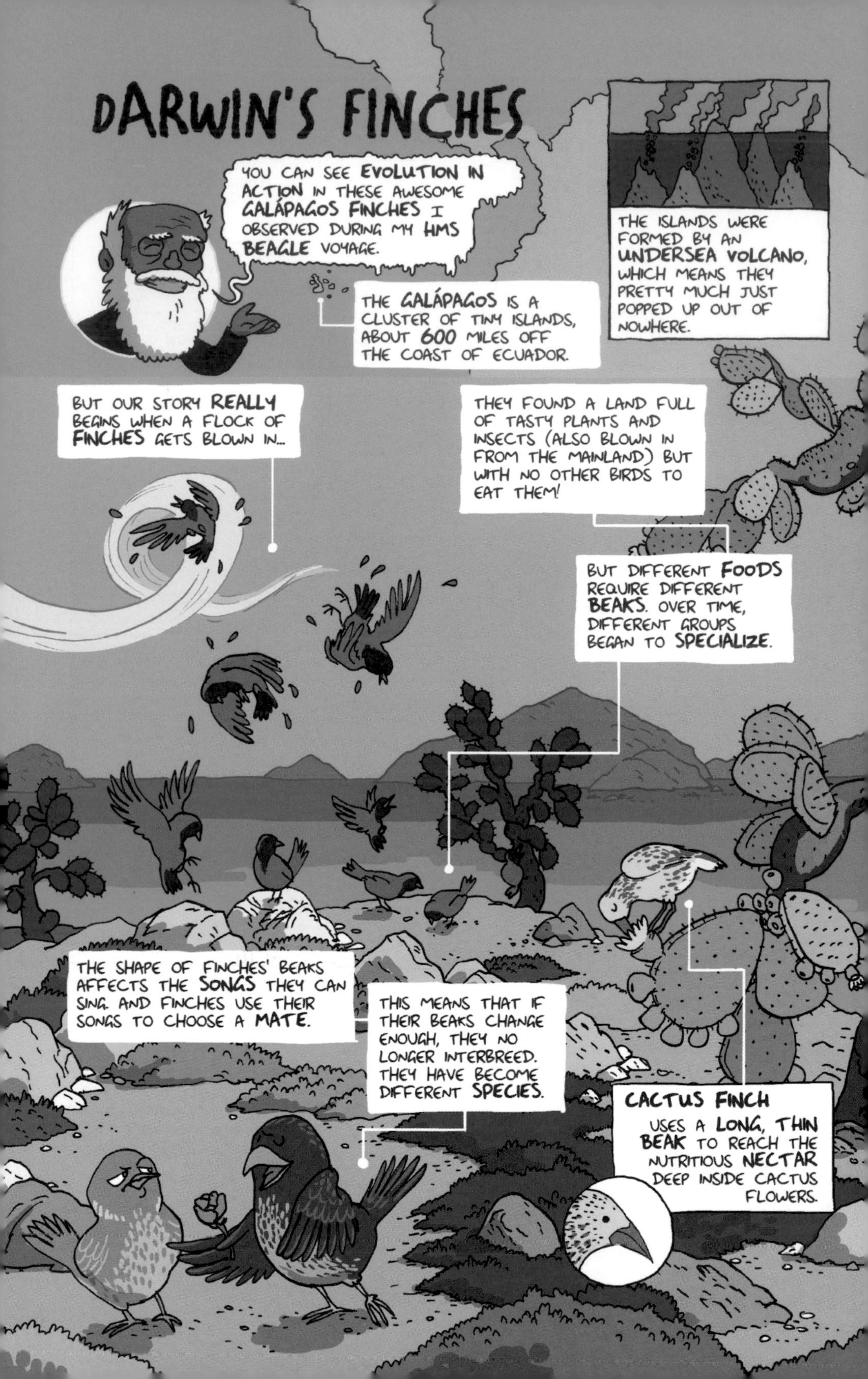
DARWIN'S FINCHES
YOU CAN SEE EVOLUTION IN ACTION IN THESE AWESOME GALÁPAGOS FINCHES I OBSERVED DURING MY HMS BEAGLE VOYAGE.
THE GALÁPAGOS IS A CLUSTER OF TINY ISLANDS, ABOUT 600 MILES OFF THE COAST OF ECUADOR.
THE ISLANDS WERE FORMED BY AN UNDERSEA VOLCANO, WHICH MEANS THEY PRETTY MUCH JUST POPPED UP OUT OF NOWHERE.
BUT OUR STORY REALLY BEGINS WHEN A FLOCK OF FINCHES GETS BLOWN IN...
THEY FOUND A LAND FULL OF TASTY PLANTS AND INSECTS (ALSO BLOWN IN FROM THE MAINLAND) BUT WITH NO OTHER BIRDS TO EAT THEM!
BUT DIFFERENT FOODS REQUIRE DIFFERENT BEAKS. OVER TIME, DIFFERENT GROUPS BEGAN TO SPECIALIZE.
THE SHAPE OF FINCHES' BEAKS AFFECTS THE SONGS THEY CAN SING. AND FINCHES USE THEIR SONGS TO CHOOSE A MATE.
THIS MEANS THAT IF THEIR BEAKS CHANGE ENOUGH, THEY NO LONGER INTERBREED. THEY HAVE BECOME DIFFERENT SPECIES.
CACTUS FINCH
USES A LONG, THIN BEAK TO REACH THE NUTRITIOUS NECTAR DEEP INSIDE CACTUS FLOWERS.

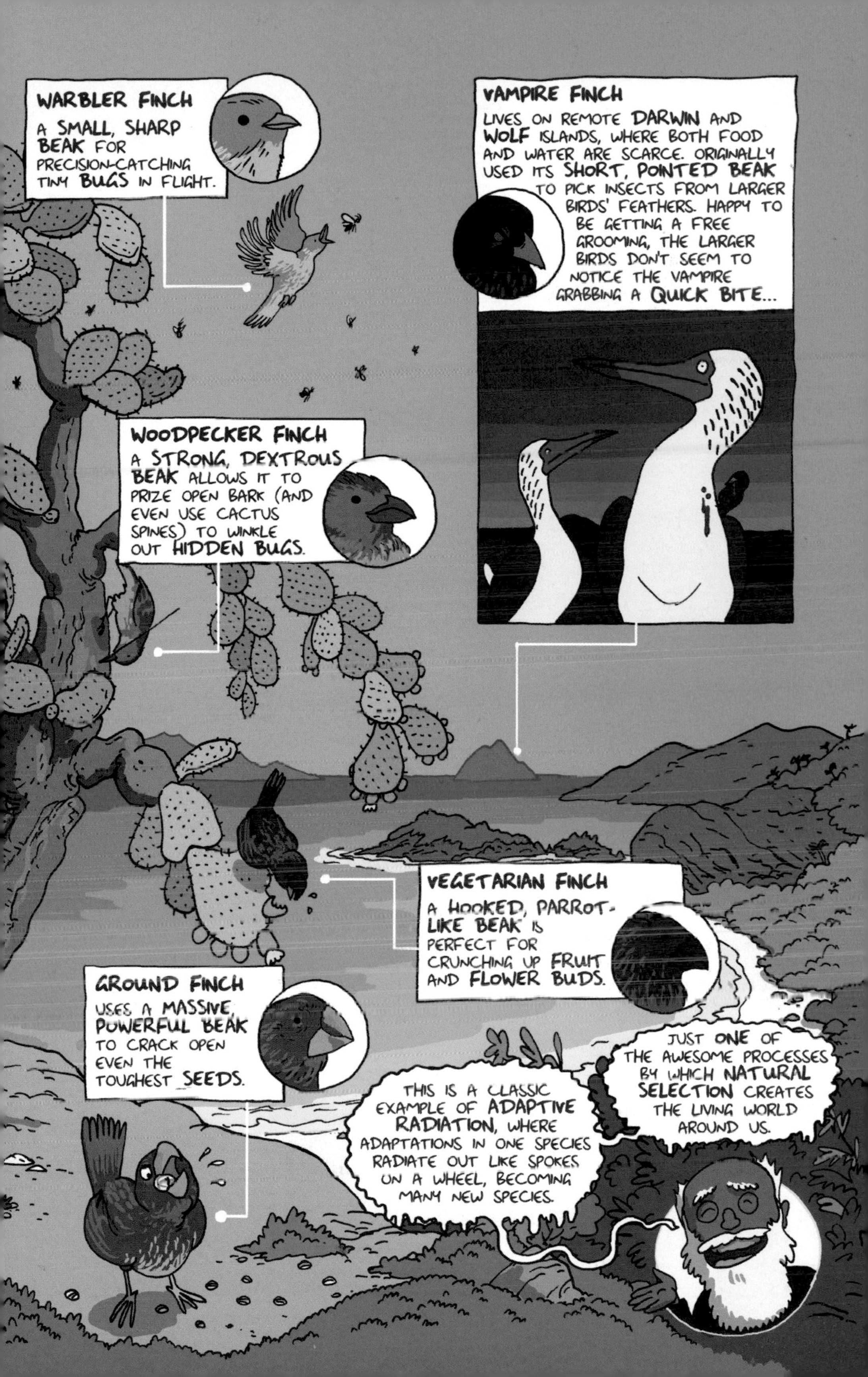
WARBLER FINCH
A SMALL, SHARP BEAK FOR PRECISION-CATCHING TINY BUGS IN FLIGHT.
VAMPIRE FINCH
LIVES ON REMOTE DARWIN AND WOLF ISLANDS, WHERE BOTH FOOD AND WATER ARE SCARCE. ORIGINALLY USED ITS SHORT, POINTED BEAK TO PICK INSECTS FROM LARGER BIRDS' FEATHERS. HAPPY TO BE GETTING A FREE GROOMING, THE LARGER BIRDS DON'T SEEM TO NOTICE THE VAMPIRE GRABBING A QUICK BITE...
WOODPECKER FINCH
A STRONG, DEXTROUS BEAK ALLOWS IT TO PRIZE OPEN BARK (AND EVEN USE CACTUS SPINES) TO WINKLE OUT HIDDEN BUGS.
VEGETARIAN FINCH
A HOOKED, PARROT-LIKE BEAK IS PERFECT FOR CRUNCHING UP FRUIT AND FLOWER BUDS.
GROUND FINCH
USES A MASSIVE, POWERFUL BEAK TO CRACK OPEN EVEN THE TOUGHEST SEEDS.
THIS IS A CLASSIC EXAMPLE OF ADAPTIVE RADIATION, WHERE ADAPTATIONS IN ONE SPECIES RADIATE OUT LIKE SPOKES ON A WHEEL, BECOMING MANY NEW SPECIES.
JUST ONE OF THE AWESOME PROCESSES BY WHICH NATURAL SELECTION CREATES THE LIVING WORLD AROUND US.

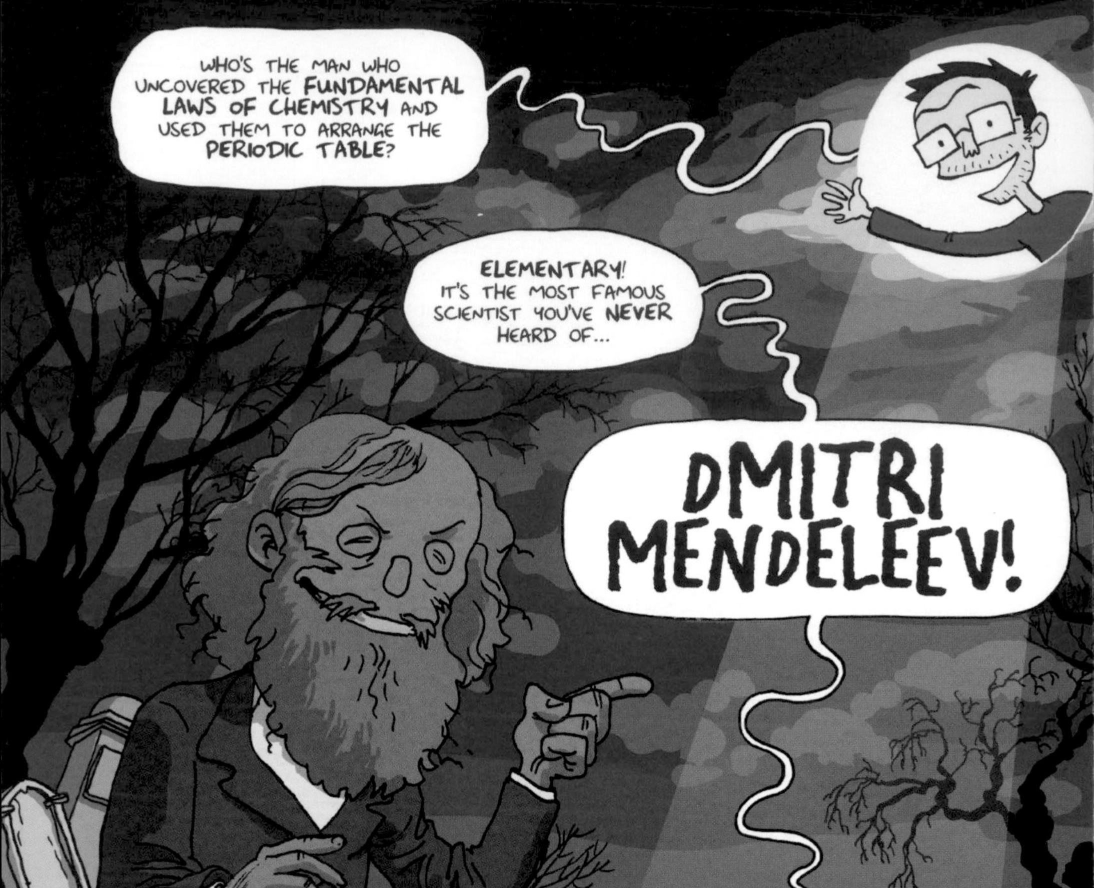
WHO'S THE MAN WHO UNCOVERED THE FUNDAMENTAL LAWS OF CHEMISTRY AND USED THEM TO ARRANGE THE PERIODIC TABLE?
ELEMENTARY! IT'S THE MOST FAMOUS SCIENTIST YOU'VE NEVER HEARD OF...
DMITRI MENDELEEV!
DMITRI MENDELEEV
CHEMIST
1834-1907

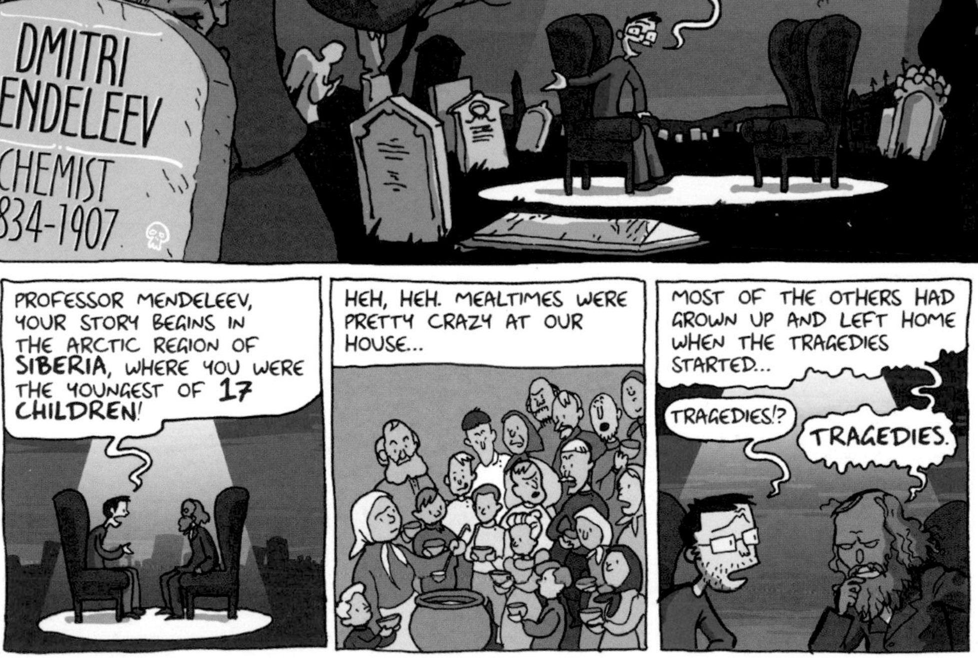
PROFESSOR MENDELEEV, YOUR STORY BEGINS IN THE ARCTIC REGION OF SIBERIA, WHERE YOU WERE THE YOUNGEST OF 17 CHILDREN!
HEH, HEH. MEALTIMES WERE PRETTY CRAZY AT OUR HOUSE...
MOST OF THE OTHERS HAD GROWN UP AND LEFT HOME WHEN THE TRAGEDIES STARTED...
TRAGEDIES!?
TRAGEDIES.

FIRST, PAPPA WENT BLIND. TO SUPPORT US, MAMMA TOOK OVER THE RUNNING OF THE FAMILY **GLASS FACTORY**.

IT WAS THERE THAT I BECAME FASCINATED WITH ALL THE WEIRD AND WONDERFUL BOTTLES AND BEAKERS WE MADE FOR CHEMISTRY EXPERIMENTS.

BUT THEN PAPPA DIED AND THE FACTORY BURNED DOWN.

OH, GEEZ. AT THE SAME TIME?

PRETTY CLOSE.

THEN, WHILE I WAS AT UNIVERSITY, MAMMA AND MY SISTERS DIED OF **TUBERCULOSIS**.

IT ALMOST KILLED ME, TOO. THE DOCTORS GAVE ME A YEAR TO LIVE.

BUT I SURVIVED AND SWORE FROM THEN ON TO DEDICATE MY LIFE TO **SCIENCE**.

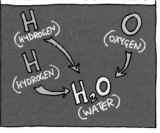

I RESEARCHED ALL SORTS OF THINGS, FROM ALCOHOL TO FERTILIZERS TO OIL. BUT IT WASN'T ENOUGH JUST TO STUDY. I ALSO WANTED TO **TEACH**, TO SHARE MY KNOWLEDGE AND MY LOVE OF SCIENCE!

WHENEVER I TRAVELED BY TRAIN, I ALWAYS WENT THIRD CLASS WITH THE POOR FARMERS, SO I COULD TELL THEM ABOUT THE LATEST AGRICULTURE RESEARCH.

I WAS TEACHING UNIVERSITY STUDENTS, TOO. BUT THERE WASN'T A CHEMISTRY TEXTBOOK IN **RUSSIAN**. SO I DECIDED TO WRITE MY OWN.

I WAS WRITING ABOUT THE ELEMENTS, WHEN I STARTED NOTICING SOME CURIOUS PATTERNS...

WAIT A MINUTE, WAIT A MINUTE. **ELEMENTS**. WHAT **ARE** ELEMENTS?

ELEMENTS ARE LIKE THE LETTERS OF THE ALPHABET, SIMPLE CHEMICALS THAT CAN COMBINE TO MAKE MORE COMPLICATED 'WORDS'.

H (HYDROGEN)

H (HYDROGEN)

O (OXYGEN)

H_2O (WATER)

89

SOME ELEMENTS, LIKE SODIUM OR POTASSIUM, **EXPLODE** ON CONTACT WITH AIR OR WATER!

LOTS ARE HARD, SHINY, AND GOOD CONDUCTORS OF **ELECTRICITY**—THE METALS.

SOME, LIKE OXYGEN OR CARBON, **DON'T** CONDUCT ELECTRICITY, BUT THEY ARE GREAT AT COMBINING WITH OTHER ELEMENTS TO MAKE NEW THINGS.

YOUR BODY IS MOSTLY CARBON AND OXYGEN.

I KNEW THERE MUST BE SOME PATTERN, SOME REASON WHY THEY SHARED SIMILAR PROPERTIES LIKE THAT, BUT **WHAT?**

I HAD THEM ALL WRITTEN OUT ON CARDS, AND I'D SPENT **YEARS** MOVING THEM AROUND, ARRANGING AND REARRANGING...

BORON HERE...

NO, WAIT, ANTIMONY HERE, BORON THERE...

BUT THEN, ONE DAY, I GOT **SO SLEEPY,** I HAD TO TAKE A NAP.

CALCIUM...

NICKEL...

MOLYBDENUM...

Z

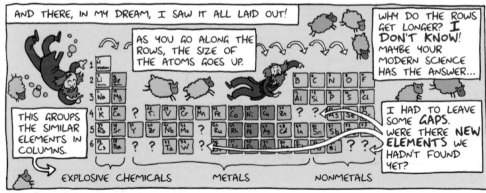

AND THERE, IN MY DREAM, I SAW IT ALL LAID OUT!

AS YOU GO ALONG THE ROWS, THE SIZE OF THE ATOMS GOES UP.

WHY DO THE ROWS GET LONGER? **I DON'T KNOW!** MAYBE YOUR MODERN SCIENCE HAS THE ANSWER...

THIS GROUPS THE SIMILAR ELEMENTS IN COLUMNS.

I HAD TO LEAVE SOME **GAPS.** WERE THERE **NEW ELEMENTS** WE HADN'T FOUND YET?

EXPLOSIVE CHEMICALS   METALS   NONMETALS

HUH!? WUZZAT!

NOT EVERYONE LIKED MY NEW SYSTEM...

WHAT'S WITH ALL THE **GAPS,** HUH? **MENDELEEEV?**

BUT WHEN THE MISSING ELEMENTS WERE FOUND, THEY HAD TO ACCEPT MY SYSTEM WAS RIGHT!

GALLIUM
Ga
FOUND 1875

GERMANIUM
Ge
FOUND 1886

SCANDIUM
Sn
FOUND 1879

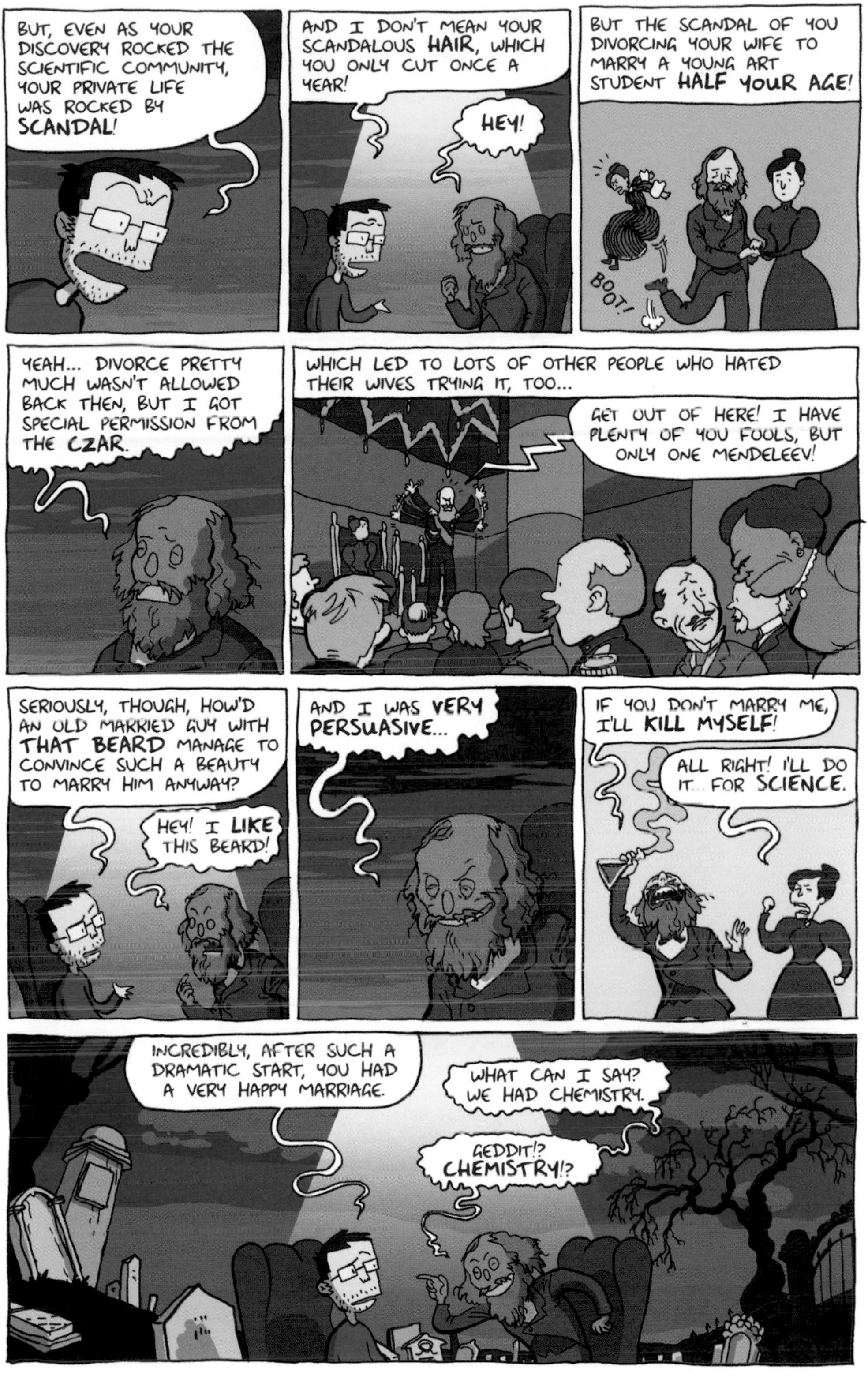
BUT, EVEN AS YOUR DISCOVERY ROCKED THE SCIENTIFIC COMMUNITY, YOUR PRIVATE LIFE WAS ROCKED BY SCANDAL!
AND I DON'T MEAN YOUR SCANDALOUS HAIR, WHICH YOU ONLY CUT ONCE A YEAR!
HEY!
BUT THE SCANDAL OF YOU DIVORCING YOUR WIFE TO MARRY A YOUNG ART STUDENT HALF YOUR AGE!
BOOT!
YEAH... DIVORCE PRETTY MUCH WASN'T ALLOWED BACK THEN, BUT I GOT SPECIAL PERMISSION FROM THE CZAR.
WHICH LED TO LOTS OF OTHER PEOPLE WHO HATED THEIR WIVES TRYING IT, TOO...
GET OUT OF HERE! I HAVE PLENTY OF YOU FOOLS, BUT ONLY ONE MENDELEEV!
SERIOUSLY, THOUGH, HOW'D AN OLD MARRIED GUY WITH THAT BEARD MANAGE TO CONVINCE SUCH A BEAUTY TO MARRY HIM ANYWAY?
HEY! I LIKE THIS BEARD!
AND I WAS VERY PERSUASIVE...
IF YOU DON'T MARRY ME, I'LL KILL MYSELF!
ALL RIGHT! I'LL DO IT... FOR SCIENCE.
INCREDIBLY, AFTER SUCH A DRAMATIC START, YOU HAD A VERY HAPPY MARRIAGE.
WHAT CAN I SAY? WE HAD CHEMISTRY.
GEDDIT!? CHEMISTRY!?

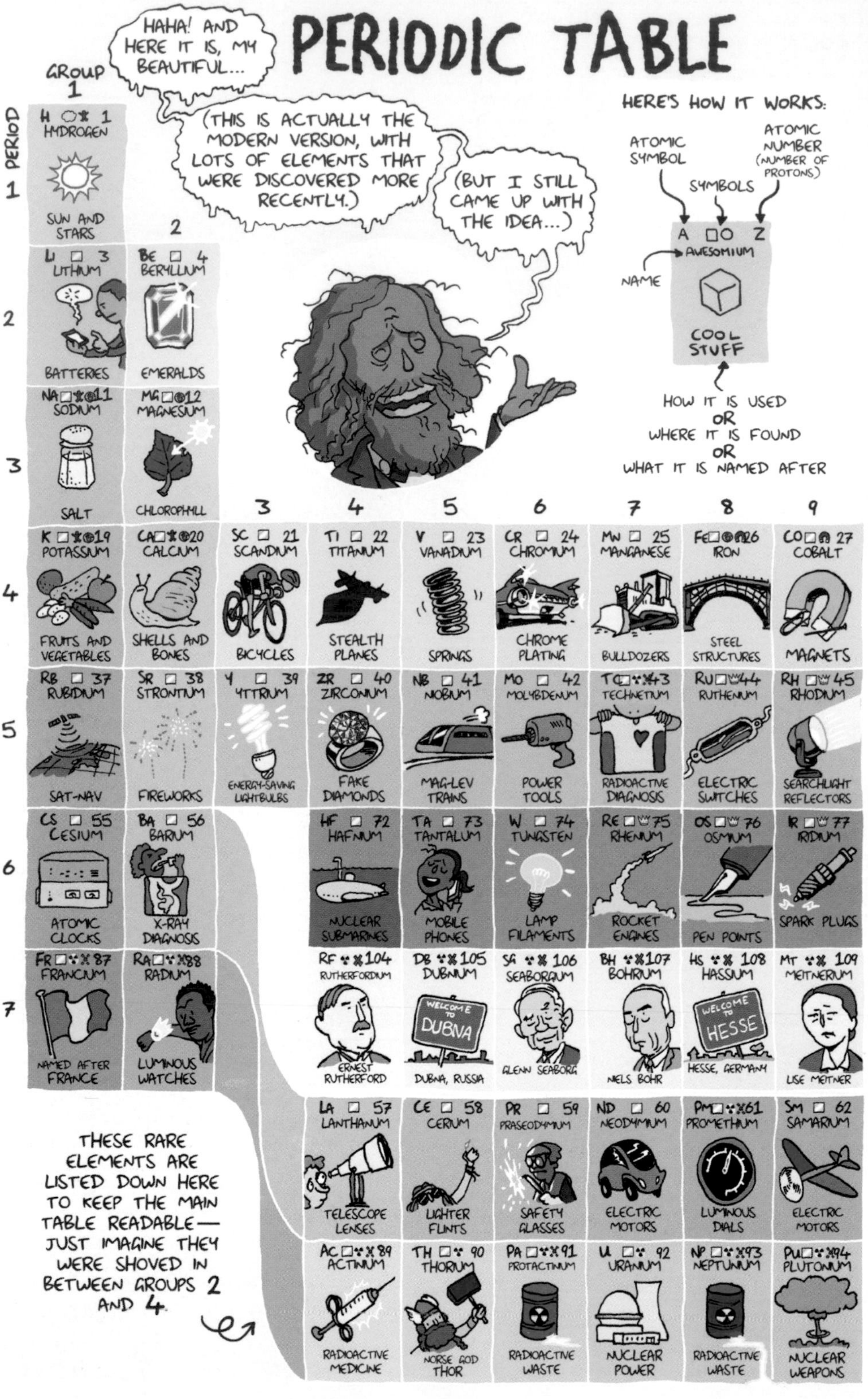
PERIODIC TABLE
HAHA! AND HERE IT IS, MY BEAUTIFUL...
(THIS IS ACTUALLY THE MODERN VERSION, WITH LOTS OF ELEMENTS THAT WERE DISCOVERED MORE RECENTLY.)
(BUT I STILL CAME UP WITH THE IDEA...)
HERE'S HOW IT WORKS:
ATOMIC SYMBOL
SYMBOLS
ATOMIC NUMBER (NUMBER OF PROTONS)
A Z
AWESOMIUM
NAME
COOL STUFF
HOW IT IS USED OR WHERE IT IS FOUND OR WHAT IT IS NAMED AFTER
GROUP 1
PERIOD
1
2
3
4
5
6
7
2
3
4
5
6
7
8
9
H 1 HYDROGEN SUN AND STARS
LI 3 LITHIUM BATTERIES
BE 4 BERYLLIUM EMERALDS
NA 11 SODIUM SALT
MG 12 MAGNESIUM CHLOROPHYLL
K 19 POTASSIUM FRUITS AND VEGETABLES
CA 20 CALCIUM SHELLS AND BONES
SC 21 SCANDIUM BICYCLES
TI 22 TITANIUM STEALTH PLANES
V 23 VANADIUM SPRINGS
CR 24 CHROMIUM CHROME PLATING
MN 25 MANGANESE BULLDOZERS
FE 26 IRON STEEL STRUCTURES
CO 27 COBALT MAGNETS
RB 37 RUBIDIUM SAT-NAV
SR 38 STRONTIUM FIREWORKS
Y 39 YTTRIUM ENERGY-SAVING LIGHTBULBS
ZR 40 ZIRCONIUM FAKE DIAMONDS
NB 41 NIOBIUM MAG-LEV TRAINS
MO 42 MOLYBDENUM POWER TOOLS
TC 43 TECHNETIUM RADIOACTIVE DIAGNOSIS
RU 44 RUTHENIUM ELECTRIC SWITCHES
RH 45 RHODIUM SEARCHLIGHT REFLECTORS
CS 55 CESIUM ATOMIC CLOCKS
BA 56 BARIUM X-RAY DIAGNOSIS
HF 72 HAFNIUM NUCLEAR SUBMARINES
TA 73 TANTALUM MOBILE PHONES
W 74 TUNGSTEN LAMP FILAMENTS
RE 75 RHENIUM ROCKET ENGINES
OS 76 OSMIUM PEN POINTS
IR 77 IRIDIUM SPARK PLUGS
FR 87 FRANCIUM NAMED AFTER FRANCE
RA 88 RADIUM LUMINOUS WATCHES
RF 104 RUTHERFORDIUM ERNEST RUTHERFORD
DB 105 DUBNIUM WELCOME TO DUBNA DUBNA, RUSSIA
SG 106 SEABORGIUM GLENN SEABORG
BH 107 BOHRIUM NIELS BOHR
HS 108 HASSIUM WELCOME TO HESSE HESSE, GERMANY
MT 109 MEITNERIUM LISE MEITNER
LA 57 LANTHANUM TELESCOPE LENSES
CE 58 CERIUM LIGHTER FLINTS
PR 59 PRASEODYMIUM SAFETY GLASSES
ND 60 NEODYMIUM ELECTRIC MOTORS
PM 61 PROMETHIUM LUMINOUS DIALS
SM 62 SAMARIUM ELECTRIC MOTORS
AC 89 ACTINIUM RADIOACTIVE MEDICINE
TH 90 THORIUM NORSE GOD THOR
PA 91 PROTACTINIUM RADIOACTIVE WASTE
U 92 URANIUM NUCLEAR POWER
NP 93 NEPTUNIUM RADIOACTIVE WASTE
PU 94 PLUTONIUM NUCLEAR WEAPONS
THESE RARE ELEMENTS ARE LISTED DOWN HERE TO KEEP THE MAIN TABLE READABLE—JUST IMAGINE THEY WERE SHOVED IN BETWEEN GROUPS 2 AND 4.

SYMBOL KEY:

- SOLID
- LIQUID
- GAS

(AT ROOM TEMPERATURE)

THE COLOR OF THE SYMBOL IS THE COLOR OF THE ELEMENT IN ITS MOST COMMON PURE FORM.

EXAMPLES:
- METALLIC SOLID
- RED LIQUID
- INVISIBLE GAS

HUMAN ELEMENTS TOP 10 ELEMENTS IN YOUR BODY

COMMON AS MUD TOP 8 ELEMENTS IN EARTH'S CRUST

MAGNETIC ATTRACTS IRON AT ROOM TEMP

NOBLE METALS CORROSION-RESISTANT

RADIOACTIVE ALL ISOTOPES ARE RADIOACTIVE

TRACE ELEMENTS SUPER-RARE: LESS THAT 1 MILLIONTH OF EARTH'S CRUST

FRANKEN-ELEMENTS NEVER OCCUR IN NATURE, MADE IN RADIATION RESEARCH LABS

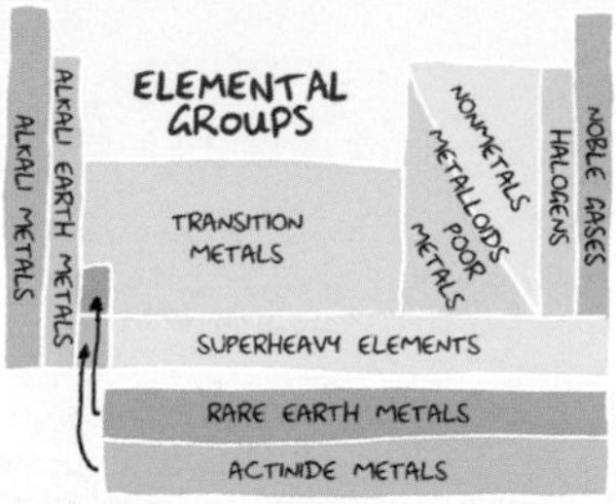

ELEMENTAL GROUPS
ALKALI METALS
ALKALI EARTH METALS
TRANSITION METALS
NONMETALS
METALLOIDS
POOR METALS
HALOGENS
NOBLE GASES
SUPERHEAVY ELEMENTS
RARE EARTH METALS
ACTINIDE METALS

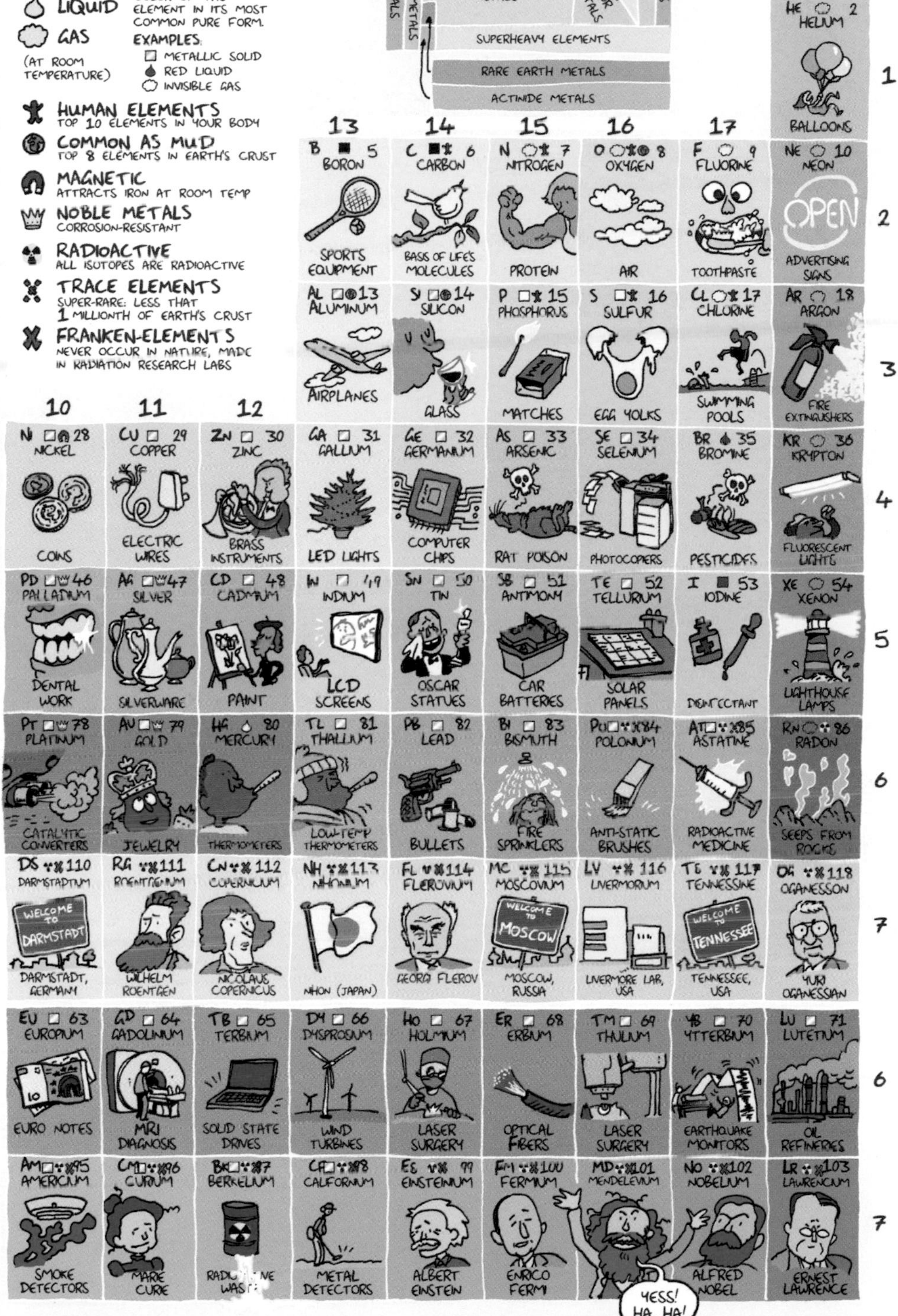

18
1
HE 2 HELIUM
BALLOONS
13
14
15
16
17
2
B 5 BORON
SPORTS EQUIPMENT
C 6 CARBON
BASIS OF LIFE'S MOLECULES
N 7 NITROGEN
PROTEIN
O 8 OXYGEN
AIR
F 9 FLUORINE
TOOTHPASTE
NE 10 NEON
OPEN
ADVERTISING SIGNS
3
AL 13 ALUMINUM
AIRPLANES
SI 14 SILICON
GLASS
P 15 PHOSPHORUS
MATCHES
S 16 SULFUR
EGG YOLKS
CL 17 CHLORINE
SWIMMING POOLS
AR 18 ARGON
FIRE EXTINGUISHERS
10
11
12
4
NI 28 NICKEL
COINS
CU 29 COPPER
ELECTRIC WIRES
ZN 30 ZINC
BRASS INSTRUMENTS
GA 31 GALLIUM
LED LIGHTS
GE 32 GERMANIUM
COMPUTER CHIPS
AS 33 ARSENIC
RAT POISON
SE 34 SELENIUM
PHOTOCOPIERS
BR 35 BROMINE
PESTICIDES
KR 36 KRYPTON
FLUORESCENT LIGHTS
5
PD 46 PALLADIUM
DENTAL WORK
AG 47 SILVER
SILVERWARE
CD 48 CADMIUM
PAINT
IN 49 INDIUM
LCD SCREENS
SN 50 TIN
OSCAR STATUES
SB 51 ANTIMONY
CAR BATTERIES
TE 52 TELLURIUM
SOLAR PANELS
I 53 IODINE
DISINFECTANT
XE 54 XENON
LIGHTHOUSE LAMPS
6
PT 78 PLATINUM
CATALYTIC CONVERTERS
AU 79 GOLD
JEWELRY
HG 80 MERCURY
THERMOMETERS
TL 81 THALLIUM
LOW-TEMP THERMOMETERS
PB 82 LEAD
BULLETS
BI 83 BISMUTH
FIRE SPRINKLERS
PO 84 POLONIUM
ANTI-STATIC BRUSHES
AT 85 ASTATINE
RADIOACTIVE MEDICINE
RN 86 RADON
SEEPS FROM ROCKS
7
DS 110 DARMSTADTIUM
WELCOME TO DARMSTADT
DARMSTADT, GERMANY
RG 111 ROENTGENIUM
WILHELM ROENTGEN
CN 112 COPERNICIUM
NICOLAUS COPERNICUS
NH 113 NIHONIUM
NIHON (JAPAN)
FL 114 FLEROVIUM
GEORGI FLEROV
MC 115 MOSCOVIUM
WELCOME TO MOSCOW
MOSCOW, RUSSIA
LV 116 LIVERMORIUM
LIVERMORE LAB, USA
TS 117 TENNESSINE
WELCOME TO TENNESSEE
TENNESSEE, USA
OG 118 OGANESSON
YURI OGANESSIAN
6
EU 63 EUROPIUM
10
EURO NOTES
GD 64 GADOLINIUM
MRI DIAGNOSIS
TB 65 TERBIUM
SOLID STATE DRIVES
DY 66 DYSPROSIUM
WIND TURBINES
HO 67 HOLMIUM
LASER SURGERY
ER 68 ERBIUM
OPTICAL FIBERS
TM 69 THULIUM
LASER SURGERY
YB 70 YTTERBIUM
EARTHQUAKE MONITORS
LU 71 LUTETIUM
OIL REFINERIES
7
AM 95 AMERICIUM
SMOKE DETECTORS
CM 96 CURIUM
MARIE CURIE
BK 97 BERKELIUM
RADIOACTIVE WASTE
CF 98 CALIFORNIUM
METAL DETECTORS
ES 99 EINSTEINIUM
ALBERT EINSTEIN
FM 100 FERMIUM
ENRICO FERMI
MD 101 MENDELEVIUM
YESS! HA, HA!
NO 102 NOBELIUM
ALFRED NOBEL
LR 103 LAWRENCIUM
ERNEST LAWRENCE

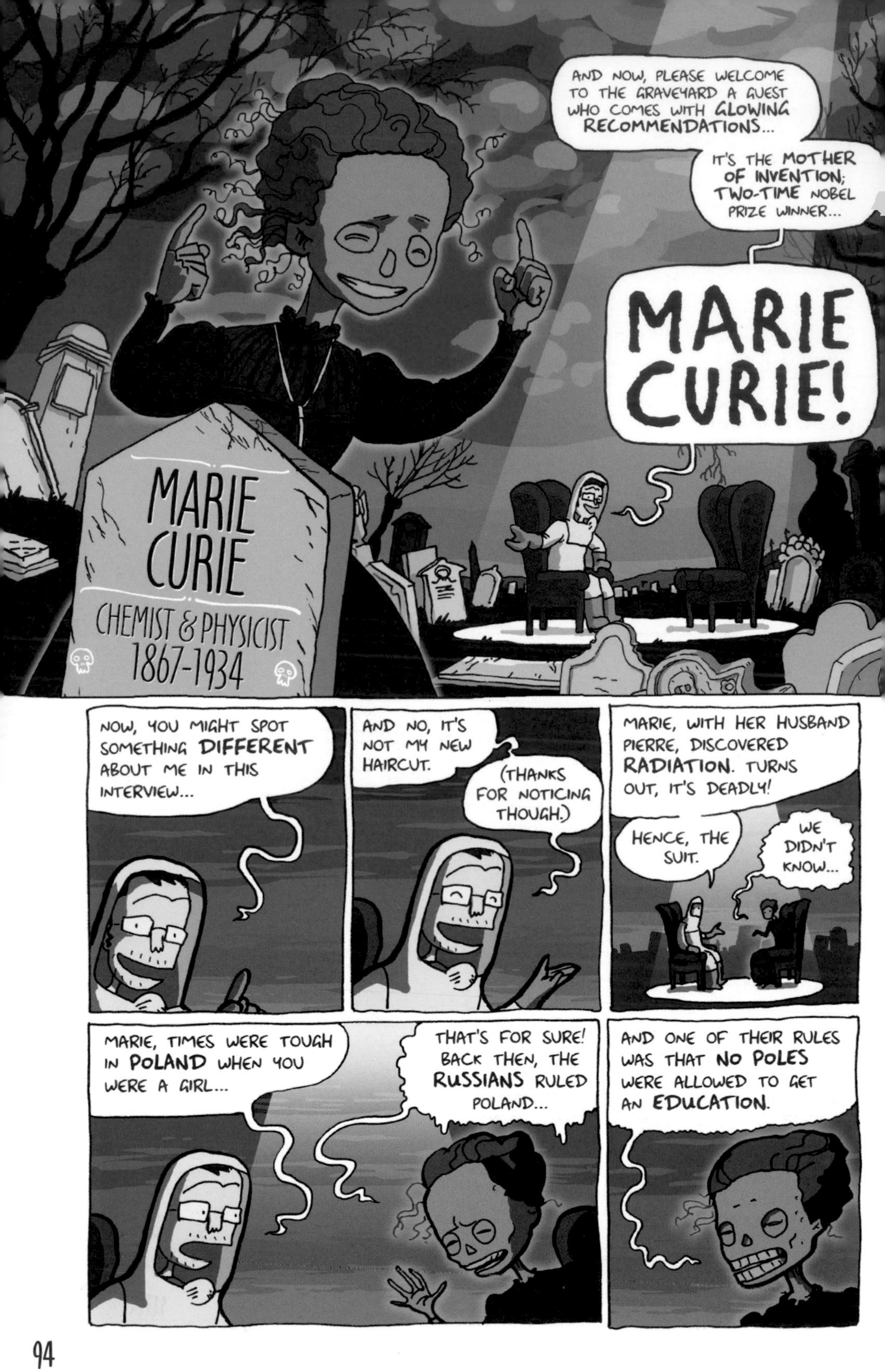
AND NOW, PLEASE WELCOME TO THE GRAVEYARD A GUEST WHO COMES WITH GLOWING RECOMMENDATIONS...
IT'S THE MOTHER OF INVENTION; TWO-TIME NOBEL PRIZE WINNER...
MARIE CURIE!
MARIE CURIE
CHEMIST & PHYSICIST
1867-1934
NOW, YOU MIGHT SPOT SOMETHING DIFFERENT ABOUT ME IN THIS INTERVIEW...
AND NO, IT'S NOT MY NEW HAIRCUT.
(THANKS FOR NOTICING THOUGH.)
MARIE, WITH HER HUSBAND PIERRE, DISCOVERED RADIATION. TURNS OUT, IT'S DEADLY!
HENCE, THE SUIT.
WE DIDN'T KNOW...
MARIE, TIMES WERE TOUGH IN POLAND WHEN YOU WERE A GIRL...
THAT'S FOR SURE! BACK THEN, THE RUSSIANS RULED POLAND...
AND ONE OF THEIR RULES WAS THAT NO POLES WERE ALLOWED TO GET AN EDUCATION.

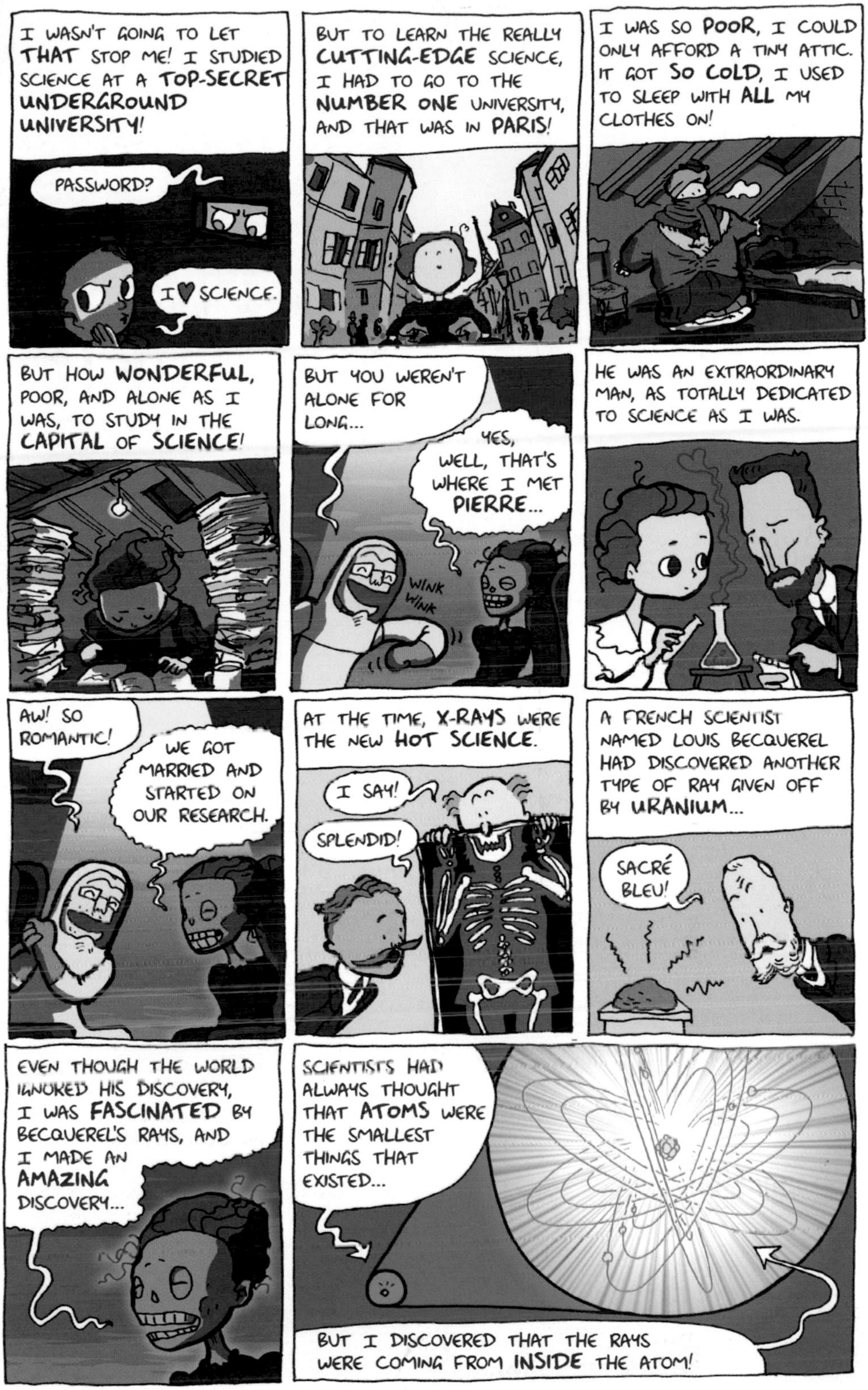
I WASN'T GOING TO LET THAT STOP ME! I STUDIED SCIENCE AT A TOP-SECRET UNDERGROUND UNIVERSITY!
PASSWORD?
I ♥ SCIENCE.
BUT TO LEARN THE REALLY CUTTING-EDGE SCIENCE, I HAD TO GO TO THE NUMBER ONE UNIVERSITY, AND THAT WAS IN PARIS!
I WAS SO POOR, I COULD ONLY AFFORD A TINY ATTIC. IT GOT SO COLD, I USED TO SLEEP WITH ALL MY CLOTHES ON!
BUT HOW WONDERFUL, POOR, AND ALONE AS I WAS, TO STUDY IN THE CAPITAL OF SCIENCE!
BUT YOU WEREN'T ALONE FOR LONG...
YES, WELL, THAT'S WHERE I MET PIERRE...
WINK WINK
HE WAS AN EXTRAORDINARY MAN, AS TOTALLY DEDICATED TO SCIENCE AS I WAS.
AW! SO ROMANTIC!
WE GOT MARRIED AND STARTED ON OUR RESEARCH.
AT THE TIME, X-RAYS WERE THE NEW HOT SCIENCE.
I SAY!
SPLENDID!
A FRENCH SCIENTIST NAMED LOUIS BECQUEREL HAD DISCOVERED ANOTHER TYPE OF RAY GIVEN OFF BY URANIUM...
SACRÉ BLEU!
EVEN THOUGH THE WORLD IGNORED HIS DISCOVERY, I WAS FASCINATED BY BECQUEREL'S RAYS, AND I MADE AN AMAZING DISCOVERY...
SCIENTISTS HAD ALWAYS THOUGHT THAT ATOMS WERE THE SMALLEST THINGS THAT EXISTED...
BUT I DISCOVERED THAT THE RAYS WERE COMING FROM INSIDE THE ATOM!

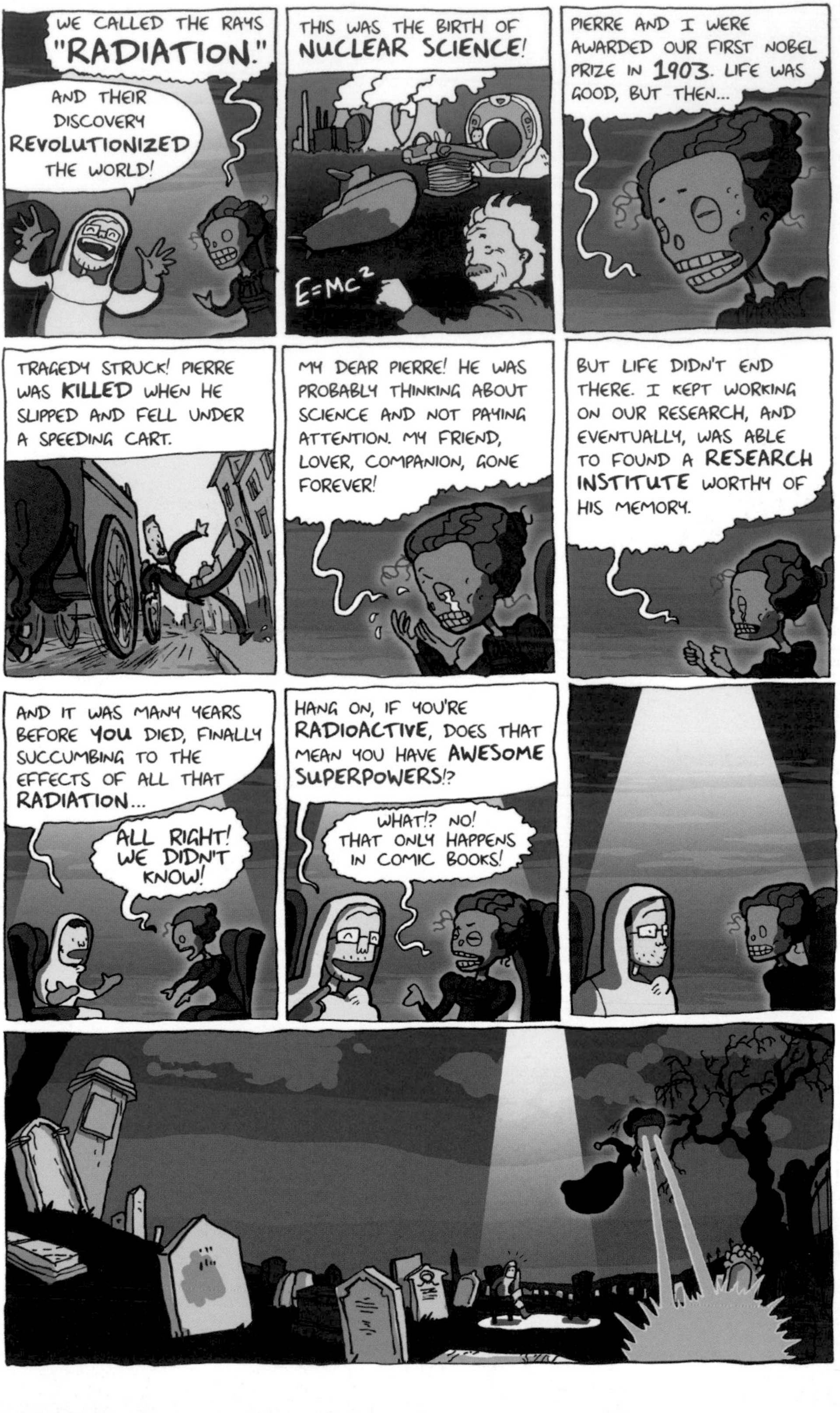
WE CALLED THE RAYS "RADIATION."
AND THEIR DISCOVERY REVOLUTIONIZED THE WORLD!
THIS WAS THE BIRTH OF NUCLEAR SCIENCE!
E=MC²
PIERRE AND I WERE AWARDED OUR FIRST NOBEL PRIZE IN 1903. LIFE WAS GOOD, BUT THEN...
TRAGEDY STRUCK! PIERRE WAS KILLED WHEN HE SLIPPED AND FELL UNDER A SPEEDING CART.
MY DEAR PIERRE! HE WAS PROBABLY THINKING ABOUT SCIENCE AND NOT PAYING ATTENTION. MY FRIEND, LOVER, COMPANION, GONE FOREVER!
BUT LIFE DIDN'T END THERE. I KEPT WORKING ON OUR RESEARCH, AND EVENTUALLY, WAS ABLE TO FOUND A RESEARCH INSTITUTE WORTHY OF HIS MEMORY.
AND IT WAS MANY YEARS BEFORE YOU DIED, FINALLY SUCCUMBING TO THE EFFECTS OF ALL THAT RADIATION...
ALL RIGHT! WE DIDN'T KNOW!
HANG ON, IF YOU'RE RADIOACTIVE, DOES THAT MEAN YOU HAVE AWESOME SUPERPOWERS!?
WHAT!? NO! THAT ONLY HAPPENS IN COMIC BOOKS!

KILLER RESEARCH

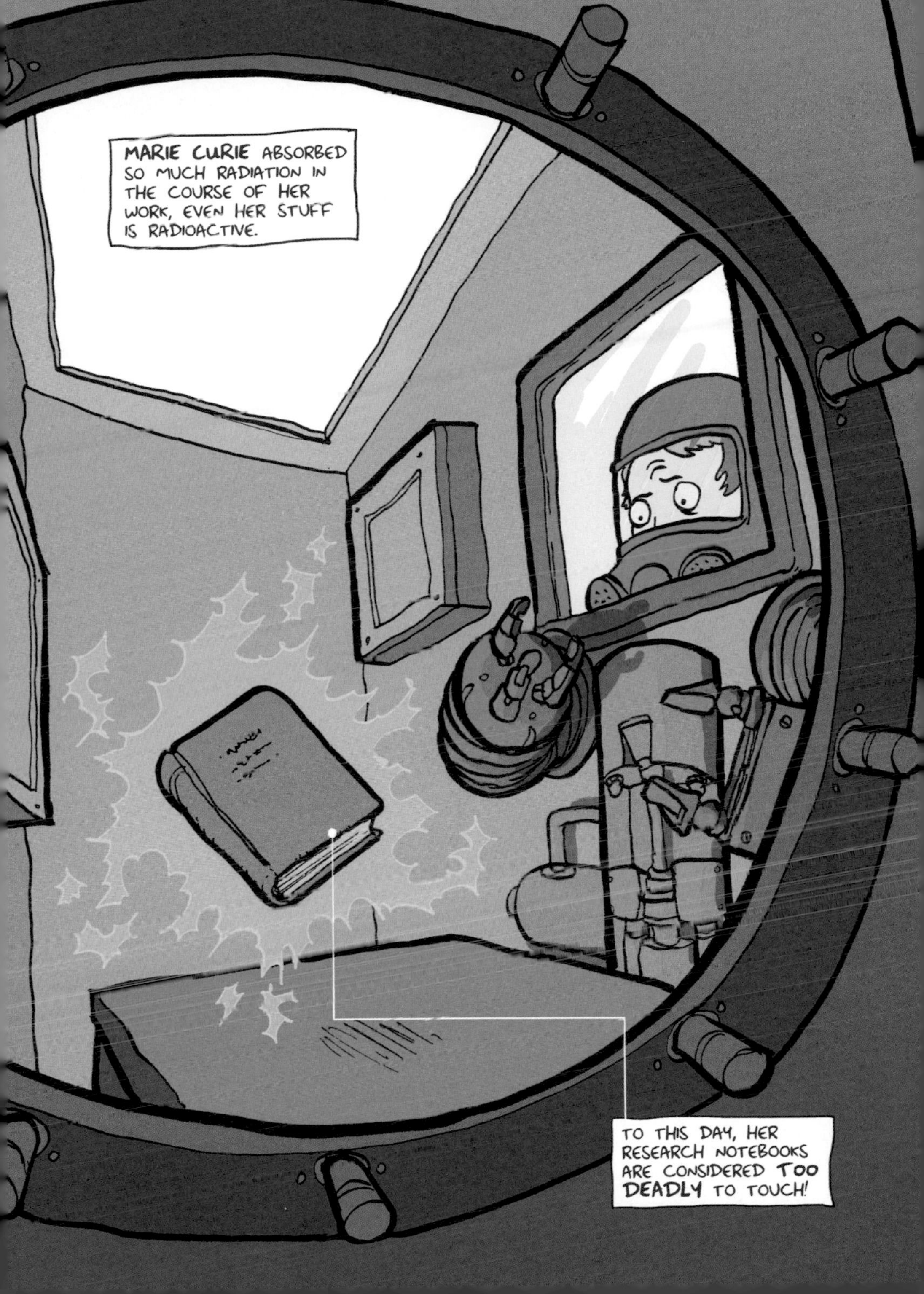
MARIE CURIE ABSORBED SO MUCH RADIATION IN THE COURSE OF HER WORK, EVEN HER STUFF IS RADIOACTIVE.
TO THIS DAY, HER RESEARCH NOTEBOOKS ARE CONSIDERED TOO DEADLY TO TOUCH!

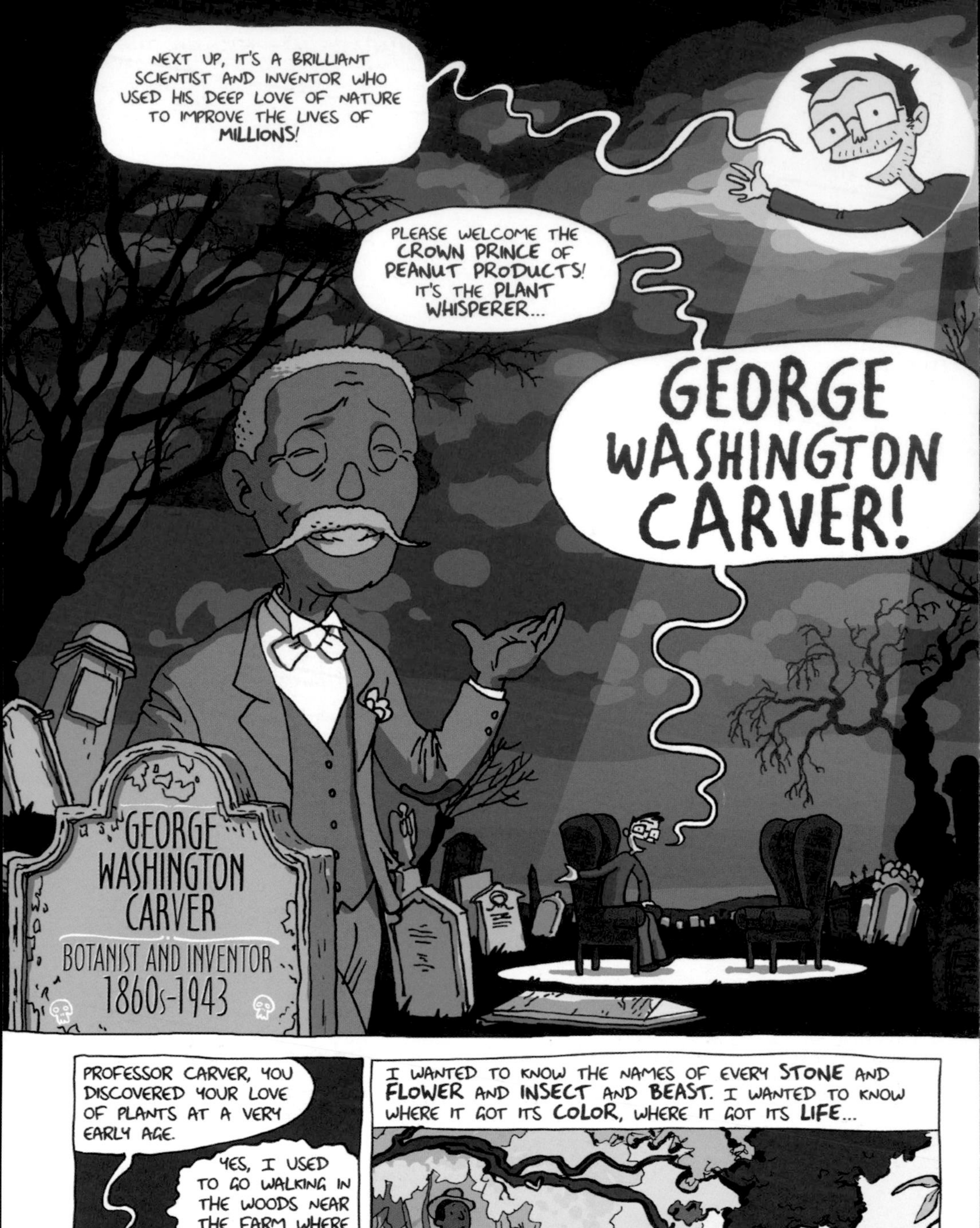
NEXT UP, IT'S A BRILLIANT SCIENTIST AND INVENTOR WHO USED HIS DEEP LOVE OF NATURE TO IMPROVE THE LIVES OF MILLIONS!
PLEASE WELCOME THE CROWN PRINCE OF PEANUT PRODUCTS! IT'S THE PLANT WHISPERER...
GEORGE WASHINGTON CARVER!
GEORGE WASHINGTON CARVER
BOTANIST AND INVENTOR
1860s-1943

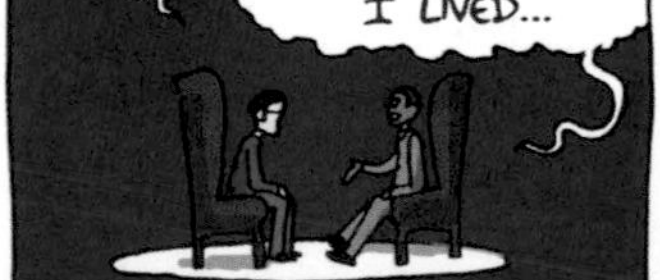
PROFESSOR CARVER, YOU DISCOVERED YOUR LOVE OF PLANTS AT A VERY EARLY AGE.
YES, I USED TO GO WALKING IN THE WOODS NEAR THE FARM WHERE I LIVED...

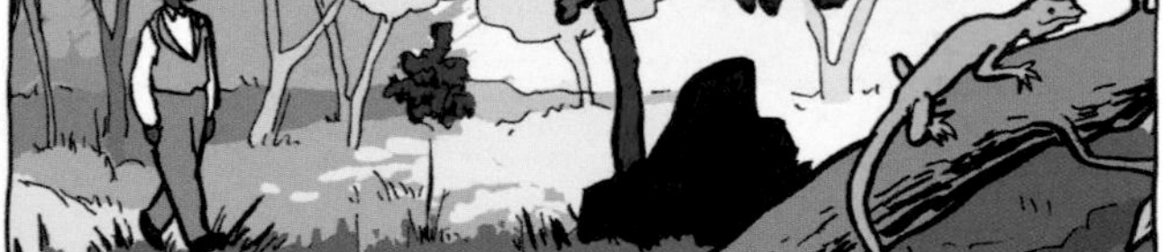
I WANTED TO KNOW THE NAMES OF EVERY STONE AND FLOWER AND INSECT AND BEAST. I WANTED TO KNOW WHERE IT GOT ITS COLOR, WHERE IT GOT ITS LIFE...

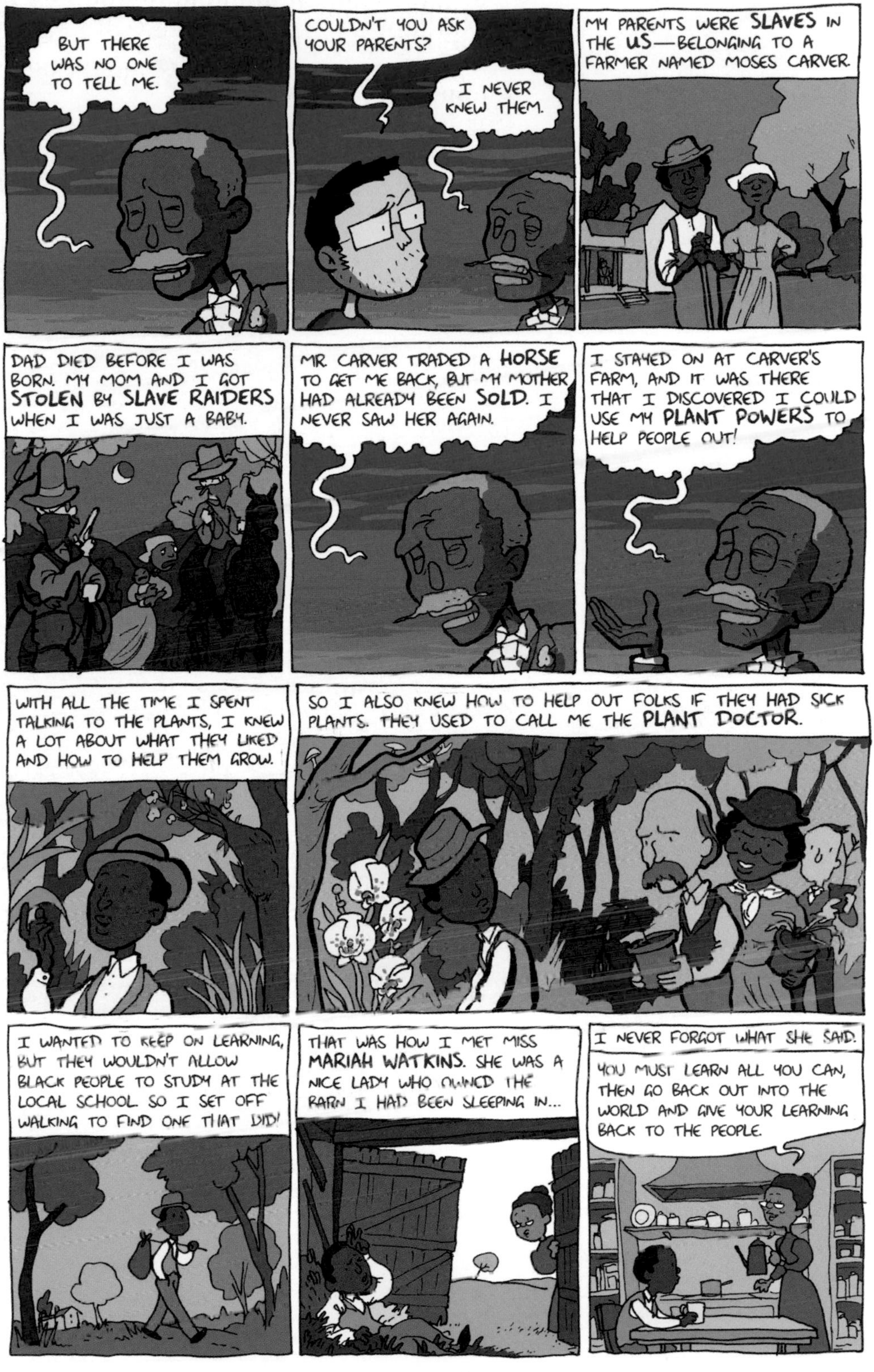

BUT THERE WAS NO ONE TO TELL ME.
COULDN'T YOU ASK YOUR PARENTS?
I NEVER KNEW THEM.
MY PARENTS WERE SLAVES IN THE US—BELONGING TO A FARMER NAMED MOSES CARVER.
DAD DIED BEFORE I WAS BORN. MY MOM AND I GOT STOLEN BY SLAVE RAIDERS WHEN I WAS JUST A BABY.
MR. CARVER TRADED A HORSE TO GET ME BACK, BUT MY MOTHER HAD ALREADY BEEN SOLD. I NEVER SAW HER AGAIN.
I STAYED ON AT CARVER'S FARM, AND IT WAS THERE THAT I DISCOVERED I COULD USE MY PLANT POWERS TO HELP PEOPLE OUT!
WITH ALL THE TIME I SPENT TALKING TO THE PLANTS, I KNEW A LOT ABOUT WHAT THEY LIKED AND HOW TO HELP THEM GROW.
SO I ALSO KNEW HOW TO HELP OUT FOLKS IF THEY HAD SICK PLANTS. THEY USED TO CALL ME THE PLANT DOCTOR.
I WANTED TO KEEP ON LEARNING, BUT THEY WOULDN'T ALLOW BLACK PEOPLE TO STUDY AT THE LOCAL SCHOOL. SO I SET OFF WALKING TO FIND ONE THAT DID!
THAT WAS HOW I MET MISS MARIAH WATKINS. SHE WAS A NICE LADY WHO OWNED THE BARN I HAD BEEN SLEEPING IN...
I NEVER FORGOT WHAT SHE SAID.
YOU MUST LEARN ALL YOU CAN, THEN GO BACK OUT INTO THE WORLD AND GIVE YOUR LEARNING BACK TO THE PEOPLE.

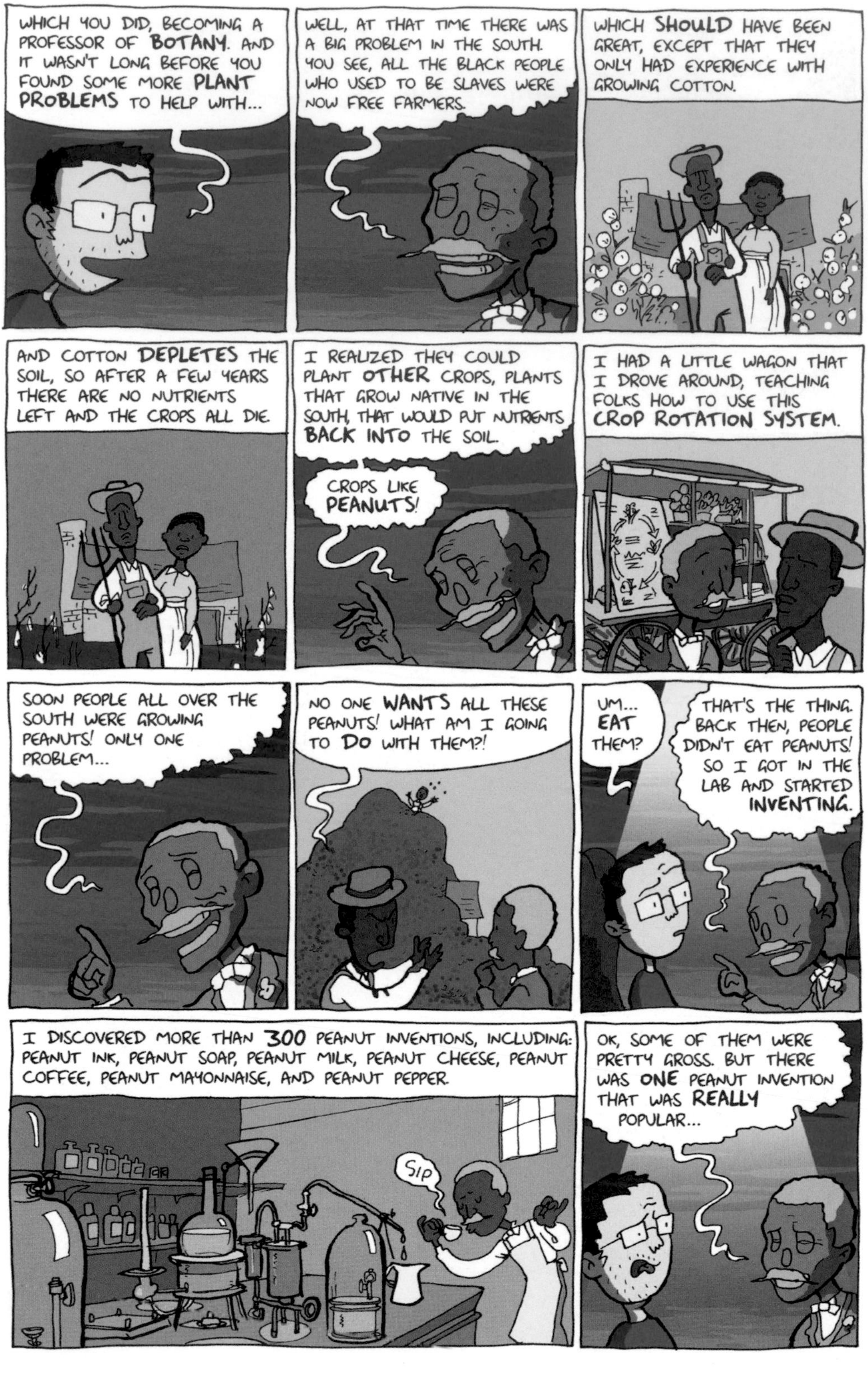
WHICH YOU DID, BECOMING A PROFESSOR OF BOTANY. AND IT WASN'T LONG BEFORE YOU FOUND SOME MORE PLANT PROBLEMS TO HELP WITH...
WELL, AT THAT TIME THERE WAS A BIG PROBLEM IN THE SOUTH. YOU SEE, ALL THE BLACK PEOPLE WHO USED TO BE SLAVES WERE NOW FREE FARMERS.
WHICH SHOULD HAVE BEEN GREAT, EXCEPT THAT THEY ONLY HAD EXPERIENCE WITH GROWING COTTON.
AND COTTON DEPLETES THE SOIL, SO AFTER A FEW YEARS THERE ARE NO NUTRIENTS LEFT AND THE CROPS ALL DIE.
I REALIZED THEY COULD PLANT OTHER CROPS, PLANTS THAT GROW NATIVE IN THE SOUTH, THAT WOULD PUT NUTRIENTS BACK INTO THE SOIL.
CROPS LIKE PEANUTS!
I HAD A LITTLE WAGON THAT I DROVE AROUND, TEACHING FOLKS HOW TO USE THIS CROP ROTATION SYSTEM.
SOON PEOPLE ALL OVER THE SOUTH WERE GROWING PEANUTS! ONLY ONE PROBLEM...
NO ONE WANTS ALL THESE PEANUTS! WHAT AM I GOING TO DO WITH THEM?!
UM... EAT THEM?
THAT'S THE THING. BACK THEN, PEOPLE DIDN'T EAT PEANUTS! SO I GOT IN THE LAB AND STARTED INVENTING.
I DISCOVERED MORE THAN 300 PEANUT INVENTIONS, INCLUDING: PEANUT INK, PEANUT SOAP, PEANUT MILK, PEANUT CHEESE, PEANUT COFFEE, PEANUT MAYONNAISE, AND PEANUT PEPPER.
SIP
OK, SOME OF THEM WERE PRETTY GROSS. BUT THERE WAS ONE PEANUT INVENTION THAT WAS REALLY POPULAR...

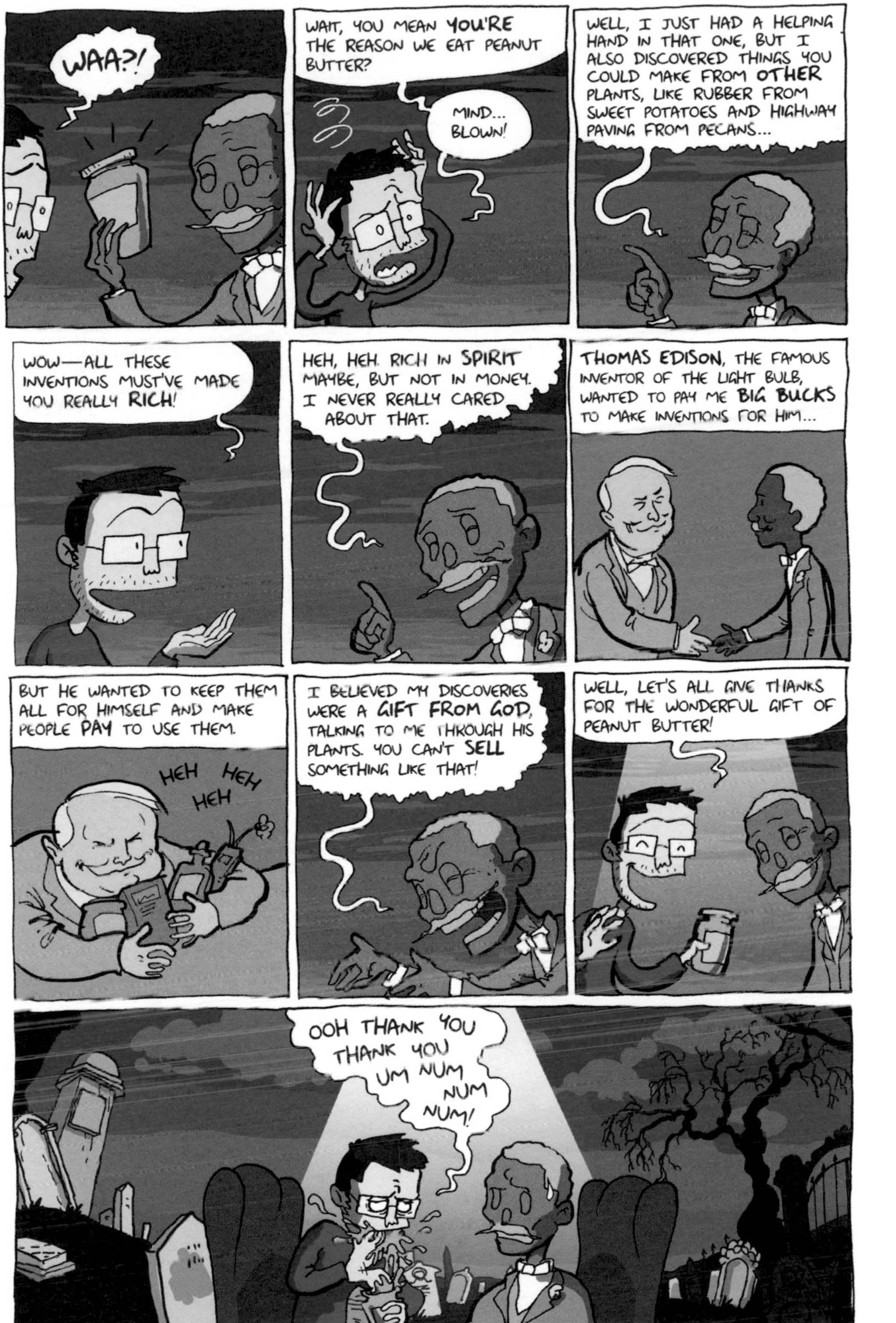
WAA?!
WAIT, YOU MEAN YOU'RE THE REASON WE EAT PEANUT BUTTER?
MIND... BLOWN!
WELL, I JUST HAD A HELPING HAND IN THAT ONE, BUT I ALSO DISCOVERED THINGS YOU COULD MAKE FROM OTHER PLANTS, LIKE RUBBER FROM SWEET POTATOES AND HIGHWAY PAVING FROM PECANS...
WOW—ALL THESE INVENTIONS MUST'VE MADE YOU REALLY RICH!
HEH, HEH. RICH IN SPIRIT MAYBE, BUT NOT IN MONEY. I NEVER REALLY CARED ABOUT THAT.
THOMAS EDISON, THE FAMOUS INVENTOR OF THE LIGHT BULB, WANTED TO PAY ME BIG BUCKS TO MAKE INVENTIONS FOR HIM...
BUT HE WANTED TO KEEP THEM ALL FOR HIMSELF AND MAKE PEOPLE PAY TO USE THEM.
HEH HEH HEH
I BELIEVED MY DISCOVERIES WERE A GIFT FROM GOD, TALKING TO ME THROUGH HIS PLANTS. YOU CAN'T SELL SOMETHING LIKE THAT!
WELL, LET'S ALL GIVE THANKS FOR THE WONDERFUL GIFT OF PEANUT BUTTER!
OOH THANK YOU THANK YOU UM NUM NUM NUM!

NUTS ABOUT NUTS!

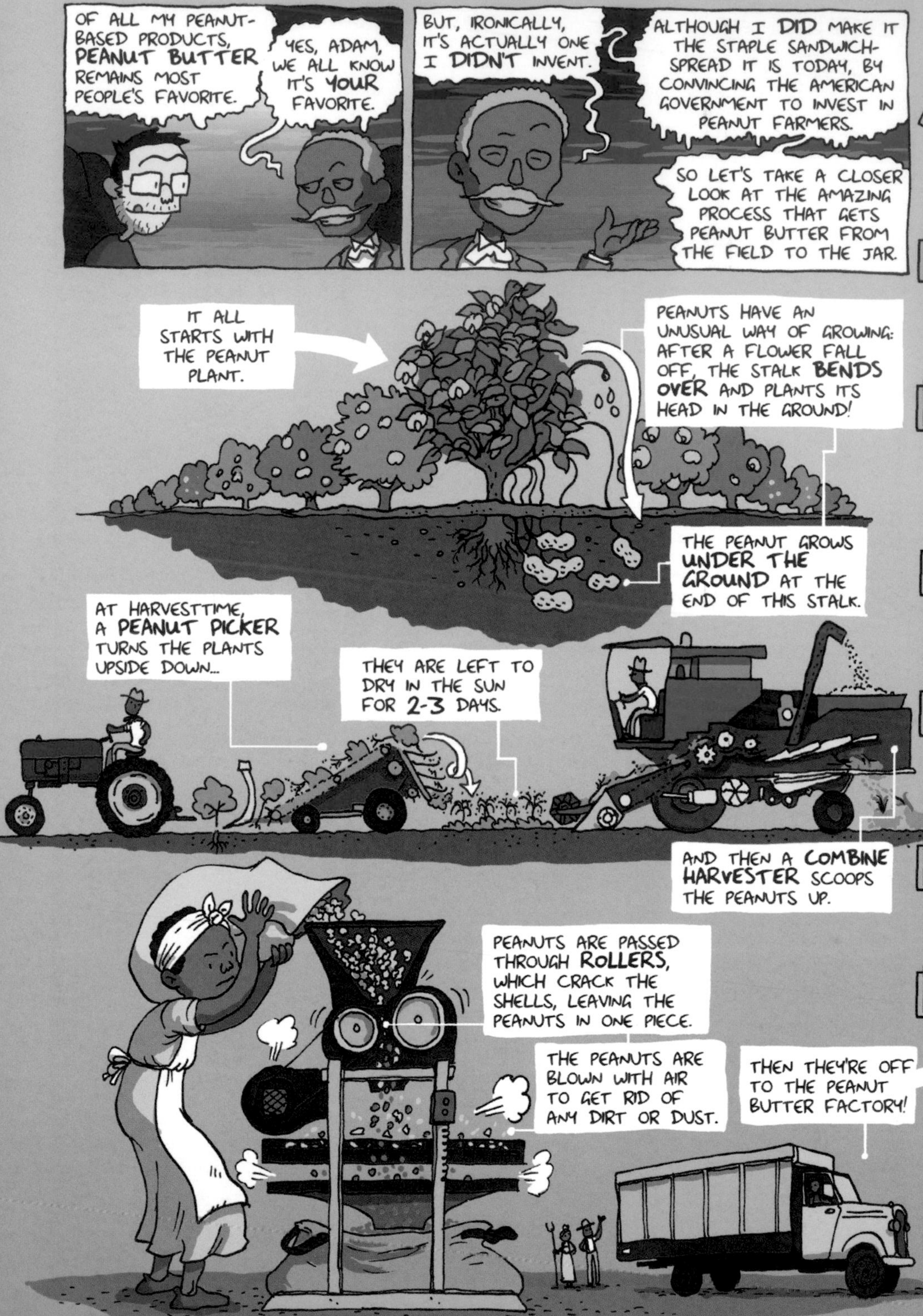

OF ALL MY PEANUT-BASED PRODUCTS, PEANUT BUTTER REMAINS MOST PEOPLE'S FAVORITE.
YES, ADAM, WE ALL KNOW IT'S YOUR FAVORITE.
BUT, IRONICALLY, IT'S ACTUALLY ONE I DIDN'T INVENT.
ALTHOUGH I DID MAKE IT THE STAPLE SANDWICH-SPREAD IT IS TODAY, BY CONVINCING THE AMERICAN GOVERNMENT TO INVEST IN PEANUT FARMERS.
SO LET'S TAKE A CLOSER LOOK AT THE AMAZING PROCESS THAT GETS PEANUT BUTTER FROM THE FIELD TO THE JAR.
IT ALL STARTS WITH THE PEANUT PLANT.
PEANUTS HAVE AN UNUSUAL WAY OF GROWING: AFTER A FLOWER FALL OFF, THE STALK BENDS OVER AND PLANTS ITS HEAD IN THE GROUND!
THE PEANUT GROWS UNDER THE GROUND AT THE END OF THIS STALK.
AT HARVESTTIME, A PEANUT PICKER TURNS THE PLANTS UPSIDE DOWN...
THEY ARE LEFT TO DRY IN THE SUN FOR 2-3 DAYS.
AND THEN A COMBINE HARVESTER SCOOPS THE PEANUTS UP.
PEANUTS ARE PASSED THROUGH ROLLERS, WHICH CRACK THE SHELLS, LEAVING THE PEANUTS IN ONE PIECE.
THE PEANUTS ARE BLOWN WITH AIR TO GET RID OF ANY DIRT OR DUST.
THEN THEY'RE OFF TO THE PEANUT BUTTER FACTORY!

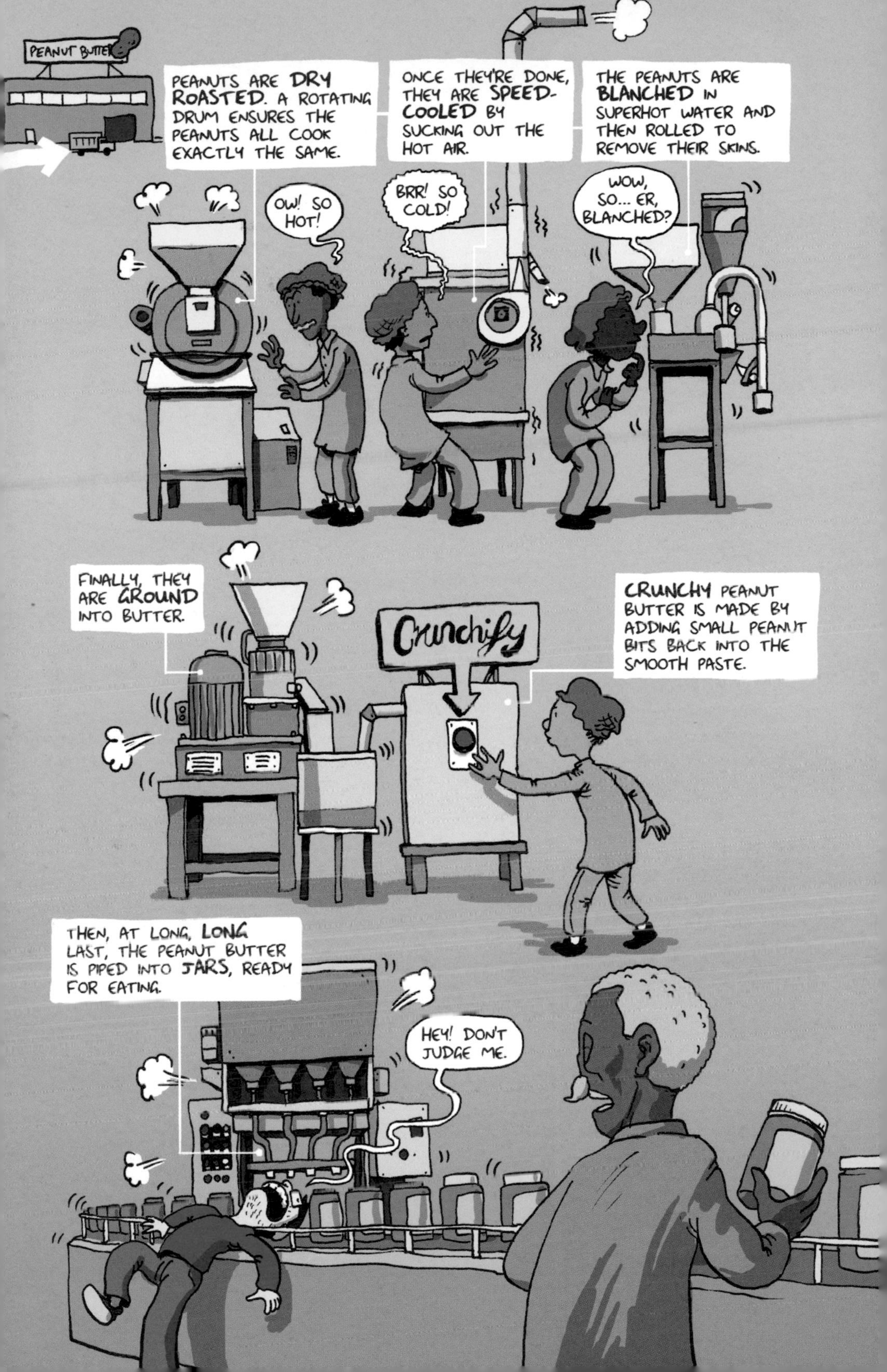
PEANUT BUTTER
PEANUTS ARE DRY ROASTED. A ROTATING DRUM ENSURES THE PEANUTS ALL COOK EXACTLY THE SAME.
OW! SO HOT!
ONCE THEY'RE DONE, THEY ARE SPEED-COOLED BY SUCKING OUT THE HOT AIR.
BRR! SO COLD!
THE PEANUTS ARE BLANCHED IN SUPERHOT WATER AND THEN ROLLED TO REMOVE THEIR SKINS.
WOW, SO... ER, BLANCHED?
FINALLY, THEY ARE GROUND INTO BUTTER.
Crunchify
CRUNCHY PEANUT BUTTER IS MADE BY ADDING SMALL PEANUT BITS BACK INTO THE SMOOTH PASTE.
THEN, AT LONG, LONG LAST, THE PEANUT BUTTER IS PIPED INTO JARS, READY FOR EATING.
HEY! DON'T JUDGE ME.

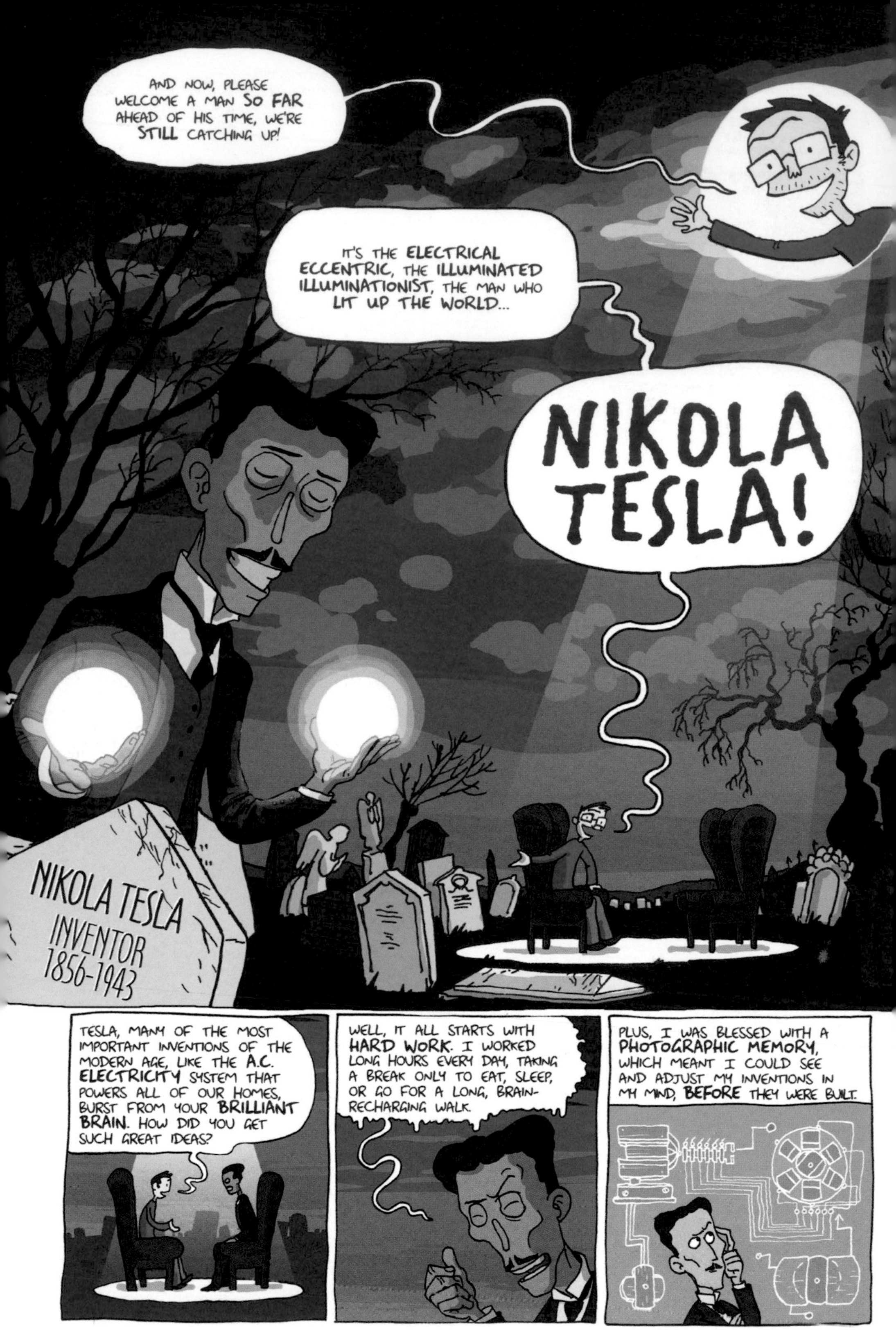
AND NOW, PLEASE WELCOME A MAN SO FAR AHEAD OF HIS TIME, WE'RE STILL CATCHING UP!
IT'S THE ELECTRICAL ECCENTRIC, THE ILLUMINATED ILLUMINATIONIST, THE MAN WHO LIT UP THE WORLD...
NIKOLA TESLA!
NIKOLA TESLA
INVENTOR
1856-1943
TESLA, MANY OF THE MOST IMPORTANT INVENTIONS OF THE MODERN AGE, LIKE THE A.C. ELECTRICITY SYSTEM THAT POWERS ALL OF OUR HOMES, BURST FROM YOUR BRILLIANT BRAIN. HOW DID YOU GET SUCH GREAT IDEAS?
WELL, IT ALL STARTS WITH HARD WORK. I WORKED LONG HOURS EVERY DAY, TAKING A BREAK ONLY TO EAT, SLEEP, OR GO FOR A LONG, BRAIN-RECHARGING WALK.
PLUS, I WAS BLESSED WITH A PHOTOGRAPHIC MEMORY, WHICH MEANT I COULD SEE AND ADJUST MY INVENTIONS IN MY MIND, BEFORE THEY WERE BUILT.

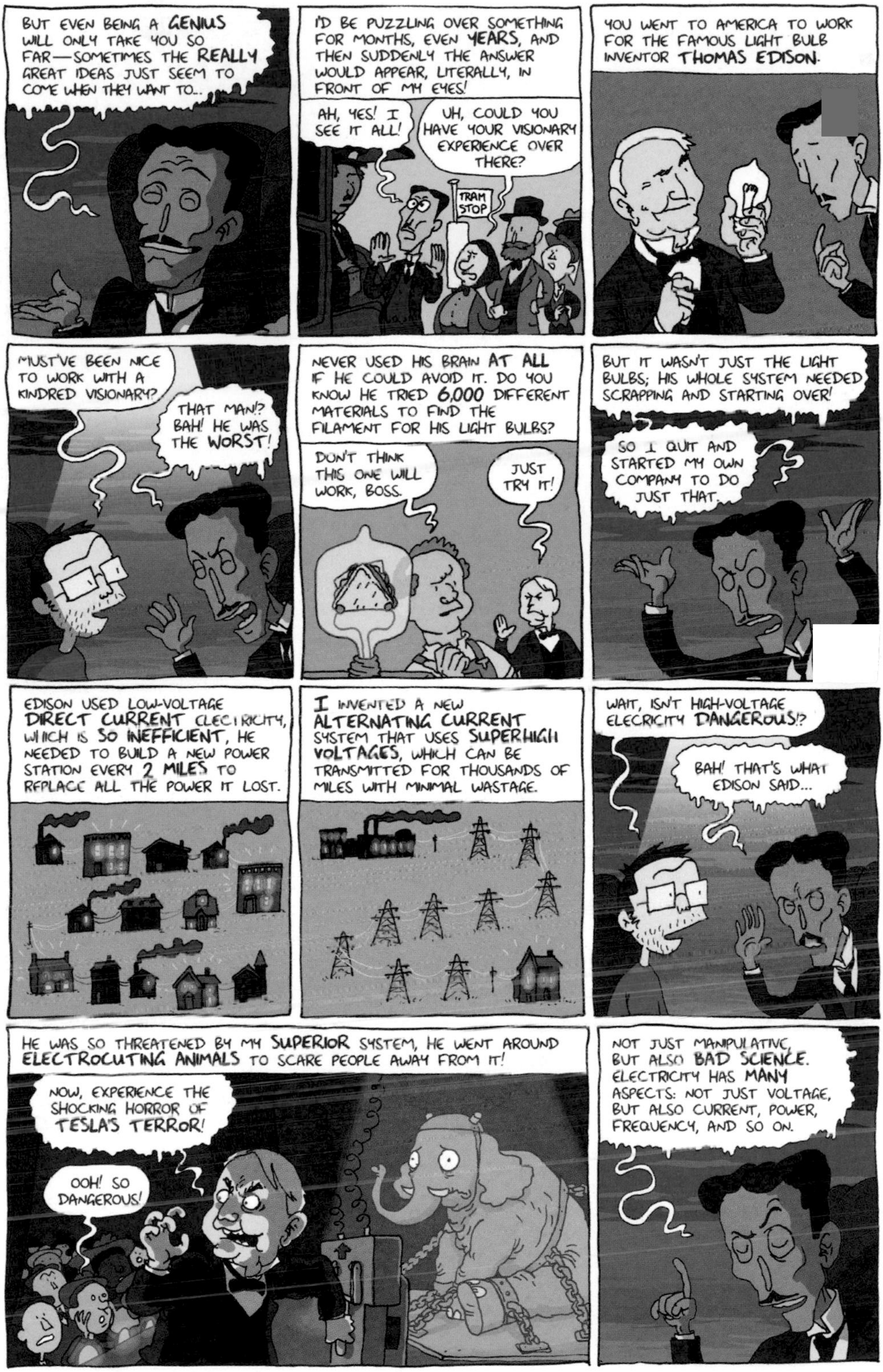

BUT EVEN BEING A GENIUS WILL ONLY TAKE YOU SO FAR—SOMETIMES THE REALLY GREAT IDEAS JUST SEEM TO COME WHEN THEY WANT TO...
I'D BE PUZZLING OVER SOMETHING FOR MONTHS, EVEN YEARS, AND THEN SUDDENLY THE ANSWER WOULD APPEAR, LITERALLY, IN FRONT OF MY EYES!
AH, YES! I SEE IT ALL!
UH, COULD YOU HAVE YOUR VISIONARY EXPERIENCE OVER THERE?
TRAM STOP
YOU WENT TO AMERICA TO WORK FOR THE FAMOUS LIGHT BULB INVENTOR THOMAS EDISON.
MUST'VE BEEN NICE TO WORK WITH A KINDRED VISIONARY?
THAT MAN!? BAH! HE WAS THE WORST!
NEVER USED HIS BRAIN AT ALL IF HE COULD AVOID IT. DO YOU KNOW HE TRIED 6,000 DIFFERENT MATERIALS TO FIND THE FILAMENT FOR HIS LIGHT BULBS?
DON'T THINK THIS ONE WILL WORK, BOSS.
JUST TRY IT!
BUT IT WASN'T JUST THE LIGHT BULBS; HIS WHOLE SYSTEM NEEDED SCRAPPING AND STARTING OVER!
SO I QUIT AND STARTED MY OWN COMPANY TO DO JUST THAT.
EDISON USED LOW-VOLTAGE DIRECT CURRENT ELECTRICITY, WHICH IS SO INEFFICIENT, HE NEEDED TO BUILD A NEW POWER STATION EVERY 2 MILES TO REPLACE ALL THE POWER IT LOST.
I INVENTED A NEW ALTERNATING CURRENT SYSTEM THAT USES SUPERHIGH VOLTAGES, WHICH CAN BE TRANSMITTED FOR THOUSANDS OF MILES WITH MINIMAL WASTAGE.
WAIT, ISN'T HIGH-VOLTAGE ELECRICITY DANGEROUS!?
BAH! THAT'S WHAT EDISON SAID...
HE WAS SO THREATENED BY MY SUPERIOR SYSTEM, HE WENT AROUND ELECTROCUTING ANIMALS TO SCARE PEOPLE AWAY FROM IT!
NOW, EXPERIENCE THE SHOCKING HORROR OF TESLA'S TERROR!
OOH! SO DANGEROUS!
NOT JUST MANIPULATIVE, BUT ALSO BAD SCIENCE. ELECTRICITY HAS MANY ASPECTS: NOT JUST VOLTAGE, BUT ALSO CURRENT, POWER, FREQUENCY, AND SO ON.

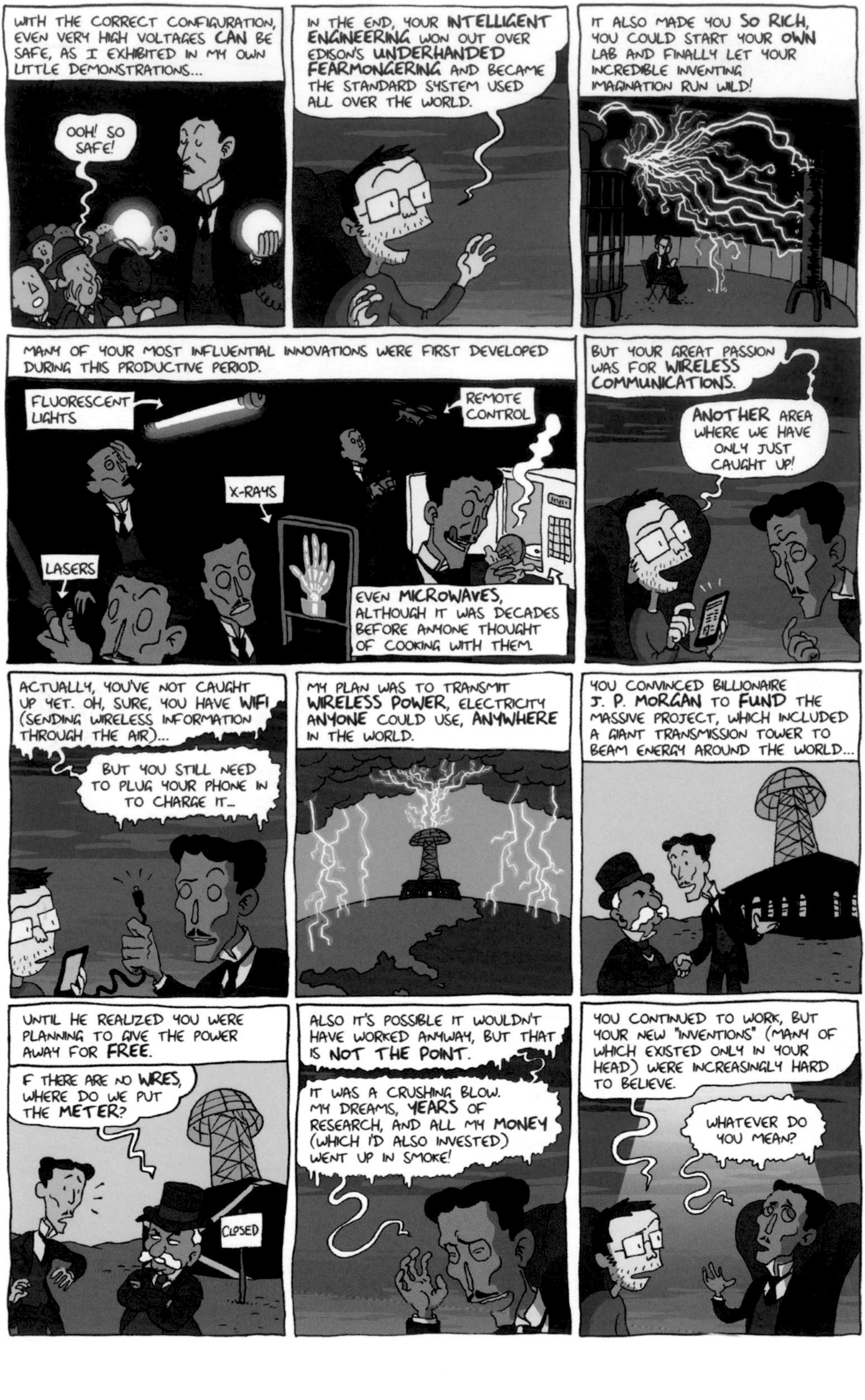

WITH THE CORRECT CONFIGURATION, EVEN VERY HIGH VOLTAGES **CAN** BE SAFE, AS I EXHIBITED IN MY OWN LITTLE DEMONSTRATIONS...
OOH! SO SAFE!
IN THE END, YOUR **INTELLIGENT ENGINEERING** WON OUT OVER EDISON'S **UNDERHANDED FEARMONGERING** AND BECAME THE STANDARD SYSTEM USED ALL OVER THE WORLD.
IT ALSO MADE YOU **SO RICH**, YOU COULD START YOUR **OWN** LAB AND FINALLY LET YOUR INCREDIBLE INVENTING IMAGINATION RUN WILD!
MANY OF YOUR MOST INFLUENTIAL INNOVATIONS WERE FIRST DEVELOPED DURING THIS PRODUCTIVE PERIOD.
FLUORESCENT LIGHTS
REMOTE CONTROL
X-RAYS
LASERS
EVEN **MICROWAVES**, ALTHOUGH IT WAS DECADES BEFORE ANYONE THOUGHT OF COOKING WITH THEM.
BUT YOUR GREAT PASSION WAS FOR **WIRELESS COMMUNICATIONS**.
ANOTHER AREA WHERE WE HAVE ONLY JUST CAUGHT UP!
ACTUALLY, YOU'VE NOT CAUGHT UP YET. OH, SURE, YOU HAVE **WIFI** (SENDING WIRELESS INFORMATION THROUGH THE AIR)...
BUT YOU STILL NEED TO PLUG YOUR PHONE IN TO CHARGE IT...
MY PLAN WAS TO TRANSMIT **WIRELESS POWER**, ELECTRICITY **ANYONE** COULD USE, **ANYWHERE** IN THE WORLD.
YOU CONVINCED BILLIONAIRE **J. P. MORGAN** TO **FUND** THE MASSIVE PROJECT, WHICH INCLUDED A GIANT TRANSMISSION TOWER TO BEAM ENERGY AROUND THE WORLD...
UNTIL HE REALIZED YOU WERE PLANNING TO GIVE THE POWER AWAY FOR **FREE**.
IF THERE ARE NO **WIRES**, WHERE DO WE PUT THE **METER**?
CLOSED
ALSO IT'S POSSIBLE IT WOULDN'T HAVE WORKED ANYWAY, BUT THAT IS **NOT THE POINT**.
IT WAS A CRUSHING BLOW. MY DREAMS, **YEARS** OF RESEARCH, AND ALL MY **MONEY** (WHICH I'D ALSO INVESTED) WENT UP IN SMOKE!
YOU CONTINUED TO WORK, BUT YOUR NEW "INVENTIONS" (MANY OF WHICH EXISTED ONLY IN YOUR HEAD) WERE INCREASINGLY HARD TO BELIEVE.
WHATEVER DO YOU MEAN?

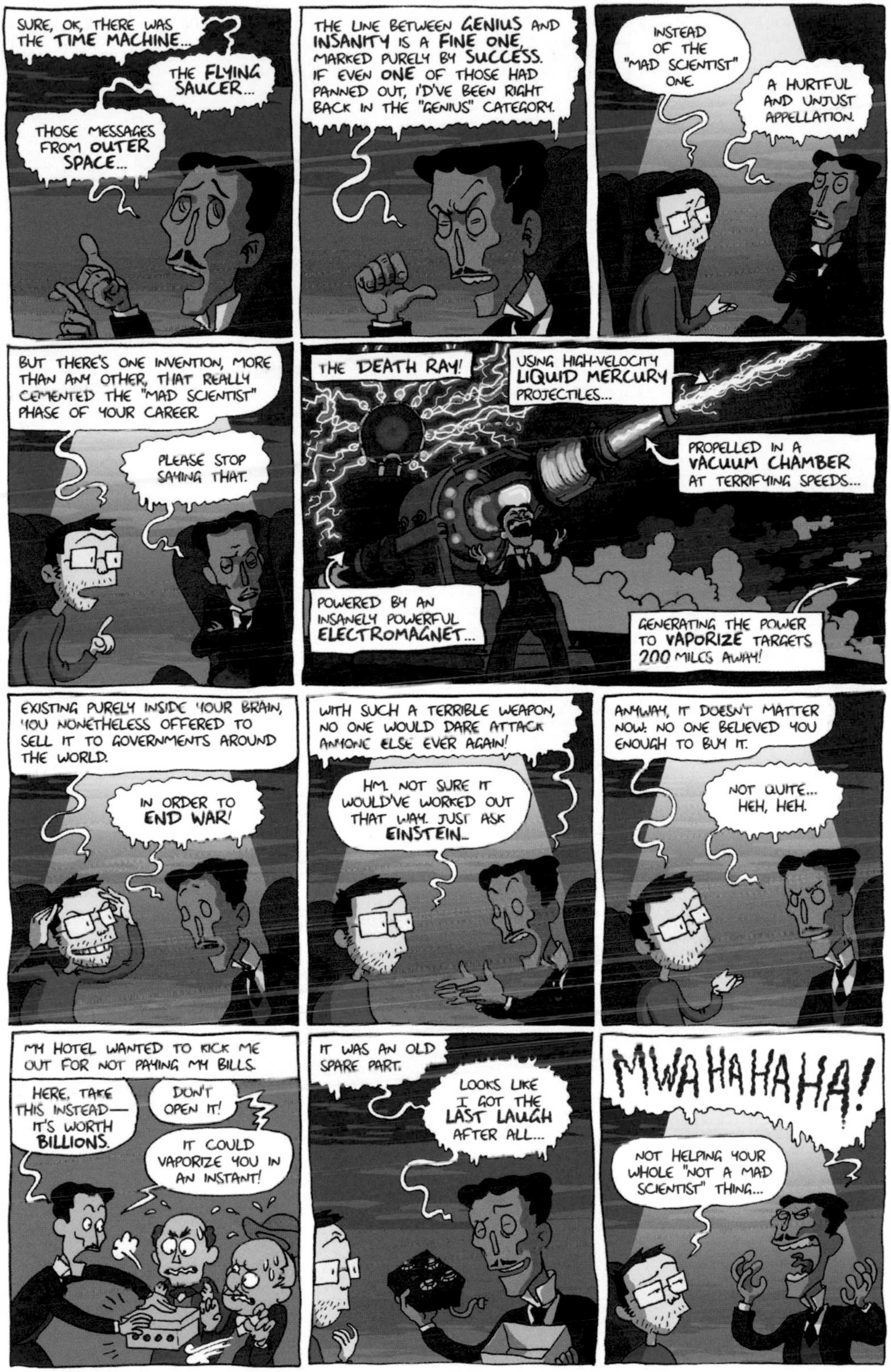
SURE, OK, THERE WAS THE TIME MACHINE...
THE FLYING SAUCER...
THOSE MESSAGES FROM OUTER SPACE...
THE LINE BETWEEN GENIUS AND INSANITY IS A FINE ONE, MARKED PURELY BY SUCCESS. IF EVEN ONE OF THOSE HAD PANNED OUT, I'D'VE BEEN RIGHT BACK IN THE "GENIUS" CATEGORY.
INSTEAD OF THE "MAD SCIENTIST" ONE.
A HURTFUL AND UNJUST APPELLATION.
BUT THERE'S ONE INVENTION, MORE THAN ANY OTHER, THAT REALLY CEMENTED THE "MAD SCIENTIST" PHASE OF YOUR CAREER.
PLEASE STOP SAYING THAT.
THE DEATH RAY!
USING HIGH-VELOCITY LIQUID MERCURY PROJECTILES...
PROPELLED IN A VACUUM CHAMBER AT TERRIFYING SPEEDS...
POWERED BY AN INSANELY POWERFUL ELECTROMAGNET...
GENERATING THE POWER TO VAPORIZE TARGETS 200 MILES AWAY!
EXISTING PURELY INSIDE YOUR BRAIN, YOU NONETHELESS OFFERED TO SELL IT TO GOVERNMENTS AROUND THE WORLD.
IN ORDER TO END WAR!
WITH SUCH A TERRIBLE WEAPON, NO ONE WOULD DARE ATTACK ANYONE ELSE EVER AGAIN!
HM. NOT SURE IT WOULD'VE WORKED OUT THAT WAY. JUST ASK EINSTEIN...
ANYWAY, IT DOESN'T MATTER NOW: NO ONE BELIEVED YOU ENOUGH TO BUY IT.
NOT QUITE... HEH, HEH.
MY HOTEL WANTED TO KICK ME OUT FOR NOT PAYING MY BILLS.
HERE, TAKE THIS INSTEAD— IT'S WORTH BILLIONS.
DON'T OPEN IT!
IT COULD VAPORIZE YOU IN AN INSTANT!
IT WAS AN OLD SPARE PART.
LOOKS LIKE I GOT THE LAST LAUGH AFTER ALL...
MWAHAHAHA!
NOT HELPING YOUR WHOLE "NOT A MAD SCIENTIST" THING...

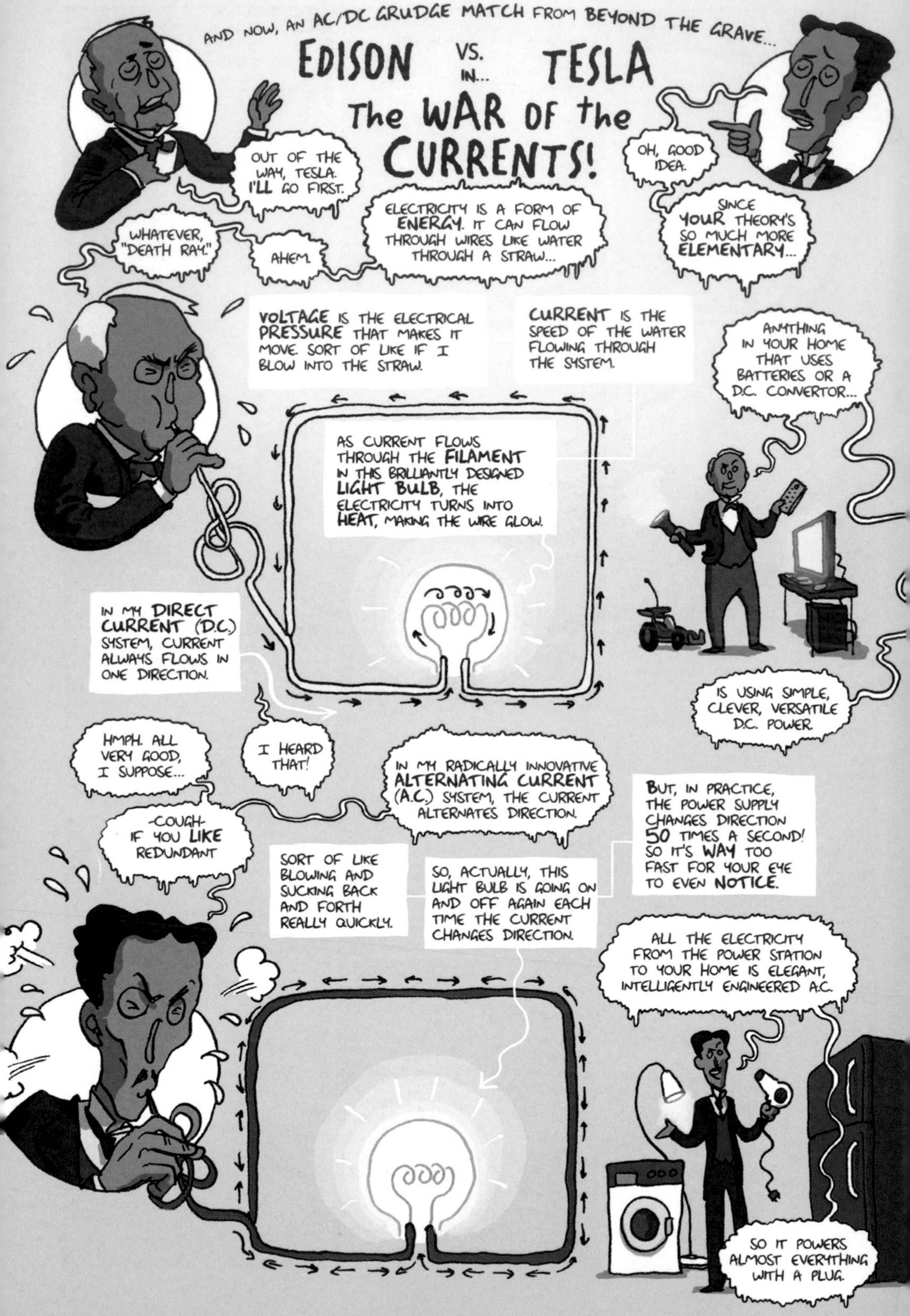
AND NOW, AN AC/DC GRUDGE MATCH FROM BEYOND THE GRAVE...
EDISON VS. TESLA IN... The WAR OF the CURRENTS!
OUT OF THE WAY, TESLA. I'LL GO FIRST.
OH, GOOD IDEA.
WHATEVER, "DEATH RAY."
AHEM.
ELECTRICITY IS A FORM OF ENERGY. IT CAN FLOW THROUGH WIRES LIKE WATER THROUGH A STRAW...
SINCE YOUR THEORY'S SO MUCH MORE ELEMENTARY...
VOLTAGE IS THE ELECTRICAL PRESSURE THAT MAKES IT MOVE. SORT OF LIKE IF I BLOW INTO THE STRAW.
CURRENT IS THE SPEED OF THE WATER FLOWING THROUGH THE SYSTEM.
ANYTHING IN YOUR HOME THAT USES BATTERIES OR A D.C. CONVERTOR...
AS CURRENT FLOWS THROUGH THE FILAMENT IN THIS BRILLIANTLY DESIGNED LIGHT BULB, THE ELECTRICITY TURNS INTO HEAT, MAKING THE WIRE GLOW.
IN MY DIRECT CURRENT (D.C.) SYSTEM, CURRENT ALWAYS FLOWS IN ONE DIRECTION.
IS USING SIMPLE, CLEVER, VERSATILE D.C. POWER.
HMPH. ALL VERY GOOD, I SUPPOSE...
I HEARD THAT!
IN MY RADICALLY INNOVATIVE ALTERNATING CURRENT (A.C.) SYSTEM, THE CURRENT ALTERNATES DIRECTION.
-COUGH- IF YOU LIKE REDUNDANT
BUT, IN PRACTICE, THE POWER SUPPLY CHANGES DIRECTION 50 TIMES A SECOND! SO IT'S WAY TOO FAST FOR YOUR EYE TO EVEN NOTICE.
SORT OF LIKE BLOWING AND SUCKING BACK AND FORTH REALLY QUICKLY.
SO, ACTUALLY, THIS LIGHT BULB IS GOING ON AND OFF AGAIN EACH TIME THE CURRENT CHANGES DIRECTION.
ALL THE ELECTRICITY FROM THE POWER STATION TO YOUR HOME IS ELEGANT, INTELLIGENTLY ENGINEERED A.C.
SO IT POWERS ALMOST EVERYTHING WITH A PLUG.

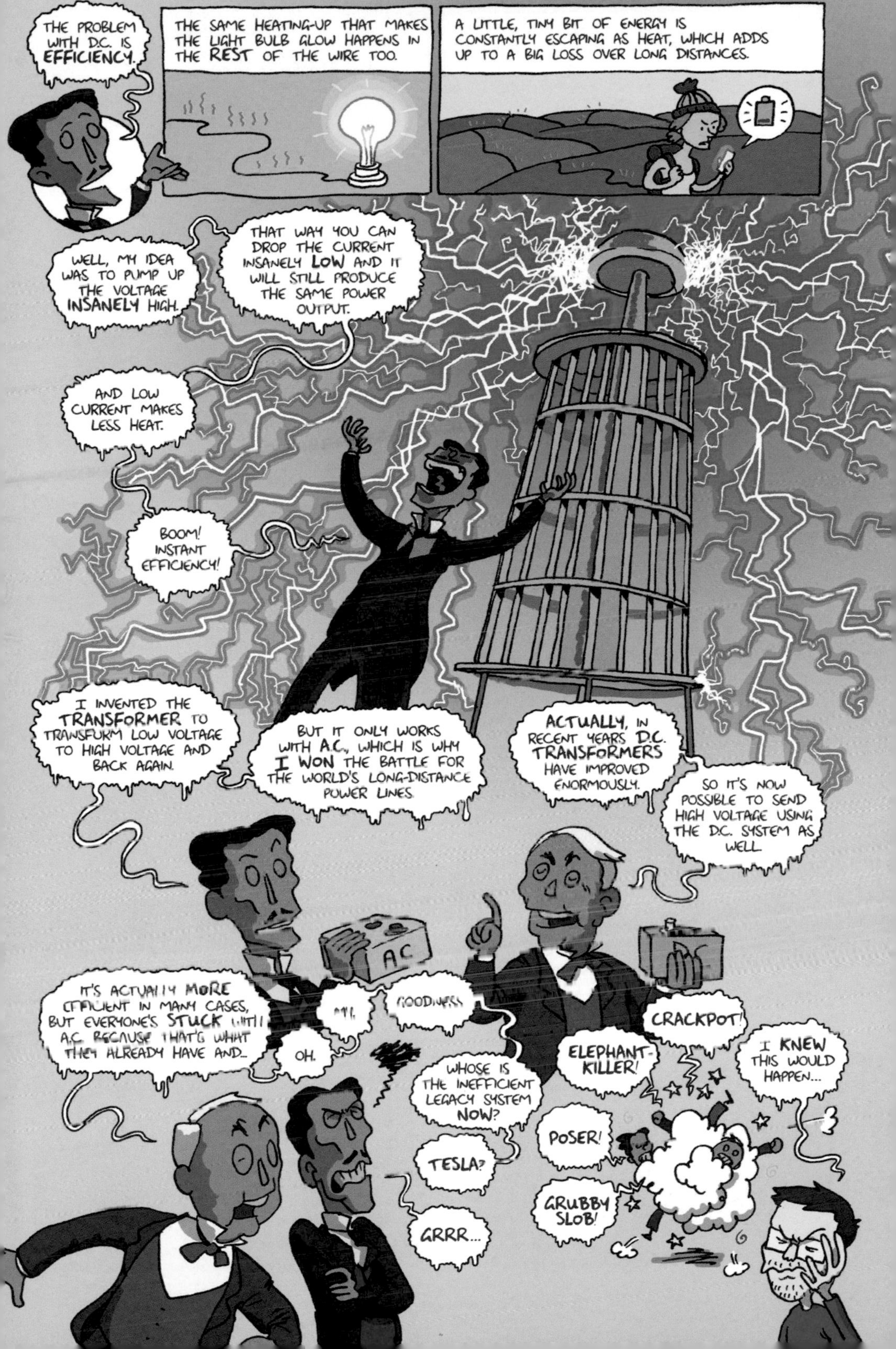

THE PROBLEM WITH D.C. IS **EFFICIENCY**.
THE SAME HEATING-UP THAT MAKES THE LIGHT BULB GLOW HAPPENS IN THE **REST** OF THE WIRE TOO.
A LITTLE, TINY BIT OF ENERGY IS CONSTANTLY ESCAPING AS HEAT, WHICH ADDS UP TO A BIG LOSS OVER LONG DISTANCES.
WELL, MY IDEA WAS TO PUMP UP THE VOLTAGE **INSANELY** HIGH.
THAT WAY YOU CAN DROP THE CURRENT INSANELY **LOW** AND IT WILL STILL PRODUCE THE SAME POWER OUTPUT.
AND LOW CURRENT MAKES LESS HEAT.
BOOM! INSTANT EFFICIENCY!
I INVENTED THE **TRANSFORMER** TO TRANSFORM LOW VOLTAGE TO HIGH VOLTAGE AND BACK AGAIN.
BUT IT ONLY WORKS WITH **A.C.**, WHICH IS WHY **I WON** THE BATTLE FOR THE WORLD'S LONG-DISTANCE POWER LINES.
ACTUALLY, IN RECENT YEARS **D.C. TRANSFORMERS** HAVE IMPROVED ENORMOUSLY.
SO IT'S NOW POSSIBLE TO SEND HIGH VOLTAGE USING THE D.C. SYSTEM AS WELL.
AC
IT'S ACTUALLY **MORE** EFFICIENT IN MANY CASES, BUT EVERYONE'S **STUCK** WITH A.C. BECAUSE THAT'S WHAT THEY ALREADY HAVE AND...
GOODNESS
OH.
WHOSE IS THE INEFFICIENT LEGACY SYSTEM **NOW**?
CRACKPOT!
ELEPHANT-KILLER!
I **KNEW** THIS WOULD HAPPEN...
TESLA?
POSER!
GRUBBY SLOB!
GRRR...

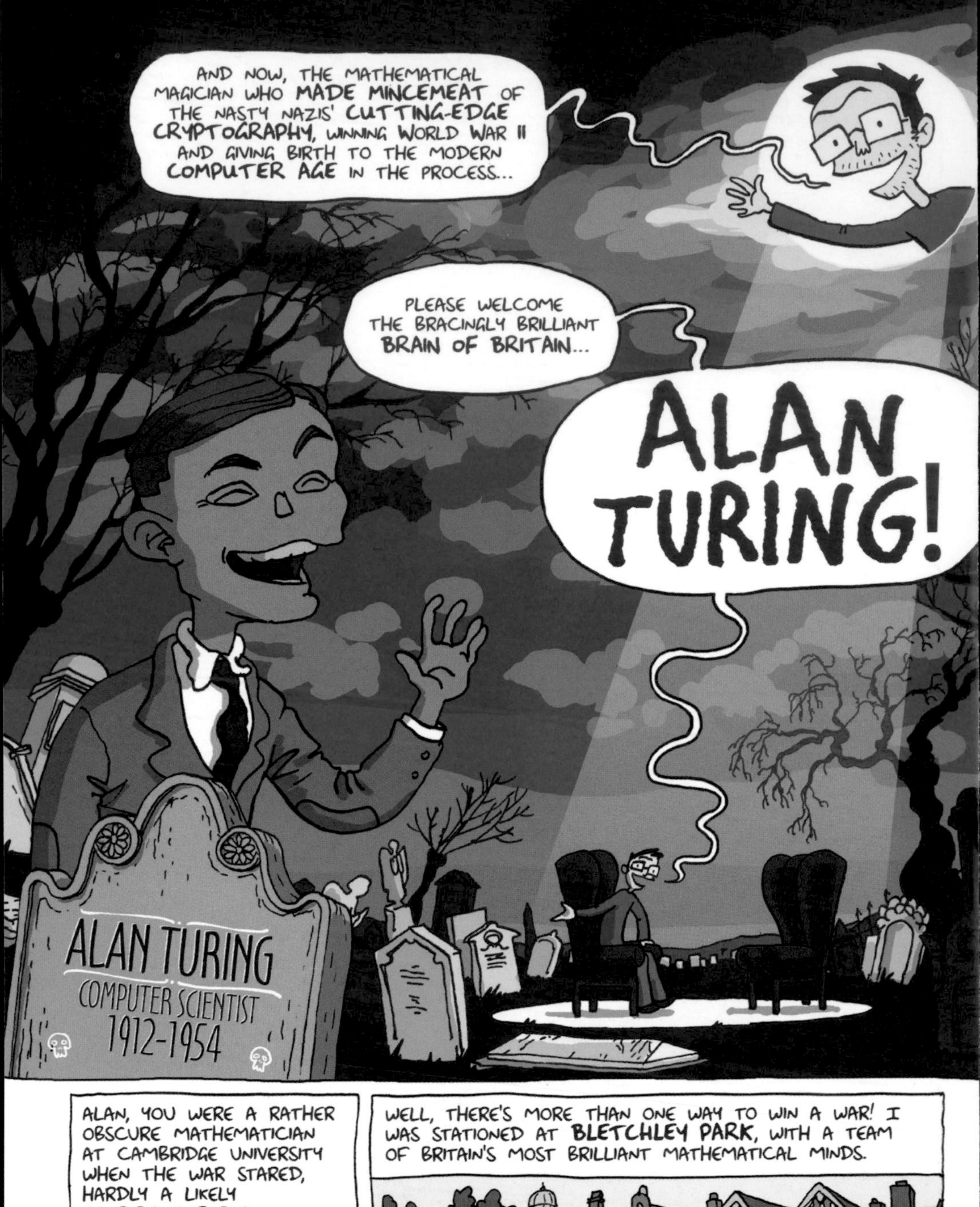
AND NOW, THE MATHEMATICAL MAGICIAN WHO MADE MINCEMEAT OF THE NASTY NAZIS' CUTTING-EDGE CRYPTOGRAPHY, WINNING WORLD WAR II AND GIVING BIRTH TO THE MODERN COMPUTER AGE IN THE PROCESS...
PLEASE WELCOME THE BRACINGLY BRILLIANT BRAIN OF BRITAIN...
ALAN TURING!
ALAN TURING
COMPUTER SCIENTIST
1912-1954
ALAN, YOU WERE A RATHER OBSCURE MATHEMATICIAN AT CAMBRIDGE UNIVERSITY WHEN THE WAR STARED, HARDLY A LIKELY CANDIDATE FOR A NAZI-SMASHING HERO!
WELL, THERE'S MORE THAN ONE WAY TO WIN A WAR! I WAS STATIONED AT BLETCHLEY PARK, WITH A TEAM OF BRITAIN'S MOST BRILLIANT MATHEMATICAL MINDS.

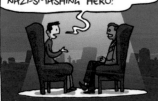

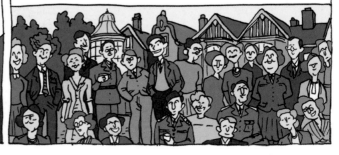

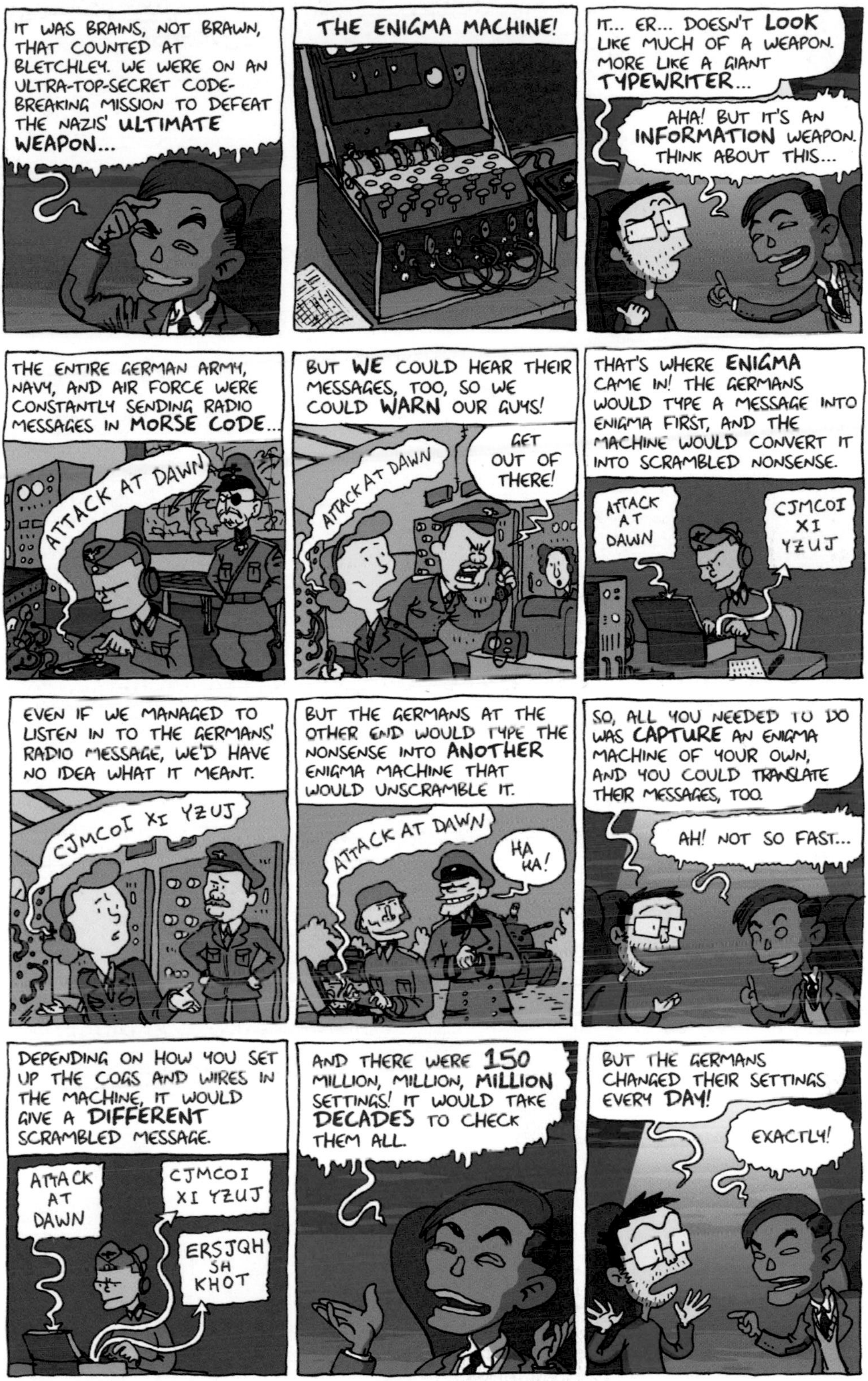
IT WAS BRAINS, NOT BRAWN, THAT COUNTED AT BLETCHLEY. WE WERE ON AN ULTRA-TOP-SECRET CODE-BREAKING MISSION TO DEFEAT THE NAZIS' ULTIMATE WEAPON...
THE ENIGMA MACHINE!
IT... ER... DOESN'T LOOK LIKE MUCH OF A WEAPON. MORE LIKE A GIANT TYPEWRITER...
AHA! BUT IT'S AN INFORMATION WEAPON. THINK ABOUT THIS...
THE ENTIRE GERMAN ARMY, NAVY, AND AIR FORCE WERE CONSTANTLY SENDING RADIO MESSAGES IN MORSE CODE...
ATTACK AT DAWN
BUT WE COULD HEAR THEIR MESSAGES, TOO, SO WE COULD WARN OUR GUYS!
ATTACK AT DAWN
GET OUT OF THERE!
THAT'S WHERE ENIGMA CAME IN! THE GERMANS WOULD TYPE A MESSAGE INTO ENIGMA FIRST, AND THE MACHINE WOULD CONVERT IT INTO SCRAMBLED NONSENSE.
ATTACK AT DAWN
CJMCOI XI YZUJ
EVEN IF WE MANAGED TO LISTEN IN TO THE GERMANS' RADIO MESSAGE, WE'D HAVE NO IDEA WHAT IT MEANT.
CJMCOI XI YZUJ
BUT THE GERMANS AT THE OTHER END WOULD TYPE THE NONSENSE INTO ANOTHER ENIGMA MACHINE THAT WOULD UNSCRAMBLE IT.
ATTACK AT DAWN
HA HA!
SO, ALL YOU NEEDED TO DO WAS CAPTURE AN ENIGMA MACHINE OF YOUR OWN, AND YOU COULD TRANSLATE THEIR MESSAGES, TOO.
AH! NOT SO FAST...
DEPENDING ON HOW YOU SET UP THE COGS AND WIRES IN THE MACHINE, IT WOULD GIVE A DIFFERENT SCRAMBLED MESSAGE.
ATTACK AT DAWN
CJMCOI XI YZUJ
ERSJQH SH KHOT
AND THERE WERE 150 MILLION, MILLION, MILLION SETTINGS! IT WOULD TAKE DECADES TO CHECK THEM ALL.
BUT THE GERMANS CHANGED THEIR SETTINGS EVERY DAY!
EXACTLY!

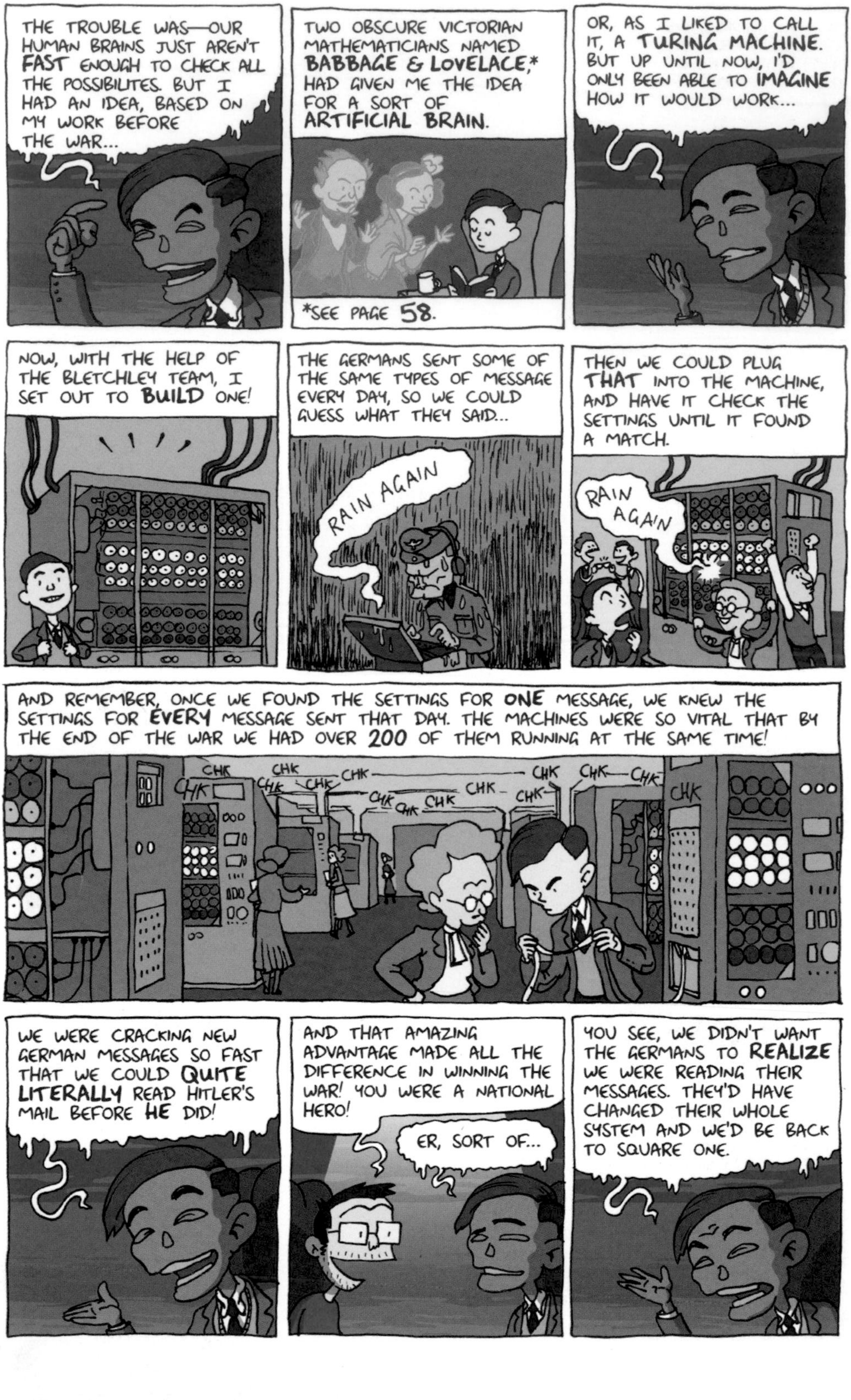
THE TROUBLE WAS—OUR HUMAN BRAINS JUST AREN'T FAST ENOUGH TO CHECK ALL THE POSSIBILITES. BUT I HAD AN IDEA, BASED ON MY WORK BEFORE THE WAR...
TWO OBSCURE VICTORIAN MATHEMATICIANS NAMED BABBAGE & LOVELACE,* HAD GIVEN ME THE IDEA FOR A SORT OF ARTIFICIAL BRAIN.
*SEE PAGE 58.
OR, AS I LIKED TO CALL IT, A TURING MACHINE. BUT UP UNTIL NOW, I'D ONLY BEEN ABLE TO IMAGINE HOW IT WOULD WORK...
NOW, WITH THE HELP OF THE BLETCHLEY TEAM, I SET OUT TO BUILD ONE!
THE GERMANS SENT SOME OF THE SAME TYPES OF MESSAGE EVERY DAY, SO WE COULD GUESS WHAT THEY SAID...
RAIN AGAIN
THEN WE COULD PLUG THAT INTO THE MACHINE, AND HAVE IT CHECK THE SETTINGS UNTIL IT FOUND A MATCH.
RAIN AGAIN
AND REMEMBER, ONCE WE FOUND THE SETTINGS FOR ONE MESSAGE, WE KNEW THE SETTINGS FOR EVERY MESSAGE SENT THAT DAY. THE MACHINES WERE SO VITAL THAT BY THE END OF THE WAR WE HAD OVER 200 OF THEM RUNNING AT THE SAME TIME!
CHK CHK CHK CHK CHK CHK CHK CHK CHK CHK CHK CHK CHK CHK CHK
WE WERE CRACKING NEW GERMAN MESSAGES SO FAST THAT WE COULD QUITE LITERALLY READ HITLER'S MAIL BEFORE HE DID!
AND THAT AMAZING ADVANTAGE MADE ALL THE DIFFERENCE IN WINNING THE WAR! YOU WERE A NATIONAL HERO!
ER, SORT OF...
YOU SEE, WE DIDN'T WANT THE GERMANS TO REALIZE WE WERE READING THEIR MESSAGES. THEY'D HAVE CHANGED THEIR WHOLE SYSTEM AND WE'D BE BACK TO SQUARE ONE.

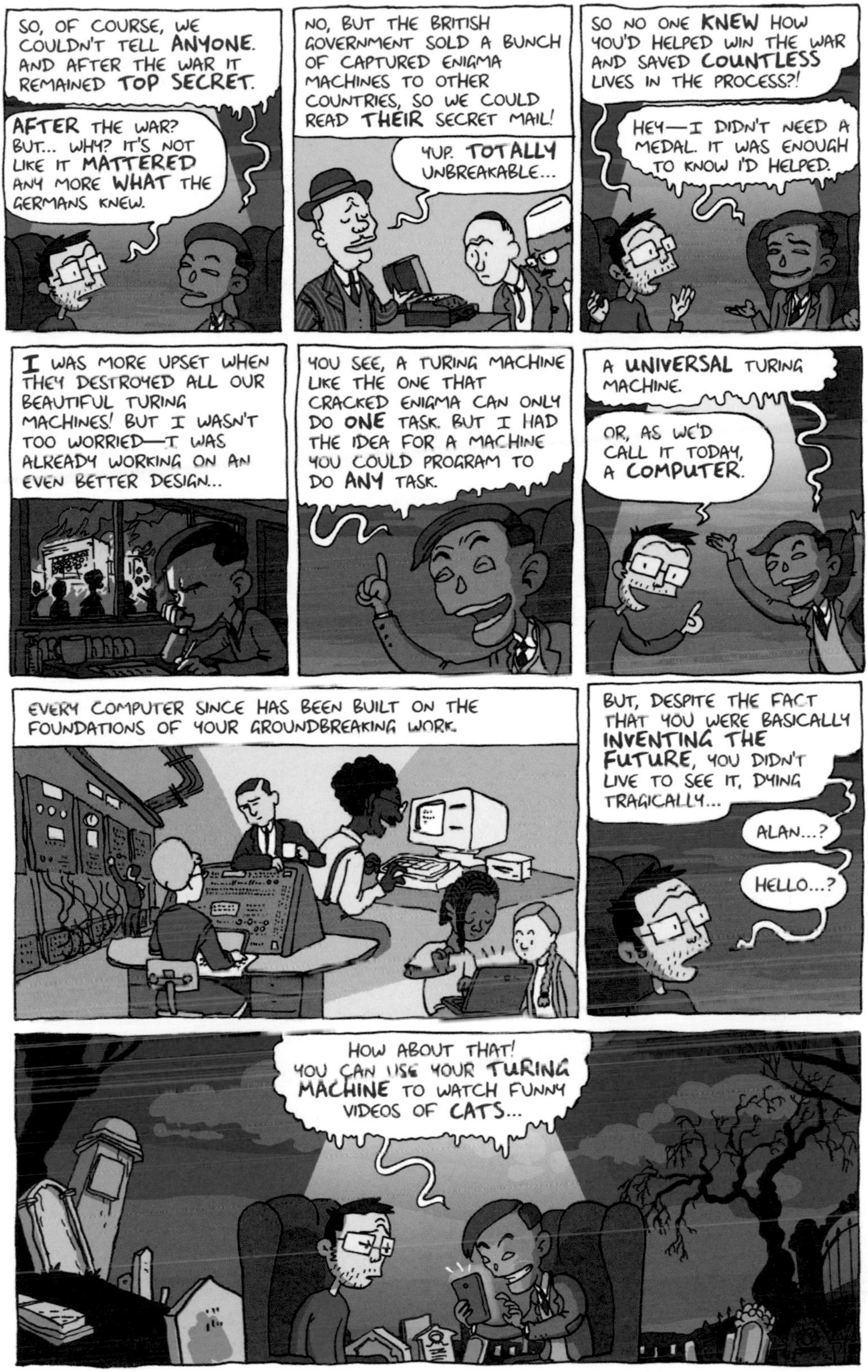
SO, OF COURSE, WE COULDN'T TELL ANYONE. AND AFTER THE WAR IT REMAINED TOP SECRET.
AFTER THE WAR? BUT... WHY? IT'S NOT LIKE IT MATTERED ANY MORE WHAT THE GERMANS KNEW.
NO, BUT THE BRITISH GOVERNMENT SOLD A BUNCH OF CAPTURED ENIGMA MACHINES TO OTHER COUNTRIES, SO WE COULD READ THEIR SECRET MAIL!
YUP. TOTALLY UNBREAKABLE...
SO NO ONE KNEW HOW YOU'D HELPED WIN THE WAR AND SAVED COUNTLESS LIVES IN THE PROCESS?!
HEY—I DIDN'T NEED A MEDAL. IT WAS ENOUGH TO KNOW I'D HELPED.
I WAS MORE UPSET WHEN THEY DESTROYED ALL OUR BEAUTIFUL TURING MACHINES! BUT I WASN'T TOO WORRIED—I WAS ALREADY WORKING ON AN EVEN BETTER DESIGN...
YOU SEE, A TURING MACHINE LIKE THE ONE THAT CRACKED ENIGMA CAN ONLY DO ONE TASK. BUT I HAD THE IDEA FOR A MACHINE YOU COULD PROGRAM TO DO ANY TASK.
A UNIVERSAL TURING MACHINE.
OR, AS WE'D CALL IT TODAY, A COMPUTER.
EVERY COMPUTER SINCE HAS BEEN BUILT ON THE FOUNDATIONS OF YOUR GROUNDBREAKING WORK.
BUT, DESPITE THE FACT THAT YOU WERE BASICALLY INVENTING THE FUTURE, YOU DIDN'T LIVE TO SEE IT, DYING TRAGICALLY...
ALAN...?
HELLO...?
HOW ABOUT THAT! YOU CAN USE YOUR TURING MACHINE TO WATCH FUNNY VIDEOS OF CATS...

AN ENIGMA WRAPPED IN A MYSTERY

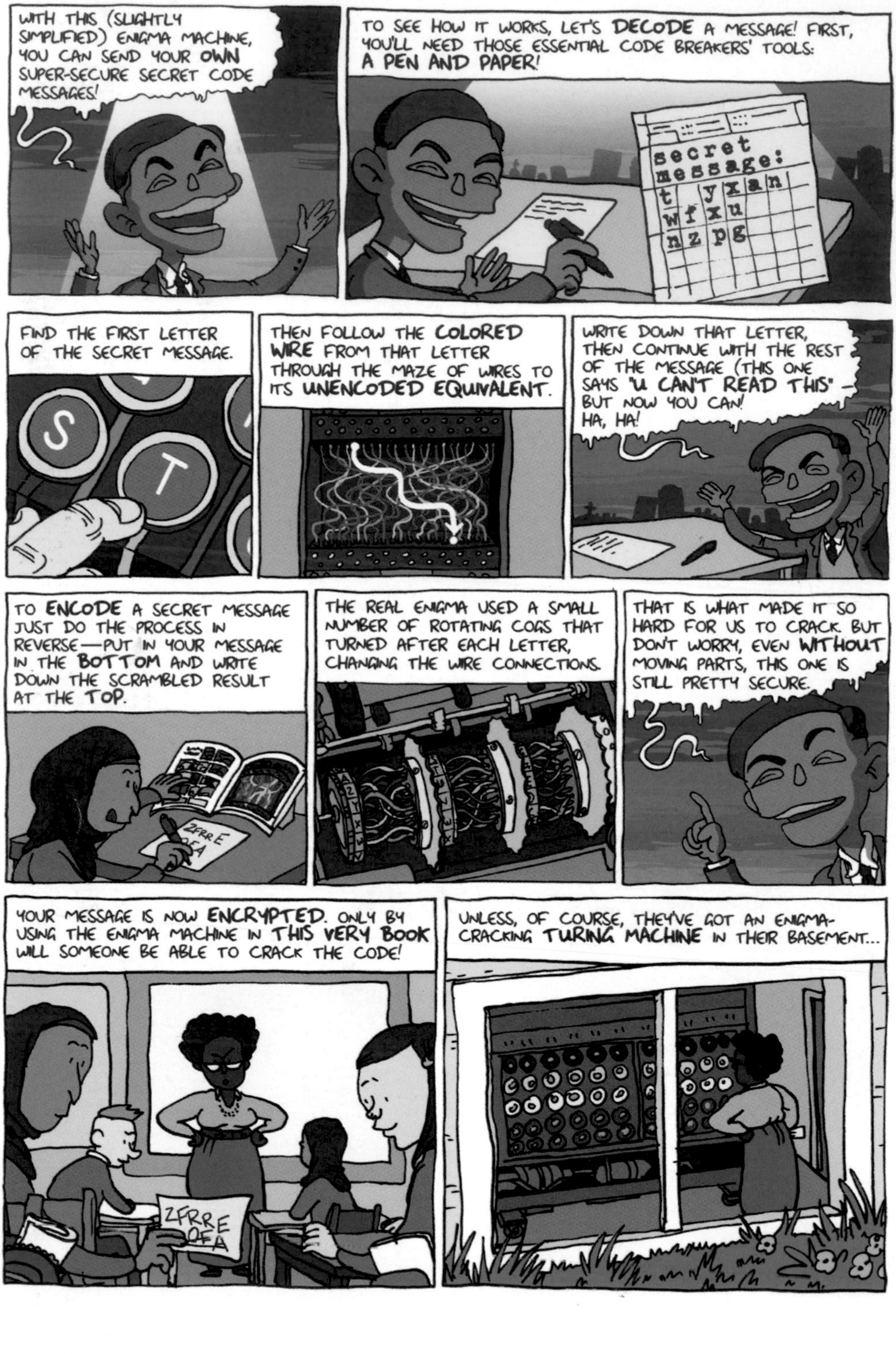

WITH THIS (SLIGHTLY SIMPLIFIED) ENIGMA MACHINE, YOU CAN SEND YOUR OWN SUPER-SECURE SECRET CODE MESSAGES!
TO SEE HOW IT WORKS, LET'S DECODE A MESSAGE! FIRST, YOU'LL NEED THOSE ESSENTIAL CODE BREAKERS' TOOLS: A PEN AND PAPER!
secret message:
t y x a n
w f x u
n z p g
FIND THE FIRST LETTER OF THE SECRET MESSAGE.
S
T
THEN FOLLOW THE COLORED WIRE FROM THAT LETTER THROUGH THE MAZE OF WIRES TO ITS UNENCODED EQUIVALENT.
WRITE DOWN THAT LETTER, THEN CONTINUE WITH THE REST OF THE MESSAGE (THIS ONE SAYS 'U CAN'T READ THIS'—BUT NOW YOU CAN! HA, HA!
TO ENCODE A SECRET MESSAGE JUST DO THE PROCESS IN REVERSE—PUT IN YOUR MESSAGE IN THE BOTTOM AND WRITE DOWN THE SCRAMBLED RESULT AT THE TOP.
THE REAL ENIGMA USED A SMALL NUMBER OF ROTATING COGS THAT TURNED AFTER EACH LETTER, CHANGING THE WIRE CONNECTIONS.
THAT IS WHAT MADE IT SO HARD FOR US TO CRACK. BUT DON'T WORRY, EVEN WITHOUT MOVING PARTS, THIS ONE IS STILL PRETTY SECURE.
YOUR MESSAGE IS NOW ENCRYPTED. ONLY BY USING THE ENIGMA MACHINE IN THIS VERY BOOK WILL SOMEONE BE ABLE TO CRACK THE CODE!
ZFRRE
OFA
UNLESS, OF COURSE, THEY'VE GOT AN ENIGMA-CRACKING TURING MACHINE IN THEIR BASEMENT...

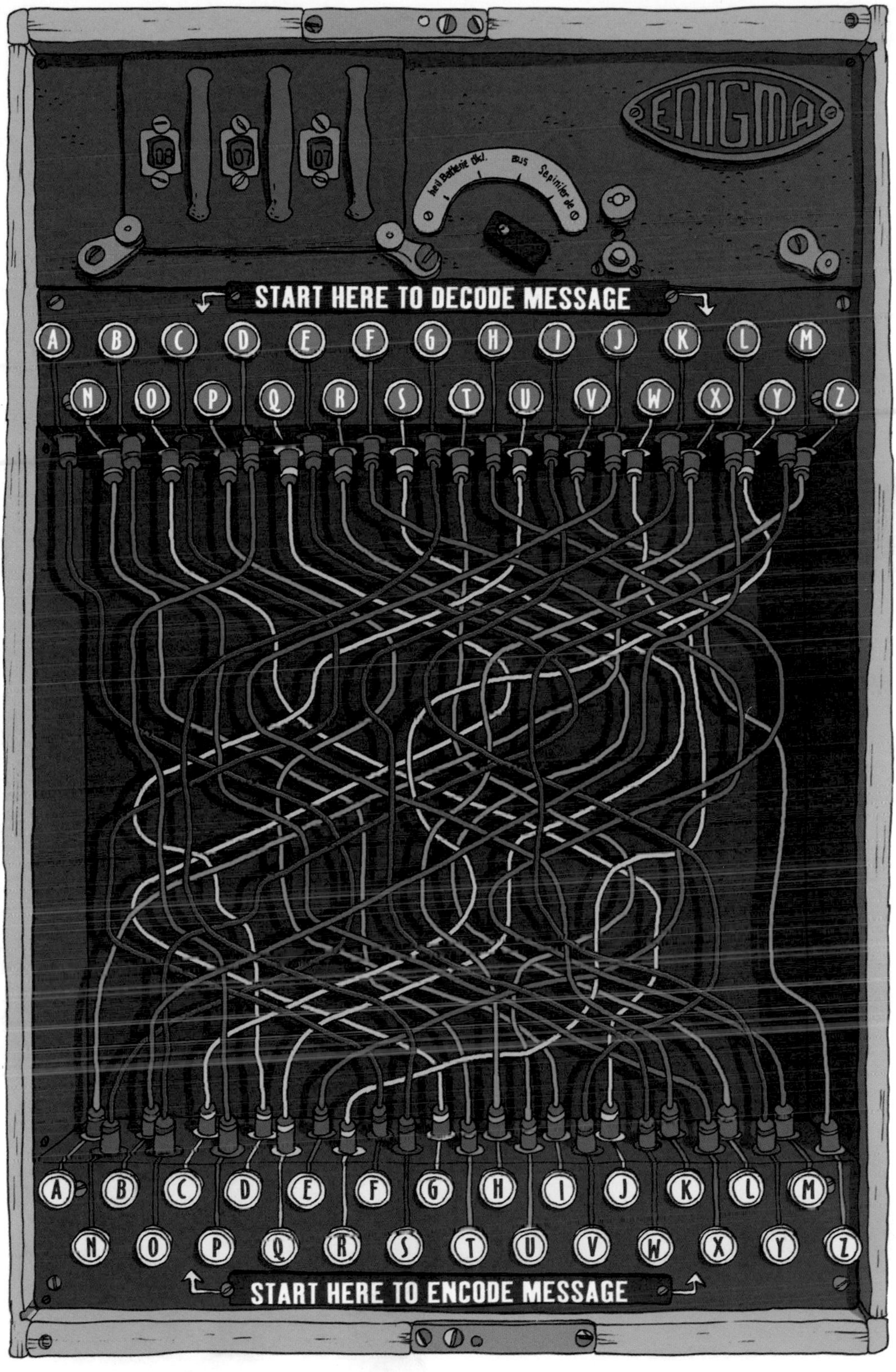

ENIGMA
08
07
07
heil Batterie (lkl.)
aus
Sepiniler ale
START HERE TO DECODE MESSAGE
A B C D E F G H I J K L M
N O P Q R S T U V W X Y Z
A B C D E F G H I J K L M
N O P Q R S T U V W X Y Z
START HERE TO ENCODE MESSAGE

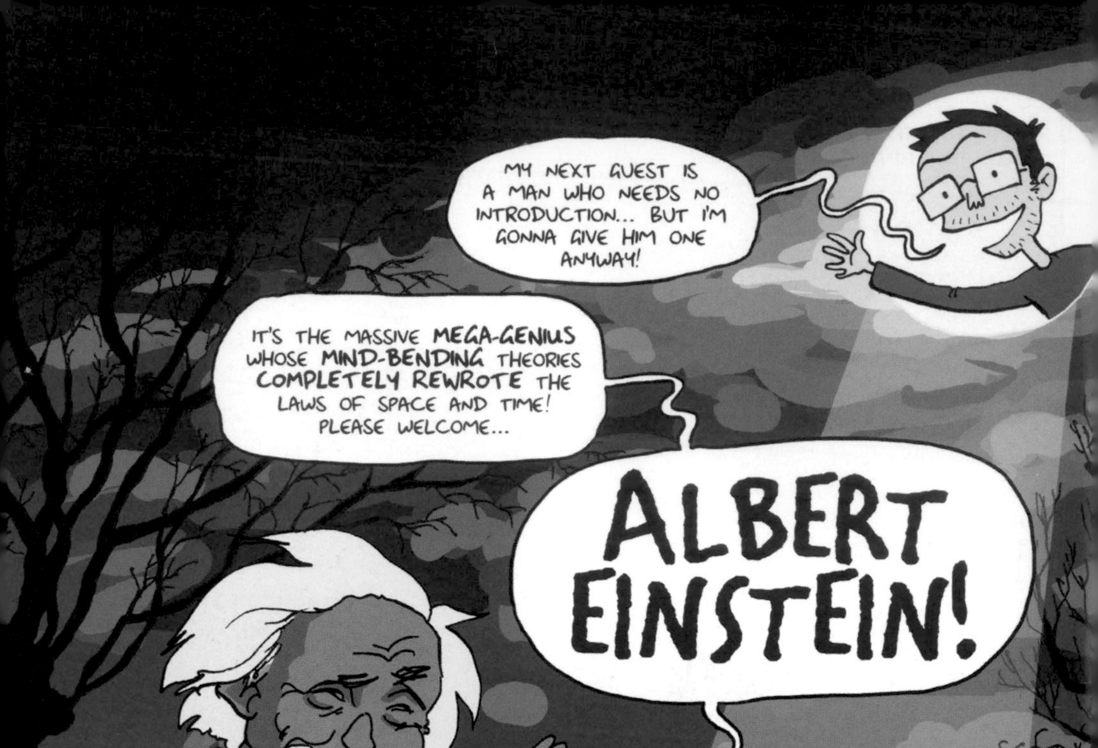
MY NEXT GUEST IS A MAN WHO NEEDS NO INTRODUCTION... BUT I'M GONNA GIVE HIM ONE ANYWAY!
IT'S THE MASSIVE MEGA-GENIUS WHOSE MIND-BENDING THEORIES COMPLETELY REWROTE THE LAWS OF SPACE AND TIME! PLEASE WELCOME...
ALBERT EINSTEIN!
ALBERT EINSTEIN
PHYSICIST
1879-1955

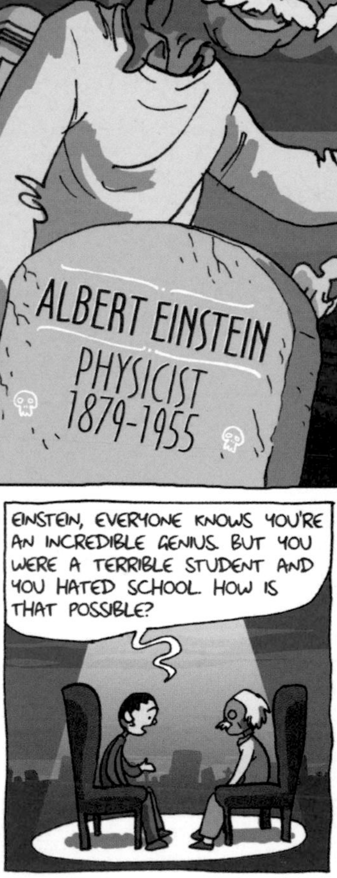
EINSTEIN, EVERYONE KNOWS YOU'RE AN INCREDIBLE GENIUS. BUT YOU WERE A TERRIBLE STUDENT AND YOU HATED SCHOOL. HOW IS THAT POSSIBLE?

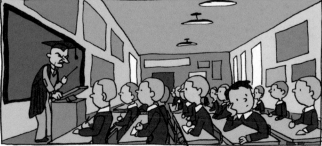

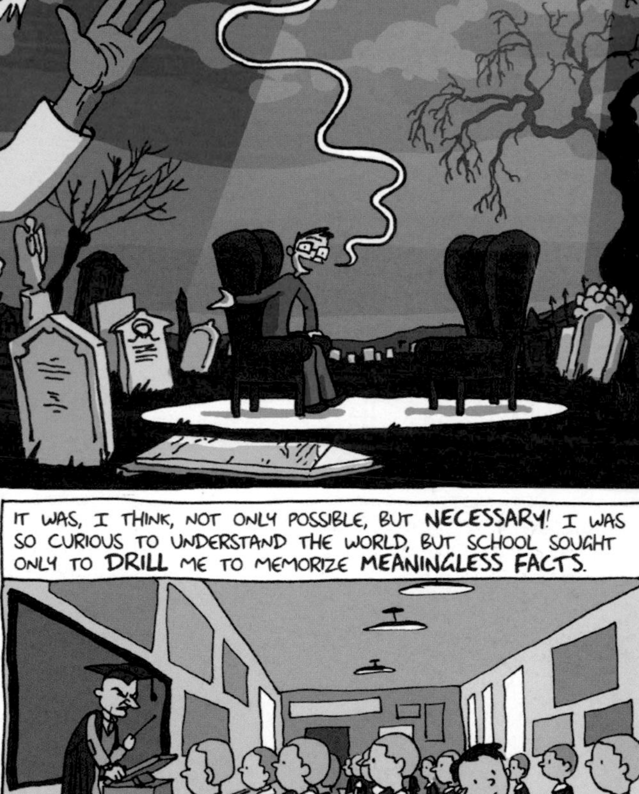
IT WAS, I THINK, NOT ONLY POSSIBLE, BUT NECESSARY! I WAS SO CURIOUS TO UNDERSTAND THE WORLD, BUT SCHOOL SOUGHT ONLY TO DRILL ME TO MEMORIZE MEANINGLESS FACTS.

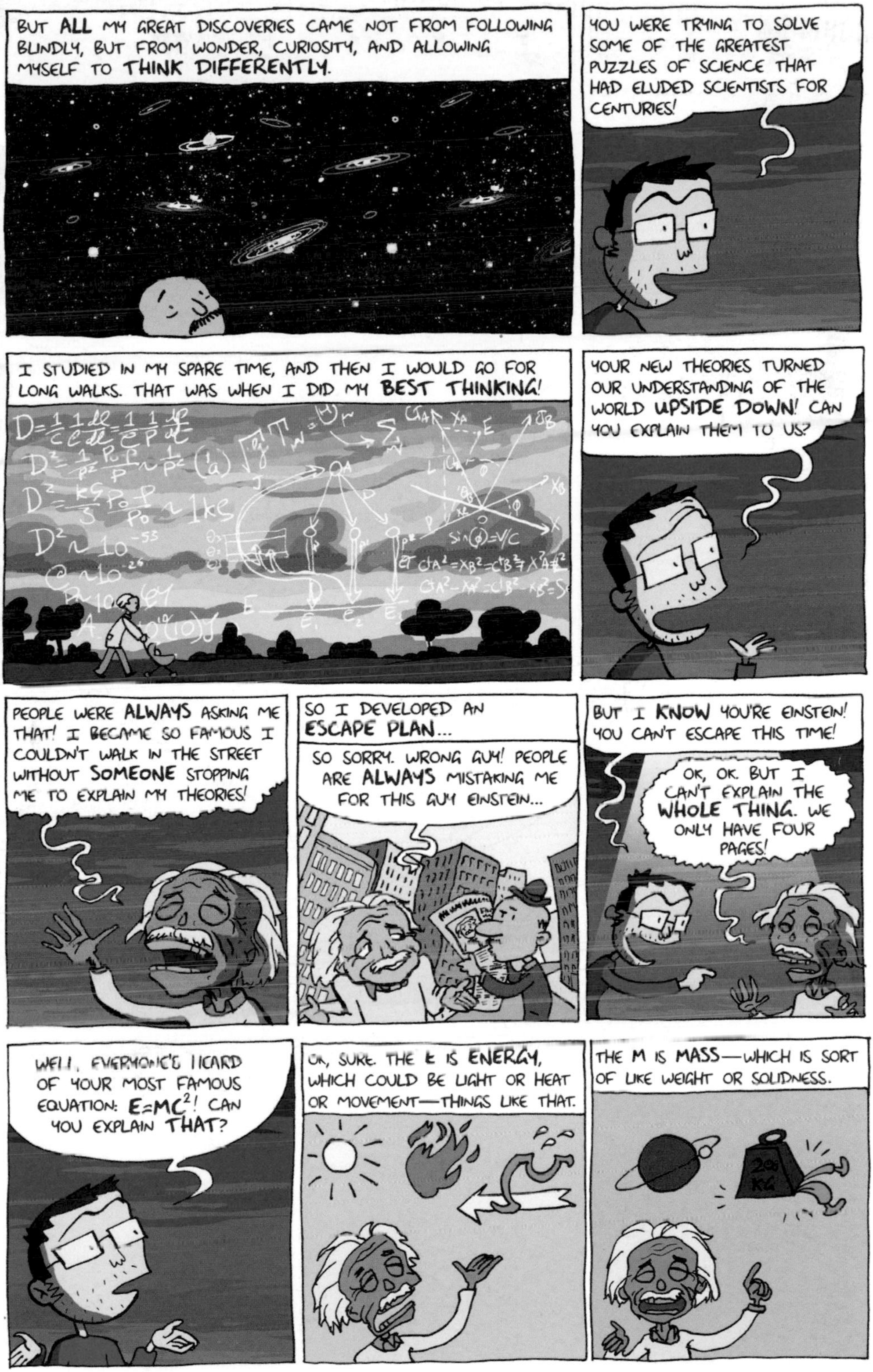

BUT ALL MY GREAT DISCOVERIES CAME NOT FROM FOLLOWING BLINDLY, BUT FROM WONDER, CURIOSITY, AND ALLOWING MYSELF TO THINK DIFFERENTLY.
YOU WERE TRYING TO SOLVE SOME OF THE GREATEST PUZZLES OF SCIENCE THAT HAD ELUDED SCIENTISTS FOR CENTURIES!
I STUDIED IN MY SPARE TIME, AND THEN I WOULD GO FOR LONG WALKS. THAT WAS WHEN I DID MY BEST THINKING!
YOUR NEW THEORIES TURNED OUR UNDERSTANDING OF THE WORLD UPSIDE DOWN! CAN YOU EXPLAIN THEM TO US?
PEOPLE WERE ALWAYS ASKING ME THAT! I BECAME SO FAMOUS I COULDN'T WALK IN THE STREET WITHOUT SOMEONE STOPPING ME TO EXPLAIN MY THEORIES!
SO I DEVELOPED AN ESCAPE PLAN...
SO SORRY. WRONG GUY! PEOPLE ARE ALWAYS MISTAKING ME FOR THIS GUY EINSTEIN...
BUT I KNOW YOU'RE EINSTEIN! YOU CAN'T ESCAPE THIS TIME!
OK, OK. BUT I CAN'T EXPLAIN THE WHOLE THING. WE ONLY HAVE FOUR PAGES!
WELL, EVERYONE'S HEARD OF YOUR MOST FAMOUS EQUATION: $E=MC^2$! CAN YOU EXPLAIN THAT?
OK, SURE. THE E IS ENERGY, WHICH COULD BE LIGHT OR HEAT OR MOVEMENT—THINGS LIKE THAT.
THE M IS MASS—WHICH IS SORT OF LIKE WEIGHT OR SOLIDNESS.
20 KG

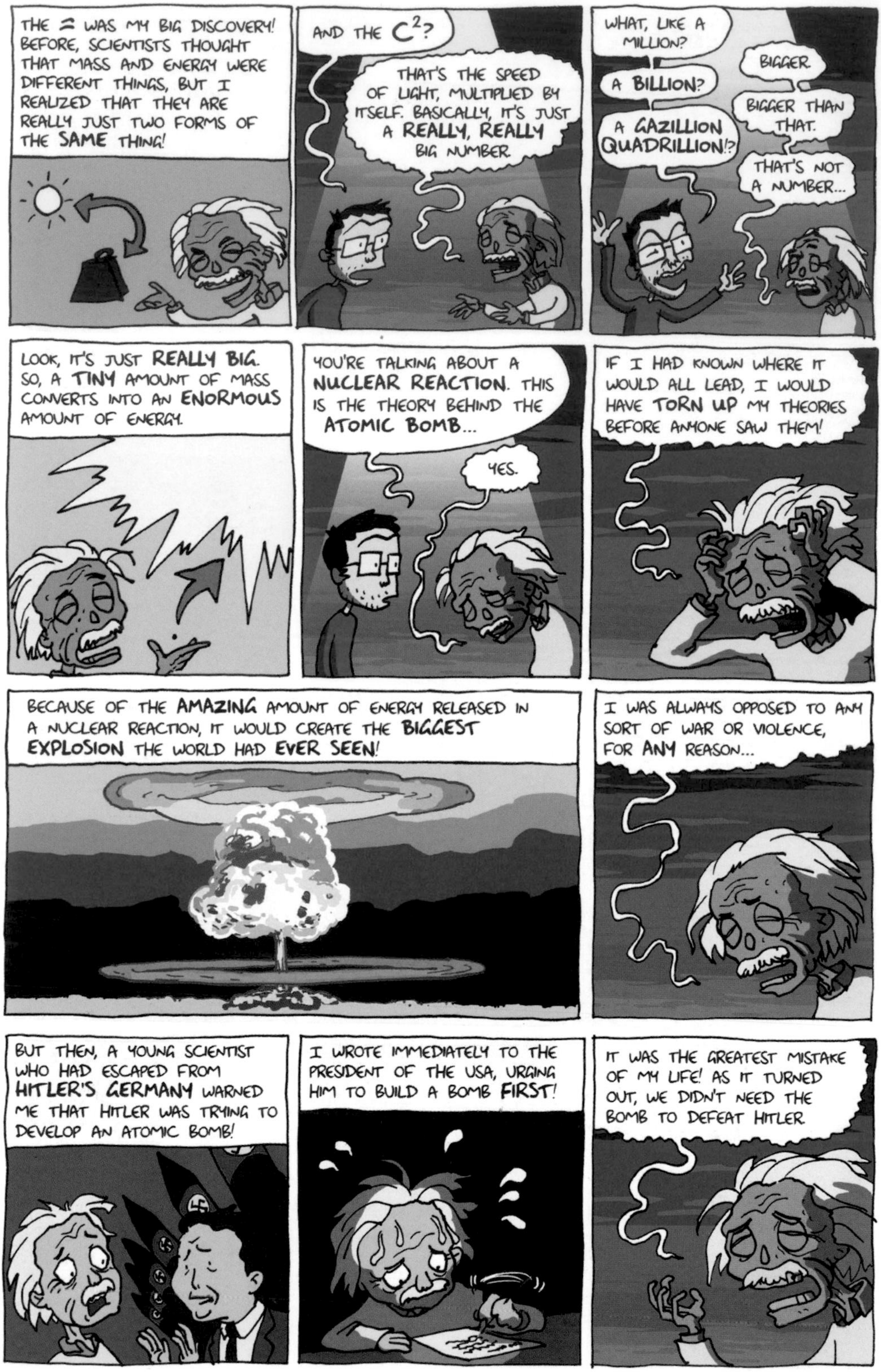
THE = WAS MY BIG DISCOVERY! BEFORE, SCIENTISTS THOUGHT THAT MASS AND ENERGY WERE DIFFERENT THINGS, BUT I REALIZED THAT THEY ARE REALLY JUST TWO FORMS OF THE SAME THING!
AND THE C^2?
THAT'S THE SPEED OF LIGHT, MULTIPLIED BY ITSELF. BASICALLY, IT'S JUST A REALLY, REALLY BIG NUMBER.
WHAT, LIKE A MILLION?
BIGGER.
A BILLION?
BIGGER THAN THAT.
A GAZILLION QUADRILLION!?
THAT'S NOT A NUMBER...
LOOK, IT'S JUST REALLY BIG. SO, A TINY AMOUNT OF MASS CONVERTS INTO AN ENORMOUS AMOUNT OF ENERGY.
YOU'RE TALKING ABOUT A NUCLEAR REACTION. THIS IS THE THEORY BEHIND THE ATOMIC BOMB...
YES.
IF I HAD KNOWN WHERE IT WOULD ALL LEAD, I WOULD HAVE TORN UP MY THEORIES BEFORE ANYONE SAW THEM!
BECAUSE OF THE AMAZING AMOUNT OF ENERGY RELEASED IN A NUCLEAR REACTION, IT WOULD CREATE THE BIGGEST EXPLOSION THE WORLD HAD EVER SEEN!
I WAS ALWAYS OPPOSED TO ANY SORT OF WAR OR VIOLENCE, FOR ANY REASON...
BUT THEN, A YOUNG SCIENTIST WHO HAD ESCAPED FROM HITLER'S GERMANY WARNED ME THAT HITLER WAS TRYING TO DEVELOP AN ATOMIC BOMB!
I WROTE IMMEDIATELY TO THE PRESIDENT OF THE USA, URGING HIM TO BUILD A BOMB FIRST!
IT WAS THE GREATEST MISTAKE OF MY LIFE! AS IT TURNED OUT, WE DIDN'T NEED THE BOMB TO DEFEAT HITLER.

THE UNITED STATES WAS STILL FIGHTING WITH JAPAN, SO IT DECIDED TO USE THE BOMB TO **TERRIFY** THE JAPANESE INTO SURRENDERING.

I WROTE TO THE PRESIDENT AGAIN, PLEADING WITH HIM **NOT** TO DROP IT ON JAPAN...

BUT IT WAS STILL USED ANYWAY...

120,000 PEOPLE WERE **VAPORIZED** INSTANTLY AND ANOTHER **65,000** DIED OF **BURNS** AND **RADIATION SICKNESS**.

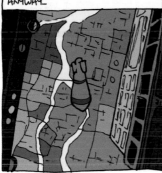

I UNCOVERED THE BEAUTIFUL, PROFOUND SECRETS OF THE UNIVERSE, AND THEIR **FIRST APPLICATION** WAS THE MOST **HORRIFIC KILLING MACHINE** EVER DEVISED.

AND YET, YOU CONTINUED WORKING!?

WHAT ELSE COULD I DO?! I DIDN'T BUILD THE BLASTED THING! AND ANYWAY, I STILL BELIEVE THAT KNOWLEDGE DOES MORE GOOD THAN EVIL.

ONE THING I REALIZED IS THAT EVEN THOUGH WE LIKE TO THINK THAT WE ARE **SEPARATE** FROM THE REST OF THE UNIVERSE, THAT IS REALLY AN **ILLUSION**.

ONLY WHEN WE REALIZE THAT WE ARE **ALL CONNECTED** WILL WE BE ABLE TO LIVE IN PEACE

AAH!

OK, MAYBE NOT **THAT** CONNECTED...

119

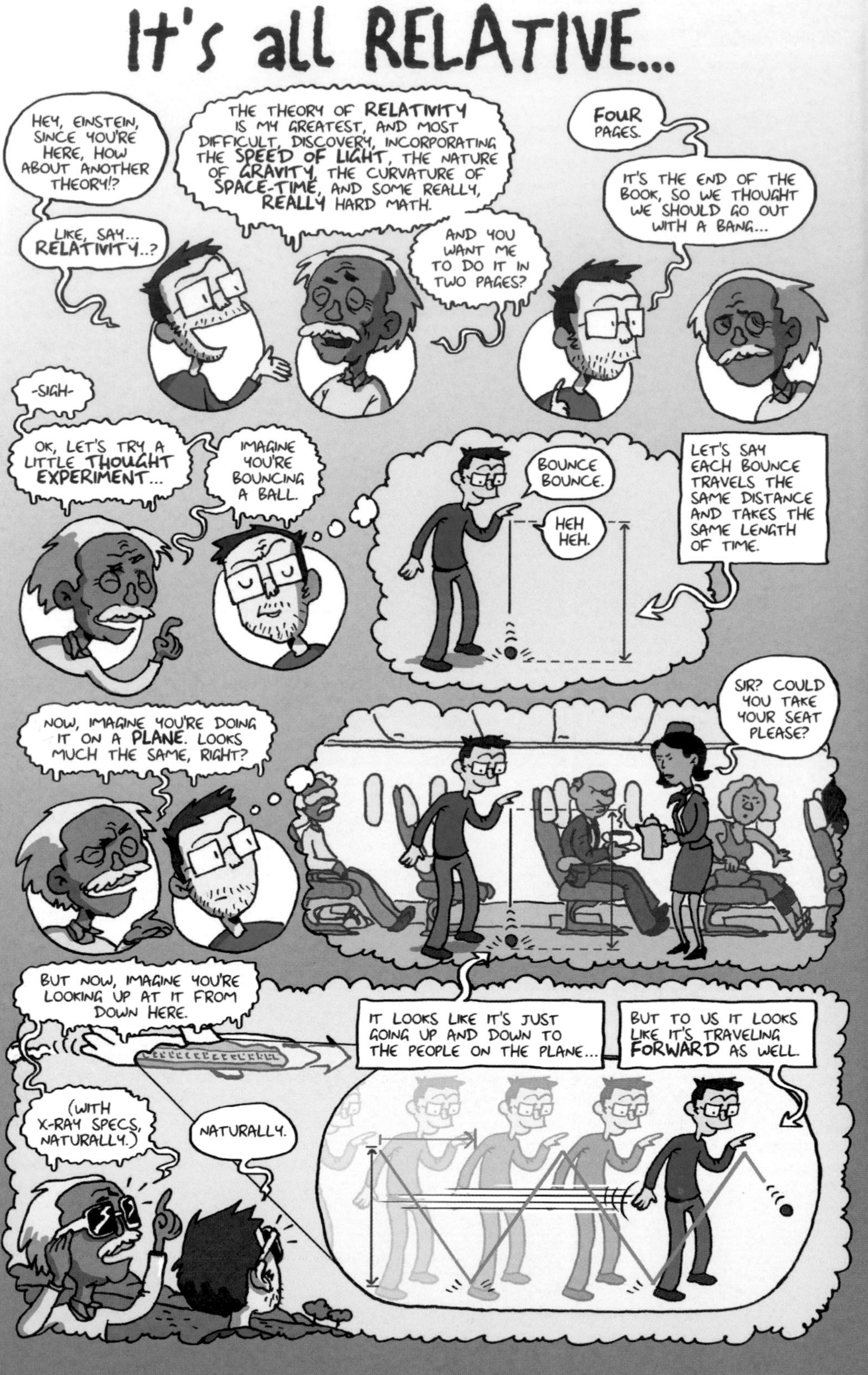
It's all RELATIVE...
HEY, EINSTEIN, SINCE YOU'RE HERE, HOW ABOUT ANOTHER THEORY!?
LIKE, SAY... RELATIVITY..?
THE THEORY OF RELATIVITY IS MY GREATEST, AND MOST DIFFICULT, DISCOVERY, INCORPORATING THE SPEED OF LIGHT, THE NATURE OF GRAVITY, THE CURVATURE OF SPACE-TIME, AND SOME REALLY, REALLY HARD MATH.
AND YOU WANT ME TO DO IT IN TWO PAGES?
FOUR PAGES.
IT'S THE END OF THE BOOK, SO WE THOUGHT WE SHOULD GO OUT WITH A BANG...
-SIGH-
OK, LET'S TRY A LITTLE THOUGHT EXPERIMENT...
IMAGINE YOU'RE BOUNCING A BALL.
BOUNCE BOUNCE.
HEH HEH.
LET'S SAY EACH BOUNCE TRAVELS THE SAME DISTANCE AND TAKES THE SAME LENGTH OF TIME.
NOW, IMAGINE YOU'RE DOING IT ON A PLANE. LOOKS MUCH THE SAME, RIGHT?
SIR? COULD YOU TAKE YOUR SEAT PLEASE?
BUT NOW, IMAGINE YOU'RE LOOKING UP AT IT FROM DOWN HERE.
IT LOOKS LIKE IT'S JUST GOING UP AND DOWN TO THE PEOPLE ON THE PLANE...
BUT TO US IT LOOKS LIKE IT'S TRAVELING FORWARD AS WELL.
(WITH X-RAY SPECS, NATURALLY.)
NATURALLY.

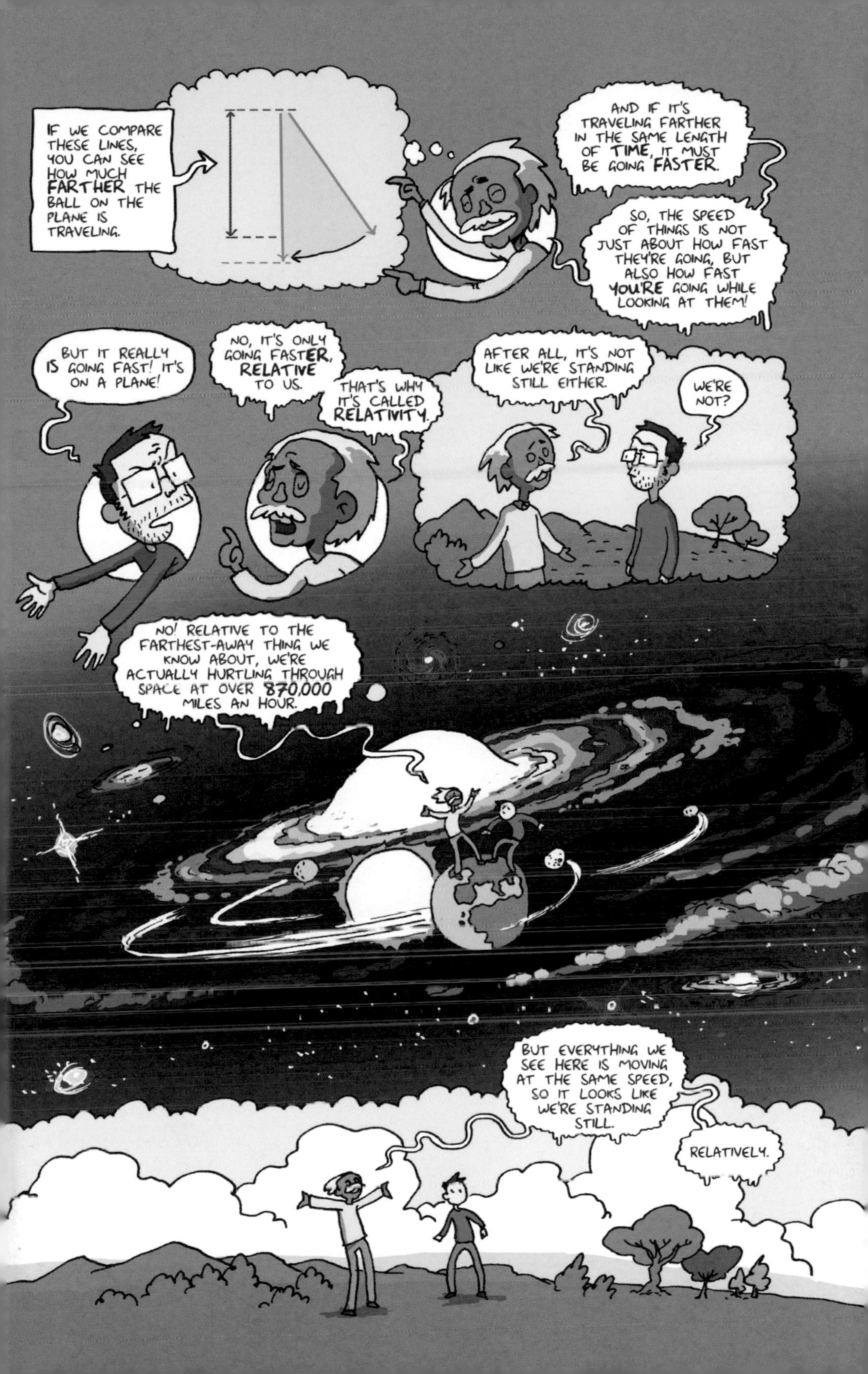
IF WE COMPARE THESE LINES, YOU CAN SEE HOW MUCH FARTHER THE BALL ON THE PLANE IS TRAVELING.
AND IF IT'S TRAVELING FARTHER IN THE SAME LENGTH OF TIME, IT MUST BE GOING FASTER.
SO, THE SPEED OF THINGS IS NOT JUST ABOUT HOW FAST THEY'RE GOING, BUT ALSO HOW FAST YOU'RE GOING WHILE LOOKING AT THEM!
BUT IT REALLY IS GOING FAST! IT'S ON A PLANE!
NO, IT'S ONLY GOING FASTER, RELATIVE TO US.
THAT'S WHY IT'S CALLED RELATIVITY.
AFTER ALL, IT'S NOT LIKE WE'RE STANDING STILL EITHER.
WE'RE NOT?
NO! RELATIVE TO THE FARTHEST-AWAY THING WE KNOW ABOUT, WE'RE ACTUALLY HURTLING THROUGH SPACE AT OVER 870,000 MILES AN HOUR.
BUT EVERYTHING WE SEE HERE IS MOVING AT THE SAME SPEED, SO IT LOOKS LIKE WE'RE STANDING STILL.
RELATIVELY.

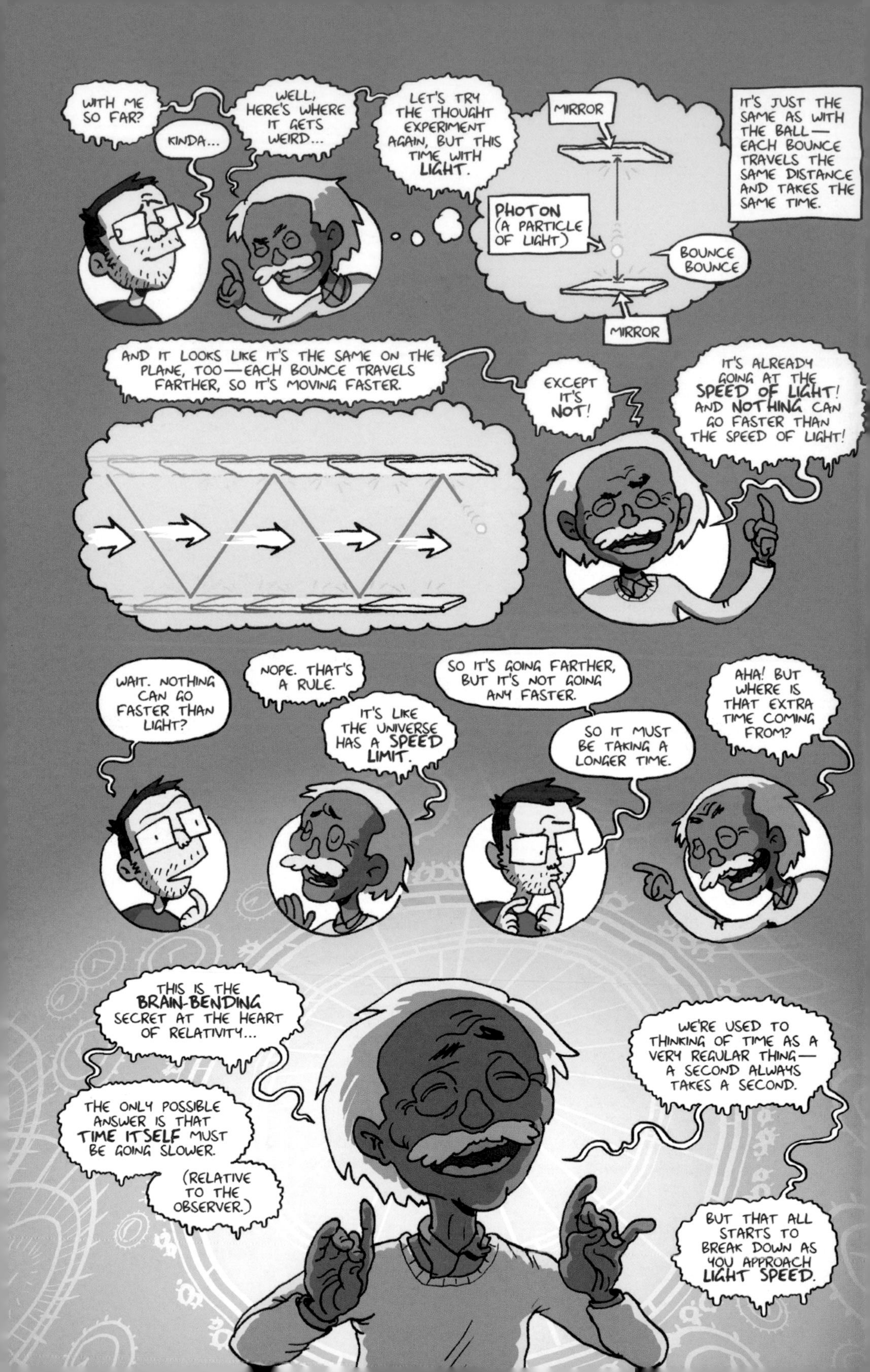
WITH ME SO FAR?
KINDA...
WELL, HERE'S WHERE IT GETS WEIRD...
LET'S TRY THE THOUGHT EXPERIMENT AGAIN, BUT THIS TIME WITH **LIGHT**.
MIRROR
PHOTON (A PARTICLE OF LIGHT)
BOUNCE BOUNCE
MIRROR
IT'S JUST THE SAME AS WITH THE BALL—EACH BOUNCE TRAVELS THE SAME DISTANCE AND TAKES THE SAME TIME.
AND IT LOOKS LIKE IT'S THE SAME ON THE PLANE, TOO—EACH BOUNCE TRAVELS FARTHER, SO IT'S MOVING FASTER.
EXCEPT IT'S **NOT**!
IT'S ALREADY GOING AT THE **SPEED OF LIGHT**! AND **NOTHING** CAN GO FASTER THAN THE SPEED OF LIGHT!
WAIT. NOTHING CAN GO FASTER THAN LIGHT?
NOPE. THAT'S A RULE.
IT'S LIKE THE UNIVERSE HAS A **SPEED LIMIT**.
SO IT'S GOING FARTHER, BUT IT'S NOT GOING ANY FASTER.
SO IT MUST BE TAKING A LONGER TIME.
AHA! BUT WHERE IS THAT EXTRA TIME COMING FROM?
THIS IS THE **BRAIN-BENDING** SECRET AT THE HEART OF RELATIVITY...
THE ONLY POSSIBLE ANSWER IS THAT **TIME ITSELF** MUST BE GOING SLOWER.
(RELATIVE TO THE OBSERVER.)
WE'RE USED TO THINKING OF TIME AS A VERY REGULAR THING—A SECOND ALWAYS TAKES A SECOND.
BUT THAT ALL STARTS TO BREAK DOWN AS YOU APPROACH **LIGHT SPEED**.

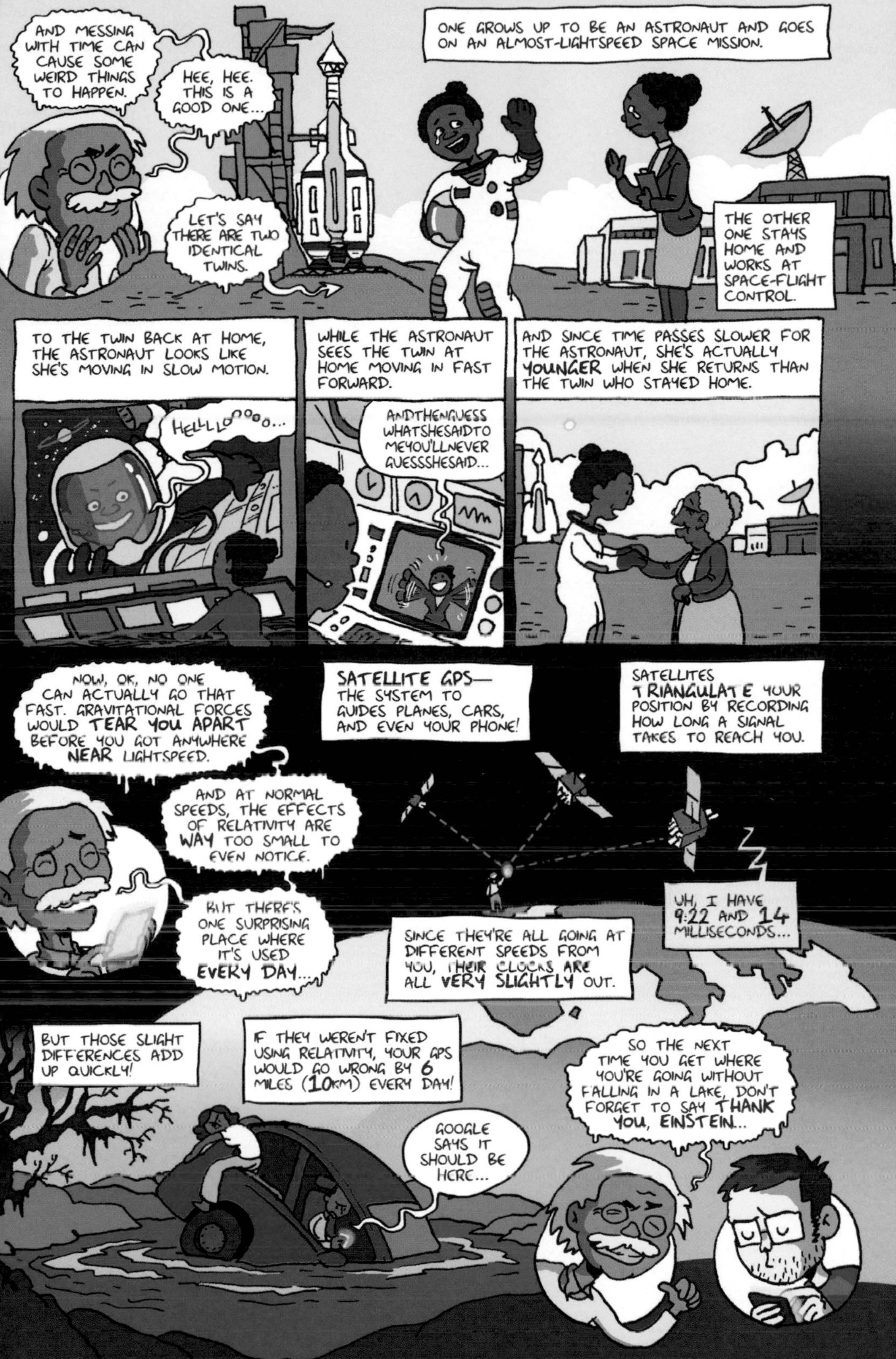
AND MESSING WITH TIME CAN CAUSE SOME WEIRD THINGS TO HAPPEN.
HEE, HEE. THIS IS A GOOD ONE...
LET'S SAY THERE ARE TWO IDENTICAL TWINS.
ONE GROWS UP TO BE AN ASTRONAUT AND GOES ON AN ALMOST-LIGHTSPEED SPACE MISSION.
THE OTHER ONE STAYS HOME AND WORKS AT SPACE-FLIGHT CONTROL.
TO THE TWIN BACK AT HOME, THE ASTRONAUT LOOKS LIKE SHE'S MOVING IN SLOW MOTION.
HELLLLOoooo...
WHILE THE ASTRONAUT SEES THE TWIN AT HOME MOVING IN FAST FORWARD.
ANDTHENGUESS WHATSHESAIDTO MEYOU'LLNEVER GUESSSHESAID...
AND SINCE TIME PASSES SLOWER FOR THE ASTRONAUT, SHE'S ACTUALLY **YOUNGER** WHEN SHE RETURNS THAN THE TWIN WHO STAYED HOME.
NOW, OK, NO ONE CAN ACTUALLY GO THAT FAST. GRAVITATIONAL FORCES WOULD **TEAR YOU APART** BEFORE YOU GOT ANYWHERE **NEAR** LIGHTSPEED.
AND AT NORMAL SPEEDS, THE EFFECTS OF RELATIVITY ARE **WAY** TOO SMALL TO EVEN NOTICE.
BUT THERE'S ONE SURPRISING PLACE WHERE IT'S USED **EVERY DAY**...
SATELLITE GPS— THE SYSTEM TO GUIDES PLANES, CARS, AND EVEN YOUR PHONE!
SATELLITES **TRIANGULATE** YOUR POSITION BY RECORDING HOW LONG A SIGNAL TAKES TO REACH YOU.
UH, I HAVE 9:22 AND 14 MILLISECONDS...
SINCE THEY'RE ALL GOING AT DIFFERENT SPEEDS FROM YOU, THEIR CLOCKS ARE ALL **VERY SLIGHTLY** OUT.
BUT THOSE SLIGHT DIFFERENCES ADD UP QUICKLY!
IF THEY WEREN'T FIXED USING RELATIVITY, YOUR GPS WOULD GO WRONG BY 6 MILES (10KM) EVERY DAY!
GOOGLE SAYS IT SHOULD BE HERE...
SO THE NEXT TIME YOU GET WHERE YOU'RE GOING WITHOUT FALLING IN A LAKE, DON'T FORGET TO SAY **THANK YOU, EINSTEIN**...

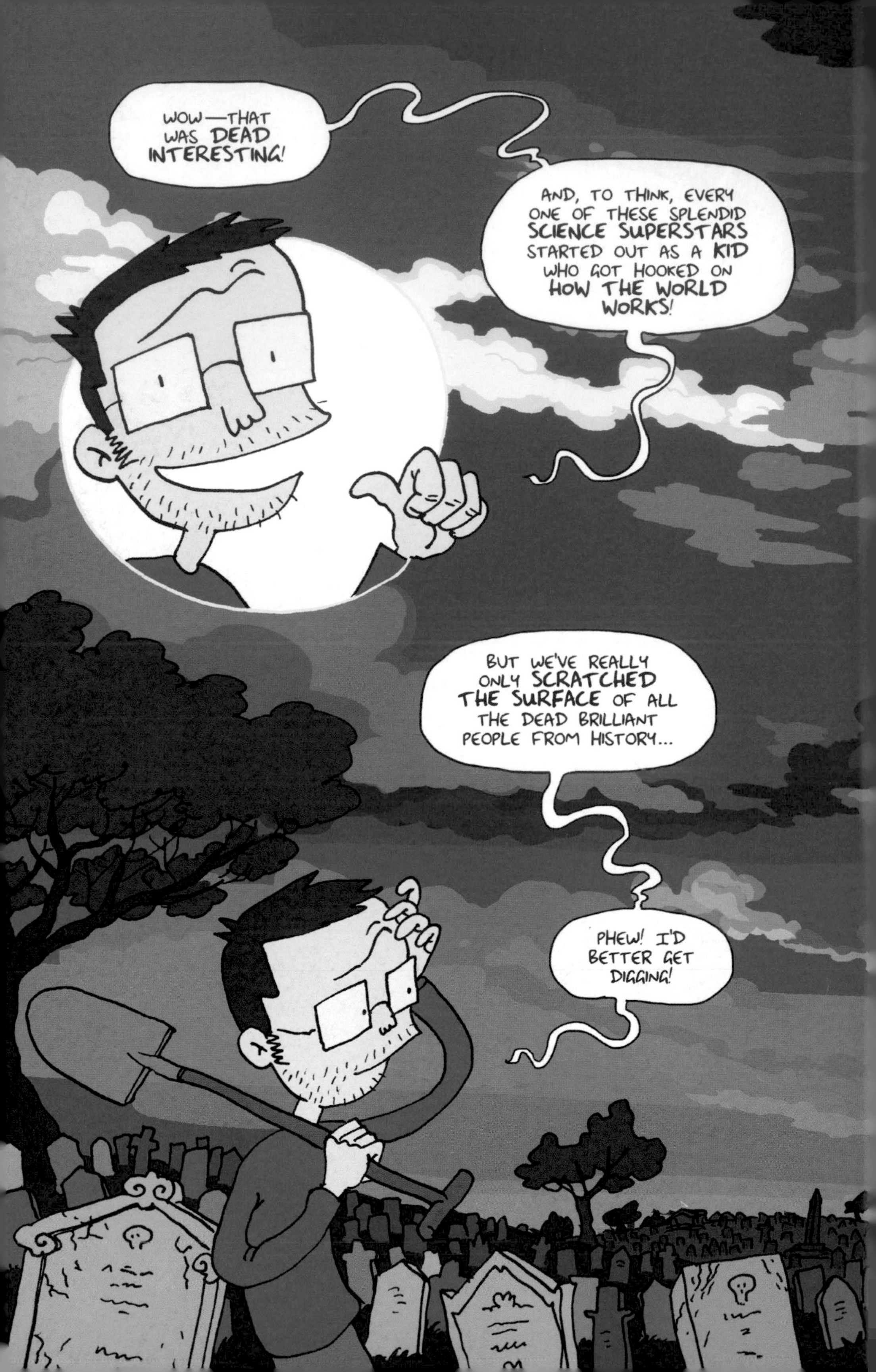
WOW—THAT WAS DEAD INTERESTING!
AND, TO THINK, EVERY ONE OF THESE SPLENDID SCIENCE SUPERSTARS STARTED OUT AS A KID WHO GOT HOOKED ON HOW THE WORLD WORKS!
BUT WE'VE REALLY ONLY SCRATCHED THE SURFACE OF ALL THE DEAD BRILLIANT PEOPLE FROM HISTORY...
PHEW! I'D BETTER GET DIGGING!

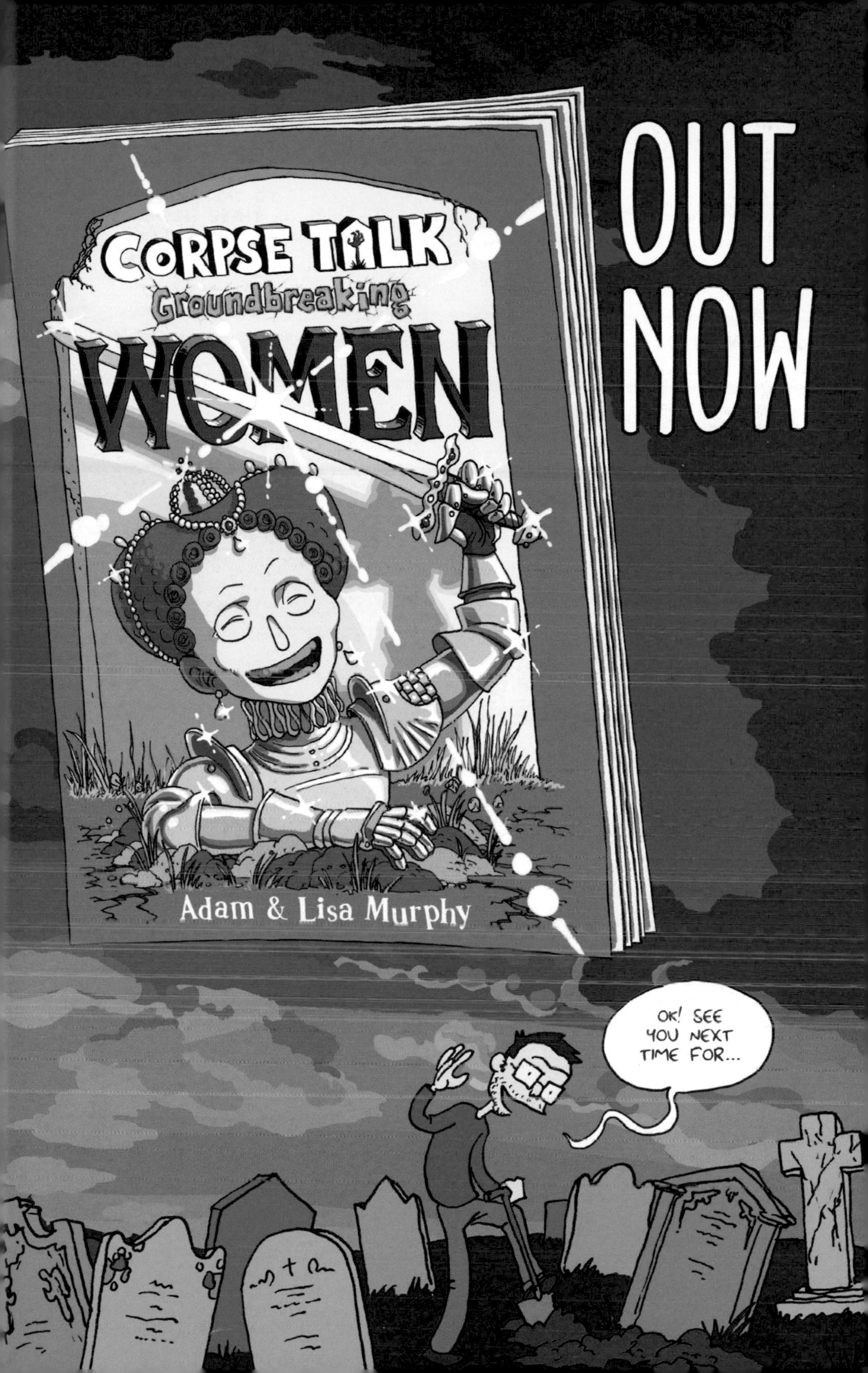
CORPSE TALK
Groundbreaking
WOMEN
Adam & Lisa Murphy
OUT NOW
OK! SEE YOU NEXT TIME FOR...

Glossary

ASTRONOMY THE STUDY OF OBJECTS IN SPACE, INCLUDING STARS, PLANETS, AND GALAXIES.

ATOMS TINY BUILDING BLOCKS THAT MAKE UP EVERYTHING IN THE UNIVERSE.

BOTANY THE STUDY OF PLANTS.

CARTHAGINIANS PEOPLE FROM THE ANCIENT CITY OF CARTHAGE, ON THE NORTH COAST OF AFRICA.

CARTOGRAPHY THE STUDY OF MAPS AND HOW THEY'RE MADE.

CHOLERA AN ILLNESS SPREAD BY UNCLEAN WATER, RESPONSIBLE FOR MILLIONS OF DEATHS WORLDWIDE.

COPROLITE FOSSILIZED POOP.

CRYPTOGRAPHY THE ART OF WRITING OR SOLVING SECRET CODES.

DISSECTION THE OPENING UP OF HUMAN OR ANIMAL BODIES TO UNDERSTAND HOW THEY WORK INSIDE.

ELEMENT A BASIC BUILDING BLOCK THAT IS MADE FROM IDENTICAL ATOMS.

ENTOMOLOGY THE STUDY OF INSECTS. SOMEONE WHO STUDIES ENTOMOLOGY IS CALLED AN ENTOMOLOGIST.

EVOLUTION THE WAY ANIMALS AND PLANTS CHANGE, OR ADAPT, OVER TIME TO SUIT THEIR ENVIRONMENT. CHARLES DARWIN CAME UP WITH THIS THEORY.

FOSSILS REMAINS OF ANIMALS OR PLANTS FROM A LONG TIME AGO THAT HAVE BEEN PRESERVED IN THE EARTH (IN ROCK, AMBER, OR ICE).

FRICTION THE FORCE CREATED WHEN TWO OBJECTS RUB AGAINST EACH OTHER, SLOWING THEM DOWN AND CREATING HEAT.

GEOLOGY THE SCIENTIFIC STUDY OF ROCKS AND THE HISTORY OF THE EARTH.

HERETIC SOMEONE WHOSE BELIEFS DIFFER TO THOSE ACCEPTED BY SOCIETY, USUALLY IN REGARDS TO RELIGION.

HYPOTHESIS A SCIENTIFIC THEORY THAT NEEDS TO BE TESTED.

JURASSIC A PERIOD 201 TO 145 MILLION YEARS AGO, WHEN DINOSAURS ROAMED THE EARTH.

METAMORPHOSIS THE PROCESS BY WHICH SOME ANIMALS, SUCH AS BUTTERFLIES AND FROGS, UNDERGO DRAMATIC CHANGES OVER THEIR LIFE CYCLE.

NATURALIST SOMEONE WHO STUDIES NATURAL HISTORY.

ORBIT THE PATH TAKEN BY AN OBJECT IN SPACE AS IT MOVES AROUND ANOTHER OBJECT.

PALEONTOLOGY THE STUDY OF FOSSILIZED ANIMALS AND PLANTS, INCLUDING DINOSAURS.

PERIODIC TABLE A TABLE THAT ORGANIZES THE ELEMENTS BASED ON THEIR NUMBER OF ATOMS.

PHILOSOPHY A METHOD OF TRYING TO UNDERSTAND THE WORLD BY ASKING A LOT OF QUESTIONS.

PHYSICIAN ANOTHER NAME FOR A MEDICAL DOCTOR.

SMALLPOX A ONCE-COMMON VIRUS, NOW ERADICATED, THAT WAS RESPONSIBLE FOR MILLIONS OF DEATHS WORLDWIDE.

TYPHUS DEADLY DISEASE CARRIED BY LICE.

VACCINATION EXPOSING SOMEONE TO A MILD FORM OF A DISEASE SO THAT THEIR BODY DEVISES WAYS OF FIGHTING THE DISEASE IN THE FUTURE.

VULCANOLOGY THE SCIENTIFIC STUDY OF VOLCANOES.

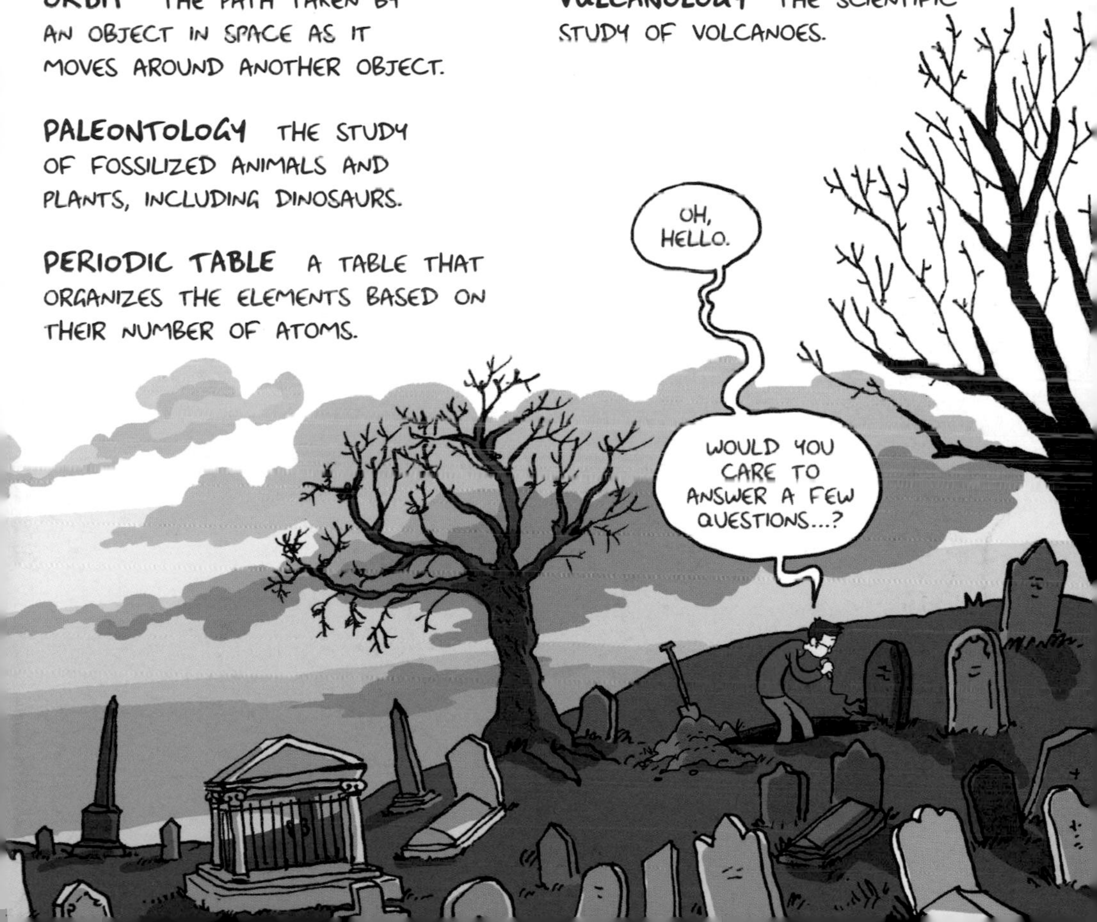
OH, HELLO.
WOULD YOU CARE TO ANSWER A FEW QUESTIONS...?

For Bev & John

Design and adaptation Paul Duffield
Additional colour flatting David B Cooper
With special thanks to Tom Fickling,
Anthony Hinton, and Joe Brady
US Senior Editor Shannon Beatty
US Editor Margaret Parrish
Senior Production Editor Nikoleta Parasaki
Senior Production Controller Inderjit Bhullar
Publishing Director Sarah Larter

First American Edition, 2020
Published in the United States by DK Publishing
1450 Broadway, Suite 801, New York, NY 10018

Text and Illustrations © Adam & Lisa Murphy, 2017, 2020

DK, a Division of Penguin Random House LLC
20 21 22 23 24 10 9 8 7 6 5 4 3 2 1
001–315773–Aug/2020

Published in Great Britain by Dorling Kindersley Limited

A catalog record for this book
is available from the Library of Congress.
ISBN: 978-1-4654-9987-5 (Paperback)
ISBN: 978-0-7440-2358-9 (Hardback)

DK books are available at special discounts when purchased
in bulk for sales promotions, premiums, fund-raising, or
educational use. For details, contact:
DK Publishing Special Markets,
1450 Broadway, Suite 801, New York, NY 10018
SpecialSales@dk.com

Printed and bound in the USA.

For the curious
www.dk.com